ENGLISH
ITALIAN

THEME-BASED
DICTIONARY

Contains over 9000 commonly
used words

Theme-based dictionary British English-Italian - 9000 words
British English collection

By Andrey Taranov

T&P Books vocabularies are intended for helping you learn, memorize and review foreign words. The dictionary is divided into themes, covering all major spheres of everyday activities, business, science, culture, etc.

The process of learning words using T&P Books' theme-based dictionaries gives you the following advantages:

- Correctly grouped source information predetermines success at subsequent stages of word memorization
- Availability of words derived from the same root allowing memorization of word units (rather than separate words)
- Small units of words facilitate the process of establishing associative links needed for consolidation of vocabulary
- Level of language knowledge can be estimated by the number of learned words

T&P Books Publishing
www.tpbooks.com

ISBN: 978-1-78400-009-7

This book is also available in E-book formats.
Please visit www.tpbooks.com or the major online bookstores.

ITALIAN THEME-BASED DICTIONARY
British English collection

T&P Books vocabularies are intended to help you learn, memorize, and review foreign words. The vocabulary contains over 9000 commonly used words arranged thematically.

- Vocabulary contains the most commonly used words
- Recommended as an addition to any language course
- Meets the needs of beginners and advanced learners of foreign languages
- Convenient for daily use, revision sessions, and self-testing activities
- Allows you to assess your vocabulary

Special features of the vocabulary

- Words are organized according to their meaning, not alphabetically
- Words are presented in three columns to facilitate the reviewing and self-testing processes
- Words in groups are divided into small blocks to facilitate the learning process
- The vocabulary offers a convenient and simple transcription of each foreign word

The vocabulary has 256 topics including:

Basic Concepts, Numbers, Colors, Months, Seasons, Units of Measurement, Clothing & Accessories, Food & Nutrition, Restaurant, Family Members, Relatives, Character, Feelings, Emotions, Diseases, City, Town, Sightseeing, Shopping, Money, House, Home, Office, Working in the Office, Import & Export, Marketing, Job Search, Sports, Education, Computer, Internet, Tools, Nature, Countries, Nationalities and more ...

TABLE OF CONTENTS

PRONUNCIATION GUIDE

Letter	Italian example	T&P phonetics alphabet	English example

Vowels

A a	anno	[a]	shorter than in ask
E e	epoca	[e], [ɛ]	absent, pet
I i	vicino	[i]	shorter than in feet
i [1]	ieri	[j]	yes, New York
O o	ora	[o], [ɔ]	drop, baught
U u	uva	[u]	book
Y y	yacht	[j]	yes, New York

Consonants

B b	bambino	[b]	baby, book
c,cc [2]	città	[ʧ]	church, French
c,cc [3]	casa	[k]	clock, kiss
D d	donna	[d]	day, doctor
F f	frutto	[f]	face, food
g, gg [4]	giorno	[ʤ]	joke, general
g, gg [5]	grande	[g]	game, gold
H h	hotel	[h]	silent [h]
J j	jazz	[ʤ]	joke, general
K k	kiwi	[k]	clock, kiss
L l	latte	[l]	lace, people
M m	madre	[m]	magic, milk
N n	notte	[n]	name, normal
P p	parco	[p]	pencil, private
Q q	quadro	[k]	clock, kiss
R r	rosa	[r]	rolled [r]
s [6]	vaso	[z]	zebra, please
S s [7]	sbarra	[z]	zebra, please
S s [8]	testa	[s]	city, boss
T t	teatro	[t]	tourist, trip
V v	vita	[v]	very, river
W w	wisky	[w]	vase, winter
X x	fax	[ks]	box, taxi
Z z [9]	zio	[ʣ]	beads, kids
Z z [10]	bronzo	[ʣ]	beads, kids
Z z [11]	marzo	[ʦ]	cats, tsetse fly

Letter	Italian example	T&P phonetics alphabet	English example

Combinations of letters

ch	chitarra	[k]	clock, kiss
gh	ghiaccio	[g]	game, gold
gn	legno	[ɲ]	canyon, new
gli [12]	figlio	[ʎ]	daily, million
gli [13]	figli	[lji]	million, billiards
sc [14]	scienza	[ʃ]	machine, shark
sc [15]	scala	[sk]	risk, sky
sch	schermo	[sk]	risk, sky

Comments

[1] between vowels
[2] before
[3] elsewhere
[4] before e,i
[5] elsewhere
[6] between wovels
[7] before
[8] elsewhere
[9] at the beginning of words
[10] after
[11] after the other consonants
[12] at the beginning and inside
[13] at the end of words
[14] before e,i
[15] elsewhere

ABBREVIATIONS
used in the dictionary

ab.	-	about
adj	-	adjective
adv	-	adverb
anim.	-	animate
as adj	-	attributive noun used as adjective
e.g.	-	for example
etc.	-	et cetera
fam.	-	familiar
fem.	-	feminine
form.	-	formal
inanim.	-	inanimate
masc.	-	masculine
math	-	mathematics
mil.	-	military
n	-	noun
pl	-	plural
pron.	-	pronoun
sb	-	somebody
sing.	-	singular
sth	-	something
v aux	-	auxiliary verb
vi	-	intransitive verb
vi, vt	-	intransitive, transitive verb
vt	-	transitive verb
m	-	masculine noun
f	-	feminine noun
m pl	-	masculine plural
f pl	-	feminine plural
m, f	-	masculine, feminine
vr	-	reflexive verb

BASIC CONCEPTS

Basic concepts. Part 1

1. Pronouns

I, me	io	['iɔ]
you	tu	['tu]
he	lui	['lyj]
she	lei	['lej]
we	noi	['nɔj]
you (to a group)	voi	['vɔj]
they	loro, essi	['lɜrɔ], ['ɛssi]

2. Greetings. Salutations. Farewells

Hello! (fam.)	Buongiorno!	[buɔn'dʒɔrnɔ]
Hello! (form.)	Salve!	['saʎvɛ]
Good morning!	Buongiorno!	[buɔn'dʒɔrnɔ]
Good afternoon!	Buon pomeriggio!	[bu'ɔn pɔmɛ'ridʒɔ]
Good evening!	Buonasera!	[buɔna'sɛra]
to say hello	salutare (vt)	[saly'tarɛ]
Hi! (hello)	Ciao! Salve!	['tʃaɔ 'saʎvɛ]
greeting (n)	saluto (m)	[sa'lytɔ]
to greet (vt)	salutare (vt)	[saly'tarɛ]
How are you?	Come va?	['kɔmɛ 'va]
What's new?	Che c'è di nuovo?	[kɛ tʃe di nu'ɔvɔ]
Bye-Bye! Goodbye!	Arrivederci!	[arrivɛ'dɛrtʃi]
See you soon!	A presto!	[a 'prɛstɔ]
Farewell!	Addio!	[ad'diɔ]
to say goodbye	congedarsi (vr)	[kɔndʒe'darsi]
Cheers!	Ciao!	['tʃaɔ]
Thank you! Cheers!	Grazie!	['gratsiɛ]
Thank you very much!	Grazie mille!	['gratsiɛ mille]
My pleasure!	Prego	['prɛgɔ]
Don't mention it!	Non c'è di che!	[nɔn tʃɛ di'kɛ]
It was nothing	Di niente	[di 'njentɛ]
Excuse me! (fam.)	Scusa!	['skuza]
Excuse me! (form.)	Scusi!	['skuzi]
to excuse (forgive)	scusare (vt)	[sku'zarɛ]
to apologize (vi)	scusarsi (vr)	[sku'zarsi]

My apologies	Chiedo scusa	['kjedɔ 'skuza]
I'm sorry!	Mi perdoni!	[mi pɛr'dɔni]
to forgive (vt)	perdonare (vt)	[pɛrdɔ'narɛ]
It's okay!	Non fa niente	[nɔn fa ni'ɛntɛ]
please (adv)	per favore	[pɛr fa'vɔrɛ]

Don't forget!	Non dimentichi!	[nɔn di'mɛntiki]
Certainly!	Certamente!	[tʃerta'mɛntɛ]
Of course not!	Certamente no!	[tʃerta'mɛntɛ nɔ]
Okay! (I agree)	D'accordo!	[dak'kɔrdɔ]
That's enough!	Basta!	['basta]

3. How to address

mister, sir	signore	[si'ɲɔrɛ]
madam	signora	[si'ɲɔra]
miss	signorina	[siɲɔ'rina]
young man	signore	[si'ɲɔrɛ]
young man (little boy)	ragazzo	[ra'gatsɔ]
miss (little girl)	ragazza	[ra'gatsa]

4. Cardinal numbers. Part 1

0 zero	zero (m)	['dzɛrɔ]
1 one	uno	['unɔ]
2 two	due	['duɛ]
3 three	tre	['trɛ]
4 four	quattro	[ku'attrɔ]

5 five	cinque	['tʃiŋkuɛ]
6 six	sei	['sɛj]
7 seven	sette	['sɛttɛ]
8 eight	otto	['ɔttɔ]
9 nine	nove	['nɔvɛ]

10 ten	dieci	['djetʃi]
11 eleven	undici	['unditʃi]
12 twelve	dodici	['dɔditʃi]
13 thirteen	tredici	['trɛditʃi]
14 fourteen	quattordici	[kuat'tɔrditʃi]

15 fifteen	quindici	[ku'inditʃi]
16 sixteen	sedici	['sɛditʃi]
17 seventeen	diciassette	[ditʃas'sɛttɛ]
18 eighteen	diciotto	[di'tʃɔttɔ]
19 nineteen	diciannove	[ditʃa'ɲɔvɛ]

20 twenty	venti	['vɛnti]
21 twenty-one	ventuno	[vɛn'tunɔ]
22 twenty-two	ventidue	[vɛnti'duɛ]
23 twenty-three	ventitre	[vɛntit'rɛ]
30 thirty	trenta	['trɛnta]

31 thirty-one	trentuno	[trɛn'tuno]
32 thirty-two	trentadue	[trɛnta'duɛ]
33 thirty-three	trentatre	[trɛntat'rɛ]

40 forty	quaranta	[kua'ranta]
41 forty-one	quarantuno	[kuaran'tuno]
42 forty-two	quarantadue	[kuaranta'duɛ]
43 forty-three	quarantatre	[kuarantat'rɛ]

50 fifty	cinquanta	[ʧiŋku'anta]
51 fifty-one	cinquantuno	[ʧiŋkuan'tuno]
52 fifty-two	cinquantadue	[ʧiŋkuanta'duɛ]
53 fifty-three	cinquantatre	[ʧiŋkuantat'rɛ]

60 sixty	sessanta	[sɛs'santa]
61 sixty-one	sessantuno	[sɛssan'tuno]
62 sixty-two	sessantadue	[sɛssanta'duɛ]
63 sixty-three	sessantatre	[sɛssantat'rɛ]

70 seventy	settanta	[sɛt'tanta]
71 seventy-one	settantuno	[sɛttan'tuno]
72 seventy-two	settantadue	[sɛttanta'duɛ]
73 seventy-three	settantatre	[sɛttantat'rɛ]

80 eighty	ottanta	[ɔt'tanta]
81 eighty-one	ottantuno	[ɔttan'tuno]
82 eighty-two	ottantadue	[ɔttanta'duɛ]
83 eighty-three	ottantatre	[ɔttantat'rɛ]

90 ninety	novanta	[nɔ'vanta]
91 ninety-one	novantuno	[nɔvan'tuno]
92 ninety-two	novantadue	[nɔvanta'duɛ]
93 ninety-three	novantatre	[nɔvantat'rɛ]

5. Cardinal numbers. Part 2

100 one hundred	cento	['ʧentɔ]
200 two hundred	duecento	[duɛ'ʧentɔ]
300 three hundred	trecento	[trɛ'ʧentɔ]
400 four hundred	quattrocento	[kuattrɔ'ʧentɔ]
500 five hundred	cinquecento	[ʧiŋkuɛ'ʧentɔ]

600 six hundred	seicento	[sɛj'ʧentɔ]
700 seven hundred	settecento	[sɛttɛ'ʧentɔ]
800 eight hundred	ottocento	[ɔttɔ'ʧentɔ]
900 nine hundred	novecento	[nɔvɛ'ʧentɔ]

1000 one thousand	mille	['mille]
2000 two thousand	duemila	[duɛ'miʎa]
3000 three thousand	tremila	[trɛ'miʎa]
10000 ten thousand	diecimila	[djeʧi'miʎa]
one hundred thousand	centomila	[ʧentɔ'miʎa]
million	milione (m)	[mi'ʎɔnɛ]
billion	miliardo (m)	[mili'ardɔ]

6. Ordinal numbers

first (adj)	primo	['primɔ]
second (adj)	secondo	[sɛ'kɔndɔ]
third (adj)	terzo	['tɛrtsɔ]
fourth (adj)	quarto	[ku'artɔ]
fifth (adj)	quinto	[ku'intɔ]

sixth (adj)	sesto	['sɛstɔ]
seventh (adj)	settimo	['sɛttimɔ]
eighth (adj)	ottavo	[ɔt'tavɔ]
ninth (adj)	nono	['nɔnɔ]
tenth (adj)	decimo	['dɛtʃimɔ]

7. Numbers. Fractions

fraction	frazione (f)	[fra'tsʲɔnɛ]
one half	un mezzo	[un 'mɛdzɔ]
one third	un terzo	[un 'tɛrtsɔ]
one quarter	un quarto	[un ku'artɔ]

one eighth	un ottavo	[un ɔt'tavɔ]
one tenth	un decimo	[un 'dɛtʃimɔ]
two thirds	due terzi	['duɛ 'tɛrtsi]
three quarters	tre quarti	['trɛ ku'arti]

8. Numbers. Basic operations

subtraction	sottrazione (f)	[sɔttra'tsʲɔnɛ]
to subtract (vi, vt)	sottrarre (vt)	[sɔtt'rarrɛ]
division	divisione (f)	[diwizi'ɔnɛ]
to divide (vt)	dividere (vt)	[di'widɛrɛ]

addition	addizione (f)	[addi'tsʲɔnɛ]
to add up (vt)	addizionare (vt)	[additsʲɔ'narɛ]
to add (vi)	addizionare (vt)	[additsʲɔ'narɛ]
multiplication	moltiplicazione (f)	[mɔʎtiplika'tsʲɔnɛ]
to multiply (vt)	moltiplicare (vt)	[mɔʎtipli'karɛ]

9. Numbers. Miscellaneous

digit, figure	cifra (f)	['tʃifra]
number	numero (m)	['numɛrɔ]
numeral	numerale (m)	[numɛ'ralɛ]
minus	meno (m)	['menɔ]
plus	più (m)	['pjy]
formula	formula (f)	['fɔrmuʎa]
calculation	calcolo (m)	['kaʎkɔlɔ]
to count (vt)	contare (vt)	[kɔn'tarɛ]

to count up	calcolare (vt)	[kaʎkɔ'ʎarɛ]
to compare (vt)	comparare (vt)	[kɔmpa'rarɛ]
How much?	Quanto?	[ku'antɔ]
How many?	Quanti?	[ku'anti]
sum, total	somma (f)	['sɔmma]
result	risultato (m)	[rizuʎ'tatɔ]
remainder	resto (m)	['rɛstɔ]
a few ...	qualche ...	[ku'aʎkɛ]
few, little (adv)	un po' di ...	[un 'pɔ di]
the rest	resto (m)	['rɛstɔ]
one and a half	uno e mezzo	['unɔ ɛ 'mɛdzɔ]
dozen	dozzina (f)	[dɔ'dzina]
in half (adv)	in due	[in 'duɛ]
equally (evenly)	in parti uguali	[in 'parti ugu'ali]
half	metà (f), mezzo (m)	[mɛ'ta], ['mɛdzɔ]
time (three ~s)	volta (f)	['vɔʎta]

10. The most important verbs. Part 1

to advise (vt)	consigliare (vt)	[kɔnsi'ʎjarɛ]
to agree (say yes)	essere d'accordo	['ɛssɛrɛ dak'kɔrdɔ]
to answer (vi, vt)	rispondere (vi, vt)	[ris'pɔndɛrɛ]
to apologize (vi)	scusarsi (vr)	[sku'zarsi]
to arrive (vi)	arrivare (vi)	[arri'varɛ]
to ask (~ oneself)	chiedere, domandare	['kjedɛrɛ], [dɔman'darɛ]
to ask (~ sb to do sth)	chiedere, domandare	['kjedɛrɛ], [dɔman'darɛ]
to be (vi)	essere (vi)	['ɛssɛrɛ]
to be afraid	avere paura	[a'vɛrɛ pa'ura]
to be hungry	avere fame	[a'vɛrɛ 'famɛ]
to be interested in ...	interessarsi di ...	[intɛrɛs'sarsi di]
to be needed	occorrere	[ɔk'kɔrrɛrɛ]
to be surprised	stupirsi (vr)	[stu'pirsi]
to be thirsty	avere sete	[a'vɛrɛ 'sɛtɛ]
to begin (vt)	cominciare (vt)	[kɔmin'tʃarɛ]
to belong to ...	appartenere (vi)	[appartɛ'nɛrɛ]
to boast (vi)	vantarsi (vr)	[van'tarsi]
to break (split into pieces)	rompere (vt)	['rɔmpɛrɛ]
to call (for help)	chiamare (vt)	[kja'marɛ]
can (v aux)	potere (v aux)	[pɔ'tɛrɛ]
to catch (vt)	afferrare (vt)	[affer'rarɛ]
to change (vt)	cambiare (vt)	[kam'bjarɛ]
to choose (select)	scegliere (vt)	['ʃɛʎjerɛ]
to come down	scendere (vi)	['ʃɛndɛrɛ]
to come in (enter)	entrare (vi)	[ɛnt'rarɛ]
to compare (vt)	comparare (vt)	[kɔmpa'rarɛ]
to complain (vi, vt)	lamentarsi (vr)	[ʎamɛn'tarsi]

to confuse (mix up)	confondere (vt)	[kon'fondɛrɛ]
to continue (vt)	continuare (vt)	[kontinu'arɛ]
to control (vt)	controllare (vt)	[kontro'ʎarɛ]
to cook (dinner)	cucinare (vi)	[kutʃi'narɛ]
to cost (vt)	costare (vt)	[kos'tarɛ]

to count (add up)	contare (vt)	[kon'tarɛ]
to count on ...	contare su ...	[kon'tarɛ su]
to create (vt)	creare (vt)	[krɛ'arɛ]
to cry (weep)	piangere (vi)	['pjandʒerɛ]

11. The most important verbs. Part 2

to deceive (vi, vt)	ingannare (vt)	[iŋa'ŋarɛ]
to decorate (tree, street)	decorare (vt)	[dɛko'rarɛ]
to defend (a country, etc.)	difendere (vt)	[di'fɛndɛrɛ]
to demand (request firmly)	esigere (vt)	[ɛ'zidʒerɛ]

to dig (vt)	scavare (vt)	[ska'varɛ]
to discuss (vt)	discutere (vt)	[dis'kutɛrɛ]
to do (vt)	fare (vt)	['farɛ]
to doubt (have doubts)	dubitare (vi)	[dubi'tarɛ]
to drop (let fall)	lasciar cadere	[ʎa'ʃar ka'dɛrɛ]

to excuse (forgive)	battaglia (f)	[bat'taʎja]
to exist (vi)	esistere (vi)	[ɛ'zistɛrɛ]
to expect (foresee)	prevedere (vt)	[prɛvɛ'dɛrɛ]
to explain (vt)	spiegare (vt)	[spje'garɛ]

to fall (vi)	cadere (vi)	[ka'dɛrɛ]
to fancy (vt)	piacere (vi)	[pja'tʃerɛ]
to find (vt)	trovare (vt)	[tro'varɛ]
to finish (vt)	finire (vt)	[fi'nirɛ]
to fly (vi)	volare (vi)	[vo'ʎarɛ]

to follow ... (come after)	seguire (vt)	[sɛgu'irɛ]
to forget (vi, vt)	dimenticare (vt)	[dimɛnti'karɛ]
to forgive (vt)	perdonare (vt)	[pɛrdo'narɛ]

to give (vt)	dare (vt)	['darɛ]
to give a hint	dare un suggerimento	[darɛ un sudʒeri'mɛnto]
to go (on foot)	andare (vi)	[an'darɛ]
to go for a swim	fare il bagno	['farɛ iʎ 'baɲo]
to go out (from ...)	uscire (vi)	[u'ʃirɛ]
to guess right	indovinare (vt)	[indowi'narɛ]

to have (vt)	avere (vt)	[a'vɛrɛ]
to have breakfast	fare colazione	['farɛ koʎa'tsione]
to have dinner	cenare (vi)	[tʃe'narɛ]
to have lunch	pranzare (vi)	[pran'tsarɛ]

to hear (vt)	sentire (vt)	[sɛn'tirɛ]
to help (vt)	aiutare (vt)	[aju'tarɛ]
to hide (vt)	nascondere (vt)	[nas'kondɛrɛ]

to hope (vi, vt)	sperare (vi, vt)	[spɛ'rarɛ]
to hunt (vi, vt)	cacciare (vt)	[ka'ʧarɛ]
to hurry (vi)	avere fretta	[a'vɛrɛ 'frɛtta]

12. The most important verbs. Part 3

to inform (vt)	informare (vt)	[infor'marɛ]
to insist (vi, vt)	insistere (vi)	[in'sistɛrɛ]
to insult (vt)	insultare (vt)	[insuʎ'tarɛ]
to invite (vt)	invitare (vt)	[inwi'tarɛ]
to joke (vi)	scherzare (vi)	[skɛr'tsarɛ]

to keep (vt)	conservare (vt)	[kɔnsɛr'varɛ]
to keep silent	tacere (vi)	[ta'ʧerɛ]
to kill (vt)	uccidere (vt)	[u'ʧidɛrɛ]
to know (sb)	conoscere	[kɔ'nɔʃɛrɛ]
to know (sth)	sapere (vt)	[sa'pɛrɛ]

to laugh (vi)	ridere (vi)	['ridɛrɛ]
to liberate (city, etc.)	liberare (vt)	[libɛ'rarɛ]
to look for ... (search)	cercare (vt)	[ʧer'karɛ]
to love (sb)	amare qn	[a'marɛ]

to make a mistake	sbagliare (vi)	[zba'ʎjarɛ]
to manage, to run	dirigere (vt)	[di'ridʒerɛ]
to mean (signify)	significare (vt)	[siɲifi'karɛ]
to mention (talk about)	menzionare (vt)	[mentsʲo'narɛ]
to miss (school, etc.)	mancare le lezioni	[ma'ŋkarɛ le le'tsʲoni]
to notice (see)	accorgersi (vr)	[ak'kɔrdʒersi]

to object (vi, vt)	obiettare (vt)	[ɔbjet'tarɛ]
to observe (see)	osservare (vt)	[ɔssɛr'varɛ]
to open (vt)	aprire (vt)	[ap'rirɛ]
to order (meal, etc.)	ordinare (vt)	[ɔrdi'narɛ]
to order (mil.)	ordinare (vt)	[ɔrdi'narɛ]
to own (possess)	possedere (vt)	[pɔssɛ'dɛrɛ]

to participate (vi)	partecipare (vi)	[partɛʧi'parɛ]
to pay (vi, vt)	pagare (vi, vt)	[pa'garɛ]
to permit (vt)	permettere (vt)	[pɛr'mettɛrɛ]
to plan (vt)	pianificare (vt)	[pjanifi'karɛ]
to play (children)	giocare (vi)	[dʒo'karɛ]
to pray (vi, vt)	pregare (vi, vt)	[prɛ'garɛ]
to prefer (vt)	preferire (vt)	[prɛfɛ'rirɛ]

to promise (vt)	promettere (vt)	[prɔ'mettɛrɛ]
to pronounce (vt)	pronunciare (vt)	[pronun'ʧarɛ]
to propose (vt)	proporre (vt)	[prɔ'pɔrrɛ]
to punish (vt)	punire (vt)	[pu'nirɛ]
to read (vi, vt)	leggere (vi, vt)	['ledʒerɛ]
to recommend (vt)	raccomandare (vt)	[rakkoman'darɛ]

to refuse (vi, vt)	rifiutarsi (vr)	[rifjy'tarsi]
to regret (be sorry)	rincrescere (vi)	[riŋk'rɛʃɛrɛ]

to rent (sth from sb)	**affittare** (vt)	[affit'tarɛ]
to repeat (say again)	**ripetere** (vt)	[ri'pɛtɛrɛ]
to reserve, to book	**riservare** (vt)	[risɛr'varɛ]
to run (vi)	**correre** (vi)	['kɔrrɛrɛ]

13. The most important verbs. Part 4

to save (rescue)	**salvare** (vt)	[saʎ'varɛ]
to say (~ thank you)	**dire** (vt)	['dirɛ]
to scold (vt)	**sgridare** (vt)	[zgri'darɛ]
to see (vt)	**vedere** (vt)	[vɛ'dɛrɛ]
to sell (vt)	**vendere** (vt)	['vɛndɛrɛ]
to send (vt)	**mandare** (vt)	[man'darɛ]
to shoot (vi)	**sparare** (vi)	[spa'rarɛ]
to shout (vi)	**gridare** (vi)	[gri'darɛ]
to show (vt)	**mostrare** (vt)	[mɔst'rarɛ]
to sign (document)	**firmare** (vt)	[fir'marɛ]
to sit down (vi)	**sedersi** (vr)	[sɛ'dɛrsi]
to smile (vi)	**sorridere** (vi)	[sor'ridɛrɛ]
to speak (vi, vt)	**parlare** (vi, vt)	[par'ʎarɛ]
to steal (money, etc.)	**rubare** (vt)	[ru'barɛ]
to stop (cease)	**cessare** (vt)	[tʃes'sarɛ]
to stop (for pause, etc.)	**fermarsi** (vr)	[fɛr'marsi]
to study (vt)	**studiare** (vt)	[studi'arɛ]
to swim (vi)	**nuotare** (vi)	[nuɔ'tarɛ]
to take (vt)	**prendere** (vt)	['prɛndɛrɛ]
to think (vi, vt)	**pensare** (vi, vt)	[pɛn'sarɛ]
to threaten (vt)	**minacciare** (vt)	[mina'tʃarɛ]
to touch (by hands)	**toccare** (vt)	[tɔk'karɛ]
to translate (vt)	**tradurre** (vt)	[tra'durrɛ]
to trust (vt)	**fidarsi** (vr)	[fi'darsi]
to try (attempt)	**tentare** (vt)	[tɛn'tarɛ]
to turn (~ to the left)	**girare** (vi)	[dʒi'rarɛ]
to underestimate (vt)	**sottovalutare** (vt)	[sottovaly'tarɛ]
to understand (vt)	**capire** (vt)	[ka'pirɛ]
to unite (vt)	**unire** (vt)	[u'nirɛ]
to wait (vt)	**aspettare** (vt)	[aspɛt'tarɛ]
to want (wish, desire)	**volere** (vt)	[vɔ'lerɛ]
to warn (vt)	**avvertire** (vt)	[avwer'tirɛ]
to work (vi)	**lavorare** (vi)	[ʎavɔ'rarɛ]
to write (vt)	**scrivere** (vt)	['skrivɛrɛ]
to write down	**annotare** (vt)	[aɲɔ'tarɛ]

14. Colours

colour	**colore** (m)	[kɔ'lɔrɛ]
shade (tint)	**sfumatura** (f)	[sfuma'tura]

| hue | tono (m) | ['tɔnɔ] |
| rainbow | arcobaleno (m) | [arkɔba'lenɔ] |

white (adj)	bianco	['bjaŋkɔ]
black (adj)	nero	['nɛrɔ]
grey (adj)	grigio	['gridʒɔ]

green (adj)	verde	['vɛrdɛ]
yellow (adj)	giallo	['dʒallɔ]
red (adj)	rosso	['rɔssɔ]

blue (adj)	blu	['bly]
light blue (adj)	azzurro	[a'dzurrɔ]
pink (adj)	rosa	['rɔza]
orange (adj)	arancione	[aran'ʧɔnɛ]
violet (adj)	violetto	[wiɔ'lettɔ]
brown (adj)	marrone	[mar'rɔnɛ]

| golden (adj) | d'oro | ['dɔrɔ] |
| silvery (adj) | argenteo | [ar'dʒentɛɔ] |

beige (adj)	beige	[bɛʒ]
cream (adj)	color crema	[kɔ'lɜr 'krɛma]
turquoise (adj)	turchese	[tur'kɛzɛ]
cherry red (adj)	rosso ciliegia (f)	['rɔssɔ ʧi'ʎjedʒa]
lilac (adj)	lilla	['liʎa]
crimson (adj)	rosso lampone	['rɔssɔ ʎam'pɔnɛ]

light (adj)	chiaro	['kjarɔ]
dark (adj)	scuro	['skurɔ]
bright (adj)	vivo, vivido	['wivɔ], ['wiwidɔ]

coloured (pencils)	colorato	[kɔlɔ'ratɔ]
colour (e.g. ~ film)	a colori	[a kɔ'lɔri]
black-and-white (adj)	bianco e nero	['bjaŋkɔ ɛ 'nɛrɔ]
plain (one colour)	in tinta unita	[in 'tinta u'nita]
multicoloured (adj)	multicolore	[muʎtikɔ'lɔrɛ]

15. Questions

Who?	Chi?	[ki]
What?	Che cosa?	[kɛ 'kɔza]
Where? (at, in)	Dove?	['dɔvɛ]
Where (to)?	Dove?	['dɔvɛ]
Where ... from?	Di dove?, Da dove?	[di 'dɔvɛ da 'dɔvɛ]
When?	Quando?	[ku'andɔ]
Why? (aim)	Perché?	[pɛr'kɛ]
Why? (reason)	Perché?	[pɛr'kɛ]

What for?	Per che cosa?	[pɛr kɛ 'kɔza]
How? (in what way)	Come?	['kɔmɛ]
What? (which?)	Che?	[kɛ]
Which?	Quale?	[ku'ale]
To whom?	A chi?	[a 'ki]

About whom?	Di chi?	[di 'ki]
About what?	Di che cosa?	[di kɛ 'kɔza]
With whom?	Con chi?	[kɔn 'ki]

How many?	Quanti?	[ku'anti]
How much?	Quanto?	[ku'antɔ]
Whose?	Di chi?	[di 'ki]

16. Prepositions

with (accompanied by)	con	[kɔn]
without	senza	['sɛntsa]
to (indicating direction)	a	[a]
about (talking ~ ...)	di	[di]
before (in time)	prima di ...	['prima di]
in front of ...	di fronte a ...	[di 'frɔntɛ a]

under (beneath, below)	sotto	['sɔttɔ]
above (over)	sopra	['sɔpra]
on (atop)	su	[su]
from (off, out of)	da, di	[da], [di]
of (made from)	di	[di]

| in (e.g. ~ ten minutes) | fra ... | [fra] |
| over (across the top of) | attraverso | [attra'vɛrsɔ] |

17. Function words. Adverbs. Part 1

Where? (at, in)	Dove?	['dɔvɛ]
here (adv)	qui	[ku'i]
there (adv)	lì	[li]

| somewhere (to be) | da qualche parte | [da ku'aʎkɛ 'partɛ] |
| nowhere (not anywhere) | da nessuna parte | [da nɛs'suna 'partɛ] |

| by (near, beside) | vicino a ... | [wi'ʧinɔ a] |
| by the window | vicino alla finestra | [wi'ʧinɔ 'aʎa fi'nɛstra] |

Where (to)?	Dove?	['dɔvɛ]
here (e.g. come ~!)	di qui	[di ku'i]
there (e.g. to go ~)	ci	[ʧi]
from here (adv)	da qui	[da ku'i]
from there (adv)	da lì	[da 'li]

| close (adv) | vicino, accanto | [wi'ʧinɔ], [a'kantɔ] |
| far (adv) | lontano | [lɔn'tanɔ] |

near (e.g. ~ Paris)	vicino a ...	[wi'ʧinɔ a]
nearby (adv)	vicino	[wi'ʧinɔ]
not far (adv)	non lontano	[nɔn lɔn'tanɔ]
left (adj)	sinistro	[si'nistrɔ]
on the left	a sinistra	[a si'nistra]

to the left	a sinistra	[a si'nistra]
right (adj)	destro	['dɛstrɔ]
on the right	a destra	[a 'dɛstra]
to the right	a destra	[a 'dɛstra]

in front (adv)	davanti	[da'vanti]
front (as adj)	anteriore	[antɛri'ɔrɛ]
ahead (in space)	avanti	[a'vanti]

behind (adv)	dietro	['djetrɔ]
from behind	da dietro	[da 'djetrɔ]
back (towards the rear)	indietro	[in'djetrɔ]

| middle | mezzo (m), centro (m) | ['mɛdzɔ], ['ʧɛntrɔ] |
| in the middle | in mezzo, al centro | [in 'mɛdzɔ], [aʎ 'ʧɛntrɔ] |

at the side	di fianco	[di 'fjaŋkɔ]
everywhere (adv)	dappertutto	[dappɛr'tuttɔ]
around (in all directions)	attorno	[at'tɔrnɔ]

from inside	da dentro	[da 'dɛntrɔ]
somewhere (to go)	da qualche parte	[da ku'aʎkɛ 'partɛ]
straight (directly)	dritto	['drittɔ]
back (e.g. come ~)	indietro	[in'djetrɔ]

| from anywhere | da qualsiasi parte | [da kuaʎsia'zi 'partɛ] |
| from somewhere | da qualche posto | [da ku'aʎkɛ 'pɔstɔ] |

firstly (adv)	in primo luogo	[in 'primɔ ly'ɔgɔ]
secondly (adv)	in secondo luogo	[in sɛ'kɔndɔ ly'ɔgɔ]
thirdly (adv)	in terzo luogo	[in 'tɛrtsɔ ly'ɔgɔ]

suddenly (adv)	all'improvviso	[allimprɔv'wizɔ]
at first (adv)	all'inizio	[alli'nitsiɔ]
for the first time	per la prima volta	[pɛr ʎa 'prima 'vɔʎta]
long before ...	molto tempo prima di...	['mɔʎtɔ 'tɛmpɔ 'prima di]
anew (over again)	di nuovo	[di nu'ɔvɔ]
for good (adv)	per sempre	[pɛr 'sɛmprɛ]

never (adv)	mai	[maj]
again (adv)	ancora	[a'ŋkɔra]
now (adv)	adesso	[a'dɛssɔ]
often (adv)	spesso	['spɛssɔ]
then (adv)	allora	[al'lɔra]
urgently (quickly)	urgentemente	[urdʒɛntɛ'mɛntɛ]
usually (adv)	di solito	[di 'sɔlitɔ]

by the way, ...	a proposito, ...	[a prɔ'pɔzitɔ]
possible (that is ~)	è possibile	[ɛ pɔ'sibilɛ]
probably (adv)	probabilmente	[prɔbabiʎ'mɛntɛ]
maybe (adv)	forse	['fɔrsɛ]
besides ...	inoltre ...	[i'nɔʎtrɛ]
that's why ...	ecco perché ...	['ɛkkɔ pɛr'kɛ]
in spite of ...	nonostante	[nɔnɔs'tantɛ]
thanks to ...	grazie a ...	['gratsiɛ a]
what (pron.)	che cosa	[kɛ 'kɔza]

that	che	[kɛ]
something	qualcosa	[kuaʎ'kɔza]
anything (something)	qualcosa	[kuaʎ'kɔza]
nothing	niente	['njentɛ]

who (pron.)	chi	[ki]
someone	qualcuno	[kuaʎ'kunɔ]
somebody	qualcuno	[kuaʎ'kunɔ]

nobody	nessuno	[nɛs'sunɔ]
nowhere (a voyage to ~)	da nessuna parte	[da nɛs'suna 'partɛ]
nobody's	di nessuno	[di nɛs'sunɔ]
somebody's	di qualcuno	[di kuaʎ'kunɔ]

so (I'm ~ glad)	così	[kɔ'zi]
also (as well)	anche	['aŋkɛ]
too (as well)	anche, pure	['aŋkɛ], ['purɛ]

18. Function words. Adverbs. Part 2

Why?	Perché?	[pɛr'kɛ]
for some reason	per qualche ragione	[pɛr ku'aʎke ra'dʒɔnɛ]
because ...	perché ...	[pɛr'kɛ]
for some purpose	per qualche motivo	[pɛr ku'aʎke mɔ'tivɔ]

and	e	[ɛ]
or	o ...	[ɔ]
but	ma	[ma]
for (e.g. ~ me)	per	[pɛr]

too (excessively)	troppo	['trɔppɔ]
only (exclusively)	solo	['sɔlɔ]
exactly (adv)	esattamente	[ɛzatta'mentɛ]
about (more or less)	circa	['tʃirka]

approximately (adv)	approssimativamente	[aprɔsimativa'mentɛ]
approximate (adj)	approssimativo	[apprɔssima'tivɔ]
almost (adv)	quasi	[ku'azi]
the rest	resto (m)	['rɛstɔ]

each (adj)	ogni	['ɔɲi]
any (no matter which)	qualsiasi	[kuaʎ'siazi]
many (adv)	molti	['mɔʎti]
much (adv)	molto	['mɔʎtɔ]
many people	molta gente	['mɔʎta 'dʒɛntɛ]
all (everyone)	tutto, tutti	['tuttɔ], ['tutti]

in exchange for ...	in cambio di ...	[in 'kambʲɔ di]
in exchange (adv)	in cambio	[in 'kambʲɔ]
by hand (made)	a mano	[a 'manɔ]
hardly (negative opinion)	poco probabile	['pɔkɔ prɔ'babile]

| probably (adv) | probabilmente | [prɔbabiʎ'mentɛ] |
| on purpose (adv) | apposta | [ap'pɔsta] |

by accident (adv)	**per caso**	[pɛr 'kazɔ]
very (adv)	**molto**	['mɔʎtɔ]
for example (adv)	**per esempio**	[pɛr ɛ'zɛmpʲɔ]
between	**fra**	[fra]
among	**fra**	[fra]
so much (such a lot)	**tanto**	['tantɔ]
especially (adv)	**soprattutto**	[sɔpra'tuttɔ]

Basic concepts. Part 2

19. Weekdays

Monday	lunedì (m)	[lynɛ'di]
Tuesday	martedì (m)	[martɛ'di]
Wednesday	mercoledì (m)	[mɛrkɔle'di]
Thursday	giovedì (m)	[dʒɔvɛ'di]
Friday	venerdì (m)	[vɛnɛr'di]
Saturday	sabato (m)	['sabatɔ]
Sunday	domenica (f)	[dɔ'mɛnika]
today (adv)	oggi	['ɔdʒi]
tomorrow (adv)	domani	[dɔ'mani]
the day after tomorrow	dopo domani	['dɔpɔ dɔ'mani]
yesterday (adv)	ieri	['jeri]
the day before yesterday	l'altro ieri	['ʎaʎtrɔ 'jeri]
day	giorno (m)	['dʒɔrnɔ]
working day	giorno (m) lavorativo	['dʒɔrnɔ ʎavɔra'tivɔ]
public holiday	giorno (m) festivo	['dʒɔrnɔ fɛs'tivɔ]
day off	giorno (m) di riposo	['dʒɔrnɔ di ri'pɔzɔ]
weekend	fine (m) settimana	['finɛ sɛtti'mana]
all day long	tutto il giorno	['tutto iʎ 'dʒɔrnɔ]
next day (adv)	l'indomani	[lindɔ'mani]
two days ago	due giorni fa	['duɛ 'dʒɔrni fa]
the day before	il giorno prima	[iʎ 'dʒɔrnɔ 'prima]
daily (adj)	quotidiano	[kuɔtidi'anɔ]
every day (adv)	ogni giorno	['ɔɲi 'dʒɔrnɔ]
week	settimana (f)	[sɛtti'mana]
last week (adv)	la settimana scorsa	[ʎa sɛtti'mana 'skɔrsa]
next week (adv)	la settimana prossima	[ʎa sɛtti'mana 'prɔssima]
weekly (adj)	settimanale	[sɛttima'nale]
every week (adv)	ogni settimana	[ɔɲi sɛtti'mana]
twice a week	due volte alla settimana	['duɛ 'vɔʎtɛ 'aʎa sɛtti'mana]
every Tuesday	ogni martedì	['ɔɲi martɛ'di]

20. Hours. Day and night

morning	mattina (f)	[mat'tina]
in the morning	di mattina	[di mat'tina]
noon, midday	mezzogiorno (m)	[mɛdzɔ'dʒɔrnɔ]
in the afternoon	nel pomeriggio	[nɛʎ pomɛ'ridʒɔ]
evening	sera (f)	['sɛra]
in the evening	di sera	[di 'sɛra]

night	notte (f)	['nɔttɛ]
at night	di notte	[di 'nɔttɛ]
midnight	mezzanotte (f)	[mɛdza'nɔttɛ]

second	secondo (m)	[sɛ'kondɔ]
minute	minuto (m)	[mi'nutɔ]
hour	ora (f)	['ɔra]
half an hour	mezzora (f)	[mɛ'dzora]
quarter of an hour	un quarto d'ora	[un ku'artɔ 'dora]
fifteen minutes	quindici minuti	[ku'inditʃi mi'nuti]
24 hours	ventiquattro ore	[vɛntiku'attrɔ 'ɔrɛ]

sunrise	levata (f) del sole	[le'vata dɛʎ 'sɔle]
dawn	alba (f)	['aʎba]
early morning	mattutino (m)	[mattu'tinɔ]
sunset	tramonto (m)	[tra'montɔ]

early in the morning	di buon mattino	[di bu'ɔn mat'tinɔ]
this morning	stamattina	[stamat'tina]
tomorrow morning	domattina	[dɔmat'tina]
this afternoon	oggi pomeriggio	['odʒi pomɛ'ridʒɔ]
in the afternoon	nel pomeriggio	[nɛʎ pomɛ'ridʒɔ]
tomorrow afternoon	domani pomeriggio	[dɔ'mani pomɛ'ridʒɔ]
tonight (this evening)	stasera	[sta'sɛra]
tomorrow night	domani sera	[dɔ'mani 'sɛra]

at 3 o'clock sharp	alle tre precise	['alle trɛ prɛ'tʃizɛ]
about 4 o'clock	verso le quattro	['vɛrsɔ le ku'attrɔ]
by 12 o'clock	per le dodici	[pɛr le 'doditʃi]

in 20 minutes	fra venti minuti	[fra 'vɛnti mi'nuti]
in an hour	fra un'ora	[fra un 'ɔra]
on time (adv)	puntualmente	[puntuaʎ'mɛntɛ]

a quarter to ...	un quarto di ...	[un ku'artɔ di]
within an hour	entro un'ora	['ɛntrɔ un 'ɔra]
every 15 minutes	ogni quindici minuti	['ɔɲi ku'inditʃi mi'nuti]
round the clock	giorno e notte	['dʒɔrnɔ ɛ 'nɔttɛ]

21. Months. Seasons

January	gennaio (m)	[dʒe'ɲajo]
February	febbraio (m)	[fɛbb'rajo]
March	marzo (m)	['martsɔ]
April	aprile (m)	[ap'rile]
May	maggio (m)	['madʒɔ]
June	giugno (m)	['dʒuɲɔ]

July	luglio (m)	['luʎɔ]
August	agosto (m)	[a'gostɔ]
September	settembre (m)	[sɛt'tɛmbrɛ]
October	ottobre (m)	[ot'tobrɛ]
November	novembre (m)	[nɔ'vɛmbrɛ]
December	dicembre (m)	[di'tʃembrɛ]

spring	primavera (f)	[prima'vɛra]
in spring	in primavera	[in prima'vɛra]
spring (as adj)	primaverile	[primavɛ'rile]
summer	estate (f)	[ɛs'tatɛ]
in summer	in estate	[in ɛs'tatɛ]
summer (as adj)	estivo	[ɛs'tivɔ]
autumn	autunno (m)	[au'tuɲɔ]
in autumn	in autunno	[in au'tuɲɔ]
autumn (as adj)	autunnale	[autu'ɲale]
winter	inverno (m)	[in'vɛrnɔ]
in winter	in inverno	[in in'vɛrnɔ]
winter (as adj)	invernale	[invɛr'nale]
month	mese (m)	['mezɛ]
this month	questo mese	[ku'ɛstɔ 'mɛzɛ]
next month	il mese prossimo	[iʎ 'mɛzɛ 'prɔssimɔ]
last month	il mese scorso	[iʎ 'mɛzɛ 'skɔrsɔ]
a month ago	un mese fa	[un 'mɛzɛ fa]
in a month	fra un mese	[fra un 'mɛzɛ]
in two months	fra due mesi	[fra 'duɛ 'mɛzi]
a whole month	un mese intero	[un 'mɛzɛ in'tɛrɔ]
all month long	per tutto il mese	[per 'tuttɔ iʎ 'mɛzɛ]
monthly (~ magazine)	mensile	[men'sile]
monthly (adv)	mensilmente	[mensiʎ'mɛntɛ]
every month	ogni mese	['ɔɲʲi 'mɛzɛ]
twice a month	due volte al mese	['duɛ 'vɔʎtɛ aʎ 'mɛzɛ]
year	anno (m)	['aɲɔ]
this year	quest'anno	[kuɛs'taɲɔ]
next year	l'anno prossimo	['ʎaɲɔ 'prɔssimɔ]
last year	l'anno scorso	['ʎaɲɔ 'skɔrsɔ]
a year ago	un anno fa	[un 'aɲɔ fa]
in a year	fra un anno	[fra un 'aɲɔ]
in two years	fra due anni	[fra 'duɛ 'aɲi]
a whole year	un anno intero	[un 'aɲɔ in'tɛrɔ]
all year long	per tutto l'anno	[per 'tuttɔ 'ʎaɲɔ]
every year	ogni anno	['ɔɲʲi 'aɲɔ]
annual (adj)	annuale	[aɲu'ale]
annually (adv)	annualmente	[aɲuaʎ'mɛntɛ]
4 times a year	quattro volte all'anno	[ku'attrɔ 'vɔʎtɛ a'ʎaɲɔ]
date (e.g. today's ~)	data (f)	['data]
date (e.g. ~ of birth)	data (f)	['data]
calendar	calendario (m)	[kalen'dariɔ]
half a year	mezz'anno (m)	[mɛ'dzaɲɔ]
six months	semestre (m)	[sɛ'mɛstrɛ]
season (summer, etc.)	stagione (f)	[sta'dʒɔnɛ]
century	secolo (m)	['sɛkɔlɔ]

22. Time. Miscellaneous

time	tempo (m)	['tɛmpɔ]
instant (n)	istante (m)	[is'tantɛ]
moment	momento (m)	[mɔ'mɛntɔ]
instant (adj)	istantaneo	[istan'tanɛɔ]
period (length of time)	periodo (m)	[pɛ'riɔdɔ]
life	vita (f)	['wita]
eternity	eternità (f)	[ɛtɛrni'ta]

epoch	epoca (f)	['ɛpɔka]
era	era (f)	['ɛra]
cycle	ciclo (m)	['tʃiklɔ]
period	periodo (m)	[pɛ'riɔdɔ]
term (short-~)	scadenza (f)	[ska'dɛntsa]

the future	futuro (m)	[fu'turɔ]
future (as adj)	futuro	[fu'turɔ]
next time	la prossima volta	[ʎa 'prɔssima 'vɔlta]

the past	passato (m)	[pas'satɔ]
past (recent)	scorso	['skɔrsɔ]
last time	la volta scorsa	[ʎa 'vɔʎta 'skɔrsa]

later (adv)	più tardi	[pjy 'tardi]
after	dopo	['dɔpɔ]
nowadays (adv)	oggigiorno	[ɔdʒi'dʒɔrnɔ]
now (adv)	adesso, ora	[a'dɛssɔ], [ɔra]
immediately (adv)	subito	['subitɔ]
soon (adv)	fra poco, presto	[fra 'pɔkɔ], ['prɛstɔ]
in advance (beforehand)	in anticipo	[in an'titʃipɔ]

a long time ago	tanto tempo fa	['tantɔ 'tɛmpɔ fa]
recently (adv)	di recente	[di rɛ'tʃɛntɛ]
destiny	destino (m)	[dɛs'tinɔ]
memories (childhood ~)	ricordi (m pl)	[ri'kɔrdi]
archives	archivio (m)	[ar'kiwiɔ]

during ...	durante ...	[du'rantɛ]
long, a long time (adv)	a lungo	[a 'lyŋɔ]
not long (adv)	per poco tempo	[pɛr 'pɔkɔ 'tɛmpɔ]
early (in the morning)	presto	['prɛstɔ]
late (not early)	tardi	['tardi]

forever (for good)	per sempre	[pɛr 'sɛmprɛ]
to start (begin)	cominciare (vt)	[kɔmin'tʃarɛ]
to postpone (vt)	posticipare (vt)	[postitʃi'parɛ]

at the same time	simultaneamente	[simultanɛa'mentɔ]
permanently (adv)	tutto il tempo	['tutto iʎ 'tɛmpɔ]
constant (noise, pain)	costante	[kɔs'tantɛ]
temporary (adj)	temporaneo	[tɛmpɔ'ranɛɔ]
sometimes (adv)	a volte	[a 'vɔʎtɛ]
rarely (adv)	raramente	[rara'mɛntɛ]
often (adv)	spesso	['spɛssɔ]

23. Opposites

rich (adj)	ricco	['rikkɔ]
poor (adj)	povero	['pɔvɛrɔ]
ill, sick (adj)	malato	[ma'ʎatɔ]
healthy (adj)	sano	['sanɔ]
big (adj)	grande	['grandɛ]
small (adj)	piccolo	['pikkɔlɔ]
quickly (adv)	rapidamente	[rapida'mɛntɛ]
slowly (adv)	lentamente	[lenta'mɛntɛ]
fast (adj)	veloce	[vɛ'lɔʧe]
slow (adj)	lento	['lentɔ]
cheerful (adj)	allegro	[al'legrɔ]
sad (adj)	triste	['tristɛ]
together (adv)	insieme	[in'sjemɛ]
separately (adv)	separatamente	[sɛparata'mɛntɛ]
aloud (to read)	ad alta voce	[ad 'aʎta 'vɔʧe]
silently (to oneself)	in silenzio	[in si'lentsiɔ]
tall (adj)	alto	['aʎtɔ]
low (adj)	basso	['bassɔ]
deep (adj)	profondo	[prɔ'fondɔ]
shallow (adj)	basso	['bassɔ]
yes	sì	[si]
no	no	[nɔ]
distant (in space)	lontano	[lɔn'tanɔ]
nearby (adj)	vicino	[wi'ʧinɔ]
far (adv)	lontano	[lɔn'tanɔ]
nearby (adv)	vicino	[wi'ʧinɔ]
long (adj)	lungo	['lyŋɔ]
short (adj)	corto	['kɔrtɔ]
good (kindhearted)	buono	[bu'ɔnɔ]
evil (adj)	cattivo	[kat'tivɔ]
married (adj)	sposato	[spɔ'zatɔ]
single (adj)	celibe	['ʧelibɛ]
to forbid (vt)	vietare (vt)	[vje'tarɛ]
to permit (vt)	permettere (vt)	[pɛr'mɛttɛrɛ]
end	fine (f)	['finɛ]
beginning	inizio (m)	[i'nitsiɔ]

| left (adj) | sinistro | [si'nistrɔ] |
| right (adj) | destro | ['dɛstrɔ] |

| first (adj) | primo | ['primɔ] |
| last (adj) | ultimo | ['uʌtimɔ] |

| crime | delitto (m) | [dɛ'litto] |
| punishment | punizione (f) | [puni'tsɪɔnɛ] |

| to order (vt) | ordinare (vt) | [ɔrdi'narɛ] |
| to obey (vi, vt) | obbedire (vi) | [ɔbbɛ'dirɛ] |

| straight (adj) | dritto | ['drittɔ] |
| curved (adj) | curvo | ['kurvɔ] |

| heaven | paradiso (m) | [para'dizɔ] |
| hell | inferno (m) | [in'fɛrnɔ] |

| to be born | nascere (vi) | ['naʃɛrɛ] |
| to die (vi) | morire (vi) | [mɔ'rirɛ] |

| strong (adj) | forte | ['fɔrtɛ] |
| weak (adj) | debole | ['dɛbɔle] |

| old (adj) | vecchio | ['vɛkkiɔ] |
| young (adj) | giovane | ['dʒɔvanɛ] |

| old (adj) | vecchio | ['vɛkkiɔ] |
| new (adj) | nuovo | [nu'ɔvɔ] |

| hard (adj) | duro | ['durɔ] |
| soft (adj) | morbido | ['mɔrbidɔ] |

| warm (adj) | caldo | ['kaʌdɔ] |
| cold (adj) | freddo | ['frɛddɔ] |

| fat (adj) | grasso | ['grassɔ] |
| slim (adj) | magro | ['magrɔ] |

| narrow (adj) | stretto | ['strɛttɔ] |
| wide (adj) | largo | ['ʌargɔ] |

| good (adj) | buono | [bu'ɔnɔ] |
| bad (adj) | cattivo | [kat'tivɔ] |

| brave (adj) | valoroso | [valɜ'rozɔ] |
| cowardly (adj) | codardo | [kɔ'dardɔ] |

24. Lines and shapes

square	quadrato (m)	[kuad'ratɔ]
square (as adj)	quadrato	[kuad'ratɔ]
circle	cerchio (m)	['tʃerkiɔ]
round (adj)	rotondo	[rɔ'tɔndɔ]

| triangle | triangolo (m) | [tri'aŋɔlɔ] |
| triangular (adj) | triangolare | [triaŋɔ'ʎarɛ] |

oval	ovale (m)	[ɔ'vale]
oval (as adj)	ovale	[ɔ'vale]
rectangle	rettangolo (m)	[rɛt'taŋɔlɔ]
rectangular (adj)	rettangolare	[rɛttaŋɔ'ʎarɛ]

pyramid	piramide (f)	[pi'ramidɛ]
rhombus	rombo (m)	['rɔmbɔ]
trapezium	trapezio (m)	[tra'pɛtsiɔ]
cube	cubo (m)	['kubɔ]
prism	prisma (m)	['prizma]

circumference	circonferenza (f)	[ʧirkɔnfɛ'rɛntsa]
sphere	sfera (f)	['sfɛra]
globe (sphere)	palla (f)	['paʎa]
diameter	diametro (m)	[di'amɛtrɔ]
radius	raggio (m)	['radʒɔ]
perimeter	perimetro (m)	[pɛ'rimɛtrɔ]
centre	centro (m)	['ʧentrɔ]

horizontal (adj)	orizzontale	[ɔridzɔn'tale]
vertical (adj)	verticale	[vɛrti'kale]
parallel (n)	parallela (f)	[paral'leʎa]
parallel (as adj)	parallelo	[paral'lelɔ]

line	linea (f)	['linɛa]
stroke	tratto (m)	['trattɔ]
straight line	linea (f) retta	['linɛa 'rɛtta]
curve (curved line)	linea (f) curva	['linɛa 'kurva]
thin (line, etc.)	sottile	[sɔt'tile]
contour (outline)	contorno (m)	[kɔn'tɔrnɔ]

intersection	intersezione (f)	[intɛrsɛ'tsiɔnɛ]
right angle	angolo (m) retto	['aŋɔlɔ 'rɛttɔ]
segment	segmento	[sɛg'mɛntɔ]
sector	settore (m)	[sɛt'tɔrɛ]
side (of triangle)	lato (m)	['ʎatɔ]
angle	angolo (m)	['aŋɔlɔ]

25. Units of measurement

weight	peso (m)	['pɛzɔ]
length	lunghezza (f)	[ly'ŋɛtsa]
width	larghezza (f)	[ʎar'gɛtsa]
height	altezza (f)	[aʎ'tɛtsa]
depth	profondità (f)	[prɔfɔndi'ta]
volume	volume (m)	[vɔ'lymɛ]
area	area (f)	['arɛa]
gram	grammo (m)	['grammɔ]
milligram	milligrammo (m)	[millig'rammɔ]
kilogram	chilogrammo (m)	[kilɔg'rammɔ]
ton	tonnellata (f)	[tɔŋɛ'ʎata]

pound	libbra (f)	['libbra]
ounce	oncia (f)	['ontʃa]
metre	metro (m)	['mɛtrɔ]
millimetre	millimetro (m)	[mil'limɛtrɔ]
centimetre	centimetro (m)	[tʃen'timɛtrɔ]
kilometre	chilometro (m)	[ki'lɔmɛtrɔ]
mile	miglio (m)	['miʎʼɔ]
inch	pollice (m)	['pɔllitʃe]
foot	piede (f)	['pjedɛ]
yard	iarda (f)	[jarda]
square metre	metro (m) quadro	['mɛtrɔ ku'adrɔ]
hectare	ettaro (m)	['ɛttarɔ]
litre	litro (m)	['litrɔ]
degree	grado (m)	['gradɔ]
volt	volt (m)	[vɔʎt]
ampere	ampere (m)	[am'pɛrɛ]
horsepower	cavallo vapore (m)	[ka'vallɔ va'pɔrɛ]
quantity	quantità (f)	[kuanti'ta]
a little bit of ...	un po' di ...	[un 'pɔ di]
half	metà (f)	[mɛ'ta]
dozen	dozzina (f)	[dɔ'dzina]
piece (item)	pezzo (m)	['pɛtsɔ]
size	dimensione (f)	[dimɛnsi'ɔnɛ]
scale (map ~)	scala (f)	['skaʎa]
minimum (adj)	minimo	['minimɔ]
the smallest (adj)	minore	[mi'nɔrɛ]
medium (adj)	medio	['mɛdiɔ]
maximum (adj)	massimo	['massimɔ]
the largest (adj)	maggiore	[ma'dʒɔrɛ]

26. Containers

jar (glass)	barattolo (m) di vetro	[ba'rattolɔ di 'vɛtrɔ]
tin, can	latta (f), lattina (f)	['ʎatta], [lat'tina]
bucket	secchio (m)	['sɛkkiɔ]
barrel	barile (m), botte (f)	[ba'rile], ['bɔttɛ]
basin (for washing)	catino (m)	[ka'tinɔ]
tank (for liquid, gas)	serbatoio (m)	[sɛrba'tɔjo]
hip flask	fiaschetta (f)	[fias'ketta]
jerrycan	tanica (f)	['tanika]
cistern (tank)	cisterna (f)	[tʃis'tɛrna]
mug	tazza (f)	['tattsa]
cup (of coffee, etc.)	tazzina (f)	[ta'tsina]
saucer	piattino (m)	[pjat'tinɔ]
glass (tumbler)	bicchiere (m)	[bik'kjerɛ]

| glass (~ of vine) | calice (m) | ['kalitʃe] |
| stew pot | casseruola (f) | [kassɛru'ɔʎa] |

| bottle (~ of wine) | bottiglia (f) | [bɔt'tiʎja] |
| neck (of the bottle) | collo (m) | ['kɔllɔ] |

carafe	caraffa (f)	[ka'raffa]
jug (earthenware)	brocca (f)	['brɔkka]
vessel (container)	recipiente (m)	[rɛtʃipi'entɛ]
pot (crock)	vaso (m) di coccio	['vazɔ di 'kɔtʃɔ]
vase	vaso (m)	['vazɔ]

bottle (~ of perfume)	boccetta (f)	[bɔ'tʃetta]
vial, small bottle	fiala (f)	[fi'aʎa]
tube (of toothpaste)	tubetto (m)	[tu'bɛttɔ]

sack (bag)	sacco (m)	['sakkɔ]
bag (paper ~, plastic ~)	sacchetto (m)	[sak'kɛttɔ]
packet (of cigarettes, etc.)	pacchetto (m)	[pak'kɛttɔ]

box (e.g. shoebox)	scatola (f)	['skatɔʎa]
crate	cassa (f)	['kassa]
basket	cesta (f)	['tʃesta]

27. Materials

material	materiale (m)	[matɛri'ale]
wood	legno (m)	['leɲɔ]
wooden (adj)	di legno	[di 'leɲɔ]

| glass (n) | vetro (m) | ['vɛtrɔ] |
| glass (as adj) | di vetro | [di 'vɛtrɔ] |

| stone (n) | pietra (f) | ['pjetra] |
| stone (as adj) | di pietra | [di 'pjetra] |

| plastic (n) | plastica (f) | ['pʎastika] |
| plastic (as adj) | di plastica | [di 'plastika] |

| rubber (n) | gomma (f) | ['gɔmma] |
| rubber (as adj) | di gomma | [di 'gɔmma] |

| material, fabric (n) | stoffa (f) | ['stɔffa] |
| fabric (as adj) | di stoffa | [di 'stɔffa] |

| paper (n) | carta (f) | ['karta] |
| paper (as adj) | di carta | [di 'karta] |

cardboard (n)	cartone (m)	[kar'tɔnɛ]
cardboard (as adj)	di cartone	[di kar'tɔnɛ]
polythene	polietilene (m)	[poliɛti'lenɛ]
cellophane	cellofan (m)	['tʃellɔfan]
linoleum	linoleum (m)	[li'nɔleum]
plywood	legno (m) compensato	['leɲɔ kɔmpɛn'satɔ]

porcelain (n)	porcellana (f)	[pɔrtʃe'ʎana]
porcelain (as adj)	di porcellana	[di pɔrtʃe'ʎana]
clay (n)	argilla (f)	[ar'dʒiʎa]
clay (as adj)	d'argilla	[dar'dʒiʎa]
ceramics (n)	ceramica (f)	[tʃe'ramika]
ceramic (as adj)	ceramico	[tʃe'ramikɔ]

28. Metals

metal (n)	metallo (m)	[mɛ'tallɔ]
metal (as adj)	metallico	[mɛ'tallikɔ]
alloy (n)	lega (f)	['lega]

gold (n)	oro (m)	['ɔrɔ]
gold, golden (adj)	d'oro	['dɔrɔ]
silver (n)	argento (m)	[ar'dʒentɔ]
silver (as adj)	d'argento	[dar'dʒentɔ]

iron (n)	ferro (m)	['fɛrrɔ]
iron (adj), made of iron	di ferro	[di 'fɛrrɔ]
steel (n)	acciaio (m)	[a'tʃajo]
steel (as adj)	d'acciaio	[da'tʃajo]
copper (n)	rame (m)	['ramɛ]
copper (as adj)	di rame	[di 'ramɛ]

aluminium (n)	alluminio (m)	[ally'miniɔ]
aluminium (as adj)	di alluminio	[ally'minikɔ]
bronze (n)	bronzo (m)	['brɔndzɔ]
bronze (as adj)	di bronzo	[di 'brɔndzɔ]

brass	ottone (m)	[ɔt'tɔnɛ]
nickel	nichel (m)	['nikɛʎ]
platinum	platino (m)	['pʎatinɔ]
mercury	mercurio (m)	[mɛr'kuriɔ]
tin	stagno (m)	['staɲɔ]
lead	piombo (m)	['pʲɔmbɔ]
zinc	zinco (m)	['dziŋkɔ]

HUMAN BEING

Human being. The body

29. Humans. Basic concepts

human being	uomo (m), essere umano (m)	[u'omɔ], ['ɛssɛrɛ u'manɔ]
man (adult male)	uomo (m)	[u'omɔ]
woman	donna (f)	['dɔŋa]
child	bambino (m)	[bam'binɔ]
girl	bambina (f)	[bam'bina]
boy	bambino (m)	[bam'binɔ]
teenager	adolescente (m, f)	[adɔle'ʃɛntɛ]
old man	vecchio (m)	['vɛkkiɔ]
old woman	vecchia (f)	['vɛkkja]

30. Human anatomy

organism	organismo (m)	[ɔrga'nizmɔ]
heart	cuore (m)	[ku'ɔrɛ]
blood	sangue (m)	['saŋuɛ]
artery	arteria (f)	[ar'tɛria]
vein	vena (f)	['vɛna]
brain	cervello (m)	[tʃer'vɛllɔ]
nerve	nervo (m)	['nɛrvɔ]
nerves	nervi (m pl)	['nɛrwi]
vertebra	vertebra (f)	['vɛrtɛbra]
spine	colonna (f) vertebrale	[kɔ'lɔŋa vɛrtɛb'rale]
stomach (organ)	stomaco (m)	['stɔmakɔ]
intestines, bowel	intestini (m pl)	[intɛs'tini]
intestine (e.g. large ~)	intestino (m)	[intɛs'tinɔ]
liver	fegato (m)	['fɛgatɔ]
kidney	rene (m)	['rɛnɛ]
bone	osso (m)	['ɔssɔ]
skeleton	scheletro (m)	['skɛletrɔ]
rib	costola (f)	['kɔstɔʎa]
skull	cranio (m)	['kraniɔ]
muscle	muscolo (m)	['muskɔlɔ]
biceps	bicipite (m)	[bitʃi'pitɛ]
triceps	tricipite (m)	[tritʃi'pitɛ]
tendon	tendine (m)	['tɛndinɛ]
joint	articolazione (f)	[artikɔʎa'tsjɔnɛ]

lungs	polmoni (m pl)	[pol'moni]
genitals	genitali (m pl)	[dʒeni'tali]
skin	pelle (f)	['pɛlle]

31. Head

head	testa (f)	['tɛsta]
face	viso (m)	['wizɔ]
nose	naso (m)	['nazɔ]
mouth	bocca (f)	['bɔkka]

eye	occhio (m)	['ɔkkiɔ]
eyes	occhi (m pl)	['ɔkki]
pupil	pupilla (f)	[pu'piʎa]
eyebrow	sopracciglio (m)	[sɔpra'tʃiʎɔ]
eyelash	ciglio (m)	['tʃiʎɔ]
eyelid	palpebra (f)	['paʎpɛbra]

tongue	lingua (f)	['liŋua]
tooth	dente (m)	['dɛntɛ]
lips	labbra (f pl)	['ʎabbra]
cheekbones	zigomi (m)	['dzigɔmi]
gum	gengiva (f)	[dʒen'dʒiva]
palate	palato (m)	[pa'ʎatɔ]

nostrils	narici (f pl)	[na'ritʃi]
chin	mento (m)	['mentɔ]
jaw	mascella (f)	[ma'ʃɛʎa]
cheek	guancia (f)	[gu'antʃa]

forehead	fronte (f)	['frɔntɛ]
temple	tempia (f)	['tɛmpia]
ear	orecchio (m)	[ɔ'rɛkkiɔ]
back of the head	nuca (f)	['nuka]
neck	collo (m)	['kɔllɔ]
throat	gola (f)	['gɔʎa]

hair	capelli (m pl)	[ka'pɛlli]
hairstyle	pettinatura (f)	[pɛttina'tura]
haircut	taglio (m)	['taʎɔ]
wig	parrucca (f)	['parrukka]

moustache	baffi (m pl)	['baffi]
beard	barba (f)	['barba]
to have (a beard, etc.)	portare (vt)	[pɔr'tarɛ]
plait	treccia (f)	['trɛtʃa]
sideboards	basette (f pl)	[ba'zɛttɛ]

red-haired (adj)	rosso	['rɔssɔ]
grey (hair)	brizzolato	[britsɔ'ʎatɔ]
bald (adj)	calvo	['kaʎvɔ]
bald patch	calvizie (f)	[kaʎ'witsiɛ]
ponytail	coda (f) di cavallo	['kɔda di ka'vaʎɔ]
fringe	frangetta (f)	[fran'dʒetta]

32. Human body

hand	**mano** (f)	['manɔ]
arm	**braccio** (m)	['bratʃɔ]
finger	**dito** (m)	['ditɔ]
thumb	**pollice** (m)	['pɔllitʃe]
little finger	**mignolo** (m)	[mi'ɲɔlɔ]
nail	**unghia** (f)	['ungja]
fist	**pugno** (m)	['puɲɔ]
palm	**palmo** (m)	['paʎmɔ]
wrist	**polso** (m)	['pɔʎsɔ]
forearm	**avambraccio** (m)	[avamb'ratʃɔ]
elbow	**gomito** (m)	['gɔmitɔ]
shoulder	**spalla** (f)	['spaʎa]
leg	**gamba** (f)	['gamba]
foot	**pianta** (f) **del piede**	['pjanta dɛʎ 'pjedɛ]
knee	**ginocchio** (m)	[dʒi'nɔkkiɔ]
calf (part of leg)	**polpaccio** (m)	[pɔʎ'patʃɔ]
hip	**anca** (f)	['aŋka]
heel	**tallone** (m)	[tal'lɔnɛ]
body	**corpo** (m)	['kɔrpɔ]
stomach	**pancia** (f)	['pantʃa]
chest	**petto** (m)	['pɛttɔ]
breast	**seno** (m)	['sɛnɔ]
flank	**fianco** (m)	['fjaŋkɔ]
back	**schiena** (f)	['skjena]
lower back	**zona** (f) **lombare**	['dzona lɔm'barɛ]
waist	**vita** (f)	['wita]
navel	**ombelico** (m)	[ɔmbɛ'likɔ]
buttocks	**natiche** (f pl)	['natikɛ]
bottom	**sedere** (m)	[sɛ'dɛrɛ]
beauty mark	**neo** (m)	['nɛɔ]
birthmark	**voglia** (f)	['vɔʎja]
tattoo	**tatuaggio** (m)	[tatu'adʒɔ]
scar	**cicatrice** (f)	[tʃikat'ritʃe]

Clothing & Accessories

33. Outerwear. Coats

clothes	vestiti (m pl)	[vɛs'titi]
outer clothing	soprabito (m)	[sɔp'rabitɔ]
winter clothing	abiti (m pl) invernali	['abiti invɛr'nali]
overcoat	cappotto (m)	[kap'pottɔ]
fur coat	pelliccia (f)	[pɛl'litʃa]
fur jacket	pellicciotto (m)	[pɛlli'tʃottɔ]
down coat	piumino (m)	[pjy'minɔ]
jacket (e.g. leather ~)	giubbotto (m), giaccha (f)	[dʒub'bottɔ], ['dʒakka]
raincoat	impermeabile (m)	[impɛrmɛ'abile]
waterproof (adj)	impermeabile	[impɛrmɛ'abile]

34. Men's & women's clothing

shirt	camicia (f)	[ka'mitʃa]
trousers	pantaloni (m pl)	[panta'lɔni]
jeans	jeans (m pl)	['dʒins]
jacket (of man's suit)	giacca (f)	['dʒakka]
suit	abito (m) da uomo	['abitɔ da u'omɔ]
dress (frock)	abito (m)	['abitɔ]
skirt	gonna (f)	['gɔŋa]
blouse	camicetta (f)	[kami'tʃetta]
knitted jacket	giacca (f) a maglia	['dʒakka a 'maʎja]
jacket (of woman's suit)	giacca (f) tailleur	['dʒaka ta'jer]
T-shirt	maglietta (f)	[ma'ʎjetta]
shorts (short trousers)	pantaloni (m pl) corti	[panta'lɔni 'kɔrti]
tracksuit	tuta (f) sportiva	['tuta spɔr'tiva]
bathrobe	accappatoio (m)	[akkappa'tɔjo]
pyjamas	pigiama (m)	[pi'dʒama]
sweater	maglione (m)	[ma'ʎjɔnɛ]
pullover	pullover (m)	[pul'lɔvɛr]
waistcoat	gilè (m)	[dʒi'le]
tailcoat	frac (m)	[frak]
dinner suit	smoking (m)	['zmɔkiŋ]
uniform	uniforme (f)	[uni'fɔrmɛ]
workwear	tuta (f) da lavoro	['tuta da ʎa'vɔrɔ]
boiler suit	salopette (f)	[salɔ'pɛtt]
coat (e.g. doctor's ~)	camice (m)	[ka'mitʃe]

35. Clothing. Underwear

underwear	biancheria (f) intima	[bjaŋkɛ'ria 'intima]
vest (singlet)	maglietta (f) intima	[mali'ɛtta 'intima]
socks	calzini (m pl)	[kaʎ'tsini]

nightgown	camicia (f) da notte	[ka'mitʃa da 'nɔttɛ]
bra	reggiseno (m)	[rɛdʒi'sɛno]
knee highs	calzini (m pl) alti	[kaʎ'tsini 'alti]
tights	collant (m)	[kɔ'ʎant]
stockings	calze (f pl)	['kaʎtse]
swimsuit, bikini	costume (m) da bagno	[kɔs'tumɛ da 'baɲɔ]

36. Headwear

hat	cappello (m)	[kap'pɛllo]
trilby hat	cappello (m) di feltro	[kap'pɛllo di feltro]
baseball cap	cappello (m) da baseball	[kap'pɛllo da 'bɛjzbɔʎ]
flatcap	coppola (f)	['kɔppɔla]

beret	basco (m)	['baskɔ]
hood	cappuccio (m)	[kap'putʃɔ]
panama hat	panama (m)	['panama]
knitted hat	berretto (m) a maglia	[bɛr'rɛttɔ a 'maʎja]

headscarf	fazzoletto (m) da capo	[fatso'lettɔ da 'kapo]
women's hat	cappellino (m) donna	[kappɛl'lino 'doŋa]

hard hat	casco (m)	['kaskɔ]
forage cap	bustina (f)	[bus'tina]
helmet	casco (m)	['kaskɔ]

bowler	bombetta (f)	[bom'bɛtta]
top hat	cilindro (m)	[tʃi'lindrɔ]

37. Footwear

footwear	calzature (f pl)	[kaʎtsa'turɛ]
ankle boots	stivaletti (m pl)	[stiva'letti]
shoes (low-heeled ~)	scarpe (f pl)	['skarpɛ]
boots (cowboy ~)	stivali (m pl)	[sti'vali]
slippers	pantofole (f pl)	[pan'tofole]

trainers	scarpe (f pl) da tennis	['skarpɛ da 'tɛɲis]
plimsolls, pumps	scarpe (f pl) da ginnastica	['skarpɛ da dʒim'nastika]
sandals	sandali (m pl)	['sandali]

cobbler	calzolaio (m)	[kaʎtso'ʎajo]
heel	tacco (m)	['takkɔ]
pair (of shoes)	paio (m)	['pajo]
shoelace	laccio (m)	['ʎatʃo]

to lace up (vt)	allacciare (vt)	[aʎa'tʃarɛ]
shoehorn	calzascarpe (m)	[kaʎtsas'karpɛ]
shoe polish	lucido (m) per le scarpe	['lytʃidɔ pɛr le 'skarpɛ]

38. Textile. Fabrics

cotton (n)	cotone (m)	[kɔ'tɔnɛ]
cotton (as adj)	di cotone	[di kɔ'tɔnɛ]
flax (n)	lino (m)	['linɔ]
flax (as adj)	di lino	[di 'linɔ]

silk (n)	seta (f)	['sɛta]
silk (as adj)	di seta	[di 'sɛta]
wool (n)	lana (f)	['ʎana]
woollen (adj)	di lana	[di 'ʎana]

velvet	velluto (m)	[vɛl'lytɔ]
suede	camoscio (m)	[ka'mɔʃɔ]
corduroy	velluto (m) a coste	[vɛl'lytɔ a 'kɔstɛ]

nylon (n)	nylon (m)	['najlɜn]
nylon (as adj)	di nylon	[di 'najlɜn]
polyester (n)	poliestere (m)	[poli'ɛstɛrɛ]
polyester (as adj)	di poliestere	[di poli'ɛstɛrɛ]

leather (n)	pelle (f)	['pɛlle]
leather (as adj)	di pelle	[di 'pɛlle]
fur (n)	pelliccia (f)	[pɛl'litʃa]
fur (e.g. ~ coat)	di pelliccia	[di pɛl'litʃa]

39. Personal accessories

gloves	guanti (m pl)	[gu'anti]
mittens	manopole (f pl)	[ma'nɔpole]
scarf (long)	sciarpa (f)	['ʃarpa]

glasses	occhiali (m pl)	[ɔk'kjali]
frame (eyeglass ~)	montatura (f)	[mɔnta'tura]
umbrella	ombrello (m)	[ɔmb'rɛllɔ]
walking stick	bastone (m)	[bas'tɔnɛ]
hairbrush	spazzola (f) per capelli	['spatsɔʎa pɛr ka'pɛlli]
fan	ventaglio (m)	[vɛn'taʎɔ]

tie (necktie)	cravatta (f)	[kra'vatta]
bow tie	cravatta (f) a farfalla	[kra'vatta a far'faʎa]
braces	bretelle (f pl)	[brɛ'tɛlle]
handkerchief	fazzoletto (m)	[fatsɔ'lettɔ]

comb	pettine (m)	['pɛttinɛ]
hair slide	fermaglio (m)	[fɛr'maʎɔ]
hairpin	forcina (f)	[for'tʃina]
buckle	fibbia (f)	['fibbja]

| belt | cintura (f) | [ʧin'tura] |
| shoulder strap | spallina (f) | [spal'lina] |

bag (handbag)	borsa (f)	['bɔrsa]
handbag	borsetta (f)	[bor'sɛtta]
rucksack	zaino (m)	['dzainɔ]

40. Clothing. Miscellaneous

fashion	moda (f)	['mɔda]
in vogue (adj)	di moda	[di 'mɔda]
fashion designer	stilista (m)	[sti'lista]

collar	collo (m)	['kɔllɔ]
pocket	tasca (f)	['taska]
pocket (as adj)	tascabile	[tas'kabile]
sleeve	manica (f)	['manika]
hanging loop	asola (f) per appendere	['azoʎa per ap'pendɛrɛ]
flies (on trousers)	patta (f)	['patta]

zip (fastener)	cerniera (f) lampo	[ʧer'ɲjera 'lampɔ]
fastener	chiusura (f)	[kjy'zura]
button	bottone (m)	[bot'tɔnɛ]
buttonhole	occhiello (m)	[ɔk'kjellɔ]
to come off (ab. button)	staccarsi (vr)	[stak'karsi]

to sew (vi, vt)	cucire (vi, vt)	[ku'ʧirɛ]
to embroider (vi, vt)	ricamare (vi, vt)	[rika'marɛ]
embroidery	ricamo (m)	[ri'kamɔ]
sewing needle	ago (m)	['agɔ]
thread	filo (m)	['filɔ]
seam	cucitura (f)	[kuʧi'tura]

to get dirty (vi)	sporcarsi (vr)	[spor'karsi]
stain (mark, spot)	macchia (f)	['makkja]
to crease, crumple (vi)	sgualcirsi (vr)	[zguaʎ'ʧirsi]
to tear (vt)	strappare (vt)	[strap'parɛ]
clothes moth	tarma (f)	['tarma]

41. Personal care. Cosmetics

toothpaste	dentifricio (m)	[dɛntif'riʧo]
toothbrush	spazzolino (m) da denti	[spatso'linɔ da 'dɛnti]
to clean one's teeth	lavarsi i denti	[ʎa'varsi i 'dɛnti]

razor	rasoio (m)	[ra'zɔjo]
shaving cream	crema (f) da barba	['krɛma da 'barba]
to shave (vi)	rasarsi (vr)	[ra'zarsi]

soap	sapone (m)	[sa'pɔnɛ]
shampoo	shampoo (m)	['ʃampɔ]
scissors	forbici (f pl)	['forbiʧi]

nail file	limetta (f)	[li'mɛtta]
nail clippers	tagliaunghie (m)	[taʎa'ungje]
tweezers	pinzette (f pl)	[pin'tsettɛ]

cosmetics	cosmetica (f)	[kɔz'mɛtika]
face pack	maschera (f) di bellezza	['maskɛra di bɛl'letsa]
manicure	manicure (m)	[mani'kyrɛ]
to have a manicure	fare la manicure	['farɛ ʎa mani'kurɛ]
pedicure	pedicure (m)	[pɛdi'kyrɛ]

make-up bag	borsa (f) del trucco	['bɔrsa dɛʎ 'trukkɔ]
face powder	cipria (f)	['ʧipria]
powder compact	portacipria (m)	[pɔrta'ʧipria]
blusher	fard (m)	[far]

perfume (bottled)	profumo (m)	[pro'fumɔ]
toilet water	acqua (f) da toeletta	['akva da tɔɛ'lɛtta]
lotion	lozione (f)	[lɔ'tsʲonɛ]
cologne	acqua (f) di Colonia	['akua di kɔ'lɔɲʲa]

eyeshadow	ombretto (m)	[ɔmb'rɛttɔ]
eyeliner	eyeliner (m)	[aj'lajnɛr]
mascara	mascara (m)	[mas'kara]

lipstick	rossetto (m)	[rɔs'sɛttɔ]
nail polish	smalto (m)	['zmaʎtɔ]
hair spray	lacca (f) per capelli	['ʎakka per ka'pɛlli]
deodorant	deodorante (m)	[dɛɔdo'rantɛ]

cream	crema (f)	['krɛma]
face cream	crema (f) per il viso	['krɛma pɛr iʎ 'wizɔ]
hand cream	crema (f) per le mani	['krɛma pɛr le 'mani]
anti-wrinkle cream	crema (f) antirughe	['krɛma anti'rugɛ]
day (as adj)	da giorno	[da 'ʤɔrnɔ]
night (as adj)	da notte	[da 'nɔttɛ]

tampon	tampone (m)	[tam'pɔnɛ]
toilet paper	carta (f) igienica	['karta i'ʤenika]
hair dryer	fon (m)	[fɔn]

42. Jewellery

jewellery	gioielli (m pl)	[ʤo'jelli]
precious (e.g. ~ stone)	prezioso	[prɛtsi'ɔzɔ]
hallmark	marchio (m)	['markiɔ]

ring	anello (m)	[a'nɛllɔ]
wedding ring	anello (m) nuziale	[a'nɛllɔ nutsi'ale]
bracelet	braccialetto (m)	[bratʃa'lettɔ]

earrings	orecchini (m pl)	[ɔrɛk'kini]
necklace (~ of pearls)	collana (f)	[kɔ'ʎana]
crown	corona (f)	[kɔ'rɔna]
bead necklace	perline (f pl)	[per'linɛ]

diamond	diamante (m)	[dia'mantɛ]
emerald	smeraldo (m)	[zmɛ'raʎdɔ]
ruby	rubino (m)	[ru'binɔ]
sapphire	zaffiro (m)	[dzaf'firɔ]
pearl	perle (f pl)	['pɛrle]
amber	ambra (f)	['ambra]

43. Watches. Clocks

watch (wristwatch)	orologio (m)	[ɔrɔ'lɔdʒɔ]
dial	quadrante (m)	[kuad'rantɛ]
hand (of clock, watch)	lancetta (f)	[ʎan'tʃetta]
metal bracelet	braccialetto (m)	[bratʃa'lettɔ]
watch strap	cinturino (m)	[tʃintu'rinɔ]

battery	pila (f)	['piʎa]
to be flat (battery)	essere scarico	['ɛssɛrɛ 'skarikɔ]
to change a battery	cambiare la pila	[kam'bjarɛ ʎa 'piʎa]
to run fast	andare avanti	[an'darɛ a'vanti]
to run slow	andare indietro	[an'darɛ indri'etrɔ]

wall clock	orologio (m) da muro	[ɔrɔ'lɔdʒɔ da 'murɔ]
hourglass	clessidra (f)	['klessidra]
sundial	orologio (m) solare	[ɔrɔ'lɔdʒɔ sɔ'ʎarɛ]
alarm clock	sveglia (f)	['zvɛʎja]
watchmaker	orologiaio (m)	[ɔrɔlɔ'dʒajo]
to repair (vt)	riparare (vt)	[ripa'rarɛ]

Food. Nutricion

44. Food

meat	carne (f)	['karnɛ]
chicken	pollo (m)	['pollo]
young chicken	pollo (m) novello	['pollo no'vɛllo]
duck	anatra (f)	['anatra]
goose	oca (f)	['ɔka]
game	cacciagione (f)	[katʃa'dʒonɛ]
turkey	tacchino (m)	[tak'kino]
pork	carne (m) di maiale	['karnɛ di ma'jale]
veal	vitello (m)	[wi'tɛllo]
lamb	carne (f) di agnello	['karnɛ di a'nɛllo]
beef	manzo (m)	['mandzo]
rabbit	coniglio (m)	[ko'niʎʲo]
sausage (salami, etc.)	salame (m)	[sa'ʎamɛ]
vienna sausage	wüsterl (m)	['wy:stɛrʎ]
bacon	pancetta (f)	[pan'tʃetta]
ham	prosciutto (m)	[pro'ʃutto]
gammon (ham)	prosciutto (m) affumicato	[pro'ʃutto affumi'kato]
pâté	pâté (m)	[pa'tɛ]
liver	fegato (m)	['fɛgato]
lard	lardo (m)	['ʎardo]
mince	carne (f) trita	['karnɛ 'trita]
tongue	lingua (f)	['liŋua]
egg	uovo (m)	[u'ovo]
eggs	uova (f pl)	[u'ova]
egg white	albume (m)	[aʎ'bumɛ]
egg yolk	tuorlo (m)	[tu'ɔrlo]
fish	pesce (m)	['pɛʃɛ]
seafood	frutti (m pl) di mare	['frutti di 'marɛ]
crustaceans	crostacei (m pl)	[kros'tatʃei]
caviar	caviale (m)	[ka'vjale]
crab	granchio (m)	['graŋkio]
prawn	gamberetto (m)	[gambɛ'rɛtto]
oyster	ostrica (f)	['ɔstrika]
spiny lobster	aragosta (f)	[ara'gosta]
octopus	polpo (m)	['poʎpo]
squid	calamaro (m)	[kaʎa'maro]
sturgeon	storione (m)	[stori'ɔnɛ]
salmon	salmone (m)	[saʎ'monɛ]
halibut	ippoglosso (m)	[ippog'lɔsso]

cod	merluzzo (m)	[mɛr'lytso]
mackerel	scombro (m)	['skombro]
tuna	tonno (m)	['tono]
eel	anguilla (f)	[aŋu'iʎa]

trout	trota (f)	['trota]
sardine	sardina (f)	[sar'dina]
pike	luccio (m)	['lytʃo]
herring	aringa (f)	[a'riŋa]

bread	pane (m)	['panɛ]
cheese	formaggio (m)	[for'madʒo]
sugar	zucchero (m)	['dzukkɛro]
salt	sale (m)	['sale]

rice	riso (m)	['rizo]
pasta	pasta (f)	['pasta]
noodles	tagliatelle (f pl)	[taʎja'tɛlle]

butter	burro (m)	['burro]
vegetable oil	olio (m) vegetale	['oʎo wedʒe'tale]
sunflower oil	olio (m) di girasole	['oʎo di dʒira'sole]
margarine	margarina (f)	[marga'rina]

| olives | olive (f pl) | [o'livɛ] |
| olive oil | olio (m) d'oliva | ['oʎo do'liva] |

milk	latte (m)	['ʎattɛ]
condensed milk	latte (m) condensato	['ʎattɛ kondɛn'sato]
yogurt	yogurt (m)	['jogurt]
sour cream	panna (f) acida	['paŋa 'atʃida]
cream (of milk)	panna (f)	['paŋa]

| mayonnaise | maionese (m) | [majo'nɛzɛ] |
| buttercream | crema (f) | ['krɛma] |

groats	cereali (m pl)	[tʃerɛ'ali]
flour	farina (f)	[fa'rina]
tinned food	cibi (m pl) in scatola	['tʃibi in 'skatola]

cornflakes	fiocchi (m pl) di mais	['fʲokki di 'mais]
honey	miele (m)	['mjele]
jam	marmellata (f)	[marmɛ'ʎata]
chewing gum	gomma (f) da masticare	['gomma da masti'karɛ]

45. Drinks

water	acqua (f)	['akua]
drinking water	acqua (f) potabile	['akua po'tabile]
mineral water	acqua (f) minerale	['akua mine'rale]

still (adj)	liscia, non gassata	['liʃa], [non gas'sata]
carbonated (adj)	gassata	[gas'sata]
sparkling (adj)	frizzante	[fri'dzantɛ]

| ice | ghiaccio (m) | ['gjatʃo] |
| with ice | con ghiaccio | [kɔn 'gjatʃo] |

non-alcoholic (adj))	analcolico	[anaʎ'kɔlikɔ]
soft drink	bevanda (f) analcolica	[bɛ'vanda anaʎ'kɔlika]
cool soft drink	bibita (f)	['bibita]
lemonade	limonata (f)	[limɔ'nata]

spirits	bevande (f pl) alcoliche	[bɛ'vandɛ aʎ'kɔlikɛ]
wine	vino (m)	['winɔ]
white wine	vino (m) bianco	['winɔ 'bjaŋkɔ]
red wine	vino (m) rosso	['winɔ 'rɔssɔ]

liqueur	liquore (m)	[liku'ɔrɛ]
champagne	champagne (m)	[ʃam'paɲ]
vermouth	vermouth (m)	['vɛrmut]

whisky	whisky	[u'iski]
vodka	vodka (f)	['vɔdka]
gin	gin (m)	[dʒin]
cognac	cognac (m)	['kɔɲjak]
rum	rum (m)	[rum]

coffee	caffè (m)	[kaf'fɛ]
black coffee	caffè (m) nero	[kaf'fɛ 'nɛrɔ]
white coffee	caffè latte (m)	[kaf'fɛ 'lattɛ]
cappuccino	cappuccino (m)	[kappu'tʃino]
instant coffee	caffè (m) solubile	[kaf'fɛ sɔ'lybile]

milk	latte (m)	['ʎattɛ]
cocktail	cocktail (m)	['kɔktɛjʎ]
milk shake	frullato (m)	[frul'latɔ]

juice	succo (m)	['sukkɔ]
tomato juice	succo (m) di pomodoro	['sukkɔ di pɔmɔ'dɔrɔ]
orange juice	succo (m) d'arancia	['sukkɔ da'rantʃa]
freshly squeezed juice	spremuta (f)	[sprɛ'muta]

beer	birra (f)	['birra]
lager	birra (f) chiara	['birra 'kjara]
bitter	birra (f) scura	['birra 'skura]

tea	tè (m)	[tɛ]
black tea	tè (m) nero	[tɛ 'nɛrɔ]
green tea	tè (m) verde	[tɛ 'vɛrdɛ]

46. Vegetables

| vegetables | ortaggi (m pl) | [ɔr'tadʒi] |
| greens | verdura (f) | [vɛr'dura] |

tomato	pomodoro (m)	[pɔmɔ'dɔrɔ]
cucumber	cetriolo (m)	[tʃetri'ɔlɔ]
carrot	carota (f)	[ka'rɔta]

potato	patata (f)	[pa'tata]
onion	cipolla (f)	[ʧi'poʎa]
garlic	aglio (m)	['aʎo]

cabbage	cavolo (m)	['kavolo]
cauliflower	cavolfiore (m)	[kavoʎ'fjorɛ]
Brussels sprouts	cavoletti (m pl) di Bruxelles	[kavo'letti di bruk'sɛʎ]
broccoli	broccolo (m)	['brokkolo]

beetroot	barbabietola (f)	[barba'bjetoʎa]
aubergine	melanzana (f)	[mɛʎan'tsana]
marrow	zucchina (f)	[dzuk'kina]
pumpkin	zucca (f)	['dzukka]
turnip	rapa (f)	['rapa]

parsley	prezzemolo (m)	[prɛ'tsɛmolo]
dill	aneto (m)	[a'nɛto]
lettuce	lattuga (f)	[ʎat'tuga]
celery	sedano (m)	['sɛdano]
asparagus	asparago (m)	[as'parago]
spinach	spinaci (m pl)	[spi'naʧi]

pea	pisello (m)	[pi'zɛllo]
beans	fave (f pl)	['favɛ]
maize	mais (m)	['mais]
kidney bean	fagiolo (m)	[fa'dʒolo]

bell pepper	peperone (m)	[pepɛ'ronɛ]
radish	ravanello (m)	[rava'nɛllo]
artichoke	carciofo (m)	[kar'ʧofo]

47. Fruits. Nuts

fruit	frutto (m)	['frutto]
apple	mela (f)	['mɛʎa]
pear	pera (f)	['pɛra]
lemon	limone (m)	[li'monɛ]
orange	arancia (f)	[a'ranʧa]
strawberry	fragola (f)	['fragoʎa]

tangerine	mandarino (m)	[manda'rino]
plum	prugna (f)	['pruɲja]
peach	pesca (f)	['pɛska]
apricot	albicocca (f)	[aʎbi'kokka]
raspberry	lampone (m)	[ʎam'ponɛ]
pineapple	ananas (m)	[ana'nas]

banana	banana (f)	[ba'nana]
watermelon	anguria (f)	[a'ɳuria]
grape	uva (f)	['uva]
sour cherry	amarena (f)	[ama'rɛna]
sweet cherry	ciliegia (f)	[ʧi'ʎjedʒa]
melon	melone (m)	[mɛ'lɔnɛ]
grapefruit	pompelmo (m)	[pom'pɛʎmo]

avocado	**avocado** (m)	[avɔ'kadɔ]
papaya	**papaia** (f)	[pa'paja]
mango	**mango** (m)	['maŋɔ]
pomegranate	**melagrana** (f)	[mɛlag'rana]

redcurrant	**ribes** (m) **rosso**	['ribɛs 'rɔssɔ]
blackcurrant	**ribes** (m) **nero**	['ribɛs 'nɛrɔ]
gooseberry	**uva** (f) **spina**	['uva 'spina]
bilberry	**mirtillo** (m)	[mir'tillɔ]
blackberry	**mora** (f)	['mɔra]

raisin	**uvetta** (f)	[u'vɛtta]
fig	**fico** (m)	['fikɔ]
date	**dattero** (m)	['dattɛrɔ]

peanut	**arachide** (f)	[a'rakidɛ]
almond	**mandorla** (f)	['mandorʎa]
walnut	**noce** (f)	['nɔtʃe]
hazelnut	**nocciola** (f)	[nɔ'tʃɔʎa]
coconut	**noce** (f) **di cocco**	['nɔtʃe di 'kɔkkɔ]
pistachios	**pistacchi** (m pl)	[pis'takki]

48. Bread. Sweets

confectionery (pastry)	**pasticceria** (f)	[pastitʃe'ria]
bread	**pane** (m)	['panɛ]
biscuits	**biscotti** (m pl)	[bis'kɔtti]

chocolate (n)	**cioccolato** (m)	[tʃɔkkɔ'ʎatɔ]
chocolate (as adj)	**al cioccolato**	[aʎ tʃɔkkɔ'ʎatɔ]
sweet	**caramella** (f)	[kara'mɛlla]
cake (e.g. cupcake)	**tortina** (f)	[tɔr'tina]
cake (e.g. birthday ~)	**torta** (f)	['tɔrta]

pie (e.g. apple ~)	**crostata** (f)	[krɔs'tata]
filling (for cake, pie)	**ripieno** (m)	[ri'pjenɔ]

whole fruit jam	**marmellata** (f)	[marmɛ'ʎata]
marmalade	**marmellata** (f) **di agrumi**	[marmɛ'ʎata di ag'rumi]
waffle	**wafer** (m)	['vafɛr]
ice-cream	**gelato** (m)	[dʒe'ʎatɔ]
pudding	**budino** (m)	[bu'dinɔ]

49. Cooked dishes

course, dish	**piatto** (m)	['pjattɔ]
cuisine	**cucina** (f)	[ku'tʃina]
recipe	**ricetta** (f)	[ri'tʃetta]
portion	**porzione** (f)	[pɔr'tsʲɔnɛ]

salad	**insalata** (f)	[insa'ʎata]
soup	**minestra** (f)	[mi'nɛstra]

clear soup (broth)	brodo (m)	['brɔdɔ]
sandwich (bread)	panino (m)	[pa'ninɔ]
fried eggs	uova (f pl) al tegamino	[u'ova aʎ tɛga'minɔ]

cutlet	cotoletta (f)	[koto'letta]
hamburger (beefburger)	hamburger (m)	[am'burger]
beefsteak	bistecca (f)	[bis'tɛkka]
roast meat	arrosto (m)	[ar'rostɔ]

garnish	contorno (m)	[kɔn'tɔrnɔ]
spaghetti	spaghetti (m pl)	[spa'gɛtti]
mash	purè (m) di patate	[pu'rɛ di pa'tatɛ]
pizza	pizza (f)	['pitsa]
porridge (oatmeal, etc.)	porridge (m)	[por'ridʒɛ]
omelette	frittata (f)	[frit'tata]

boiled (e.g. ~ beef)	bollito	[bol'litɔ]
smoked (adj)	affumicato	[affumi'katɔ]
fried (adj)	fritto	['frittɔ]
dried (adj)	secco	['sɛkkɔ]
frozen (adj)	congelato	[kɔndʒe'ʎatɔ]
pickled (adj)	sottoaceto	[sottɔa'ʧɛtɔ]

sweet (sugary)	dolce	['dɔʎʧe]
salty (adj)	salato	[sa'ʎatɔ]
cold (adj)	freddo	['frɛddɔ]
hot (adj)	caldo	['kaʎdɔ]
bitter (adj)	amaro	[a'marɔ]
tasty (adj)	buono, gustoso	[bu'ɔnɔ], [gus'tozɔ]

to cook (in boiling water)	cuocere, preparare (vt)	[ku'ɔʧɛrɛ], [prepa'rarɛ]
to cook (dinner)	cucinare (vi)	[kuʧi'narɛ]
to fry (vt)	friggere (vt)	['fridʒɛrɛ]
to heat up (food)	riscaldare (vt)	[riskaʎ'darɛ]

to salt (vt)	salare (vt)	[sa'ʎarɛ]
to pepper (vt)	pepare (vt)	[pɛ'parɛ]
to grate (vt)	grattugiare (vt)	[grattu'dʒarɛ]
peel (n)	buccia (f)	['buʧa]
to peel (vt)	sbucciare (vt)	[zbu'ʧarɛ]

50. Spices

salt	sale (m)	['sale]
salty (adj)	salato	[sa'ʎatɔ]
to salt (vt)	salare (vt)	[sa'ʎarɛ]

black pepper	pepe (m) nero	['pɛpɛ 'nɛrɔ]
red pepper	peperoncino (m)	[pɛperɔn'ʧinɔ]
mustard	senape (f)	[sɛ'napɛ]
horseradish	cren (m)	['krɛn]

| condiment | condimento (m) | [kɔndi'mɛntɔ] |
| spice | spezie (f pl) | ['spɛtsiɛ] |

sauce	**salsa** (f)	['saʎsa]
vinegar	**aceto** (m)	[a'ʧeto]

anise	**anice** (m)	['aniʧe]
basil	**basilico** (m)	[ba'ziliko]
cloves	**chiodi** (m pl) **di garofano**	[ki'odi di ga'rofano]
ginger	**zenzero** (m)	['ʣenʣero]
coriander	**coriandolo** (m)	[kori'andolo]
cinnamon	**cannella** (f)	[ka'ɳɛʎa]

sesame	**sesamo** (m)	[sɛzamo]
bay leaf	**alloro** (m)	[al'lɜro]
paprika	**paprica** (f)	['paprika]
caraway	**cumino, comino** (m)	[ku'mino], [ko'mino]
saffron	**zafferano** (m)	[ʣaffe'rano]

51. Meals

food	**cibo** (m)	['ʧibo]
to eat (vi, vt)	**mangiare** (vi, vt)	[man'ʤarɛ]

breakfast	**colazione** (f)	[koʎa'tsʲonɛ]
to have breakfast	**fare colazione**	['farɛ koʎa'tsʲonɛ]
lunch	**pranzo** (m)	['pranʦo]
to have lunch	**pranzare** (vi)	[pran'ʦarɛ]
dinner	**cena** (f)	['ʧena]
to have dinner	**cenare** (vi)	[ʧe'narɛ]

appetite	**appetito** (m)	[appɛ'tito]
Enjoy your meal!	**Buon appetito!**	[bu'on appɛ'tito]

to open (~ a bottle)	**aprire** (vt)	[ap'rirɛ]
to spill (liquid)	**rovesciare** (vt)	[rove'ʃarɛ]
to spill out (vi)	**rovesciarsi** (vi)	[rove'ʃarsi]

to boil (vi)	**bollire** (vi)	[bol'lirɛ]
to boil (vt)	**far bollire**	[far bol'lirɛ]
boiled (~ water)	**bollito**	[bol'lito]
to chill (vt)	**raffreddare** (vt)	[raffre'darɛ]
to chill (vi)	**raffreddarsi** (vr)	[raffred'darsi]

taste, flavour	**gusto** (m)	['gusto]
aftertaste	**retrogusto** (m)	[rɛtro'gusto]

to be on a diet	**essere a dieta**	['ɛssɛrɛ a di'ɛta]
diet	**dieta** (f)	[di'ɛta]
vitamin	**vitamina** (f)	[wita'mina]
calorie	**caloria** (f)	[kalɜ'ria]
vegetarian (n)	**vegetariano** (m)	[vɛʤetari'ano]
vegetarian (adj)	**vegetariano**	[vɛʤetari'ano]

fats (nutrient)	**grassi** (m pl)	['grassi]
proteins	**proteine** (f pl)	[protɛ'inɛ]
carbohydrates	**carboidrati** (m pl)	[karbɔid'rati]

slice (of lemon, ham)	fetta (f), fettina (f)	['fetta], [fet'tina]
piece (of cake, pie)	pezzo (m)	['pɛtsɔ]
crumb (of bread)	briciola (f)	['britʃoʎa]

52. Table setting

spoon	cucchiaio (m)	[kuk'kjajo]
knife	coltello (m)	[koʎ'tɛllɔ]
fork	forchetta (f)	[for'kɛtta]

cup (of coffee)	tazza (f)	['tattsa]
plate (dinner ~)	piatto (m)	['pjattɔ]
saucer	piattino (m)	[pjat'tinɔ]
serviette	tovagliolo (m)	[tɔva'ʎɔlɔ]
toothpick	stuzzicadenti (m)	[stuttsika'dɛnti]

53. Restaurant

restaurant	ristorante (m)	[ristɔ'rantɛ]
coffee bar	caffè (m)	[kaf'fɛ]
pub, bar	pub (m), bar (m)	[pab], [bar]
tearoom	sala (f) da tè	['saʎa da 'tɛ]

waiter	cameriere (m)	[kamɛ'rjerɛ]
waitress	cameriera (f)	[kamɛ'rjera]
barman	barista (m)	[ba'rista]

menu	menù (m)	[me'nu]
wine list	carta (f) dei vini	['karta dɛi 'wini]
to book a table	prenotare un tavolo	[prɛnɔ'tarɛ un 'tavɔlɔ]

course, dish	piatto (m)	['pjattɔ]
to order (meal)	ordinare (vt)	[ɔrdi'narɛ]
to make an order	fare un'ordinazione	['farɛ unɔrdina'tsʲonɛ]

aperitif	aperitivo (m)	[apɛri'tivɔ]
starter	antipasto (m)	[anti'pastɔ]
dessert, sweet	dolce (m)	['doʎtʃe]

bill	conto (m)	['kontɔ]
to pay the bill	pagare il conto	[pa'garɛ iʎ 'kontɔ]
to give change	dare il resto	['darɛ iʎ 'rɛstɔ]
tip	mancia (f)	['mantʃa]

Family, relatives and friends

54. Personal information. Forms

name, first name	nome (m)	['nɔmɛ]
family name	cognome (m)	[kɔ'ɲɔmɛ]
date of birth	data (f) di nascita	['data di 'naʃita]
place of birth	luogo (m) di nascita	[ly'ɔgɔ di 'naʃita]
nationality	nazionalità (f)	[natsjonali'ta]
place of residence	domicilio (m)	[dɔmi'ʧilio]
country	paese (m)	[pa'ɛzɛ]
profession (occupation)	professione (f)	[prɔfɛs'sjonɛ]
gender, sex	sesso (m)	['sɛssɔ]
height	statura (f)	[sta'tura]
weight	peso (m)	['pɛzɔ]

55. Family members. Relatives

mother	madre (f)	['madrɛ]
father	padre (m)	['padrɛ]
son	figlio (m)	['fiʎɔ]
daughter	figlia (f)	['fiʎja]
younger daughter	figlia (f) minore	['fiʎja mi'nɔrɛ]
younger son	figlio (m) minore	['fiʎɔ mi'nɔrɛ]
eldest daughter	figlia (f) maggiore	['fiʎja ma'dʒɔrɛ]
eldest son	figlio (m) maggiore	['fiʎɔ ma'dʒɔrɛ]
brother	fratello (m)	[fra'tɛllɔ]
sister	sorella (f)	[sɔ'rɛʎa]
cousin (masc.)	cugino (m)	[ku'dʒinɔ]
cousin (fem.)	cugina (f)	[ku'dʒina]
mummy	mamma (f)	['mamma]
dad, daddy	papà (m)	[pa'pa]
parents	genitori (m pl)	[dʒeni'tori]
child	bambino (m)	[bam'binɔ]
children	bambini (m pl)	[bam'bini]
grandmother	nonna (f)	['nɔŋa]
grandfather	nonno (m)	['nɔŋɔ]
grandson	nipote (m)	[ni'pɔtɛ]
granddaughter	nipote (f)	[ni'pɔtɛ]
grandchildren	nipoti (pl)	[ni'poti]
uncle	zio (m)	['ʦio]
aunt	zia (f)	['ʦia]

| nephew | nipote (m) | [ni'potɛ] |
| niece | nipote (f) | [ni'potɛ] |

mother-in-law	suocera (f)	[su'ɔtʃera]
father-in-law	suocero (m)	[su'ɔtʃerɔ]
son-in-law	genero (m)	['dʒenɛrɔ]
stepmother	matrigna (f)	[mat'riɲja]
stepfather	patrigno (m)	[pat'riɲ'ɔ]

infant	neonato (m)	[nɛɔ'natɔ]
baby (infant)	infante (m)	[in'fantɛ]
little boy, kid	bimbo (m)	['bimbɔ]

wife	moglie (f)	['mɔʎje]
husband	marito (m)	[ma'ritɔ]
spouse (husband)	coniuge (m)	['kɔɲjydʒe]
spouse (wife)	coniuge (f)	['kɔɲjydʒe]

married (masc.)	sposato	[spɔ'zatɔ]
married (fem.)	sposata	[spɔ'zata]
single (unmarried)	celibe	['tʃelibɛ]
bachelor	scapolo (m)	['skapɔlɔ]
divorced (masc.)	divorziato	[divɔrtsi'atɔ]
widow	vedova (f)	['vɛdɔva]
widower	vedovo (m)	['vɛdɔvɔ]

relative	parente (m)	[pa'rɛntɛ]
close relative	parente (m) stretto	[pa'rɛntɛ 'strɛttɔ]
distant relative	parente (m) lontano	[pa'rɛntɛ lɔn'tanɔ]
relatives	parenti (m pl)	[pa'rɛnti]

orphan (boy)	orfano (m)	['ɔrfanɔ]
orphan (girl)	orfana (f)	['ɔrfana]
guardian (of minor)	tutore (m)	[tu'tɔrɛ]
to adopt (a boy)	adottare (vt)	[adɔt'tarɛ]
to adopt (a girl)	adottare (vt)	[adɔt'tarɛ]

56. Friends. Colleagues

friend (masc.)	amico (m)	[a'mikɔ]
friend (fem.)	amica (f)	[a'mika]
friendship	amicizia (f)	[ami'tʃitsia]
to be friends	essere amici	['ɛssɛrɛ a'mitʃi]

pal (masc.)	amico (m)	[a'mikɔ]
pal (fem.)	amica (f)	[a'mika]
partner	partner (m)	['partnɛr]

chief (boss)	capo (m)	['kapɔ]
superior	capo (m), superiore (m)	['kapɔ], [supɛ'rɔrɛ]
subordinate	subordinato (m)	[subɔrdi'natɔ]
colleague	collega (m)	[kɔl'lega]
acquaintance (person)	conoscente (m)	[kɔnɔ'ʃɛntɛ]
fellow traveller	compagno (m) di viaggio	[kɔm'paɲ'ɔ di wi'jadʒɔ]

classmate	compagno (m) di classe	[kɔm'paɲɔ di 'kʎassɛ]
neighbour (masc.)	vicino (m)	[wi'tʃinɔ]
neighbour (fem.)	vicina (f)	[wi'tʃina]
neighbours	vicini (m pl)	[wi'tʃini]

57. Man. Woman

woman	donna (f)	['dɔŋa]
girl (young woman)	ragazza (f)	[ra'gatsa]
bride	sposa (f)	['spɔza]

beautiful (adj)	bella	['bɛʎa]
tall (adj)	alta	['aʎta]
slender (adj)	snella	['znɛʎa]
short (adj)	bassa	['bassa]

| blonde (n) | bionda (f) | ['bʲɔnda] |
| brunette (n) | bruna (f) | ['bruna] |

ladies' (adj)	da donna	[da 'dɔŋa]
virgin (girl)	vergine (f)	['vɛrdʒinɛ]
pregnant (adj)	incinta	[in'tʃinta]

man (adult male)	uomo (m)	[u'omɔ]
blonde haired man	biondo (m)	['bʲɔndɔ]
dark haired man	bruno (m)	['brunɔ]
tall (adj)	alto	['aʎtɔ]
short (adj)	basso	['bassɔ]

rude (rough)	sgarbato	[sgar'batɔ]
stocky (adj)	tozzo	['tɔtsɔ]
robust (adj)	robusto	[rɔ'bustɔ]
strong (adj)	forte	['fɔrtɛ]
strength	forza (f)	['fɔrtsa]

stout, fat (adj)	corpulento	[kɔrpu'lentɔ]
swarthy (adj)	bruno	['brunɔ]
well-built (adj)	snello	['znɛllɔ]
elegant (adj)	elegante	[ɛle'gantɛ]

58. Age

age	età (f)	[ɛ'ta]
youth (young age)	giovinezza (f)	[dʒɔwi'netsa]
young (adj)	giovane	['dʒɔvanɛ]

| younger (adj) | più giovane | [pjy 'dʒɔvanɛ] |
| older (adj) | più vecchio | [pjy 'vɛkkiɔ] |

young man	giovane (m)	['dʒɔvanɛ]
teenager	adolescente (m, f)	[adɔle'ʃɛntɛ]
guy, fellow	ragazzo (m)	[ra'gatsɔ]

| old man | vecchio (m) | ['vɛkkiɔ] |
| old woman | vecchia (f) | ['vɛkkja] |

adult	adulto (m)	[a'duʎtɔ]
middle-aged (adj)	di mezza età	[di 'mɛdza ɛ'ta]
elderly (adj)	anziano	[antsi'anɔ]
old (adj)	vecchio	['vɛkkiɔ]

| to retire (from job) | andare in pensione | [an'darɛ in pɛnsi'ɔnɛ] |
| pensioner | pensionato (m) | [pɛnsiɔ'natɔ] |

59. Children

child	bambino (m)	[bam'binɔ]
children	bambini (m pl)	[bam'bini]
twins	gemelli (m pl)	[dʒe'mɛlli]

cradle	culla (f)	['kuʎa]
rattle	sonaglio (m)	[sɔ'naʎɔ]
nappy	pannolino (m)	[paɲɔ'linɔ]

dummy, comforter	tettarella (f)	[tɛtta'rɛʎa]
pram	carrozzina (f)	[karrɔ'tsina]
nursery	scuola (f) materna	[sku'ɔʎa ma'tɛrna]
babysitter	baby-sitter (m, f)	[bɛbi'sitɛr]

childhood	infanzia (f)	[in'fantsia]
doll	bambola (f)	['bambɔʎa]
toy	giocattolo (m)	[dʒɔ'kattɔlɔ]
construction set	gioco (m) di costruzione	['dʒɔkɔ di kɔnstru'tsiɔnɛ]

well-bred (adj)	educato	[ɛdu'katɔ]
ill-bred (adj)	maleducato	[maledu'katɔ]
spoilt (adj)	viziato	[witsi'atɔ]

to be naughty	essere disubbidiente	['ɛssɛrɛ dizubidi'ɛntɛ]
mischievous (adj)	birichino	[biri'kinɔ]
mischievousness	birichinata (f)	[biriki'nata]
mischievous child	monello (m)	[mɔ'nɛllɔ]

| obedient (adj) | ubbidiente | [ubidi'ɛntɛ] |
| disobedient (adj) | disubbidiente | [dizubidi'ɛntɛ] |

docile (adj)	docile	['dɔtʃilɛ]
clever (intelligent)	intelligente	[intɛlli'dʒɛntɛ]
child prodigy	bambino (m) prodigio	[bam'binɔ prɔ'didʒɔ]

60. Married couples. Family life

to kiss (vt)	baciare (vt)	[ba'tʃarɛ]
to kiss (vi)	baciarsi (vr)	[ba'tʃarsi]
family (n)	famiglia (f)	[fa'miʎja]

family (as adj)	familiare	[fami'ʎjarɛ]
couple	coppia (f)	['kɔppja]
marriage (state)	matrimonio (m)	[matri'mɔniɔ]
hearth (home)	focolare (m) domestico	[fokɔ'ʎarɛ dɔ'mɛstikɔ]
dynasty	dinastia (f)	[dinas'tia]

| date | appuntamento (m) | [appunta'mɛntɔ] |
| kiss | bacio (m) | ['batʃɔ] |

love (for sb)	amore (m)	[a'mɔrɛ]
to love (sb)	amare	[a'marɛ]
beloved	amato	[a'matɔ]

tenderness	tenerezza (f)	[tɛnɛ'rɛtsa]
tender (affectionate)	dolce, tenero	['dɔʎtʃe], ['tɛnɛrɔ]
faithfulness	fedeltà (f)	[fɛdɛʎ'ta]
faithful (adj)	fedele	[fɛ'dɛle]
care (attention)	premura (f)	[prɛ'mura]
caring (~ father)	premuroso	[prɛmu'rɔzɔ]

newlyweds	sposi (m pl) novelli	['spɔzi nɔ'vɛlli]
honeymoon	luna (f) di miele	['lyna di 'mjele]
to get married (ab. woman)	sposarsi (vr)	[spɔ'zarsi]
to get married (ab. man)	sposarsi (vr)	[spɔ'zarsi]

wedding	nozze (f pl)	['nɔtse]
golden wedding	nozze (f pl) d'oro	['nɔtse 'dɔrɔ]
anniversary	anniversario (m)	[aɲivɛr'sariɔ]

| lover (masc.) | amante (m) | [a'mantɛ] |
| mistress | amante (f) | [a'mantɛ] |

adultery	adulterio (m)	[aduʎ'tɛriɔ]
to commit adultery	commettere adulterio	[kɔm'mɛttɛrɛ aduʎ'tɛriɔ]
jealous (adj)	geloso	[dʒe'lɔzɔ]
to be jealous	essere geloso	['ɛssɛrɛ dʒe'lɔzɔ]
divorce	divorzio (m)	[di'vɔrtsiɔ]
to divorce (vi)	divorziare (vi)	[divɔrtsi'arɛ]

to quarrel (vi)	litigare (vi)	[liti'garɛ]
to be reconciled	fare pace	['farɛ 'patʃe]
together (adv)	insieme	[in'sjemɛ]
sex	sesso (m)	['sɛssɔ]

happiness	felicità (f)	[fɛlitʃi'ta]
happy (adj)	felice	[fɛ'litʃe]
misfortune (accident)	disgrazia (f)	[disg'ratsia]
unhappy (adj)	infelice	[infɛ'litʃɛ]

Character. Feelings. Emotions

61. Feelings. Emotions

feeling (emotion)	sentimento (m)	[sɛnti'mɛntɔ]
feelings	sentimenti (m pl)	[sɛnti'mɛnti]
to feel (vt)	sentire (vt)	[sɛn'tirɛ]
hunger	fame (f)	['famɛ]
to be hungry	avere fame	[a'vɛrɛ 'famɛ]
thirst	sete (f)	['sɛtɛ]
to be thirsty	avere sete	[a'vɛrɛ 'sɛtɛ]
sleepiness	sonnolenza (f)	[sɔŋɔ'lentsa]
to feel sleepy	avere sonno	[a'vɛrɛ 'sɔŋɔ]
tiredness	stanchezza (f)	[sta'ŋkɛtsa]
tired (adj)	stanco	['staŋkɔ]
to get tired	stancarsi (vr)	[sta'ŋkarsi]
mood (humour)	umore (m)	[u'mɔrɛ]
boredom	noia (f)	['nɔja]
to be bored	annoiarsi (vr)	[aŋɔ'jarsi]
seclusion	isolamento (f)	[izɔʎa'mɛntɔ]
to seclude oneself	isolarsi (vr)	[izɔ'ʎarsi]
to worry (make anxious)	preoccupare (vt)	[prɛɔkku'parɛ]
to be worried	essere preoccupato	['ɛssɛrɛ prɛɔkku'patɔ]
worrying (n)	agitazione (f)	[adʒita'tsʲɔnɛ]
anxiety	preoccupazione (f)	[prɛɔkkupa'tsʲɔnɛ]
preoccupied (adj)	preoccupato	[prɛɔkku'patɔ]
to be nervous	essere nervoso	['ɛssɛrɛ nɛr'vɔzɔ]
to panic (vi)	andare in panico	[an'darɛ in 'panikɔ]
hope	speranza (f)	[spɛ'rantsa]
to hope (vi, vt)	sperare (vi, vt)	[spɛ'rarɛ]
certainty	certezza (f)	[tʃer'tɛtsa]
certain, sure (adj)	sicuro	[si'kurɔ]
uncertainty	incertezza (f)	[intʃer'tɛtsa]
uncertain (adj)	incerto	[in'tʃertɔ]
drunk (adj)	ubriaco	[ubri'akɔ]
sober (adj)	sobrio	['sɔbriɔ]
weak (adj)	debole	['dɛbole]
happy (adj)	fortunato	[fortu'natɔ]
to scare (vt)	spaventare (vt)	[spavɛn'tarɛ]
fury (madness)	rabbia (f)	['rabbja]
rage (fury)	rabbia (f)	['rabbja]
depression	depressione (f)	[dɛprɛssi'ɔnɛ]
discomfort	disagio (m)	[di'zadʒɔ]

comfort	conforto (m)	[kɔn'fɔrtɔ]
to regret (be sorry)	rincrescere (vi)	[riŋk'reʃɛrɛ]
regret	rincrescimento (m)	[riŋkreʃi'mɛntɔ]
bad luck	sfortuna (f)	[sfɔr'tuna]
sadness	tristezza (f)	[tris'tɛttsa]

shame (feeling)	vergogna (f)	[vɛr'gɔɲa]
merriment, fun	allegria (f)	[alleg'ria]
enthusiasm	entusiasmo (m)	[ɛntuzi'azmɔ]
enthusiast	entusiasta (m)	[ɛntuzi'asta]
to show enthusiasm	mostrare entusiasmo	[mɔst'rarɛ ɛntuzi'azmɔ]

62. Character. Personality

character	carattere (m)	[ka'rattɛrɛ]
character flaw	difetto (m)	[di'fɛttɔ]
mind, reason	battaglia (f)	[bat'taʎja]
mind	mente (f)	['mɛntɛ]
reason	intelletto (m)	[intɛl'lɛttɔ]

conscience	coscienza (f)	[kɔ'ʃɛntsa]
habit (custom)	abitudine (f)	[abi'tudinɛ]
ability	capacità (f)	[kapatʃi'ta]
can (e.g. ~ swim)	sapere (vt)	[sa'pɛrɛ]

patient (adj)	paziente	[patsi'entɛ]
impatient (adj)	impaziente	[impatsi'entɛ]
curious (inquisitive)	curioso	[kuri'ɔzɔ]
curiosity	curiosità (f)	[kuriɔzi'ta]

modesty	modestia (f)	[mɔ'dɛstia]
modest (adj)	modesto	[mɔ'dɛstɔ]
immodest (adj)	immodesto	[immɔ'dɛstɔ]

| lazy (adj) | pigro | ['pigrɔ] |
| lazy person (masc.) | poltrone (m) | [pɔʎt'rɔnɛ] |

cunning (n)	furberia (f)	[furbɛ'ria]
cunning (as adj)	furbo	['furbɔ]
distrust	diffidenza (f)	[diffi'dɛntsa]
distrustful (adj)	diffidente	[diffi'dɛntɛ]

generosity	generosità (f)	[dʒenɛrɔzi'ta]
generous (adj)	generoso	[dʒenɛ'rɔzɔ]
talented (adj)	di talento	[di ta'lentɔ]
talent	talento (m)	[ta'lentɔ]

courageous (adj)	coraggioso	[kɔra'dʒozɔ]
courage	coraggio (m)	[kɔ'radʒɔ]
honest (adj)	onesto	[ɔ'nɛstɔ]
honesty	onestà (f)	[ɔnɛs'ta]

| careful (cautious) | prudente | [pru'dɛntɛ] |
| courageous (adj) | valoroso | [valɜ'rɔzɔ] |

| serious (adj) | serio | ['sɛrio] |
| strict (severe, stern) | severo | [sɛ'vɛrɔ] |

decisive (adj)	deciso	[dɛ'tʃizɔ]
indecisive (adj)	indeciso	[indɛ'tʃizɔ]
shy, timid (adj)	timido	['timidɔ]
shyness, timidity	timidezza (f)	[timi'dɛtsa]

confidence (trust)	fiducia (f)	[fi'dutʃa]
to believe (trust)	fidarsi (vr)	[fi'darsi]
trusting (naïve)	fiducioso	[fidu'tʃozɔ]

sincerely (adv)	sinceramente	[sintʃera'mɛntɛ]
sincere (adj)	sincero	[sin'tʃerɔ]
sincerity	sincerità (f)	[sintʃeri'ta]
open (person)	aperto	[a'pɛrtɔ]

calm (adj)	tranquillo	[traŋku'illɔ]
frank (sincere)	sincero	[sin'tʃerɔ]
naïve (adj)	ingenuo	[in'dʒenuɔ]
absent-minded (adj)	distratto	[dist'rattɔ]
funny (amusing)	buffo	['buffɔ]

greed	avidità (f)	[awidi'ta]
greedy (adj)	avido	['awidɔ]
stingy (adj)	avaro	[a'varɔ]
evil (adj)	cattivo	[kat'tivɔ]
stubborn (adj)	testardo	[tɛs'tardɔ]
unpleasant (adj)	antipatico	[anti'patikɔ]

selfish person (masc.)	egoista (m)	[ɛgɔ'ista]
selfish (adj)	egoistico	[ɛgɔ'istikɔ]
coward	codardo (m)	[kɔ'dardɔ]
cowardly (adj)	codardo	[kɔ'dardɔ]

63. Sleep. Dreams

to sleep (vi)	dormire (vi)	[dor'mirɛ]
sleep, sleeping	sonno (m)	['sɔŋɔ]
dream	sogno (m)	['sɔɲɔ]
to dream (in sleep)	sognare (vi)	[sɔ'ɲjarɛ]
sleepy (adj)	sonnolento	[sɔŋɔ'lentɔ]

bed	letto (m)	['lettɔ]
mattress	materasso (m)	[matɛ'rassɔ]
blanket (eiderdown)	coperta (f)	[kɔ'pɛrta]
pillow	cuscino (m)	[ku'ʃinɔ]
sheet	lenzuolo (m)	[lentsu'ɔlɔ]

insomnia	insonnia (f)	[in'sɔɲia]
sleepless (adj)	insonne	[in'sɔŋɛ]
sleeping pill	sonnifero (m)	[sɔ'ɲifɛrɔ]
to take a sleeping pill	prendere il sonnifero	['prɛndɛrɛ iʎ sɔ'ɲifɛrɔ]
to feel sleepy	avere sonno	[a'vɛrɛ 'sɔŋɔ]

to yawn (vi)	sbadigliare (vi)	[zbadi'ʎjarɛ]
to go to bed	andare a letto	[an'darɛ a 'lettɔ]
to make up the bed	fare il letto	['farɛ iʎ 'lettɔ]
to fall asleep	addormentarsi (vr)	[addɔrmɛn'tarsi]

nightmare	incubo (m)	['iŋkubɔ]
snoring	russare (m)	[rus'sarɛ]
to snore (vi)	russare (vi)	[rus'sarɛ]

alarm clock	sveglia (f)	['zvɛʎja]
to wake (vt)	svegliare (vt)	[zvɛ'ʎjarɛ]
to wake up	svegliarsi (vr)	[zvɛ'ʎjarsi]
to get up (vi)	alzarsi (vr)	[aʎ'tsarsi]
to wash oneself	lavarsi (vr)	[ʎa'varsi]

64. Humour. Laughter. Gladness

humour (wit, fun)	umorismo (m)	[umɔ'rizmɔ]
sense of humour	senso (m) dello humour	['sɛnsɔ del'lɜ u'mur]
to have fun	divertirsi (vr)	[divɛr'tirsi]
cheerful (adj)	allegro	[al'legrɔ]
merriment, fun	allegria (f)	[alleg'ria]

smile	sorriso (m)	[sɔr'rizɔ]
to smile (vi)	sorridere (vi)	[sɔr'ridɛrɛ]
to start laughing	mettersi a ridere	['mɛttɛrsi a 'ridɛrɛ]
to laugh (vi)	ridere (vi)	['ridɛrɛ]
laugh, laughter	riso (m)	['rizɔ]

anecdote	aneddoto (m)	[a'ŋɛdɔtɔ]
funny (amusing)	divertente	[divɛr'tɛntɛ]
funny (comical)	ridicolo	[ri'dikɔlɔ]

to joke (vi)	scherzare (vi)	[skɛr'tsarɛ]
joke (verbal)	scherzo (m)	['skɛrtsɔ]
joy (emotion)	gioia (f)	['dʒɔja]
to rejoice (vi)	rallegrarsi (vr)	[ralleg'rarsi]
glad, cheerful (adj)	allegro	[al'legrɔ]

65. Discussion, conversation. Part 1

communication	comunicazione (f)	[kɔmunika'tsjɔnɛ]
to communicate	comunicare (vi)	[kɔmuni'karɛ]

conversation	conversazione (f)	[kɔnwersa'tsjɔnɛ]
dialogue	dialogo (m)	[di'alɜgɔ]
discussion (discourse)	discussione (f)	[diskus'sjɔnɛ]
debate	dibattito (m)	[di'battitɔ]
to debate (vi)	discutere (vi)	[dis'kutɛrɛ]

interlocutor	interlocutore (m)	[intɛrlɜku'tɔrɛ]
topic (theme)	tema (m)	['tɛma]

point of view	punto (m) di vista	['punto di 'wista]
opinion (viewpoint)	opinione (f)	[ɔpini'ɔnɛ]
speech (talk)	discorso (m)	[dis'kɔrsɔ]

discussion (of report, etc.)	discussione (f)	[diskus's-ɔnɛ]
to discuss (vt)	discutere (vt)	[dis'kutɛrɛ]
talk (conversation)	conversazione (f)	[kɔnwersa'ts-ɔnɛ]
to talk (vi)	conversare (vi)	[kɔnvɛr'sarɛ]
meeting	incontro (m)	[i'ŋkontrɔ]
to meet (vi, vt)	incontrarsi (vr)	[iŋkont'rarsi]

proverb	proverbio (m)	[prɔ'vɛrbiɔ]
saying	detto (m)	['dɛttɔ]
riddle (poser)	indovinello (m)	[indɔwi'nɛllɔ]
to ask a riddle	fare un indovinello	['farɛ un indɔwi'nɛllɔ]
password	parola (f) d'ordine	[pa'rɔʎa 'dɔrdinɛ]
secret	segreto (m)	[sɛg'rɛtɔ]

oath (vow)	giuramento (m)	[dʒura'mɛntɔ]
to swear (an oath)	giurare (vi)	[dʒu'rarɛ]
promise	promessa (f)	[prɔ'mɛssa]
to promise (vt)	promettere (vt)	[prɔ'mɛttɛrɛ]

advice (counsel)	consiglio (m)	[kɔn'siʎɔ]
to advise (vt)	consigliare (vt)	[kɔnsi'ʎjarɛ]
to listen (to parents)	ubbidire (vi)	[ubi'dirɛ]

news	notizia (f)	[nɔ'tiʦia]
sensation (news)	sensazione (f)	[sɛnsa'ts-ɔnɛ]
information (facts)	informazioni (f pl)	[informa'ts-ɔni]
conclusion (decision)	conclusione (f)	[kɔŋklyzi'ɔnɛ]
voice	voce (f)	['vɔʧe]
compliment	complimento (m)	[kɔmpli'mɛntɔ]
kind (nice)	gentile	[dʒen'tile]

word	parola (f)	[pa'rɔʎa]
phrase	frase (f)	['frazɛ]
answer	risposta (f)	[ris'posta]

truth	verità (f)	[vɛri'ta]
lie	menzogna (f)	[men'ʦɔŋja]

thought	pensiero (m)	[pɛn'sjerɔ]
idea (inspiration)	idea (f), pensiero (m)	[i'dɛa], [pɛn'sjerɔ]
fantasy	fantasia (f)	[fanta'zia]

66. Discussion, conversation. Part 2

respected (adj)	rispettato	[rispɛt'tatɔ]
to respect (vt)	rispettare (vt)	[rispɛt'tarɛ]
respect	rispetto (m)	[ris'pɛttɔ]
Dear ...	Egregio ...	[ɛg'redʒɔ]
to introduce (present)	presentare (vt)	[prɛzɛn'tarɛ]
intention	intenzione (f)	[intɛn'ts-ɔnɛ]

to intend (have in mind)	avere intenzione	[a'vɛrɛ intɛn'tsʲonɛ]
wish	augurio (m)	[au'gurio]
to wish (~ good luck)	augurare (vt)	[augu'rarɛ]

surprise (astonishment)	sorpresa (f)	[sɔrp'rɛza]
to surprise (amaze)	sorprendere (vt)	[sɔrp'rɛndɛrɛ]
to be surprised	stupirsi (vr)	[stu'pirsi]

to give (vt)	dare (vt)	['darɛ]
to take (get hold of)	prendere (vt)	['prɛndɛrɛ]
to give back	rendere (vt)	['rɛndɛrɛ]
to return (give back)	restituire (vt)	[rɛstitu'irɛ]

to apologize (vi)	scusarsi (vr)	[sku'zarsi]
apology	scusa (f)	['skuza]
to forgive (vt)	perdonare (vt)	[pɛrdɔ'narɛ]

to talk (speak)	parlare (vi, vt)	[par'ʎarɛ]
to listen (vi)	ascoltare (vi)	[askoʎ'tarɛ]
to hear out	ascoltare fino in fondo	[askoʎ'tarɛ 'finɔ in 'fondɔ]
to understand (vt)	capire (vt)	[ka'pirɛ]

to show (display)	mostrare (vt)	[mɔst'rarɛ]
to look at ...	guardare (vt)	[guar'darɛ]
to call (with one's voice)	chiamare (vt)	[kja'marɛ]
to disturb (vt)	disturbare (vt)	[distur'barɛ]
to pass (to hand sth)	consegnare (vt)	[kɔnsɛ'ɲjarɛ]

demand (request)	richiesta (f)	[ri'kjesta]
to request (ask)	chiedere (vt)	['kjedɛrɛ]
demand (firm request)	esigenza (f)	[ɛzi'dʒentsa]
to demand (request firmly)	esigere (vt)	[ɛ'zidʒerɛ]

to tease (nickname)	stuzzicare (vt)	[stutsi'karɛ]
to mock (deride)	canzonare (vt)	[kantsɔ'narɛ]
mockery, derision	burla (f), beffa (f)	['burʎa], ['bɛffa]
nickname	soprannome (m)	[sɔpra'ɲomɛ]

allusion	allusione (f)	[ally'zʲonɛ]
to allude (vi)	alludere (vi)	[al'lydɛrɛ]
to imply (vt)	intendere (vt)	[in'tɛndɛrɛ]

| description | descrizione (f) | [dɛskri'tsʲonɛ] |
| to describe (vt) | descrivere (vt) | [dɛsk'rivɛrɛ] |

| praise (compliments) | lode (f) | ['lɔdɛ] |
| to praise (vt) | lodare (vt) | [lɔ'darɛ] |

disappointment	delusione (f)	[dɛly'zʲonɛ]
to disappoint (vt)	deludere (vt)	[dɛ'lydɛrɛ]
to be disappointed	rimanere deluso	[rima'nɛrɛ dɛ'lyzɔ]

supposition	supposizione (f)	[suppozi'tsʲonɛ]
to suppose (assume)	supporre (vt)	[sup'porrɛ]
warning (caution)	avvertimento (m)	[avverti'mɛntɔ]
to warn (vt)	avvertire (vt)	[avwer'tirɛ]

67. Discussion, conversation. Part 3

to talk into (convince)	persuadere (vt)	[pɛrsua'dɛrɛ]
to calm down (vt)	tranquillizzare (vt)	[traŋkuillit'zarɛ]
silence (~ is golden)	silenzio (m)	[si'lentsiɔ]
to keep silent	tacere (vi)	[ta'ʧerɛ]
to whisper (vi, vt)	sussurrare (vt)	[sussur'rarɛ]
whisper	sussurro (m)	[sus'surrɔ]
frankly, sincerely (adv)	francamente	[fraŋka'mɛntɛ]
in my opinion ...	secondo me ...	[sɛ'kondɔ mɛ]
detail (of the story)	dettaglio (m)	[dɛt'taʎɔ]
detailed (adj)	dettagliato	[dɛtta'ʎjatɔ]
in detail (adv)	dettagliatamente	[dɛttaʎjata'mɛntɛ]
hint, clue	suggerimento (m)	[sudʒeri'mɛntɔ]
to give a hint	suggerire (vt)	[sudʒe'rirɛ]
look (glance)	sguardo (m)	[zgu'ardɔ]
to have a look	gettare uno sguardo	[dʒet'tarɛ 'unɔ zgu'ardɔ]
fixed (look)	fisso	['fissɔ]
to blink (vi)	battere le palpebre	['battɛrɛ le 'paʎpɛbrɛ]
to wink (vi)	ammiccare (vi)	[ammik'karɛ]
to nod (in assent)	accennare col capo	[aʧe'ɲarɛ koʎ 'kapɔ]
sigh	sospiro (m)	[sɔs'pirɔ]
to sigh (vi)	sospirare (vi)	[sɔspi'rarɛ]
to shudder (vi)	sussultare (vi)	[susuʎ'tarɛ]
gesture	gesto (m)	['dʒestɔ]
to touch (one's arm, etc.)	toccare (vt)	[tok'karɛ]
to seize (by the arm)	afferrare (vt)	[affer'rarɛ]
to tap (on the shoulder)	picchiettare (vt)	[pikjet'tarɛ]
Look out!	Attenzione!	[attɛn'tsʲonɛ]
Really?	Davvero?	[dav'vɛrɔ]
Are you sure?	Sei sicuro?	[sɛj si'kurɔ]
Good luck!	Buona fortuna!	[bu'ɔna for'tuna]
I see!	Capito!	[ka'pitɔ]
It's a pity!	Peccato!	[pɛk'katɔ]

68. Agreement. Refusal

consent (mutual ~)	accordo (m)	[ak'kɔrdɔ]
to agree (say yes)	essere d'accordo	['ɛssɛrɛ dak'kɔrdɔ]
approval	approvazione (f)	[approva'tsʲonɛ]
to approve (vt)	approvare (vt)	[apprɔ'varɛ]
refusal	rifiuto (m)	[ri'fjytɔ]
to refuse (vi, vt)	rifiutarsi (vr)	[rifjy'tarsi]
Great!	Perfetto!	[pɛr'fɛttɔ]
All right!	Va bene!	[va 'bɛnɛ]

Okay! (I agree)	D'accordo!	[dak'kɔrdɔ]
forbidden (adj)	vietato, proibito	[vje'tatɔ], [prɔi'bitɔ]
it's forbidden	è proibito	[ɛ prɔi'bitɔ]
it's impossible	è impossibile	[ɛ impɔs'sibile]
incorrect (adj)	sbagliato	[zba'ʎjatɔ]

to reject (~ a demand)	respingere (vt)	[rɛs'pindʒɛrɛ]
to support (cause, idea)	sostenere (vt)	[sɔstɛ'nɛrɛ]
to accept (~ an apology)	accettare (vt)	[atʃet'tarɛ]

to confirm (vt)	confermare (vt)	[kɔnfɛr'marɛ]
confirmation	conferma (f)	[kɔn'fɛrma]
permission	permesso (m)	[pɛr'mɛssɔ]
to permit (vt)	permettere (vt)	[pɛr'mɛttɛrɛ]
decision	decisione (f)	[dɛtʃizi'ɔnɛ]
to say nothing	non dire niente	[nɔn 'dirɛ 'njentɛ]

condition (term)	condizione (f)	[kɔndi'tsɨɔnɛ]
excuse (pretext)	pretesto (m)	[prɛ'tɛstɔ]
praise (compliments)	lode (f)	['lɔdɛ]
to praise (vt)	lodare (vt)	[lɔ'darɛ]

69. Success. Good luck. Failure

success	successo (m)	[su'tʃessɔ]
successfully (adv)	con successo	[kɔn su'tʃessɔ]
successful (adj)	ben riuscito	[bɛn riu'ʃitɔ]
good luck	fortuna (f)	[for'tuna]
Good luck!	Buona fortuna!	[bu'ɔna for'tuna]
lucky (e.g. ~ day)	felice, fortunato	[fe'litʃe], [fortu'natɔ]
lucky (fortunate)	fortunato	[fortu'natɔ]

failure	fiasco (m)	[fi'askɔ]
misfortune	disdetta (f)	[diz'dɛtta]
bad luck	sfortuna (f)	[sfor'tuna]
unsuccessful (adj)	fallito	[fal'litɔ]
catastrophe	disastro (m)	[di'zastrɔ]

pride	orgoglio (m)	[ɔr'gɔʎɔ]
proud (adj)	orgoglioso	[ɔrgɔ'ʎozɔ]
to be proud	essere fiero di ...	['ɛssɛre 'fjerɔ di]
winner	vincitore (m)	[wintʃi'tɔrɛ]
to win (vi)	vincere (vi)	['wintʃerɛ]
to lose (not win)	perdere (vi)	['pɛrdɛrɛ]
try	tentativo (m)	[tɛnta'tivɔ]
to try (vi)	tentare (vi)	[tɛn'tarɛ]
chance (opportunity)	chance (f)	[ʃans]

70. Quarrels. Negative emotions

| shout (scream) | grido (m) | ['gridɔ] |
| to shout (vi) | gridare (vi) | [gri'darɛ] |

to start to cry out	mettersi a gridare	['mɛttɛrsi a gri'darɛ]
quarrel	litigio (m)	[li'tidʒo]
to quarrel (vi)	litigare (vi)	[liti'garɛ]
fight (scandal)	lite (f)	['litɛ]
to have a fight	litigare (vi)	[liti'garɛ]
conflict	conflitto (m)	[konf'litto]
misunderstanding	fraintendimento (m)	[fraintɛndi'mɛnto]

insult	insulto (m)	[in'suʎto]
to insult (vt)	insultare (vt)	[insuʎ'tarɛ]
insulted (adj)	offeso	[of'fɛzo]
offence (to take ~)	offesa (f)	[of'fɛza]
to offend (vt)	offendere (vt)	[of'fɛndɛrɛ]
to take offence	offendersi (vr)	[of'fɛndɛrsi]

indignation	indignazione (f)	[indiɲja'tsjonɛ]
to be indignant	indignarsi (vr)	[indi'ɲjarsi]
complaint	lamentela (f)	[ʎamen'tɛla]
to complain (vi, vt)	lamentarsi (vr)	[ʎamɛn'tarsi]

apology	scusa (f)	['skuza]
to apologize (vi)	scusarsi (vr)	[sku'zarsi]
to beg pardon	chiedere scusa	['kjedɛrɛ 'skuza]

criticism	critica (f)	['kritika]
to criticize (vt)	criticare (vt)	[kriti'karɛ]
accusation	accusa (f)	[ak'kuza]
to accuse (vt)	accusare (vt)	[akku'zarɛ]

revenge	vendetta (f)	[vɛn'dɛtta]
to avenge (vt)	vendicare (vt)	[vɛndi'karɛ]
to pay back	vendicarsi (vr)	[vɛndi'karsi]

disdain	disprezzo (m)	[disp'rɛtso]
to despise (vt)	disprezzare (vt)	[disprɛ'tsarɛ]
hatred, hate	odio (m)	['ɔdio]
to hate (vt)	odiare (vt)	[odi'arɛ]

nervous (adj)	nervoso	[nɛr'vozo]
to be nervous	essere nervoso	['ɛssɛrɛ nɛr'vozo]
angry (mad)	arrabbiato	[arrab'bjato]
to make angry	fare arrabbiare	['farɛ arrab'bjarɛ]

humiliation	umiliazione (f)	[umilia'tsjonɛ]
to humiliate (vt)	umiliare (vt)	[umili'arɛ]
to humiliate oneself	umiliarsi (vr)	[umili'arsi]

| shock | shock (m) | [ʃɔk] |
| to shock (vt) | scandalizzare (vt) | [skandali'dzarɛ] |

| trouble (annoyance) | problema (m) | [prɔb'lema] |
| unpleasant (adj) | spiacevole | [spja'tʃevole] |

fear (dread)	spavento (m), paura (f)	[spa'vɛnto], [pa'ura]
terrible (storm, heat)	terribile	[tɛr'ribile]
scary (e.g. ~ story)	spaventoso	[spavɛn'tozo]

| horror | orrore (m) | [ɔr'rɔrɛ] |
| awful (crime, news) | orrendo | [ɔrrɛndɔ] |

to begin to tremble	cominciare a tremare	[kɔmin'tʃarɛ a trɛ'marɛ]
to cry (weep)	piangere (vi)	['pjandʒerɛ]
to start crying	mettersi a piangere	['mɛttɛrsi a 'pjandʒerɛ]
tear	lacrima (f)	['ʎakrima]

fault	colpa (f)	['kɔʎpa]
guilt (feeling)	senso (m) di colpa	['sɛnsɔ di 'kɔʎpa]
dishonour	vergogna (f)	[vɛr'gɔɲa]
protest	protesta (f)	[prɔ'tɛsta]
stress	stress (m)	['strɛss]

to disturb (vt)	disturbare (vt)	[distur'barɛ]
to be furious	essere arrabbiato	['ɛssɛrɛ arrab'bjatɔ]
angry (adj)	arrabbiato	[arrab'bjatɔ]
to end (e.g. relationship)	porre fine a ...	['pɔrrɛ 'finɛ a]
to swear (at sb)	rimproverare (vt)	[rimprɔvɛ'rarɛ]

to be scared	spaventarsi (vr)	[spavɛn'tarsi]
to hit (strike with hand)	colpire (vt)	[kɔʎ'pirɛ]
to fight (vi)	picchiarsi (vr)	[pik'kjarsi]

to settle (a conflict)	regolare (vt)	[rɛgo'ʎarɛ]
discontented (adj)	scontento	[skɔn'tɛntɔ]
furious (adj)	furioso	[furi'ɔzɔ]

| It's not good! | Non sta bene! | [nɔn sta 'bɛnɛ] |
| It's bad! | Fa male! | [fa 'male] |

Medicine

71. Diseases

illness	malattia (f)	[maʎat'tia]
to be ill	essere malato	['ɛssɛrɛ ma'ʎato]
health	salute (f)	[sa'lytɛ]

runny nose (coryza)	raffreddore (m)	[raffrɛd'dorɛ]
tonsillitis	tonsillite (f)	[tɔnsil'litɛ]
cold (illness)	raffreddore (m)	[raffrɛd'dorɛ]
to catch a cold	raffreddarsi (vr)	[raffrɛd'darsi]

bronchitis	bronchite (f)	[brɔ'ŋkitɛ]
pneumonia	polmonite (f)	[polmɔ'nitɛ]
flu, influenza	influenza (f)	[infly'ɛntsa]

short-sighted (adj)	miope	['miɔpɛ]
long-sighted (adj)	presbite	['prɛzbitɛ]
squint	strabismo (m)	[stra'bizmɔ]
squint-eyed (adj)	strabico	['strabikɔ]
cataract	cateratta (f)	[katɛ'ratta]
glaucoma	glaucoma (m)	[gʎau'kɔma]

stroke	ictus (m) cerebrale	['iktus tʃeleb'ralɛ]
heart attack	attacco (m) di cuore	[at'takɔ di ku'ɔrɛ]
myocardial infarction	infarto (m) miocardico	[in'fartɔ miɔkar'dikɔ]
paralysis	paralisi (f)	[pa'ralizi]
to paralyse (vt)	paralizzare (vt)	[parali'dzarɛ]

allergy	allergia (f)	[aller'dʒia]
asthma	asma (f)	['azma]
diabetes	diabete (m)	[dia'bɛtɛ]

toothache	mal (m) di denti	[maʎ di 'dɛnti]
caries	carie (f)	['kariɛ]

diarrhoea	diarrea (f)	[diar'rɛa]
constipation	stitichezza (f)	[stiti'kɛtsa]
stomach upset	disturbo (m) gastrico	[dis'turbɔ 'gastrikɔ]
food poisoning	intossicazione (f) alimentare	[intɔsika'tsʲɔnɛ alimen'tarɛ]
to have a food poisoning	intossicarsi (vr)	[intɔssi'karsi]

arthritis	artrite (f)	[art'ritɛ]
rickets	rachitide (f)	[ra'kitidɛ]
rheumatism	reumatismo (m)	[rɛuma'tizmɔ]
atherosclerosis	aterosclerosi (f)	[atɛroskle'rɔzi]

gastritis	gastrite (f)	[gast'ritɛ]
appendicitis	appendicite (f)	[appɛndi'tʃitɛ]

| cholecystitis | colecistite (f) | [kɔletʃis'titɛ] |
| ulcer | ulcera (f) | ['uʌtʃera] |

measles	morbillo (m)	[mɔr'billɔ]
German measles	rosolia (f)	[rɔzɔ'lia]
jaundice	itterizia (f)	[ittɛ'ritsia]
hepatitis	epatite (f)	[ɛpa'titɛ]

schizophrenia	schizofrenia (f)	[skidzɔfrɛ'nia]
rabies (hydrophobia)	rabbia (f)	['rabbja]
neurosis	nevrosi (f)	[nɛv'rɔzi]
concussion	commozione (f) cerebrale	[kɔmmɔ'tsʲɔnɛ tʃerɛb'rale]

cancer	cancro (m)	['kaŋkrɔ]
sclerosis	sclerosi (f)	[skle'rɔzi]
multiple sclerosis	sclerosi (f) multipla	[skle'rɔzi 'muʌtipʌa]

alcoholism	alcolismo (m)	[aʌkɔ'lizmɔ]
alcoholic (n)	alcolizzato (m)	[aʌkɔli'dzatɔ]
syphilis	sifilide (f)	[si'filidɛ]
AIDS	AIDS (m)	['aids]

tumour	tumore (m)	[tu'mɔrɛ]
fever	febbre (f)	['fɛbbrɛ]
malaria	malaria (f)	[ma'ʌaria]
gangrene	cancrena (f)	[kaŋk'rɛna]
seasickness	mal (m) di mare	[maʌ di 'marɛ]
epilepsy	epilessia (f)	[ɛpiles'sia]

epidemic	epidemia (f)	[ɛpidɛ'mia]
typhus	tifo (m)	['tifɔ]
tuberculosis	tubercolosi (f)	[tuberkɔ'lɔzi]
cholera	colera (m)	[kɔ'lera]
plague (bubonic ~)	peste (f)	['pɛstɛ]

72. Symptoms. Treatments. Part 1

symptom	sintomo (m)	['sintɔmɔ]
temperature	temperatura (f)	[tɛmpɛra'tura]
fever	febbre (f) alta	['fɛbbrɛ 'aʌta]
pulse	polso (m)	['pɔʌsɔ]

giddiness	capogiro (m)	[kapɔ'dʒirɔ]
hot (adj)	caldo	['kaʌdɔ]
shivering	brivido (m)	['briwidɔ]
pale (e.g. ~ face)	pallido	['pallidɔ]

cough	tosse (f)	['tɔssɛ]
to cough (vi)	tossire (vi)	[tɔs'sirɛ]
to sneeze (vi)	starnutire (vi)	[starnu'tirɛ]
faint	svenimento (m)	[zvɛni'mɛntɔ]
to faint (vi)	svenire (vi)	[zvɛ'nirɛ]
bruise (hématome)	livido (m)	['liwidɔ]
bump (lump)	bernoccolo (m)	[ber'nɔkkɔlɔ]

to bruise oneself	farsi un livido	['farsi un 'liwido]
bruise	contusione (f)	[kontuzi'onɛ]
to get bruised	farsi male	['farsi 'male]

to limp (vi)	zoppicare (vi)	[dzoppi'karɛ]
dislocation	slogatura (f)	[zlɔga'tura]
to dislocate (vt)	slogarsi (vr)	[zlɔ'garsi]
fracture	frattura (f)	[frat'tura]
to have a fracture	fratturarsi (vr)	[frattu'rarsi]

cut (e.g. paper ~)	taglio (m)	['taʎo]
to cut oneself	tagliarsi (vr)	[ta'ʎjarsi]
bleeding	emorragia (f)	[ɛmorra'dʒia]

burn (injury)	scottatura (f)	[skotta'tura]
to burn oneself	scottarsi (vr)	[skot'tarsi]

to prick (vt)	pungere (vt)	['pundʒerɛ]
to prick oneself	pungersi (vr)	['pundʒersi]
to injure (vt)	ferire (vt)	[fɛ'rirɛ]
injury	ferita (f)	[fɛ'rita]
wound	lesione (f)	[le'zjonɛ]
trauma	trauma (m)	['trauma]

to be delirious	delirare (vi)	[dɛli'rarɛ]
to stutter (vi)	tartagliare (vi)	[tarta'ʎjarɛ]
sunstroke	colpo (m) di sole	['koʎpo di 'solе]

73. Symptoms. Treatments. Part 2

pain	dolore (m), male (m)	[do'lɔrɛ], ['male]
splinter (in foot, etc.)	scheggia (f)	['skɛdʒa]

sweat (perspiration)	sudore (m)	[su'dɔrɛ]
to sweat (perspire)	sudare (vi)	[su'darɛ]
vomiting	vomito (m)	['vomito]
convulsions	convulsioni (f pl)	[konvul'sjoni]

pregnant (adj)	incinta	[in'tʃinta]
to be born	nascere (vi)	['naʃɛrɛ]
delivery, labour	parto (m)	['parto]
to labour (vi)	essere in travaglio	['ɛssɛrɛ in tra'vaʎo]
abortion	aborto (m)	[a'bɔrto]

respiration	respirazione (f)	[rɛspira'tsjonɛ]
inhalation	inspirazione (f)	[inspira'tsjonɛ]
exhalation	espirazione (f)	[ɛspira'tsjonɛ]
to breathe out	espirare (vi)	[ɛspi'rarɛ]
to breathe in	inspirare (vi)	[inspi'rarɛ]

disabled person	invalido (m)	[in'valido]
cripple	storpio (m)	['stɔrpjo]
drug addict	drogato (m)	[dro'gato]
deaf (adj)	sordo	['sɔrdo]

| dumb (adj) | muto | ['muto] |
| deaf-and-dumb (adj) | sordomuto | [sɔrdɔ'mutɔ] |

mad, insane (adj)	matto	['mattɔ]
madman	matto (m)	['mattɔ]
madwoman	matta (f)	['matta]
to go insane	impazzire (vi)	[impa'tsirɛ]

gene	gene (m)	['dʒenɛ]
immunity	immunità (f)	[immuni'ta]
hereditary (adj)	ereditario	[ɛrɛdi'tariɔ]
congenital (adj)	innato	[i'ɲatɔ]

virus	virus (m)	['wirus]
microbe	microbo (m)	['mikrɔbɔ]
bacterium	batterio (m)	[bat'tɛriɔ]
infection	infezione (f)	[infɛ'tsjɔnɛ]

74. Symptoms. Treatments. Part 3

| hospital | ospedale (m) | [ɔspɛ'dale] |
| patient | paziente (m) | [patsi'entɛ] |

diagnosis	diagnosi (f)	[di'aɲɔzi]
cure	cura (f)	['kura]
medical treatment	battaglia (f)	[bat'taʎja]
to get treatment	curarsi (vr)	[ku'rarsi]
to treat (vt)	curare (vt)	[ku'rarɛ]
to nurse (look after)	accudire un malato	[akku'dirɛ un ma'ʎatɔ]
care	assistenza (f)	[assis'tɛntsa]

operation, surgery	operazione (f)	[ɔpɛra'tsjɔnɛ]
to bandage (head, limb)	bendare (vt)	[bɛn'darɛ]
bandaging	fasciatura (f)	[faɕa'tura]

vaccination	vaccinazione (f)	[vatʃina'tsjɔnɛ]
to vaccinate (vt)	vaccinare (vt)	[vatʃi'narɛ]
injection, shot	iniezione (f)	[inje'tsjɔnɛ]
to give an injection	fare una puntura	['farɛ 'una pun'tura]

attack	attacco (m)	[at'takkɔ]
amputation	amputazione (f)	[amputa'tsjɔnɛ]
to amputate (vt)	amputare (vt)	[ampu'tarɛ]
coma	coma (m)	['kɔma]
to be in a coma	essere in coma	['ɛssɛrɛ in 'kɔma]
intensive care	rianimazione (f)	[rianima'tsjɔnɛ]

to recover (~ from flu)	guarire (vi)	[gua'rirɛ]
state (patient's ~)	stato (f)	['statɔ]
consciousness	conoscenza (f)	[kɔnɔ'ʃɛntsa]
memory (faculty)	memoria (f)	[mɛ'mɔria]

| to extract (tooth) | estrarre (vt) | [ɛst'rarrɛ] |
| filling | otturazione (f) | [ɔttura'tsjɔnɛ] |

to fill (a tooth)	otturare (vt)	[ottu'rarɛ]
hypnosis	ipnosi (f)	[ip'nɔzi]
to hypnotize (vt)	ipnotizzare (vt)	[ipnoti'dzarɛ]

75. Doctors

doctor	medico (m)	['mɛdikɔ]
nurse	infermiera (f)	[infɛr'mjera]
private physician	medico (m) personale	['mɛdikɔ pɛrsɔ'nale]

dentist	dentista (m)	[dɛn'tista]
ophthalmologist	oculista (m)	[ɔku'lista]
general practitioner	internista (m)	[intɛr'nista]
surgeon	chirurgo (m)	[ki'rurgɔ]

psychiatrist	psichiatra (m)	[psiki'atra]
paediatrician	pediatra (m)	[pɛdi'atra]
psychologist	psicologo (m)	[psi'kɔlɔgɔ]
gynaecologist	ginecologo (m)	[dʒine'kɔlɔgɔ]
cardiologist	cardiologo (m)	[kardi'ɔlɔgɔ]

76. Medicine. Drugs. Accessories

medicine, drug	medicina (f)	[mɛdi'ʧina]
remedy	rimedio (m)	[ri'mɛdiɔ]
prescription	prescrizione (f)	[prɛskri'ʦjɔnɛ]

tablet, pill	compressa (f)	[kɔmp'rɛssa]
ointment	unguento (m)	[uŋu'ɛntɔ]
ampoule	fiala (f)	[fi'aʎa]
mixture	pozione (f)	[pɔ'ʦjɔnɛ]
syrup	sciroppo (m)	[ʃi'rɔppɔ]
pill	pillola (f)	['pillʒʎa]
powder	polverina (f)	[pɔʎvɛ'rina]

bandage	benda (f)	['bɛnda]
cotton wool	ovatta (f)	[ɔ'vatta]
iodine	iodio (m)	[i'ɔdiɔ]

plaster	cerotto (m)	[ʧe'rɔttɔ]
eyedropper	contagocce (m)	[kɔnta'gɔʧe]
thermometer	termometro (m)	[tɛr'mɔmɛtrɔ]
syringe	siringa (f)	[si'riŋa]

| wheelchair | sedia (f) a rotelle | ['sɛdia a rɔ'tɛllɛ] |
| crutches | stampelle (f pl) | [stam'pɛllе] |

painkiller	analgesico (m)	[anaʎ'dʒɛzikɔ]
laxative	lassativo (m)	[lassa'tivɔ]
spirit (ethanol)	alcol (m)	[aʎ'kɔʎ]
medicinal herbs	erba (f) officinale	['ɛrba ɔffiʧi'nale]
herbal (~ tea)	alle erbe	[al'lɛrbɛ]

77. Smoking. Tobacco products

tobacco	tabacco (m)	[ta'bakkɔ]
cigarette	sigaretta (f)	[siga'rɛtta]
cigar	sigaro (m)	['sigarɔ]
pipe	pipa (f)	['pipa]
packet (of cigarettes)	pacchetto (m)	[pak'kɛttɔ]
matches	fiammiferi (m pl)	[fjam'miferi]
matchbox	scatola (f) di fiammiferi	['skatoʎa di fjam'miferi]
lighter	accendino (m)	[atʃen'dinɔ]
ashtray	portacenere (m)	[pɔrta'tʃenɛrɛ]
cigarette case	portasigarette (m)	[pɔrtasiga'rɛttɛ]
cigarette holder	bocchino (m)	[bɔk'kinɔ]
filter	filtro (m)	['fiʎtrɔ]
to smoke (vi, vt)	fumare (vi, vt)	[fu'marɛ]
to light a cigarette	accendere una sigaretta	[a'tʃendɛrɛ una siga'rɛtta]
smoking	fumo (m)	['fumɔ]
smoker	fumatore (m)	[fuma'tɔrɛ]
cigarette end	cicca (f)	['tʃikka]
smoke, fumes	fumo (m)	['fumɔ]
ash	cenere (f)	['tʃenɛrɛ]

HUMAN HABITAT

City

78. City. Life in the city

city, town	città (f)	[tʃit'ta]
capital	capitale (f)	[kapi'tale]
village	villaggio (m)	[wi'ʎadʒɔ]
city map	mappa (f) della città	['mappa 'dɛʎa tʃit'ta]
city centre	centro (m) della città	['tʃentrɔ 'dɛʎa tʃit'ta]
suburb	sobborgo (m)	[sɔb'bɔrgɔ]
suburban (adj)	suburbano	[subur'banɔ]
outskirts	periferia (f)	[pɛrife'ria]
environs (suburbs)	dintorni (m pl)	[din'tɔrni]
quarter	isolato (m)	[izɔ'ʎatɔ]
residential quarter	quartiere (m) residenziale	[kuar'tʲerɛ rɛzidɛntsi'ale]
traffic	traffico (m)	['traffikɔ]
traffic lights	semaforo (m)	[sɛ'mafɔrɔ]
public transport	trasporti (m pl) urbani	[tras'pɔrti ur'bani]
crossroads	incrocio (m)	[iŋk'rɔtʃɔ]
zebra crossing	passaggio (m) pedonale	[pas'sadʒɔ pɛdɔ'nale]
pedestrian subway	sottopassaggio (m)	[sɔttɔpas'sadʒɔ]
to cross (vt)	attraversare (vt)	[attravɛr'sarɛ]
pedestrian	pedone (m)	[pɛ'dɔnɛ]
pavement	marciapiede (m)	[martʃa'pjedɛ]
bridge	ponte (m)	['pɔntɛ]
embankment	banchina (f)	[ba'ŋkina]
allée	vialetto (m)	[wia'lettɔ]
park	parco (m)	['parkɔ]
boulevard	boulevard (m)	[buʎ'var]
square	piazza (f)	['pjatsa]
avenue (wide street)	viale (m), corso (m)	[wi'alɛ], ['kɔrsɔ]
street	via (f), strada (f)	['wia], ['strada]
lane	vicolo (m)	['wikɔlɔ]
dead end	vicolo (m) cieco	['wikɔlɔ 'tʃjekɔ]
house	casa (f)	['kaza]
building	edificio (m)	[ɛdi'fitʃɔ]
skyscraper	grattacielo (m)	[gratta'tʃelɔ]
facade	facciata (f)	[fa'tʃata]
roof	tetto (m)	['tɛttɔ]

window	finestra (f)	[fi'nɛstra]
arch	arco (m)	['arkɔ]
column	colonna (f)	[kɔ'lɔŋa]
corner	angolo (m)	['aŋɔlo]

shop window	vetrina (f)	[vɛt'rina]
shop sign	insegna (f)	[in'sɛɲja]
poster	cartellone (m)	[kartɛl'lɔnɛ]
advertising poster	cartellone (m) pubblicitario	[kartɛl'lɔnɛ pubblitʃi'tariɔ]
hoarding	tabellone (m) pubblicitario	[tabɛl'lɔnɛ pubblitʃi'tariɔ]

rubbish	pattume (m), spazzatura (f)	[pat'tumɛ], [spatsa'tura]
rubbish bin	pattumiera (f)	[pattu'mjera]
to litter (vi)	sporcare (vi)	[spor'karɛ]
rubbish dump	discarica (f) di rifiuti	[dis'karika di ri'fjyti]

telephone box	cabina (f) telefonica	[ka'bina tɛle'fonika]
street light	lampione (m)	[lam'pɔnɛ]
bench (park ~)	panchina (f)	[pa'ŋkina]

policeman	poliziotto (m)	[politsi'ɔttɔ]
police	polizia (f)	[poli'tsia]
beggar	mendicante (m)	[mendi'kantɛ]
homeless	barbone (m)	[bar'bɔnɛ]

79. Urban institutions

shop	negozio (m)	[nɛ'gɔtsiɔ]
chemist, pharmacy	farmacia (f)	[farma'tʃia]
optician	ottica (f)	['ɔttika]
shopping centre	centro (m) commerciale	['tʃentrɔ kɔmmɛr'tʃale]
supermarket	supermercato (m)	[supɛrmɛr'katɔ]

bakery	panetteria (f)	[panɛttɛ'ria]
baker	fornaio (m)	[for'najo]
cake shop	pasticceria (f)	[pastitʃe'ria]
grocery shop	drogheria (f)	[drogɛ'ria]
butcher shop	macelleria (f)	[matʃelle'ria]

| greengrocer | fruttivendolo (m) | [frutti'vɛndolɔ] |
| market | mercato (m) | [mɛr'katɔ] |

coffee bar	caffè (m)	[kaf'fɛ]
restaurant	ristorante (m)	[risto'rantɛ]
pub	birreria (f), pub (m)	[birrɛ'ria], [pab]
pizzeria	pizzeria (f)	[pitsɛ'ria]

hairdresser	salone (m) di parrucchiere	[sa'lɔnɛ di parruk'kjerɛ]
post office	ufficio (m) postale	[uf'fitʃo pɔs'tale]
dry cleaners	lavanderia (f) a secco	[ʎavandɛ'ria a 'sɛkkɔ]
photo studio	studio (m) fotografico	['studio fotog'rafikɔ]

| shoe shop | negozio (m) di scarpe | [nɛ'gɔtsiɔ di 'skarpɛ] |
| bookshop | libreria (f) | [librɛ'ria] |

sports shop	negozio (m) sportivo	[nɛ'gotsio spor'tivo]
clothing repair	riparazione (f) di abiti	[ripara'tsione di 'abiti]
formal wear hire	noleggio (m) di abiti	[no'ledʒo di 'abiti]
DVD rental shop	noleggio DVD (m)	[no'ledʒo divu'di]

circus	circo (m)	['tʃirko]
zoo	zoo (m)	['dzo:]
cinema	cinema (m)	['tʃinɛma]
museum	museo (m)	[mu'zɛo]
library	biblioteca (f)	[biblio'tɛka]

theatre	teatro (m)	[tɛ'atro]
opera	teatro (m) dell'opera	[tɛ'atro dɛʎ 'opera]
nightclub	nightclub (m)	['najtklɛb]
casino	casinò (m)	[kazi'no]

mosque	moschea (f)	[mos'kɛa]
synagogue	sinagoga (f)	[sina'goga]
cathedral	cattedrale (f)	[kattɛd'rale]
temple	tempio (m)	['tɛmpio]
church	chiesa (f)	['kjeza]

institute	istituto (m)	[isti'tuto]
university	università (f)	[univɛrsi'ta]
school	scuola (f)	[sku'oʎa]

prefecture	prefettura (f)	[prɛfɛt'tura]
town hall	municipio (m)	[muni'tʃipio]
hotel	albergo (m)	[aʎ'bɛrgo]
bank	banca (f)	['baŋka]

embassy	ambasciata (f)	[amba'ʃata]
travel agency	agenzia (f) di viaggi	[adʒen'tsia di wi'jadʒi]
information office	ufficio (m) informazioni	[uf'fitʃo informatsi'oni]
money exchange	ufficio (m) dei cambi	[uf'fitʃo dɛi 'kambi]

| underground, tube | metropolitana (f) | [metropoli'tana] |
| hospital | ospedale (m) | [ospɛ'dale] |

| petrol station | distributore (m) di benzina | [distribu'torɛ di ben'dzina] |
| car park | parcheggio (m) | [par'kɛdʒo] |

80. Signs

shop sign	insegna (f)	[in'sɛɲa]
notice (written text)	iscrizione (f)	[iskri'tsione]
poster	cartellone (m)	[kartɛl'lone]
direction sign	segnale (m) di direzione	[se'ɲale di dirɛ'tsione]
arrow (sign)	freccia (f)	['frɛtʃa]

caution	avvertimento (m)	[avwerti'mɛnto]
warning sign	avvertimento (m)	[avwerti'mɛnto]
to warn (vt)	avvertire (vt)	[avwer'tirɛ]
closing day	giorno (m) di riposo	['dʒorno di ri'pozo]

77

| timetable (schedule) | orario (m) | [ɔ'rarjɔ] |
| opening hours | orario (m) di apertura | [ɔ'rarjɔ di apɛr'tura] |

WELCOME!	BENVENUTI!	[bɛnvɛ'nuti]
ENTRANCE	ENTRATA	[ɛnt'rata]
WAY OUT	USCITA	[u'ʃita]

PUSH	SPINGERE	['spindʒɛrɛ]
PULL	TIRARE	[ti'rarɛ]
OPEN	APERTO	[a'pɛrtɔ]
CLOSED	CHIUSO	['kjyzɔ]

| WOMEN | DONNE | ['dɔŋɛ] |
| MEN | UOMINI | [u'omini] |

DISCOUNTS	SCONTI	['skɔnti]
SALE	SALDI	['saʎdi]
NEW!	NOVITÀ!	[nɔwi'ta]
FREE	GRATIS	['gratis]

ATTENTION!	ATTENZIONE!	[attɛn'tsjɔnɛ]
NO VACANCIES	COMPLETO	[kɔmp'letɔ]
RESERVED	RISERVATO	[risɛr'vatɔ]

ADMINISTRATION	AMMINISTRAZIONE	[aministra'tsjɔnɛ]
STAFF ONLY	RISERVATO	[risɛr'vatɔ
	AL PERSONALE	aʎ pɛrsɔ'nale]

BEWARE OF THE DOG!	ATTENTI AL CANE	[at'tɛnti aʎ 'kanɛ]
NO SMOKING	VIETATO FUMARE!	[vje'tatɔ fu'marɛ]
DO NOT TOUCH!	NON TOCCARE!	[nɔn tɔk'karɛ]

DANGEROUS	PERICOLOSO	[pɛrikɔ'lɜzɔ]
DANGER	PERICOLO	[pɛ'rikɔlɔ]
HIGH TENSION	ALTA TENSIONE	['aʎta tɛnsi'ɔnɛ]
NO SWIMMING!	DIVIETO DI BALNEAZIONE	[di'vjetɔ di baʎnɛa'tsjɔnɛ]
OUT OF ORDER	GUASTO	[gu'astɔ]

FLAMMABLE	INFIAMMABILE	[infjam'mabile]
FORBIDDEN	VIETATO	[vje'tatɔ]
NO TRESPASSING!	VIETATO L'INGRESSO	[vje'tatɔ liŋ'rɛsɔ]
WET PAINT	VERNICE FRESCA	[vɛr'nitʃe 'frɛska]

81. Urban transport

bus, coach	autobus (m)	['autɔbus]
tram	tram (m)	[tram]
trolleybus	filobus (m)	['filɔbus]
route (of bus)	itinerario (m)	[itine'rarjɔ]
number (e.g. bus ~)	numero (m)	['numɛrɔ]

to go by ...	andare in ...	[an'darɛ in]
to get on (~ the bus)	salire su ...	[sa'lirɛ su]
to get off ...	scendere da ...	['ʃɛndɛrɛ da]

stop (e.g. bus ~)	fermata (f)	[fɛr'mata]
next stop	prossima fermata (f)	['prɔssima fɛr'mata]
terminus	capolinea (m)	[kapɔ'linɛa]
timetable	orario (m)	[ɔ'rariɔ]
to wait (vt)	aspettare (vt)	[aspɛt'tarɛ]
ticket	biglietto (m)	[bi'ʎjettɔ]
fare	prezzo (m) del biglietto	['prɛtsɔ dɛʎ bi'ʎjettɔ]
cashier	cassiere (m)	[kas'sjerɛ]
ticket inspection	controllo (m) dei biglietti	[kɔnt'rɔllɔ dei bi'ʎjeti]
inspector	bigliettaio (m)	[biʎjet'tajo]
to be late (for ...)	essere in ritardo	['ɛssɛrɛ in ri'tardɔ]
to miss (~ the train, etc.)	perdere (vt)	['pɛrdɛrɛ]
to be in a hurry	avere fretta	[a'vɛrɛ 'frɛtta]
taxi, cab	taxi (m)	['taksi]
taxi driver	taxista (m)	[tak'sista]
by taxi	in taxi	[in 'taksi]
taxi rank	parcheggio (m) di taxi	[par'kɛdʒɔ di 'taksi]
to call a taxi	chiamare un taxi	[kja'marɛ un 'taksi]
to take a taxi	prendere un taxi	['prɛndɛrɛ un 'taksi]
traffic	traffico (m)	['traffikɔ]
traffic jam	ingorgo (m)	[i'ŋɔrgɔ]
rush hour	ore (f pl) di punta	['ɔrɛ di 'punta]
to park (vi)	parcheggiarsi (vr)	[parkɛ'dʒarsi]
to park (vt)	parcheggiare (vt)	[parkɛ'dʒarɛ]
car park	parcheggio (m)	[par'kɛdʒɔ]
underground, tube	metropolitana (f)	[metrɔpɔli'tana]
station	stazione (f)	[sta'tsʲonɛ]
to take the tube	prendere la metropolitana	['prɛndɛrɛ ʎa metrɔpɔli'tana]
train	treno (m)	['trɛnɔ]
train station	stazione (f) ferroviaria	[sta'tsʲonɛ fɛrrɔ'vʲaria]

82. Sightseeing

monument	monumento (m)	[mɔnu'mɛntɔ]
fortress	fortezza (f)	[fɔr'tɛtsa]
palace	palazzo (m)	[pa'ʎatsɔ]
castle	castello (m)	[kas'tɛllɔ]
tower	torre (f)	['tɔrrɛ]
mausoleum	mausoleo (m)	[mauzɔ'leɔ]
architecture	architettura (f)	[arkitɛt'tura]
medieval (adj)	medievale	[mɛdiɛ'vale]
ancient (adj)	antico	[an'tikɔ]
national (adj)	nazionale	[natsiɔ'nale]
well-known (adj)	famoso	[fa'mɔzɔ]
tourist	turista (m)	[tu'rista]
guide (person)	guida (f)	[gu'ida]

excursion	escursione (f)	[ɛskursi'ɔnɛ]
to show (vt)	fare vedere	['farɛ ve'dɛrɛ]
to tell (vt)	raccontare (vt)	[rakkɔn'tarɛ]

to find (vt)	trovare (vt)	[trɔ'varɛ]
to get lost	perdersi (vr)	['pɛrdɛrsi]
map (e.g. underground ~)	mappa (f)	['mappa]
map (e.g. city ~)	piantina (f)	[pjan'tina]

souvenir, gift	souvenir (m)	[suvɛ'nir]
gift shop	negozio (m)	[nɛ'gɔtsiɔ
	di articoli da regalo	di ar'tikɔli da rɛ'galɔ]
to take pictures	fare foto	['farɛ 'fotɔ]
to be photographed	farsi fotografare	['farsi fotogra'farɛ]

83. Shopping

to buy (purchase)	comprare (vt)	[kɔmp'rarɛ]
purchase	acquisto (m)	[aku'istɔ]
to go shopping	fare acquisti	['farɛ aku'isti]
shopping	shopping (m)	['ʃɔppiŋ]

| to be open (ab. shop) | essere aperto | ['ɛssɛrɛ a'pɛrtɔ] |
| to be closed | essere chiuso | ['ɛssɛrɛ 'kjyzɔ] |

footwear	calzature (f pl)	[kaʎtsa'turɛ]
clothes, clothing	abbigliamento (m)	[abbiʎja'mɛntɔ]
cosmetics	cosmetica (f)	[kɔz'mɛtika]
food products	alimentari (m pl)	[alimɛn'tari]
gift, present	regalo (m)	[rɛ'galɔ]

| shop assistant (masc.) | commesso (m) | [kɔm'mɛssɔ] |
| shop assistant (fem.) | commessa (f) | [kɔm'mɛssa] |

cash desk	cassa (f)	['kassa]
mirror	specchio (m)	['spɛkkiɔ]
counter (in shop)	banco (m)	['baŋkɔ]
fitting room	camerino (m)	[kamɛ'rinɔ]

to try on	provare (vt)	[prɔ'varɛ]
to fit (ab. dress, etc.)	stare bene	['starɛ 'bɛnɛ]
to fancy (vt)	piacere (vi)	[pja'tʃɛrɛ]

price	prezzo (m)	['prɛtsɔ]
price tag	etichetta (f) del prezzo	[eti'ketta dɛʎ 'prɛtsɔ]
to cost (vt)	costare (vt)	[kɔs'tarɛ]
How much?	Quanto?	[ku'antɔ]
discount	sconto (m)	['skontɔ]

inexpensive (adj)	no muy caro	[nɔ muj 'karɔ]
cheap (adj)	a buon mercato	[a bu'ɔn mɛr'katɔ]
expensive (adj)	caro	['karɔ]
It's expensive	È caro	[ɛ 'karɔ]
hire (n)	noleggio (m)	[nɔ'ledʒɔ]

to hire (~ a dinner jacket)	noleggiare (vt)	[nɔle'dʒarɛ]
credit	credito (m)	['krɛditɔ]
on credit (adv)	a credito	[a 'krɛditɔ]

84. Money

money	soldi (m pl)	['sɔʎdi]
exchange	cambio (m)	['kambʲɔ]
exchange rate	corso (m) di cambio	['kɔrsɔ di 'kambʲɔ]
cashpoint	bancomat (m)	['baŋkɔmat]
coin	moneta (f)	[mɔ'nɛta]

| dollar | dollaro (m) | ['dɔʎarɔ] |
| euro | euro (m) | ['ɛurɔ] |

lira	lira (f)	['lira]
Deutschmark	marco (m)	['markɔ]
franc	franco (m)	['fraŋkɔ]
pound sterling	sterlina (f)	[stɛr'lina]
yen	yen (m)	[jen]

debt	debito (m)	['dɛbitɔ]
debtor	debitore (m)	[dɛbi'tɔrɛ]
to lend (money)	prestare (vt)	[pres'tarɛ]
to borrow (vi, vt)	prendere in prestito	['prɛndɛrɛ in 'prɛstitɔ]

bank	banca (f)	['baŋka]
account	conto (m)	['kɔntɔ]
to deposit into the account	versare sul conto	[vɛr'sare suʎ 'kɔntɔ]
to withdraw (vt)	prelevare dal conto	[prɛle'varɛ daʎ 'kɔntɔ]

credit card	carta (f) di credito	['karta di 'krɛditɔ]
cash	contanti (m pl)	[kɔn'tanti]
cheque	assegno (m)	[as'seɲʲɔ]
to write a cheque	emettere un assegno	[ɛ'mɛttɛrɛ un as'seɲʲɔ]
chequebook	libretto (m) di assegni	[lib'rɛttɔ di as'seɲʲi]

wallet	portafoglio (m)	[pɔrta'fɔʎɔ]
purse	borsellino (m)	[bɔrsɛl'linɔ]
billfold	portamonete (m)	[pɔrtamɔ'nɛtɛ]
safe	cassaforte (f)	[kassa'fɔrtɛ]

heir	erede (m)	[ɛ'rɛdɛ]
inheritance	eredità (f)	[ɛrɛdi'ta]
fortune (wealth)	fortuna (f)	[fɔr'tuna]

lease, let	affitto (m)	[af'fittɔ]
rent money	affitto (m)	[af'fittɔ]
to rent (sth from sb)	affittare (vt)	[affit'tarɛ]

price	prezzo (m)	['prɛtsɔ]
cost	costo (m), prezzo (m)	['kɔstɔ], ['prɛtsɔ]
sum	somma (f)	['sɔmma]
to spend (vt)	spendere (vt)	['spɛndɛrɛ]

expenses	spese (f pl)	['spɛzɛ]
to economize (vi, vt)	economizzare (vi, vt)	[ɛkonomi'dzarɛ]
economical	economico	[ɛko'nomiko]

to pay (vi, vt)	pagare (vi, vt)	[pa'garɛ]
payment	pagamento (m)	[paga'mɛnto]
change (give the ~)	resto (m)	['rɛsto]

tax	imposta (f)	[im'posta]
fine	multa (f), ammenda (f)	['muʎta], [am'mɛnda]
to fine (vt)	multare (vt)	[muʎ'tarɛ]

85. Post. Postal service

post office	posta (f), ufficio (m) postale	['posta], [uf'fiʧo pos'talɛ]
post (letters, etc.)	posta (f)	['posta]
postman	postino (m)	[pos'tino]
opening hours	orario (m) di apertura	[o'rario di apɛr'tura]

letter	lettera (f)	['lettɛra]
registered letter	raccomandata (f)	[rakkoman'data]
postcard	cartolina (f)	[karto'lina]
telegram	telegramma (m)	[tɛleg'ramma]
parcel	pacco (m) postale	['pakko pos'talɛ]
money transfer	vaglia (m) postale	['vaʎja pos'talɛ]

to receive (vt)	ricevere (vt)	[ri'ʧevɛrɛ]
to send (vt)	spedire (vt)	[spɛ'dirɛ]
sending	invio (m)	[in'wio]

address	indirizzo (m)	[indi'ritso]
postcode	codice (m) postale	['koditʃe pos'talɛ]
sender	mittente (m)	[mit'tɛntɛ]
receiver, addressee	destinatario (m)	[dɛstina'tario]

| name | nome (m) | ['nomɛ] |
| family name | cognome (m) | [ko'ɲlomɛ] |

rate (of postage)	tariffa (f)	[ta'riffa]
standard (adj)	ordinario	[ordi'nario]
economical (adj)	standard	['standar]

weight	peso (m)	['pɛzo]
to weigh up (vt)	pesare (vt)	[pɛ'zarɛ]
envelope	busta (f)	['busta]
postage stamp	francobollo (m)	[fraŋko'bollo]

Dwelling. House. Home

86. House. Dwelling

house	casa (f)	['kaza]
at home (adv)	a casa	[a 'kaza]
courtyard	cortile (m)	[kor'tile]
fence	recinto (m)	[rɛ'ʧinto]
brick (n)	mattone (m)	[mat'tonɛ]
brick (as adj)	di mattoni	[di mat'toni]
stone (n)	pietra (f)	['pjetra]
stone (as adj)	di pietra	[di 'pjetra]
concrete (n)	beton (m)	[bɛ'ton]
concrete (as adj)	di beton	[di bɛ'ton]
new (adj)	nuovo	[nu'ɔvɔ]
old (adj)	vecchio	['vɛkkiɔ]
decrepit (house)	fatiscente	[fati'ʃɛntɛ]
modern (adj)	moderno	[mɔ'dɛrnɔ]
multistorey (adj)	a molti piani	[a 'mɔʎti 'pjani]
high (adj)	alto	['aʎtɔ]
floor, storey	piano (m)	['pjanɔ]
single-storey (adj)	di un piano	[di un 'pjanɔ]
ground floor	pianoterra (m)	[pjanɔ'tɛrra]
top floor	ultimo piano (m)	['uʎtimɔ pi'anɔ]
roof	tetto (m)	['tɛttɔ]
chimney (stack)	ciminiera (f)	[ʧimi'njera]
roof tiles	tegola (f)	['tɛgɔʎa]
tiled (adj)	di tegole	[di 'tɛgɔle]
loft (attic)	soffitta (f)	[sof'fitta]
window	finestra (f)	[fi'nɛstra]
glass	vetro (m)	['vɛtrɔ]
window ledge	davanzale (m)	[davan'ʦale]
shutters	imposte (f pl)	[im'postɛ]
wall	muro (m)	['murɔ]
balcony	balcone (m)	[baʎ'konɛ]
downpipe	tubo (m) pluviale	['tubɔ ply'vʲale]
upstairs (to be ~)	su, di sopra	[su], [di 'sopra]
to go upstairs	andare di sopra	[an'darɛ di 'sopra]
to come down	scendere (vi)	['ʃɛndɛrɛ]
to move (to new premises)	trasferirsi (vr)	[trasfɛ'rirsi]

87. House. Entrance. Lift

entrance	entrata (f)	[ɛntˈrata]
stairs (stairway)	scala (f)	[ˈskaʎa]
steps	gradini (m pl)	[graˈdini]
banisters	ringhiera (f)	[riŋʰˈera]
lobby (hotel ~)	hall (f)	[ɔʎ]

postbox	cassetta (f) della posta	[kasˈsɛtta ˈdɛʎa ˈposta]
rubbish container	secchio (m) della spazzatura	[ˈsɛkkiɔ ˈdɛʎa spatsaˈtura]
refuse chute	scivolo (m) per la spazzatura	[ˈʃivɔlɔ per ʎa spatsaˈtura]

lift	ascensore (m)	[aʃɛnˈsɔrɛ]
goods lift	montacarichi (m)	[mɔntaˈkariki]
lift cage	cabina (f) di ascensore	[kaˈbina dɛ aʃɛnˈsɔrɛ]
to take the lift	prendere l'ascensore	[ˈprɛndɛrɛ ʎaʃɛnˈsɔrɛ]

flat	appartamento (m)	[appartaˈmɛntɔ]
residents, inhabitants	inquilini (m pl)	[iŋkuiˈlini]
neighbours	vicini (m pl)	[wiˈtʃini]

88. House. Electricity

electricity	elettricità (f)	[ɛlettritʃiˈta]
light bulb	lampadina (f)	[ʎampaˈdina]
switch	interruttore (m)	[interrutˈtorɛ]
fuse	fusibile (m)	[fuˈzibile]

cable, wire (electric ~)	filo (m)	[ˈfilɔ]
wiring	impianto (m) elettrico	[impiˈjantɔ ɛˈlettrikɔ]
electricity meter	contatore (m) dell'elettricità	[kɔntaˈtɔrɛ ˈdɛllɛlettritʃiˈta]
readings	lettura, indicazione (f)	[letˈtura], [indikaˈtsʲɔnɛ]

89. House. Doors. Locks

door	porta (f)	[ˈporta]
vehicle gate	cancello (m)	[kanˈtʃɛllɔ]
handle, doorknob	maniglia (f)	[maˈniʎja]
to unlock (unbolt)	togliere il catenaccio	[ˈtoʎjerɛ iʎ katɛˈnatʃɔ]
to open (vt)	aprire (vt)	[apˈrirɛ]
to close (vt)	chiudere (vt)	[ˈkjydɛrɛ]

key	chiave (f)	[ˈkjavɛ]
bunch (of keys)	mazzo (m)	[ˈmatsɔ]
to creak (door hinge)	cigolare (vi)	[tʃigɔˈʎarɛ]
creak	cigolio (m)	[tʃigɔˈliɔ]
hinge (of door)	cardine (m)	[ˈkardinɛ]
doormat	zerbino (m)	[dzɛrˈbinɔ]

door lock	serratura (f)	[sɛrraˈtura]
keyhole	buco (m) della serratura	[ˈbukɔ ˈdɛʎa sɛrraˈtura]

bolt (sliding bar)	chiavistello (m)	[kjawis'tɛllɔ]
door latch	catenaccio (m)	[katɛ'natʃɔ]
padlock	lucchetto (m)	[lyk'kɛttɔ]

to ring (~ the door bell)	suonare (vt)	[suɔ'narɛ]
ringing (sound)	suono (m)	[su'ɔnɔ]
doorbell	campanello (m)	[kampa'nɛllɔ]
button	pulsante (m)	[puʎ'santɛ]
knock (at the door)	bussata (f)	[bus'sata]
to knock (vi)	bussare (vi)	[bus'sarɛ]

code	codice (m)	['kɔditʃe]
code lock	serratura (f) a codice	[sɛrra'tura a 'kɔditʃe]
door phone	citofono (m)	[tʃi'tɔfɔnɔ]
number (on the door)	numero (m)	['numɛrɔ]
doorplate	targhetta (f)	[tar'getta]
peephole	spioncino (m)	[spi̯on'tʃinɔ]

90. Country house

village	villaggio (m)	[wi'ʎadʒɔ]
vegetable garden	orto (m)	['ɔrtɔ]
fence	recinto (m)	[rɛ'tʃintɔ]
paling	steccato (m)	[stɛk'katɔ]
wicket gate	cancelletto (m)	[kantʃel'lɛttɔ]

granary	granaio (m)	[gra'najo]
cellar	cantina (f), scantinato (m)	[kan'tina], [skanti'natɔ]
shed (in garden)	capanno (m)	[ka'paɲɔ]
well (water)	pozzo (m)	['pɔtsɔ]

stove (wood-fired ~)	stufa (f)	['stufa]
to heat the stove	attizzare (vt)	[atti'dzarɛ]
firewood	legna (f) da ardere	['leɲa da 'ardɛrɛ]
log (firewood)	ciocco (m)	['tʃɔkkɔ]

veranda	veranda (f)	[vɛ'randa]
terrace (patio)	terrazza (f)	[tɛr'ratsa]
front steps	scala (f) d'ingresso	['skaʎa diŋ'rɛssɔ]
swing (hanging seat)	altalena (f)	[aʎta'lena]

91. Villa. Mansion

country house	casa (f) di campagna	['kaza di kam'paɲja]
villa (by sea)	villa (f)	['wiʎa]
wing (of building)	ala (f)	['aʎa]

garden	giardino (m)	[dʒar'dinɔ]
park	parco (m)	['parkɔ]
tropical glasshouse	serra (f)	['sɛrra]
to look after (garden, etc.)	prendersi cura di	['prɛndɛrsi 'kura di]
swimming pool	piscina (f)	[pi'ʃina]

gym	**palestra** (f)	[pa'lestra]
tennis court	**campo** (m) **da tennis**	['kampo da 'tɛnis]
home cinema room	**stanza** (f) **dell'home cinema**	['stantza dɛ'ʎɔm 'sinɛma]
garage	**garage** (m)	[ga'raʒ]
private property	**proprietà** (f) **privata**	[proprie'ta pri'vata]
private land	**terreno** (m) **privato**	[tɛr'rɛno pri'vato]
warning (caution)	**avvertimento** (m)	[avwerti'mɛnto]
warning sign	**cartello** (m) **di avvertimento**	['kartɛllo di avɛrti'mɛnto]
security	**sicurezza** (f)	[siku'rɛtsa]
security guard	**guardia** (f) **giurata**	[gu'ardia dʒu'rata]
burglar alarm	**allarme** (f) **antifurto**	[a'ʎarmɛ anti'furto]

92. Castle. Palace

castle	**castello** (m)	[kas'tɛllo]
palace	**palazzo** (m)	[pa'ʎatso]
fortress	**fortezza** (f)	[for'tɛtsa]
wall (round castle)	**muro** (m)	['muro]
tower	**torre** (f)	['torrɛ]
main tower, donjon	**torre** (f) **principale**	['torrɛ printʃi'pale]
portcullis	**saracinesca** (f)	[saratʃi'nɛska]
subterranean passage	**tunnel** (m)	['tuŋɛl]
moat	**fossato** (m)	[fos'sato]
chain	**catena** (f)	[ka'tɛna]
arrow loop	**feritoia** (f)	[fɛri'toja]
magnificent (adj)	**magnifico**	[ma'ŋifiko]
majestic (adj)	**maestoso**	[maɛs'tozo]
impregnable (adj)	**inespugnabile**	[inɛspu'ŋjabile]
knightly (adj)	**cavalleresco**	[kavalle'rɛsko]
medieval (adj)	**medievale**	[mɛdiɛ'vale]

93. Flat

flat	**appartamento** (m)	[apparta'mɛnto]
room	**camera** (f), **stanza** (f)	['kamɛra], ['stantsa]
bedroom	**camera** (f) **da letto**	['kamɛra da 'letto]
dining room	**sala** (f) **da pranzo**	['saʎa da 'prantso]
living room	**salotto** (m)	[sa'lɔtto]
study	**studio** (m)	['studio]
entry room	**ingresso** (m)	[iŋ'rɛsso]
bathroom	**bagno** (m)	['baɲo]
water closet	**gabinetto** (m)	[gabi'nɛtto]
ceiling	**soffitto** (m)	[sof'fitto]
floor	**pavimento** (m)	[pawi'mɛnto]
corner	**angolo** (m)	['aŋolo]

94. Flat. Cleaning

to clean (vi, vt)	pulire (vt)	[pu'lirɛ]
to put away (to stow)	mettere via	['mɛttɛrɛ 'wia]
dust	polvere (f)	['pɔʎvɛrɛ]
dusty (adj)	impolverato	[impɔʎvɛ'ratɔ]
to dust (vt)	spolverare (vt)	[spɔʎvɛ'rarɛ]
vacuum cleaner	aspirapolvere (m)	[aspira'pɔʎvɛrɛ]
to vacuum (vt)	passare l'aspirapolvere	[pas'sarɛ ʎaspira'pɔʎvɛrɛ]

to sweep (vi, vt)	spazzare (vi, vt)	[spa'ʦarɛ]
sweepings	spazzatura (f)	[spaʦa'tura]
order	ordine (m)	['ɔrdinɛ]
disorder, mess	disordine (m)	[di'sɔrdinɛ]

mop	frettazzo (m)	[frɛt'taʦɔ]
duster	strofinaccio (m)	[strofi'natʃo]
broom	scopa (f)	['skɔpa]
dustpan	paletta (f)	[pa'letta]

95. Furniture. Interior

furniture	mobili (m pl)	['mɔbili]
table	tavolo (m)	['tavɔlɔ]
chair	sedia (f)	['sɛdia]
bed	letto (m)	['lettɔ]
sofa, settee	divano (m)	[di'vanɔ]
armchair	poltrona (f)	[pɔʎt'rona]

bookcase	libreria (f)	[librɛ'ria]
shelf	ripiano (m)	[ri'pjanɔ]
set of shelves	scaffale (m)	[ska'falе]

wardrobe	armadio (m)	[ar'madiɔ]
coat rack	attaccapanni (m) da parete	[attakka'paɲi da pa'rɛtɛ]
coat stand	appendiabiti (m) da terra	[apendi'abiti da tɛrra]

chest of drawers	comò (m)	[kɔ'mɔ]
coffee table	tavolino (m) da salotto	[tavɔ'lina da sa'lottɔ]

mirror	specchio (m)	['spɛkkiɔ]
carpet	tappeto (m)	[tap'pɛtɔ]
small carpet	tappetino (m)	[tap'pɛtinɔ]

fireplace	camino (m)	[ka'minɔ]
candle	candela (f)	[kan'dɛʎa]
candlestick	candeliere (m)	[kandɛ'ʎjerɛ]

drapes	tende (f pl)	['tɛndɛ]
wallpaper	carta (f) da parati	['karta da pa'rati]
blinds (jalousie)	tende (f pl) alla veneziana	['tɛndɛ aʎa vɛnɛʦi'ana]
table lamp	lampada (f) da tavolo	['ʎampada da 'tavɔlɔ]
wall lamp	lampada (f) da parete	['ʎampada da pa'rɛtɛ]

standard lamp	lampada (f) a stelo	['ʎampada a 'stɛlɔ]
chandelier	lampadario (m)	[ʎampa'dariɔ]

leg (of chair, table)	gamba (f)	['gamba]
armrest	bracciolo (m)	['bratʃolɔ]
back	spalliera (f)	[spa'ʎjera]
drawer	cassetto (m)	[kas'sɛttɔ]

96. Bedding

bedclothes	biancheria (f) da letto	[bʲaŋke'ria da 'lɛttɔ]
pillow	cuscino (m)	[ku'ʃinɔ]
pillowslip	federa (f)	['fɛdɛra]
blanket (eiderdown)	coperta (f)	[kɔ'pɛrta]
sheet	lenzuolo (m)	[lentsu'ɔlɔ]
bedspread	copriletto (m)	[kɔpri'lettɔ]

97. Kitchen

kitchen	cucina (f)	[ku'tʃina]
gas	gas (m)	[gas]
gas cooker	fornello (m) a gas	[fɔr'nɛllɔ a gas]
electric cooker	fornello (m) elettrico	[fɔr'nɛllɔ ɛ'lettrikɔ]
oven	forno (m)	['fɔrnɔ]
microwave oven	forno (m) a microonde	['fɔrnɔ a mikrɔ'ɔndɛ]

refrigerator	frigorifero (m)	[frigɔ'rifɛrɔ]
freezer	congelatore (m)	[kɔndʒeʎa'tɔrɛ]
dishwasher	lavastoviglie (f)	[ʎavastɔ'wiʎje]

mincer	tritacarne (m)	[trita'karnɛ]
juicer	spremifrutta (m)	[sprɛmif'rutta]
toaster	tostapane (m)	[tɔsta'panɛ]
mixer	mixer (m)	['miksɛr]

coffee maker	macchina (f) da caffè	['makkina da kaf'fɛ]
coffee pot	caffettiera (f)	[kaffɛt'tʲera]
coffee grinder	macinacaffè (m)	[matʃinakaf'fɛ]

kettle	bollitore (m)	[bɔlli'tɔrɛ]
teapot	teiera (f)	[tɛ'jera]
lid	coperchio (m)	[kɔ'pɛrkiɔ]
tea strainer	colino (m) da tè	[kɔ'linɔ da tɛ]

spoon	cucchiaio (m)	[kuk'kjajo]
teaspoon	cucchiaino (m) da tè	[kukkia'inɔ da 'tɛ]
tablespoon	cucchiaio (m)	[kuk'kjajo]
fork	forchetta (f)	[fɔr'kɛtta]
knife	coltello (m)	[kɔʎ'tɛllɔ]

tableware (dishes)	stoviglie (f pl)	[stɔ'wiʎje]
plate (dinner ~)	piatto (m)	['pjattɔ]

saucer	piattino (m)	[pjat'tino]
shot glass	bicchiere (m) da vino	[bik'kjɛrɛ da 'wino]
glass (~ of water)	bicchiere (m)	[bik'kjɛrɛ]
cup	tazzina (f)	[ta'tsina]

sugar bowl	zuccheriera (f)	[dzukkɛ'rjera]
salt shaker	saliera (f)	[sa'ʎjera]
pepper shaker	pepiera (f)	[pɛpi'ɛra]
butter dish	burriera (f)	[bur'rjera]

stew pot	pentola (f)	['pɛntoʎa]
frying pan	padella (f)	[pa'dɛʎa]
ladle	mestolo (m)	['mɛstolo]
colander	colapasta (m)	[koʎa'pasta]
tray	vassoio (m)	[vas'sojo]

bottle	bottiglia (f)	[bot'tiʎja]
jar (glass)	barattolo (m) di vetro	[ba'rattolo di 'vɛtro]
tin, can	latta (f), lattina (f)	['ʎatta], [lat'tina]

bottle opener	apribottiglie (m)	[apribot'tiʎje]
tin opener	apriscatole (m)	[apris'katole]
corkscrew	cavatappi (m)	[kava'tappi]
filter	filtro (m)	['fiʎtro]
to filter (vt)	filtrare (vt)	[fiʎt'rarɛ]

| rubbish, refuse | spazzatura (f) | [spatsa'tura] |
| rubbish bin | pattumiera (f) | [pattu'mjera] |

98. Bathroom

bathroom	bagno (m)	['baɲʲo]
water	acqua (f)	['akua]
tap	rubinetto (m)	[rubi'nɛtto]
hot water	acqua (f) calda	['akua 'kaʎda]
cold water	acqua (f) fredda	['akua 'frɛdda]

| toothpaste | dentifricio (m) | [dɛntif'ritʃo] |
| to clean one's teeth | lavarsi i denti | [ʎa'varsi i 'dɛnti] |

to shave (vi)	rasarsi (vr)	[ra'zarsi]
shaving foam	schiuma (f) da barba	[ski'juma da 'barba]
razor	rasoio (m)	[ra'zojo]

to wash (clean)	lavare (vt)	[ʎa'varɛ]
to have a bath	fare un bagno	['farɛ un 'baɲʲo]
shower	doccia (f)	['dotʃa]
to have a shower	fare una doccia	['farɛ una 'dotʃa]

bath (tub)	vasca (f) da bagno	['vaska da 'baɲʲo]
toilet	water (m)	['vatɛr]
sink (washbasin)	lavandino (m)	[ʎavan'dino]
soap	sapone (m)	[sa'ponɛ]
soap dish	porta (m) sapone	['porta sa'ponɛ]

sponge	spugna (f)	['spuɲja]
shampoo	shampoo (m)	['ʃampɔ]
towel	asciugamano (m)	[aʃuga'manɔ]
bathrobe	accappatoio (m)	[akkappa'tojo]

laundry (process)	bucato (m)	[bu'katɔ]
washing machine	lavatrice (f)	[ʎavat'ritʃe]
to do the laundry	fare il bucato	['farɛ iʎ bu'katɔ]
washing powder	detersivo (m) per il bucato	[dɛtɛr'sivɔ pɛr iʎ bu'katɔ]

99. Household appliances

TV, telly	televisore (m)	[tɛlewi'zɔrɛ]
tape recorder	registratore (m) a nastro	[rɛdʒistra'tɔrɛ a 'nastrɔ]
video	videoregistratore (m)	[widɛɔrɛdʒistra'tɔrɛ]
radio	radio (f)	['radiɔ]
player (CD, MP3, etc.)	lettore (m)	[let'tɔrɛ]

video projector	videoproiettore (m)	[widɛɔprɔjet'tɔrɛ]
home cinema	home cinema (m)	['ɔum 'tʃinema]
DVD player	lettore (m) DVD	[let'tɔrɛ divu'di]
amplifier	amplificatore (m)	[amplifika'tɔrɛ]
video game console	console (f) video giochi	['kɔnsɔle 'widɛɔ 'dʒɔki]

video camera	videocamera (f)	[widɛɔ'kamɛra]
camera (photo)	macchina (f) fotografica	['makkina fotɔg'rafika]
digital camera	fotocamera (f) digitale	[fotɔ'kamɛra didʒi'tale]

vacuum cleaner	aspirapolvere (m)	[aspira'pɔʎvɛrɛ]
iron (e.g. steam ~)	ferro (m) da stiro	['fɛrrɔ da 'stirɔ]
ironing board	asse (f) da stiro	['assɛ da 'stirɔ]

telephone	telefono (m)	[tɛ'lefɔnɔ]
mobile phone	telefonino (m)	[tɛlefɔ'ninɔ]
typewriter	macchina (f) da scrivere	['makkina da 'skrivɛrɛ]
sewing machine	macchina (f) da cucire	['makkina da ku'tʃirɛ]

microphone	microfono (m)	[mik'rɔfɔnɔ]
headphones	cuffia (f)	['kuffia]
remote control (TV)	telecomando (m)	[tɛlekɔ'mandɔ]

CD, compact disc	CD (m)	[tʃi'di]
cassette	cassetta (f)	[kas'sɛtta]
vinyl record	disco (m)	['diskɔ]

100. Repairs. Renovation

renovations	lavori (m pl) di restauro	[la'vɔri di rɛs'taurɔ]
to renovate (vt)	rinnovare (vt)	[riɲɔ'varɛ]
to repair (vt)	riparare (vt)	[ripa'rarɛ]
to put in order	mettere in ordine	['mɛttɛrɛ in 'ɔrdinɛ]
to redo (do again)	rifare (vt)	[ri'farɛ]

paint	vernice (f), pittura (f)	[vɛrˈnitʃɛ], [pitˈtura]
to paint (~ a wall)	pitturare (vt)	[pittuˈrare]
house painter	imbianchino (m)	[imbjaˈŋkinɔ]
brush	pennello (m)	[pɛˈŋɛllɔ]

| whitewash | imbiancatura (f) | [imbjaŋkaˈtura] |
| to whitewash (vt) | imbiancare (vt) | [imbjaˈŋkarɛ] |

wallpaper	carta (f) da parati	[ˈkarta da paˈrati]
to wallpaper (vt)	tappezzare (vt)	[tappɛˈtsarɛ]
varnish	vernice (f)	[vɛrˈnitʃe]
to varnish (vt)	verniciare (vt)	[vɛrniˈtʃarɛ]

101. Plumbing

water	acqua (f)	[ˈakua]
hot water	acqua (f) calda	[ˈakua ˈkaʎda]
cold water	acqua (f) fredda	[ˈakua ˈfrɛdda]
tap	rubinetto (m)	[rubiˈnɛttɔ]

drop (of water)	goccia (f)	[ˈgɔtʃa]
to drip (vi)	gocciolare (vi)	[gɔtʃɔˈʎarɛ]
to leak (ab. pipe)	perdere (vi)	[ˈpɛrdɛrɛ]
leak (pipe ~)	perdita (f)	[ˈpɛrdita]
puddle	pozza (f)	[ˈpɔtsa]

pipe	tubo (m)	[ˈtubɔ]
valve	valvola (f)	[ˈvaʎvɔʎa]
to be clogged up	intasarsi (vr)	[intaˈzarsi]

tools	strumenti (m pl)	[struˈmɛnti]
adjustable spanner	chiave (f) inglese	[kiˈjavɛ iŋˈlezɛ]
to unscrew, untwist (vt)	svitare (vt)	[zwiˈtarɛ]
to screw (tighten)	avvitare (vt)	[avwiˈtarɛ]

to unclog (vt)	stasare (vt)	[staˈzarɛ]
plumber	idraulico (m)	[idˈraulikɔ]
basement	seminterrato (m)	[sɛminterˈratɔ]
sewerage (system)	fognatura (f)	[foɲaˈtura]

102. Fire. Conflagration

fire (to catch ~)	fuoco (m)	[fuˈɔkɔ]
flame	fiamma (f)	[ˈfjamma]
spark	scintilla (f)	[ʃinˈtiʎa]
smoke (from fire)	fumo (m)	[ˈfumɔ]
torch (flaming stick)	fiaccola (f)	[ˈfjakkɔʎa]
campfire	falò (m)	[faˈlɔ]

petrol	benzina (f)	[benˈdzina]
paraffin	cherosene (m)	[kɛrɔˈzɛnɛ]
flammable (adj)	combustibile	[kɔmbusˈtibile]

| explosive (adj) | esplosivo | [ɛsploˈzivɔ] |
| NO SMOKING | VIETATO FUMARE! | [vjeˈtatɔ fuˈmarɛ] |

safety	sicurezza (f)	[sikuˈrɛtsa]
danger	pericolo (m)	[pɛˈrikɔlɔ]
dangerous (adj)	pericoloso	[pɛrikoˈlɜzɔ]

to catch fire	prendere fuoco	[ˈprɛndɛrɛ fuˈɔkɔ]
explosion	esplosione (f)	[ɛsplozi'ɔnɛ]
to set fire	incendiare (vt)	[intʃenˈdʲarɛ]
incendiary (arsonist)	incendiario (m)	[intʃendi'ariɔ]
arson	incendio (m) doloso	[inˈtʃendiɔ dɔˈlɜzɔ]

to blaze (vi)	divampare (vi)	[divamˈparɛ]
to burn (be on fire)	bruciare (vi)	[bruˈtʃarɛ]
to burn down	bruciarsi (vr)	[bruˈtʃarsi]

to call the fire brigade	chiamare i pompieri	[kjaˈmarɛ i pɔmˈpjeri]
firefighter	pompiere (m)	[pɔmˈpjerɛ]
fire engine	autopompa (f)	[autoˈpompa]
fire brigade	corpo (m) dei pompieri	[ˈkɔrpɔ dɛi pɔmˈpjeri]
fire engine ladder	autoscala (f) da pompieri	[autosˈkala da pɔmˈpjeri]

fire hose	manichetta (f)	[maniˈkɛtta]
fire extinguisher	estintore (m)	[ɛstinˈtɔrɛ]
helmet	casco (m)	[ˈkaskɔ]
siren	sirena (f)	[siˈrɛna]

to call out	gridare (vi)	[griˈdarɛ]
to call for help	chiamare in aiuto	[kjaˈmarɛ in aˈjutɔ]
rescuer	soccorritore (m)	[sɔkkorriˈtɔrɛ]
to rescue (vt)	salvare (vt)	[saʎˈvarɛ]

to arrive (vi)	arrivare (vi)	[arriˈvarɛ]
to extinguish (vt)	spegnere (vt)	[ˈspɛɲerɛ]
water	acqua (f)	[ˈakua]
sand	sabbia (f)	[ˈsabbja]

ruins (destruction)	rovine (f pl)	[rɔˈwinɛ]
to collapse (building, etc.)	crollare (vi)	[krɔˈʎarɛ]
to fall down (vi)	cadere (vi)	[kaˈdɛrɛ]
to cave in (ceiling, floor)	collassare (vi)	[kɔʎaˈsarɛ]

| fragment (piece of wall, etc.) | frammento (m) | [framˈmɛntɔ] |
| ash | cenere (f) | [ˈtʃenɛrɛ] |

| to suffocate (die) | asfissiare (vi) | [asfisˈsjarɛ] |
| to be killed (perish) | morire, perire (vi) | [mɔˈrirɛ], [pɛˈrirɛ] |

HUMAN ACTIVITIES

Job. Business. Part 1

103. Office. Working in the office

office (of firm)	ufficio (m)	[uf'fitʃo]
office (of director, etc.)	ufficio (m)	[uf'fitʃo]
reception	portineria (f)	[portinɛ'ria]
secretary	segretario (m)	[sɛgrɛ'tarjo]
director	direttore (m)	[dirɛt'tɔrɛ]
manager	manager (m)	['mɛnɛdʒer]
accountant	contabile (m)	[kɔn'tabile]
employee	impiegato (m)	[impje'gatɔ]
furniture	mobili (m pl)	['mɔbili]
desk	scrivania (f)	[skriva'nia]
desk chair	poltrona (f)	[pɔʌt'rɔna]
chest of drawers	cassettiera (f)	[kassɛt't'era]
coat stand	appendiabiti (m) da terra	[apendi'abiti da tɛrra]
computer	computer (m)	[kɔm'pjytɛr]
printer	stampante (f)	[stam'pantɛ]
fax machine	fax (m)	[faks]
photocopier	fotocopiatrice (f)	[fotɔkɔpjat'ritʃe]
paper	carta (f)	['karta]
office supplies	cancelleria (f)	[kantʃelle'rija]
mouse mat	tappetino (m) del mouse	[tap'pɛtinɔ dɛʌ 'maus]
sheet of paper	foglio (m)	['foʌ'ɔ]
folder, binder	cartella (f)	[kar'tɛʌa]
catalogue	catalogo (m)	[ka'talɔgɔ]
directory (of addresses)	elenco (m) del telefono	[ɛ'leŋkɔ dɛʌ tɛ'lefɔnɔ]
documentation	documentazione (f)	[dokumɛnta'tsʲɔnɛ]
brochure	opuscolo (m)	[ɔ'puskɔlɔ]
leaflet	volantino (m)	[vɔʌan'tinɔ]
sample	campione (m)	[kampi'ɔnɛ]
training meeting	formazione (f)	[fɔrma'tsʲɔnɛ]
meeting (of managers)	riunione (f)	[riu'ɲʲɔnɛ]
lunch time	pausa (f) pranzo	['pauza 'prantsɔ]
to make a copy	copiare (vt)	[kɔ'pjarɛ]
to make copies	fare copie	['farɛ 'kɔpje]
to receive a fax	ricevere un fax	[ri'tʃevɛrɛ un faks]
to send a fax	spedire un fax	[spɛ'dirɛ un faks]
to ring (telephone)	telefonare (vi, vt)	[tɛlefɔ'narɛ]

| to answer (vt) | rispondere (vi, vt) | [ris'pondɛrɛ] |
| to put through | passare (vt) | [pas'sarɛ] |

to arrange, to set up	fissare (vt)	[fis'sarɛ]
to demonstrate (vt)	dimostrare (vt)	[dimɔst'rarɛ]
to be absent	essere assente	['ɛssɛrɛ as'sɛntɛ]
absence	assenza (f)	[as'sɛntsa]

104. Business processes. Part 1

occupation	occupazione (f)	[ɔkkupa'tsɔnɛ]
firm	ditta (f)	['ditta]
company	compagnia (f)	[kɔmpa'nia]
corporation	corporazione (f)	[kɔrpɔra'tsɔnɛ]
enterprise	impresa (f)	[imp'rɛza]
agency	agenzia (f)	[adʒen'tsia]

agreement (contract)	accordo (m)	[ak'kɔrdɔ]
contract	contratto (m)	[kɔnt'rattɔ]
deal	affare (m)	[af'farɛ]
order (to place an ~)	ordine (m)	['ɔrdinɛ]
term (of contract)	termine (m) dell'accordo	['tɛrminɛ dɛʎ ak'kɔrdɔ]

wholesale (adv)	all'ingrosso	[alliŋ'rɔssɔ]
wholesale (adj)	all'ingrosso	[alliŋ'rɔssɔ]
wholesale (n)	vendita (f) all'ingrosso	['vɛndita alliŋ'rɔssɔ]
retail (adj)	al dettaglio	[aʎ dɛt'taʎɔ]
retail (n)	vendita (f) al dettaglio	['vɛndita aʎ dɛt'taʎɔ]

competitor	concorrente (m)	[kɔŋkɔr'rɛntɛ]
competition	concorrenza (f)	[kɔŋkɔr'rɛntsa]
to compete (vi)	competere (vi)	[kɔm'pɛtɛrɛ]

| partner (associate) | socio (m), partner (m) | ['sɔtʃɔ], ['partnɛr] |
| partnership | partenariato (m) | [partɛnari'atɔ] |

crisis	crisi (f)	['krizi]
bankruptcy	bancarotta (f)	[baŋka'rɔtta]
to go bankrupt	fallire (vi)	[fal'lirɛ]
difficulty	difficoltà (f)	[diffikɔʎ'ta]
problem	problema (m)	[prɔb'lema]
catastrophe	disastro (m)	[di'zastrɔ]

economy	economia (f)	[ɛkɔnɔ'mia]
economic (~ growth)	economico	[ɛkɔ'nɔmikɔ]
economic recession	recessione (f) economica	[rɛtʃessi'ɔnɛ ɛkɔ'nɔmika]

| goal (aim) | scopo (m), obiettivo (m) | ['skɔpɔ], [ɔbjet'tivɔ] |
| task | incarico (m) | [i'ŋkarikɔ] |

to trade (vi)	commerciare (vi)	[kɔmmɛr'tʃarɛ]
network (distribution ~)	rete (f)	['rɛtɛ]
inventory (stock)	giacenza (f)	[dʒia'tʃɛntsa]
assortment	assortimento (m)	[assɔrti'mɛntɔ]

leader	leader (m), capo (m)	['lidɛr], ['kapɔ]
large (~ company)	grande	['grandɛ]
monopoly	monopolio (m)	[mɔnɔ'pɔliɔ]

theory	teoria (f)	[tɛɔ'ria]
practice	pratica (f)	['pratika]
experience (in my ~)	esperienza (f)	[ɛspɛri'ɛntsa]
trend (tendency)	tendenza (f)	[tɛn'dɛntsa]
development	sviluppo (m)	[zwi'lyppɔ]

105. Business processes. Part 2

| profitability | profitto (m) | [prɔ'fittɔ] |
| profitable (adj) | profittevole | [prɔfit'tɛvɔle] |

delegation (group)	delegazione (f)	[dɛlega'tsʲɔnɛ]
salary	stipendio (m)	[sti'pɛndiɔ]
to correct (an error)	correggere (vt)	[kɔr'rɛdʒɛrɛ]
business trip	viaggio (m) d'affari	['vjadʒɔ daf'fari]
commission	commissione (f)	[kɔmmisi'ɔnɛ]

to control (vt)	controllare (vt)	[kɔntrɔ'ʎarɛ]
conference	conferenza (f)	[kɔnfɛ'rɛntsa]
licence	licenza (f)	[li'tʃentsa]
reliable (~ partner)	affidabile	[affi'dabile]

initiative (undertaking)	iniziativa (f)	[initsia'tiva]
norm (standard)	norma (f)	['nɔrma]
circumstance	circostanza (f)	[tʃirkɔs'tantsa]
duty (of employee)	mansione (f)	[mansi'ɔnɛ]

enterprise	impresa (f)	[imp'rɛza]
organization (process)	organizzazione (f)	[ɔrganidza'tsʲɔnɛ]
organized (adj)	organizzato	[ɔrgani'dzatɔ]
cancellation	annullamento (m)	[aɲuʎa'mɛntɔ]
to cancel (call off)	annullare (vt)	[aɲu'ʎarɛ]
report (official ~)	rapporto (m)	[rap'pɔrtɔ]

patent	brevetto (m)	[brɛ'vɛttɔ]
to patent (obtain patent)	brevettare (vt)	[brɛvɛt'tarɛ]
to plan (vt)	pianificare (vt)	[pjanifi'karɛ]

bonus (money)	premio (m)	['prɛmiɔ]
professional (adj)	professionale	[prɔfessiɔ'nale]
procedure	procedura (f)	[prɔtʃe'dura]

to examine (contract, etc.)	esaminare (vt)	[ɛzami'narɛ]
calculation	calcolo (m)	['kaʎkɔlɔ]
reputation	reputazione (f)	[rɛputa'tsʲɔnɛ]
risk	rischio (m)	['riskiɔ]

to manage, to run	dirigere (vt)	[di'ridʒɛrɛ]
information	informazioni (f pl)	[infɔrma'tsʲɔni]
property	proprietà (f)	[prɔprie'ta]

union	unione (f)	[uni'ɔnɛ]
life insurance	assicurazione (f) sulla vita	[assikura'tsjɔnɛ 'suʎa 'wita]
to insure (vt)	assicurare (vt)	[assiku'rarɛ]
insurance	assicurazione (f)	[assikura'tsjɔnɛ]

auction	asta (f)	['asta]
to notify (inform)	avvisare (vt)	[avvi'zarɛ]
management (process)	gestione (f)	[dʒes'tjɔnɛ]
service (~ industry)	servizio (m)	[sɛr'witsjɔ]

forum	forum (m)	['fɔrum]
to function (vi)	funzionare (vi)	[funtsjɔ'narɛ]
stage (phase)	stadio (m)	['stadjɔ]
legal (~ services)	giuridico	[dʒu'ridikɔ]
lawyer (legal expert)	esperto (m) legale	[ɛs'pertɔ le'galɛ]

106. Production. Works

plant	stabilimento (m)	[stabili'mɛntɔ]
factory	fabbrica (f)	['fabbrika]
workshop	officina (f) di produzione	[ɔfi'tʃina di prɔdu'tsjɔnɛ]
production site	stabilimento (m)	[stabili'mɛntɔ]

industry	industria (f)	[in'dustria]
industrial (adj)	industriale	[industri'ale]
heavy industry	industria (f) pesante	[in'dustria pɛ'zantɛ]
light industry	industria (f) leggera	[in'dustria le'dʒera]

products	prodotti (m pl)	[prɔ'dɔtti]
to produce (vt)	produrre (vt)	[prɔ'durrɛ]
raw materials	materia (f) prima	[ma'tɛria 'prima]

foreman	caposquadra (m)	[kapɔsku'adra]
workers team	squadra (f)	[sku'adra]
worker	operaio (m)	[ɔpɛ'rajo]

working day	giorno (m) lavorativo	['dʒɔrnɔ ʎavora'tivɔ]
pause	pausa (f)	['pauza]
meeting	riunione (f)	[riu'njɔnɛ]
to discuss (vt)	discutere (vt)	[dis'kutɛrɛ]

plan	piano (m)	['pjanɔ]
to fulfil the plan	eseguire il piano	[ɛzɛgu'irɛ iʎ 'pjanɔ]
rate of output	tasso (m) di produzione	['tassɔ di prɔdu'tsjɔnɛ]
quality	qualità (f)	[kuali'ta]
checking (control)	controllo (m)	[kɔnt'rɔllɔ]
quality control	controllo (m) di qualità	[kɔnt'rɔllɔ di kuali'ta]

safety of work	sicurezza (f) sul lavoro	[siku'rɛtsa suʎ ʎa'vɔrɔ]
discipline	disciplina (f)	[diʃip'lina]
infraction	infrazione (f)	[infra'tsjɔnɛ]
to violate (rules)	violare (vt)	[wiɔ'ʎarɛ]
strike	sciopero (m)	['ʃɔperɔ]
striker	scioperante (m)	[ʃɔpɛ'rantɛ]

| to be on strike | fare sciopero | ['farɛ 'ʃopɛrɔ] |
| trade union | sindacato (m) | [sinda'katɔ] |

to invent (machine, etc.)	inventare (vt)	[invɛn'tarɛ]
invention	invenzione (f)	[invɛn'tsʲɔnɛ]
research	ricerca (f)	[ri'tʃerka]
to improve (make better)	migliorare (vt)	[miʎʲɔ'rarɛ]
technology	tecnologia (f)	[tɛknɔlɔ'dʒia]
technical drawing	disegno (m) tecnico	[di'zɛɲʲɔ 'tɛknikɔ]

load, cargo	carico (m)	['karikɔ]
loader (person)	caricatore (m)	[karika'tɔrɛ]
to load (vehicle, etc.)	caricare (vt)	[kari'karɛ]
loading (process)	caricamento (m)	[karika'mɛntɔ]
to unload (vi, vt)	scaricare (vt)	[skari'karɛ]
unloading	scarico (m)	['skarikɔ]

transport	trasporto (m)	[tras'pɔrtɔ]
transport company	società (f) di trasporti	[sɔtʃe'ta di tras'pɔrti]
to transport (vt)	trasportare (vt)	[traspɔr'tarɛ]

wagon	vagone (m) merci	[va'gɔnɛ 'mɛrtʃi]
cistern	cisterna (f)	[tʃis'tɛrna]
lorry	camion (m)	['kamʲɔn]

| machine tool | macchina (f) utensile | ['makkina u'tɛnsile] |
| mechanism | meccanismo (m) | [mɛkka'nizmɔ] |

industrial waste	rifiuti (m pl) industriali	[ri'fjyti industri'ali]
packing (process)	imballaggio (m)	[imba'ʎadʒɔ]
to pack (vt)	imballare (vt)	[imba'ʎarɛ]

107. Contract. Agreement

contract	contratto (m)	[kɔnt'rattɔ]
agreement	accordo (m)	[ak'kɔrdɔ]
addendum	allegato (m)	[alle'gatɔ]

to sign a contract	firmare un contratto	[fir'marɛ un kɔnt'rattɔ]
signature	firma (f)	['firma]
to sign (vt)	firmare (vt)	[fir'marɛ]
stamp (seal)	timbro (m)	['timbrɔ]

subject of contract	oggetto (m) del contratto	[ɔ'dʒettɔ dɛʎ kɔnt'rattɔ]
clause	clausola (f)	['klauzɔʎa]
parties (in contract)	parti (f pl)	['parti]
legal address	sede (f) legale	['sɛdɛ le'gale]

to break the contract	sciogliere un contratto	['ʃoliɛrɛ un kɔnt'rattɔ]
commitment	obbligo (m)	['ɔbbligɔ]
responsibility	responsabilità (f)	[rɛspɔnsabili'ta]
force majeure	forza (f) maggiore	['fɔrtsa ma'dʒɔrɛ]
dispute	discussione (f)	[diskus'sʲɔnɛ]
penalties	sanzioni (f pl)	[santsi'ɔni]

108. Import & Export

import	importazione (f)	[importa'tsjone]
importer	importatore (m)	[importa'tore]
to import (vt)	importare (vt)	[impor'tare]
import (e.g. ~ goods)	d'importazione	[dimporta'tsjone]
exporter	esportatore (m)	[εsporta'tore]
to export (vi, vt)	esportare (vt)	[εspor'tare]
goods	merce (f)	['mεrtʃe]
consignment, lot	carico (m)	['kariko]
weight	peso (m)	['pεzo]
volume	volume (m)	[vo'lymε]
cubic metre	metro (m) cubo	['mεtro 'kubo]
manufacturer	produttore (m)	[produt'tore]
transport company	società (f) di trasporti	[sotʃe'ta di tras'porti]
container	container (m)	[kon'tεjnεr]
border	frontiera (f)	[fron'tjera]
customs	dogana (f)	[do'gana]
customs duty	dazio (m) doganale	['datsio doga'nalε]
customs officer	doganiere (m)	[doga'njerε]
smuggling	contrabbando (m)	[kontrab'bando]
contraband (goods)	merci (f pl) contrabbandate	['mεrtʃi kontraban'datε]

109. Finances

share, stock	azione (f)	[a'tsjone]
bond (certificate)	obbligazione (f)	[obbliga'tsjone]
bill of exchange	cambiale (f)	[kam'bjale]
stock exchange	borsa (f)	['borsa]
stock price	quotazione (f)	[kuota'tsjone]
to become cheaper	diminuire di prezzo	[diminu'irε di 'prεtso]
to rise in price	aumentare di prezzo	[aumen'tarε di 'prεtso]
share	quota (f)	[ku'ota]
controlling interest	pacchetto (m) di maggioranza	[pak'kεtto di madʒo'rantsa]
investment	investimento (m)	[invεsti'mεnto]
to invest (vt)	investire (vt)	[invεs'tirε]
percent	percento (m)	[pεr'tʃεnto]
interest (on investment)	interessi (m pl)	[intε'rεssi]
profit	profitto (m)	[pro'fitto]
profitable (adj)	redditizio	[rεdi'titsio]
tax	imposta (f)	[im'posta]
currency (foreign ~)	valuta (f)	[va'lyta]

| national (adj) | nazionale | [natsio'nale] |
| exchange (currency ~) | cambio (m) | ['kambio] |

| accountant | contabile (m) | [kon'tabile] |
| accounting | ufficio (m) contabilità | [uf'fitʃo kontabili'ta] |

bankruptcy	bancarotta (f)	[baŋka'rotta]
collapse, ruin	fallimento (m)	[falli'mento]
ruin	rovina (f)	[ro'wina]
to be ruined	andare in rovina	[an'darɛ in ro'wina]
inflation	inflazione (f)	[infʎa'tsione]
devaluation	svalutazione (f)	[zvalyta'tsione]

capital	capitale (m)	[kapi'tale]
income	reddito (m)	['rɛddito]
turnover	giro (m) di affari	['dʒiro di af'fari]
resources	risorse (f pl)	[ri'sorsɛ]
monetary resources	mezzi (m pl) finanziari	['mɛdzi finantsi'ari]
overheads	spese (f pl) generali	['spezɛ dʒenɛ'rali]
to reduce (expenses)	ridurre (vt)	[ri'durrɛ]

110. Marketing

marketing	marketing (m)	['markɛtiŋ]
market	mercato (m)	[mɛr'kato]
market segment	segmento (m) di mercato	[seg'mɛnto di mer'kato]
product	prodotto (m)	[pro'dotto]
goods	merce (f)	['mɛrtʃe]

brand	battaglia (f)	[bat'taʎja]
trademark	marchio (m) di fabbrica	['markio di 'fabrika]
logotype	logotipo (m)	[logo'tipo]
logo	logo (m)	[logo]

demand	domanda (f)	[do'manda]
supply	offerta (f)	[of'fɛrta]
need	bisogno (m)	[bi'zoɲo]
consumer	consumatore (m)	[konsuma'torɛ]

analysis	analisi (f)	[a'nalizi]
to analyse (vt)	analizzare (vt)	[anali'dzarɛ]
positioning	posizionamento (m)	[pozitsiona'mɛnto]
to position (vt)	posizionare (vt)	[pozitsio'narɛ]

price	prezzo (m)	['prɛtso]
pricing policy	politica (f) dei prezzi	[po'litika 'dɛi 'prɛtsi]
pricing	determinazione (f) dei prezzi	[dɛtɛrmina'tsione dɛʎ 'prɛtsi]

111. Advertising

| advertising | pubblicità (f) | [pubblitʃi'ta] |
| to advertise (vt) | pubblicizzare (vt) | [pubblitʃi'dzarɛ] |

budget	bilancio (m)	[bi'ʎantʃo]
ad, advertisement	annuncio (m)	[a'ɲuntʃo]
TV advertising	pubblicità (f) televisiva	[pubbliʧi'ta telewi'ziva]
radio advertising	pubblicità (f) radiofonica	[pubbliʧi'ta radio'fonika]
outdoor advertising	pubblicità (f) esterna	[pubbliʧi'ta ɛs'tɛrna]

mass medias	mass media (m pl)	[mass 'mɛdia]
periodical (n)	periodico (m)	[pɛri'ɔdikɔ]
image (public appearance)	immagine (f)	[im'madʒinɛ]

| slogan | slogan (m) | [zlɔgan] |
| motto (maxim) | motto (m) | ['mɔttɔ] |

campaign	campagna (f)	[kam'paɲja]
advertising campaign	campagna (f) pubblicitaria	[kam'paɲja pubbliʧi'taria]
target group	gruppo (m) di riferimento	['gruppɔ dɛ rifɛri'mɛntɔ]

business card	biglietto (m) da visita	[bi'ʎjettɔ da wi'zita]
leaflet	volantino (m)	[vɔʎan'tinɔ]
brochure	opuscolo (m)	[ɔ'puskɔlɔ]
pamphlet	depliant (m)	[dɛpli'an]
newsletter	bollettino (m)	[bollet'tinɔ]

shop sign	insegna (f)	[in'sɛɲja]
poster	cartellone (m)	[kartɛl'lɔnɛ]
hoarding	tabellone (m) pubblicitario	[tabɛl'lɔnɛ pubbliʧi'tariɔ]

112. Banking

| bank | banca (f) | ['baŋka] |
| branch (of bank, etc.) | filiale (f) | [fili'ale] |

| consultant | consulente (m) | [kɔnsu'lentɛ] |
| manager (director) | direttore (m) | [dirɛt'tɔrɛ] |

bank account	conto (m) bancario	['kɔntɔ ba'ŋkariɔ]
account number	numero (m) del conto	['numɛrɔ dɛʎ 'kɔntɔ]
current account	conto (m) corrente	['kɔntɔ kor'rentɛ]
deposit account	conto (m) di risparmio	['kɔntɔ di ris'parmiɔ]

to open an account	aprire un conto	[ap'rirɛ un 'kɔntɔ]
to close the account	chiudere il conto	['kjydɛrɛ iʎ 'kɔntɔ]
to deposit into the account	versare sul conto	[vɛr'sare suʎ 'kɔntɔ]
to withdraw (vt)	prelevare dal conto	[prɛle'varɛ daʎ 'kɔntɔ]

deposit	deposito (m)	[dɛ'pozitɔ]
to make a deposit	depositare (vt)	[dɛpozi'tarɛ]
wire transfer	trasferimento (m) telegrafico	[trasfɛri'mɛntɔ tɛleg'rafikɔ]
to wire (money)	rimettere i soldi	[ri'mɛttɛrɛ i 'sɔʎdi]

sum	somma (f)	['sɔmma]
How much?	Quanto?	[ku'antɔ]
signature	firma (f)	['firma]
to sign (vt)	firmare (vt)	[fir'marɛ]

credit card	carta (f) di credito	['karta di 'krɛdito]
code	codice (m)	['koditʃe]
credit card number	numero (m) della carta di credito	['numɛro 'dɛʎa 'karta di 'krɛdito]
cashpoint	bancomat (m)	['baŋkomat]

cheque	assegno (m)	[as'seɲo]
to write a cheque	emettere un assegno	[ɛ'mɛttɛrɛ un as'seɲo]
chequebook	libretto (m) di assegni	[lib'rɛtto di as'seɲʎi]

loan (bank ~)	prestito (m)	['prɛstito]
to apply for a loan	fare domanda per un prestito	['farɛ do'manda pɛr un 'prɛstito]
to get a loan	ottenere un prestito	[ottɛ'nɛrɛ un 'prɛstito]
to give a loan	concedere un prestito	[kon'tʃedɛrɛ un 'prɛstito]
guarantee	garanzia (f)	[garan'tsia]

113. Telephone. Phone conversation

telephone	telefono (m)	[tɛ'lefono]
mobile phone	telefonino (m)	[tɛlefo'nino]
answering machine	segreteria (f) telefonica	[sɛgrɛtɛ'ria tɛle'fonika]

| to ring (telephone) | telefonare (vi, vt) | [tɛlefo'narɛ] |
| call, ring | chiamata (f) | [kja'mata] |

to dial a number	comporre un numero	[kom'porrɛ un 'numɛro]
Hello!	Pronto!	['pronto]
to ask (vt)	chiedere, domandare	['kjedɛrɛ], [doman'darɛ]
to answer (vi, vt)	rispondere (vi, vt)	[ris'pondɛrɛ]

to hear (vt)	udire, sentire (vt)	[u'dirɛ], [sɛn'tirɛ]
well (adv)	bene	['bɛnɛ]
not well (adv)	male	['male]
noises (interference)	disturbi (m pl)	[dis'turbi]

receiver	cornetta (f)	[kor'nɛtta]
to pick up (~ the phone)	alzare la cornetta	[aʎ'tsarɛ ʎa kor'nɛtta]
to hang up (~ the phone)	riattaccare la cornetta	[riattak'karɛ ʎa kor'nɛtta]

engaged (adj)	occupato	[okku'pato]
to ring (ab. phone)	squillare (vi)	[skui'ʎarɛ]
telephone book	elenco (m) telefonico	[ɛ'leŋko tɛle'foniko]

local (adj)	locale	[lɔ'kale]
trunk (e.g. ~ call)	interurbano	[intɛrur'bano]
international (adj)	internazionale	[intɛrnatsʲo'nale]

114. Mobile telephone

| mobile phone | telefonino (m) | [tɛlefo'nino] |
| display | schermo (m) | ['skɛrmo] |

| button | tasto (m) | ['tastɔ] |
| SIM card | scheda SIM (f) | ['skɛda 'sim] |

battery	pila (f)	['piʎa]
to be flat (battery)	essere scarico	['ɛssɛrɛ 'skarikɔ]
charger	caricabatteria (m)	[karikabattɛ'ria]

menu	menù (m)	[me'nu]
settings	impostazioni (f pl)	[impɔsta'tsiɔni]
tune (melody)	melodia (f)	[mɛlɜ'dia]
to select (vt)	scegliere (vt)	['ʃeʎjerɛ]

calculator	calcolatrice (f)	[kaʎkɔʎat'ritʃe]
answering machine	segreteria (f) telefonica	[sɛgrɛtɛ'ria tɛle'fɔnika]
alarm clock	sveglia (f)	['zvɛʎja]
contacts	contatti (m pl)	[kɔn'tatti]

| SMS (text message) | messaggio (m) SMS | [mes'sadʒɔ ɛsɛ'mɛsɛ] |
| subscriber | abbonato (m) | [abbɔ'natɔ] |

115. Stationery

| ballpoint pen | penna (f) a sfera | [peɲa a 'sfɛra] |
| fountain pen | penna (f) stilografica | ['pɛɲa stilɔg'rafika] |

pencil	matita (f)	[ma'tita]
highlighter	evidenziatore (m)	[ɛwidɛntsja'tɔrɛ]
felt-tip pen	pennarello (m)	[peɲa'rɛllɔ]

| notepad | taccuino (m) | [takku'inɔ] |
| diary | agenda (f) | [a'dʒɛnda] |

ruler	righello (m)	[ri'gɛllɔ]
calculator	calcolatrice (f)	[kaʎkɔʎat'ritʃe]
rubber	gomma (f) per cancellare	['gɔmma pɛr kantʃe'ʎarɛ]
drawing pin	puntina (f)	[pun'tina]
paper clip	graffetta (f)	[graf'fɛtta]

glue	colla (f)	['kɔʎa]
stapler	pinzatrice (f)	[pintsat'ritʃe]
hole punch	perforatrice (f)	[pɛrforat'ritʃɛ]
pencil sharpener	temperamatite (m)	[tɛmpɛrama'titɛ]

116. Various kinds of documents

account (report)	resoconto (m)	[rɛzɔ'kɔntɔ]
agreement	accordo (m)	[ak'kɔrdɔ]
application form	modulo (m) di richiesta	['mɔdulɔ di riki'ɛsta]
authentic (adj)	autentico	[au'tɛntikɔ]
badge (identity tag)	tesserino (m)	[tɛssɛ'rinɔ]
business card	biglietto (m) da visita	[bi'ʎjettɔ da wi'zita]
certificate (~ of quality)	certificato (m)	[tʃertifi'katɔ]

cheque (e.g. draw a ~)	assegno (m)	[as'sɛɲɔ]
bill (in restaurant)	conto (m)	['kɔntɔ]
constitution	costituzione (f)	[kɔstitu'tsɔnɛ]

contract	contratto (m)	[kɔnt'rattɔ]
copy	copia (f)	['kɔpia]
copy (of contract, etc.)	copia (f)	['kɔpia]

customs declaration	dichiarazione (f)	[dikjara'tsɔnɛ]
document	documento (m)	[dɔku'mɛntɔ]
driving licence	patente (f) di guida	[pa'tɛntɛ di gu'ida]
addendum	allegato (m)	[alle'gatɔ]
form	modulo (m)	['mɔdulɔ]

identity card, ID	carta (f) d'identità	['karta didɛnti'ta]
inquiry (request)	richiesta (f) di informazioni	[riki'ɛsta di informa'tsɔnɛ]
invitation card	biglietto (m) d'invito	[bi'ʎjettɔ din'witɔ]
invoice	fattura (f)	[fat'tura]

law	legge (f)	['ledʒe]
letter (mail)	lettera (f)	['lettɛra]
letterhead	carta (f) intestata	['karta intɛs'tata]
list (of names, etc.)	lista (f)	['lista]
manuscript	manoscritto (m)	[manɔsk'rittɔ]
newsletter	bollettino (m)	[bɔllet'tinɔ]
note (short message)	appunto (m), nota (f)	[ap'puntɔ], ['nɔta]

pass (for worker, visitor)	lasciapassare (m)	[ʎaʃapas'sarɛ]
passport	passaporto (m)	[passa'pɔrtɔ]
permit	permesso (m)	[pɛr'mɛssɔ]
curriculum vitae, CV	curriculum vitae (f)	[kur'rikulym 'witɛ]
debt note, IOU	nota (f) di addebito	['nɔta di ad'dɛbitɔ]
receipt (for purchase)	ricevuta (f)	[ritʃe'vuta]
till receipt	scontrino (m)	[skɔnt'rinɔ]
report	rapporto (m)	[rap'pɔrtɔ]

to show (ID, etc.)	mostrare (vt)	[mɔst'rarɛ]
to sign (vt)	firmare (vt)	[fir'marɛ]
signature	firma (f)	['firma]
stamp (seal)	timbro (m)	['timbrɔ]
text	testo (m)	['tɛstɔ]
ticket (for entry)	biglietto (m)	[bi'ʎjettɔ]

| to cross out | cancellare (vt) | [kantʃe'ʎarɛ] |
| to fill in (~ a form) | riempire (vt) | [riɛm'pirɛ] |

| waybill | bolla (f) di consegna | ['bɔʎa di kɔn'sɛɲa] |
| will (testament) | testamento (m) | [tɛsta'mɛntɔ] |

117. Kinds of business

accounting services	servizi (m pl) di contabilità	[sɛr'witsi di kɔntabili'ta]
advertising	pubblicità (f)	[pubbliʧi'ta]
advertising agency	agenzia (f) pubblicitaria	[adʒen'tsia pubbliʧi'taria]

| air-conditioners | condizionatori (m pl) d'aria | [kɔnditsʲɔna'tɔri 'daria] |
| airline | compagnia (f) aerea | [kɔmpa'nia a'ɛrɛa] |

alcoholic drinks	bevande (f pl) alcoliche	[bɛ'vandɛ aʎ'kɔlikɛ]
antiques	antiquariato (m)	[antikuari'atɔ]
art gallery	galleria (f) d'arte	[galle'ria 'dartɛ]
audit services	società (f) di revisione contabile	[sɔtʃɛ'ta di rɛwi'zɔnɛ kɔn'tabile]

banks	imprese (f pl) bancarie	[imp'rɛzɛ ba'ŋkariɛ]
beauty salon	salone (m) di bellezza	[sa'lɔnɛ di bɛl'letsa]
bookshop	libreria (f)	[librɛ'ria]
brewery	birreria (f)	[birrɛ'ria]
business centre	business centro (m)	['biznɛs 'ʧɛntrɔ]
business school	scuola (f) di commercio	[sku'ɔla di kɔm'mɛrʧɔ]

casino	casinò (m)	[kazi'nɔ]
chemist, pharmacy	farmacia (f)	[farma'ʧia]
cinema	cinema (m)	['ʧinɛma]
construction	edilizia (f)	[ɛdi'litsia]
consulting	consulenza (f)	[kɔnsu'lentsa]

dentistry	odontoiatria (f)	[ɔdɔntɔjat'ria]
design	design (m)	[di'zajn]
dry cleaners	lavanderia (f) a secco	[ʎavandɛ'ria a 'sɛkkɔ]

employment agency	agenzia (f) di collocamento	[adʒen'tsia di kɔlloka'mɛntɔ]
financial services	servizi (m pl) finanziari	[sɛr'witsi finantsi'ari]
food products	industria (f) alimentare	[in'dustria alimen'tarɛ]
furniture (for house)	mobili (m pl)	['mɔbili]
garment	abbigliamento (m)	[abbiʎja'mɛntɔ]
hotel	albergo, hotel (m)	[aʎ'bɛrgɔ], [ɔ'tɛʎ]

ice-cream	gelato (m)	[dʒe'ʎatɔ]
industry	industria (f)	[in'dustria]
insurance	assicurazione (f)	[assikura'tsʲɔnɛ]
Internet	internet (m)	['intɛrnɛt]
investment	investimenti (m pl)	[invɛsti'mɛnti]
jeweller	gioielliere (m)	[dʒɔje'ʎjerɛ]
jewellery	gioielli (m pl)	[dʒɔ'jelli]

laundry (room, shop)	lavanderia (f)	[ʎavandɛ'ria]
legal adviser	consulente (m) legale	[kɔnsu'lentɛ le'gale]
light industry	industria (f) leggera	[in'dustria le'dʒera]

magazine	rivista (f)	[ri'wista]
mail-order selling	vendite (f pl) per corrispondenza	['vɛnditɛ per kɔrrispon'dentsa]
medicine	medicina (f)	[mɛdi'ʧina]
museum	museo (m)	[mu'zɛɔ]

news agency	agenzia (f) di stampa	[adʒen'tsia di 'stampa]
newspaper	giornale (m)	[dʒɔr'nale]
nightclub	nightclub (m)	['najtklɛb]
oil (petroleum)	petrolio (m)	[pɛt'rɔliɔ]
parcels service	corriere (m) espresso	[kɔr'rjerɛ ɛsp'rɛssɔ]

pharmaceuticals	farmaci (m pl)	['farmatʃi]
printing (industry)	stampa (f)	['stampa]
pub	bar (m)	[bar]
publishing house	casa (f) editrice	['kaza ɛdit'ritʃe]

radio	radio (f)	['radiɔ]
real estate	beni (m pl) immobili	['bɛni im'mɔbili]
restaurant	ristorante (m)	[risto'rantɛ]

security agency	agenzia (f) di sicurezza	[adʒen'tsia di sigu'rɛtsa]
shop	negozio (m)	[nɛ'gɔtsiɔ]
sport	sport (m)	[spɔrt]
stock exchange	borsa (f)	['bɔrsa]
supermarket	supermercato (m)	[supɛrmɛr'katɔ]
swimming pool	piscina (f)	[pi'ʃina]

tailors	sartoria (f)	[sarto'ria]
television	televisione (f)	[tɛlewizi'ɔnɛ]
theatre	teatro (m)	[tɛ'atrɔ]
trade	commercio (m)	[kɔm'mɛrtʃo]
transport companies	mezzi (m pl) di trasporto	['mɛdzi di trans'pɔrtɔ]
travel	viaggio (m)	['vjadʒɔ]

undertakers	agenzia (f) di pompe funebri	[adʒen'tsia di 'pɔmpɛ 'funɛbri]
veterinary surgeon	veterinario (m)	[vɛtɛri'nariɔ]
warehouse	deposito, magazzino (m)	[dɛ'pɔzitɔ], [maga'dzinɔ]
waste collection	trattamento (m) dei rifiuti	[tratta'mɛntɔ dɛi rifi'juti]

Job. Business. Part 2

118. Show. Exhibition

exhibition, show	fiera (f)	['fjera]
trade show	fiera (f) campionaria	['fjera kamp'o'narija]
participation	partecipazione (f)	[partɛtʃipa'ts'onɛ]
to participate (vi)	partecipare (vi)	[partɛtʃi'parɛ]
participant (exhibitor)	partecipante (m)	[partɛtʃi'pantɛ]
director	direttore (m)	[dirɛt'torɛ]
organizer's office	ufficio (m) organizzativo	[uf'fitʃo organidza'tivo]
organizer	organizzatore (m)	[organidza'torɛ]
to organize (vt)	organizzare (vt)	[organi'dzarɛ]
participation form	domanda (f) di partecipazione	[do'manda di partɛtʃipa'ts'onɛ]
to fill in (vt)	riempire (vt)	[riɛm'pirɛ]
details	dettagli (m pl)	[dɛt'taʎi]
information	informazione (f)	[informa'ts'onɛ]
price	prezzo (m)	['prɛtso]
including	incluso	[iŋk'lyzo]
to include (vt)	includere (vt)	[iŋk'lydɛrɛ]
to pay (vi, vt)	pagare (vi, vt)	[pa'garɛ]
registration fee	quota (f) d'iscrizione	[ku'ota diskri'ts'onɛ]
entrance	entrata (f)	[ɛnt'rata]
pavilion, hall	padiglione (m)	[padi'ʎonɛ]
to register (vt)	registrare (vt)	[rɛdʒist'rarɛ]
badge (identity tag)	tesserino (m)	[tɛssɛ'rino]
stand	stand (m)	[stɛnd]
to reserve, to book	prenotare, riservare	[prɛno'tarɛ], [rizɛr'varɛ]
display case	vetrina (f)	[vɛt'rina]
spotlight	faretto (m)	[fa'rɛtto]
design	design (m)	[di'zajn]
to place (put, set)	collocare (vt)	[kollɔ'karɛ]
to be placed	collocarsi (vr)	[kollɔ'karsi]
distributor	distributore (m)	[distribu'torɛ]
supplier	fornitore (m)	[forni'torɛ]
to supply (vt)	fornire (vt)	[for'nirɛ]
country	paese (m)	[pa'ɛzɛ]
foreign (adj)	straniero	[stra'njero]
product	prodotto (m)	[pro'dotto]
association	associazione (f)	[assotʃa'ts'onɛ]

conference hall	sala (f) conferenze	['saʎa kɔnfɛ'rɛntsɛ]
congress	congresso (m)	[kɔn'rɛssɔ]
contest (competition)	concorso (m)	[kɔ'ŋkɔrsɔ]
visitor	visitatore (m)	[wizita'tɔrɛ]
to visit (attend)	visitare (vt)	[wizi'tarɛ]
customer	cliente (m)	[kli'ɛntɛ]

119. Mass Media

newspaper	giornale (m)	[dʒor'nale]
magazine	rivista (f)	[ri'wista]
press (printed media)	stampa (f)	['stampa]
radio	radio (f)	['radiɔ]
radio station	stazione (f) radio	[sta'tsɨɔnɛ 'radiɔ]
television	televisione (f)	[tɛlewizi'ɔnɛ]
presenter, host	presentatore (m)	[prɛzɛnta'tɔrɛ]
newsreader	annunciatore (m)	[aɲuntʃa'tɔrɛ]
commentator	commentatore (m)	[kɔmmɛnta'tɔrɛ]
journalist	giornalista (m)	[dʒorna'lista]
correspondent (reporter)	corrispondente (m)	[korrispon'dɛntɛ]
press photographer	fotocronista (m)	[fɔtɔkrɔ'nista]
reporter	cronista (m)	[krɔ'nista]
editor	redattore (m)	[rɛdat'tɔrɛ]
editor-in-chief	redattore capo (m)	[rɛdat'tɔrɛ 'kapɔ]
to subscribe (to ...)	abbonarsi a ...	[abbɔ'narsi]
subscription	abbonamento (m)	[abbɔna'mɛntɔ]
subscriber	abbonato (m)	[abbɔ'natɔ]
to read (vi, vt)	leggere (vi, vt)	['lɛdʒɛrɛ]
reader	lettore (m)	[let'tɔrɛ]
circulation (of newspaper)	tiratura (f)	[tira'tura]
monthly (adj)	mensile	[men'sile]
weekly (adj)	settimanale	[sɛttima'nale]
issue (edition)	numero (m)	['numɛrɔ]
new (~ issue)	fresco (m)	['frɛskɔ]
headline	testata (f)	[tɛs'tata]
short article	trafiletto (m)	[trafi'lettɔ]
column (regular article)	rubrica (f)	[rub'rika]
article	articolo (m)	[ar'tikɔlɔ]
page	pagina (f)	['padʒina]
reportage, report	servizio (m)	[sɛr'witsiɔ]
event	evento (m)	[ɛ'vɛntɔ]
sensation (news)	sensazione (f)	[sɛnsa'tsɨɔnɛ]
scandal	scandalo (m)	['skandalɔ]
scandalous (adj)	scandaloso	[skanda'lɔzɔ]
great (~ scandal)	enorme, grande	[ɛ'nɔrmɛ], ['grandɛ]
programme	trasmissione (f)	[trazmissi'ɔnɛ]

interview	intervista (f)	[intɛr'wista]
live broadcast	trasmissione (f) in diretta	[trazmissi'ɔnɛ in di'rɛtta]
channel	canale (m)	[ka'nale]

120. Agriculture

agriculture	agricoltura (f)	[agrikoʎ'tura]
peasant (masc.)	contadino (m)	[kɔnta'dinɔ]
peasant (fem.)	contadina (f)	[kɔnta'dina]
farmer	fattore (m)	[fat'tɔrɛ]

| tractor | trattore (m) | [trat'tɔrɛ] |
| combine, harvester | mietitrebbia (f) | [mjetit'rɛbbia] |

plough	aratro (m)	[a'ratrɔ]
to plough (vi, vt)	arare (vt)	[a'rarɛ]
ploughland	terreno (m) coltivato	[tɛr'rɛnɔ kɔʎti'vatɔ]
furrow (in field)	solco (m)	['sɔʎkɔ]

to sow (vi, vt)	seminare (vt)	[sɛmi'narɛ]
seeder	seminatrice (f)	[sɛminat'ritʃe]
sowing (process)	semina (f)	['sɛmina]

| scythe | falce (f) | ['faʎtʃɛ] |
| to mow, to scythe | falciare (vt) | [faʎ'tʃarɛ] |

| shovel (tool) | pala (f) | ['paʎa] |
| to dig (cultivate) | scavare (vt) | [ska'varɛ] |

hoe	zappa (f)	['tsappa]
to hoe, to weed	zappare (vt)	[tsap'parɛ]
weed (plant)	erbaccia (f)	[ɛr'batʃa]

watering can	innaffiatoio (m)	[iɲaffja'tojo]
to water (plants)	innaffiare (vt)	[iɲaf'fiarɛ]
watering (act)	innaffiamento (m)	[iɲaffia'mɛntɔ]

| pitchfork | forca (f) | ['fɔrka] |
| rake | rastrello (m) | [rast'rɛllɔ] |

fertilizer	concime (m)	[kɔn'tʃimɛ]
to fertilize (vt)	concimare (vt)	[kɔntʃi'marɛ]
manure (fertilizer)	letame (m)	[le'tamɛ]

field	campo (m)	['kampɔ]
meadow	prato (m)	['pratɔ]
vegetable garden	orto (m)	['ɔrtɔ]
orchard (e.g. apple ~)	frutteto (m)	[frut'tɛtɔ]

to pasture (vt)	pascolare (vt)	[paskɔ'larɛ]
herdsman	pastore (m)	[pas'tɔrɛ]
pastureland	pascolo (m)	['paskɔlɔ]
cattle breeding	allevamento (m) di bestiame	[alleva'mɛntɔ di bɛs'tiamɛ]
sheep farming	allevamento (m) di pecore	[alleva'mɛntɔ di 'pɛkɔrɛ]

plantation	piantagione (f)	[pjanta'dʒɔnɛ]
row (garden bed ~s)	filare (m)	[fi'ʎarɛ]
greenhouse (hotbed)	serra (f) da orto	['sɛrra da 'ɔrtɔ]

| drought (lack of rain) | siccità (f) | [sitʃi'ta] |
| dry (~ summer) | secco, arido | ['sɛkkɔ], ['arridɔ] |

| cereal plants | cereali (m pl) | [tʃerɛ'ali] |
| to harvest, to gather | raccogliere (vt) | [rak'koʎjerɛ] |

miller (person)	mugnaio (m)	[mu'ɲjajo]
mill (e.g. gristmill)	mulino (m)	[mu'linɔ]
to grind (grain)	macinare (vt)	[matʃi'narɛ]
flour	farina (f)	[fa'rina]
straw	paglia (f)	['paʎja]

121. Building. Building process

building site	cantiere (m) edile	[kan'tʲerɛ 'ɛdile]
to build (vt)	costruire (vt)	[kɔstru'irɛ]
building worker	operaio (m) edile	[ɔpɛ'rajo ɛ'dile]

project	progetto (m)	[prɔ'dʒettɔ]
architect	architetto (m)	[arki'tɛttɔ]
worker	operaio (m)	[ɔpɛ'rajo]

foundations (of building)	fondamenta (f pl)	[fɔnda'mɛnta]
roof	tetto (m)	['tɛttɔ]
foundation pile	palo (m) di fondazione	['palɔ di fɔnda'tsʲɔnɛ]
wall	muro (m)	['murɔ]

| reinforcing bars | barre (f pl) di rinforzo | ['barrɛ di rin'fɔrtsɔ] |
| scaffolding | impalcatura (f) | [impaʎka'tura] |

concrete	beton (m)	[bɛ'tɔn]
granite	granito (m)	[gra'nitɔ]
stone	pietra (f)	['pjetra]
brick	mattone (m)	[mat'tɔnɛ]

sand	sabbia (f)	['sabbja]
cement	cemento (m)	[tʃe'mɛntɔ]
plaster (for walls)	intonaco (m)	[in'tɔnakɔ]
to plaster (vt)	intonacare (vt)	[intɔna'karɛ]
paint	pittura (f)	[pit'tura]
to paint (~ a wall)	pitturare (vt)	[pittu'rare]
barrel	botte (f)	['bɔttɛ]

crane	gru (f)	[gru]
to lift (vt)	sollevare (vt)	[sɔlle'varɛ]
to lower (vt)	abbassare (vt)	[abbas'sarɛ]

bulldozer	bulldozer (m)	[buʎdɔ'dzɛr]
excavator	scavatrice (f)	[skavat'ritʃe]
scoop, bucket	cucchiaia (f)	[kuk'kjaja]

| to dig (excavate) | scavare (vt) | [ska'varɛ] |
| hard hat | casco (m) | ['kaskɔ] |

122. Science. Research. Scientists

science	scienza (f)	[ʃi'ɛntsa]
scientific (adj)	scientifico	[ʃiɛn'tifikɔ]
scientist	scienziato (m)	[ʃiɛntsi'atɔ]
theory	teoria (f)	[tɛɔ'ria]

axiom	assioma (m)	[assi'ɔma]
analysis	analisi (f)	[a'nalizi]
to analyse (vt)	analizzare (vt)	[anali'dzarɛ]
argument (strong ~)	argomento (m)	[argɔ'mɛntɔ]
substance (matter)	sostanza (f)	[sɔs'tantsa]

hypothesis	ipotesi (f)	[i'potɛzi]
dilemma	dilemma (m)	[di'lemma]
dissertation	tesi (f)	['tɛzi]
dogma	dogma (m)	['dɔgma]

doctrine	dottrina (f)	[dott'rina]
research	ricerca (f)	[ri'tʃerka]
to do research	fare ricerche	['farɛ ri'tʃerkɛ]
testing	prova (f)	['prɔva]
laboratory	laboratorio (m)	[ʎabɔra'tɔriɔ]

method	metodo (m)	['mɛtɔdɔ]
molecule	molecola (f)	[mɔ'lekɔʎa]
monitoring	monitoraggio (m)	[mɔnitɔ'radʒɔ]
discovery (act, event)	scoperta (f)	[skɔ'pɛrta]

postulate	postulato (m)	[pɔstu'ʎatɔ]
principle	principio (m)	[prin'tʃipiɔ]
forecast	previsione (f)	[prɛwizi'ɔnɛ]
to forecast (vt)	fare previsioni	[farɛ prɛwizi'ɔni]

synthesis	sintesi (f)	['sintɛzi]
trend (tendency)	tendenza (f)	[tɛn'dɛntsa]
theorem	teorema (m)	[tɛɔ'rɛma]

teachings	insegnamento (m)	[insɛ'ɲamɛntɔ]
fact	fatto (m)	['fattɔ]
expedition	spedizione (f)	[spɛdi'tsɔnɛ]
experiment	esperimento (m)	[ɛspɛri'mɛntɔ]

academician	accademico (m)	[akka'dɛmikɔ]
bachelor (e.g. ~ of Arts)	laureato (m)	[laurе'atɔ]
doctor (PhD)	dottore (m)	[dot'tɔrɛ]
Associate Professor	professore (m) associato	[prɔfes'sɔrɛ assɔtʃi'atɔ]
Master (e.g. ~ of Arts)	Master (m)	['mastɛr]
professor	professore (m)	[prɔfɛs'sɔrɛ]

Professions and occupations

123. Job search. Dismissal

job	lavoro (m)	[ʎa'vɔrɔ]
personnel	organico (m)	[ɔr'ganikɔ]
career	carriera (f)	[kar'rjera]
prospect	prospettiva (f)	[prɔspɛt'tiva]
skills (mastery)	abilità (f pl)	[abili'ta]
selection (for job)	selezione (f)	[sɛle'tslonɛ]
employment agency	agenzia (f) di collocamento	[adʒen'tsia di kɔllɔka'mɛntɔ]
curriculum vitae, CV	curriculum vitae (f)	[kur'rikulym 'witɛ]
interview (for job)	colloquio (m)	[kɔl'lɔkuiɔ]
vacancy	posto (m) vacante	['pɔstɔ va'kantɛ]
salary, pay	salario (m)	[sa'ʎariɔ]
fixed salary	stipendio (m) fisso	[sti'pendiɔ 'fissɔ]
pay, compensation	compenso (m)	[kɔm'pɛnsɔ]
position (job)	carica (f)	['karika]
duty (of employee)	mansione (f)	[mansi'ɔnɛ]
range of duties	mansioni (f pl) di lavoro	[mansi'ɔni di ʎa'vɔrɔ]
busy (I'm ~)	occupato	[ɔkku'patɔ]
to fire (dismiss)	licenziare (vt)	[litʃentsi'arɛ]
dismissal	licenziamento (m)	[litʃentsia'mɛntɔ]
unemployment	disoccupazione (f)	[disɔkkupa'tslonɛ]
unemployed (n)	disoccupato (m)	[disɔkku'patɔ]
retirement	pensionamento (m)	[penslona'mɛntɔ]
to retire (from job)	andare in pensione	[an'darɛ in pɛnsi'ɔnɛ]

124. Business people

director	direttore (m)	[dirɛt'tɔrɛ]
manager (director)	dirigente (m)	[diri'dʒɛntɛ]
boss	capo (m)	['kapɔ]
superior	capo (m), superiore (m)	['kapɔ], [supɛ'rlorɛ]
superiors	capi (m pl)	['kapi]
president	presidente (m)	[prɛzi'dɛntɛ]
chairman	presidente (m)	[prɛzi'dɛntɛ]
deputy (substitute)	vice (m)	['witʃe]
assistant	assistente (m)	[assis'tɛntɛ]
secretary	segretario (m)	[sɛgrɛ'tariɔ]

personal assistant	assistente (m) personale	[assis'tɛntɛ pɛrsɔ'nalɛ]
businessman	uomo (m) d'affari	[u'ɔmɔ daf'fari]
entrepreneur	imprenditore (m)	[imprɛndi'tɔrɛ]
founder	fondatore (m)	[fɔnda'tɔrɛ]
to found (vt)	fondare (vt)	[fɔn'darɛ]

founding member	socio (m)	['sɔtʃɔ]
partner	partner (m)	['partnɛr]
shareholder	azionista (m)	[atsiɔ'nista]

millionaire	milionario (m)	[miʎɔ'nariɔ]
billionaire	miliardario (m)	[miʎar'dariɔ]
owner, proprietor	proprietario (m)	[prɔpriɛ'tariɔ]
landowner	latifondista (m)	[ʎatifɔn'dista]

client	cliente (m)	[kli'ɛntɛ]
regular client	cliente (m) abituale	[kli'ɛntɛ abitu'alɛ]
buyer (customer)	compratore (m)	[kɔmpra'tɔrɛ]
visitor	visitatore (m)	[wizita'tɔrɛ]

professional (n)	professionista (m)	[prɔfɛssiɔ'nista]
expert	esperto (m)	[ɛs'pɛrtɔ]
specialist	specialista (m)	[spɛtʃa'lista]

| banker | banchiere (m) | [ban'kjerɛ] |
| broker | broker (m) | ['brɔkɛr] |

cashier	cassiere (m)	[kas'sjerɛ]
accountant	contabile (m)	[kɔn'tabile]
security guard	guardia (f) giurata	[gu'ardia dʒu'rata]

investor	investitore (m)	[invɛsti'tɔrɛ]
debtor	debitore (m)	[dɛbi'tɔrɛ]
creditor	creditore (m)	[krɛdi'tɔrɛ]
borrower	mutuatario (m)	[mutua'tariɔ]

| importer | importatore (m) | [impɔrta'tɔrɛ] |
| exporter | esportatore (m) | [ɛspɔrta'tɔrɛ] |

manufacturer	produttore (m)	[prɔdut'tɔrɛ]
distributor	distributore (m)	[distribu'tɔrɛ]
middleman	intermediario (m)	[intɛrmɛdi'ariɔ]

consultant	consulente (m)	[kɔnsu'lentɛ]
representative	rappresentante (m)	[rapprɛzɛn'tantɛ]
agent	agente (m)	[a'dʒɛntɛ]
insurance agent	assicuratore (m)	[assikura'tɔrɛ]

125. Service professions

cook	cuoco (m)	[ku'ɔkɔ]
chef	capocuoco (m)	[kapɔku'ɔkɔ]
baker	fornaio (m)	[fɔr'najɔ]
barman	barista (m)	[ba'rista]

waiter	**cameriere** (m)	[kamɛ'rjerɛ]
waitress	**cameriera** (f)	[kamɛ'rjera]

lawyer, barrister	**avvocato** (m)	[avvo'kato]
lawyer (legal expert)	**esperto** (m) **legale**	[ɛs'pertɔ le'galɛ]
notary	**notaio** (m)	[nɔ'tajo]

electrician	**elettricista** (m)	[ɛlettri'ʧista]
plumber	**idraulico** (m)	[id'raulikɔ]
carpenter	**falegname** (m)	[fale'ɲjamɛ]

masseur	**massaggiatore** (m)	[massadʒa'tɔrɛ]
masseuse	**massaggiatrice** (f)	[massadʒat'riʧe]
doctor	**medico** (m)	['mɛdikɔ]

taxi driver	**taxista** (m)	[tak'sista]
driver	**autista** (m)	[au'tista]
delivery man	**fattorino** (m)	[fattɔ'rinɔ]

chambermaid	**cameriera** (f)	[kamɛ'rjera]
security guard	**guardia** (f) **giurata**	[gu'ardia dʒu'rata]
stewardess	**hostess** (f)	['ɔstɛss]

teacher (in primary school)	**insegnante** (m, f)	[insɛ'ɲjantɛ]
librarian	**bibliotecario** (m)	[bibliotɛ'kario]
translator	**traduttore** (m)	[tradut'tɔrɛ]
interpreter	**interprete** (m)	[in'tɛrprɛtɛ]
guide	**guida** (f)	[gu'ida]

hairdresser	**parrucchiere** (m)	[parruk'kjerɛ]
postman	**postino** (m)	[pɔs'tinɔ]
shop assistant (masc.)	**commesso** (m)	[kɔm'mɛssɔ]

gardener	**giardiniere** (m)	[dʒardi'ɲjerɛ]
servant (in household)	**domestico** (m)	[dɔ'mɛstikɔ]
maid	**domestica** (f)	[dɔ'mɛstika]
cleaner (cleaning lady)	**donna** (f) **delle pulizie**	['dɔɲa 'dɛlle puli'tsiɛ]

126. Military professions and ranks

private	**soldato** (m) **semplice**	[sɔʎ'datɔ 'sɛmpliʧɛ]
sergeant	**sergente** (m)	[sɛr'dʒentɛ]
lieutenant	**tenente** (m)	[tɛ'nɛntɛ]
captain	**capitano** (m)	[kapi'tanɔ]

major	**maggiore** (m)	[ma'dʒɔrɛ]
colonel	**colonnello** (m)	[kɔlɔ'ɲɛllɔ]
general	**generale** (m)	[dʒenɛ'rale]
marshal	**maresciallo** (m)	[marɛ'ʃallɔ]
admiral	**ammiraglio** (m)	[ammi'raʎɔ]

military man	**militare** (m)	[mili'tarɛ]
soldier	**soldato** (m)	[sɔʎ'datɔ]
officer	**ufficiale** (m)	[uffi'ʧale]

commander	comandante (m)	[kɔman'dantɛ]
border guard	guardia (f) di frontiera	[gu'ardia di frɔn'tʲera]
radio operator	marconista (m)	[markɔ'nista]
scout (searcher)	esploratore (m)	[ɛsplɜra'tɔrɛ]
pioneer (sapper)	geniere (m)	[dʒeni'erɛ]
marksman	tiratore (m)	[tira'tɔrɛ]
navigator	navigatore (m)	[nawiga'tɔrɛ]

127. Officials. Priests

| king | re (m) | [rɛ] |
| queen | regina (f) | [rɛ'dʒina] |

| prince | principe (m) | ['printʃipɛ] |
| princess | principessa (f) | [printʃi'pɛssa] |

| tsar, czar | zar (m) | [tsar] |
| czarina | zarina (f) | [tsa'rina] |

president	presidente (m)	[prɛzi'dɛntɛ]
Minister	ministro (m)	[mi'nistrɔ]
prime minister	primo ministro (m)	['primɔ mi'nistrɔ]
senator	senatore (m)	[sɛna'tɔrɛ]

diplomat	diplomatico (m)	[diplɜ'matikɔ]
consul	console (m)	['kɔnsɔle]
ambassador	ambasciatore (m)	[ambaʃa'tɔrɛ]
advisor (military ~)	consigliere (m)	[kɔnsi'ʎjerɛ]

official (civil servant)	funzionario (m)	[funtsiɔ'nariɔ]
prefect	prefetto (m)	[prɛ'fɛttɔ]
mayor	sindaco (m)	['sindakɔ]

| judge | giudice (m) | ['dʒuditʃe] |
| prosecutor | procuratore (m) | [prɔkura'tɔrɛ] |

missionary	missionario (m)	[missiɔ'nariɔ]
monk	monaco (m)	['mɔnakɔ]
abbot	abate (m)	[a'batɛ]
rabbi	rabbino (m)	[rab'binɔ]

vizier	visir (m)	[wi'zir]
shah	scià (m)	['ʃa]
sheikh	sceicco (m)	[ʃɛ'ikkɔ]

128. Agricultural professions

beekeeper	apicoltore (m)	[apikɔʎ'tɔrɛ]
herdsman	pastore (m)	[pas'tɔrɛ]
agronomist	agronomo (m)	[ag'rɔnɔmɔ]
cattle breeder	allevatore (m) di bestiame	[alleva'tɔrɛ di bɛs'tʲamɛ]
veterinary surgeon	veterinario (m)	[vɛtɛri'nariɔ]

farmer	fattore (m)	[fat'tɔrɛ]
winemaker	vinificatore (m)	[winifika'tɔrɛ]
zoologist	zoologo (m)	[ʣɔ'ɔlɔgɔ]
cowboy	cowboy (m)	[kau'bɔj]

129. Art professions

| actor | attore (m) | [at'tɔrɛ] |
| actress | attrice (f) | [att'riʧe] |

| singer (masc.) | cantante (m) | [kan'tantɛ] |
| singer (fem.) | cantante (f) | [kan'tantɛ] |

| dancer (masc.) | danzatore (m) | [danʦa'tɔrɛ] |
| dancer (fem.) | ballerina (f) | [balle'rina] |

| performing artist (masc.) | artista (m) | [ar'tista] |
| performing artist (fem.) | artista (f) | [ar'tista] |

musician	musicista (m)	[muzi'ʧista]
pianist	pianista (m)	[pia'nista]
guitar player	chitarrista (m)	[kitar'rista]

conductor (of musicians)	direttore (m) d'orchestra	[dirɛt'tɔrɛ dor'kɛstra]
composer	compositore (m)	[kɔmpozi'tɔrɛ]
impresario	impresario (m)	[imprɛ'zariɔ]

film director	regista (m)	[rɛ'ʤista]
producer	produttore (m)	[prɔdut'tɔrɛ]
scriptwriter	sceneggiatore (m)	[ʃɛnɛʤa'tɔrɛ]
critic	critico (m)	['kritikɔ]

writer	scrittore (m)	[skrit'tɔrɛ]
poet	poeta (m)	[pɔ'ɛta]
sculptor	scultore (m)	[skuʎ'tɔrɛ]
artist (painter)	pittore (m)	[pit'tɔrɛ]

juggler	giocoliere (m)	[ʤɔkɔ'ʎjerɛ]
clown	pagliaccio (m)	[pa'ʎjaʧɔ]
acrobat	acrobata (m)	[ak'rɔbata]
magician	prestigiatore (m)	[prɛstiʤa'tɔrɛ]

130. Various professions

doctor	medico (m)	['mɛdikɔ]
nurse	infermiera (f)	[infɛr'mjera]
psychiatrist	psichiatra (m)	[psiki'atra]
stomatologist	dentista (m)	[dɛn'tista]
surgeon	chirurgo (m)	[ki'rurgɔ]

| astronaut | astronauta (m) | [astrɔ'nauta] |
| astronomer | astronomo (m) | [ast'rɔnɔmɔ] |

driver (of taxi, etc.)	autista (m)	[au'tista]
train driver	macchinista (m)	[makki'nista]
mechanic	meccanico (m)	[mɛk'kaniko]

miner	minatore (m)	[mina'tɔrɛ]
worker	operaio (m)	[ɔpɛ'rajo]
metalworker	operaio (m) metallurgico	[ɔpɛ'rajo metal'lurdʒiko]
joiner (carpenter)	falegname (m)	[fale'ɲjamɛ]
turner	tornitore (m)	[tɔrni'tɔrɛ]
building worker	operaio (m) edile	[ɔpɛ'rajo ɛ'dile]
welder	saldatore (m)	[saʎda'tɔrɛ]

professor (title)	professore (m)	[prɔfɛs'sɔrɛ]
architect	architetto (m)	[arki'tɛtto]
historian	storico (m)	['stɔriko]
scientist	scienziato (m)	[ʃiɛntsi'ato]
physicist	fisico (m)	['fiziko]
chemist (scientist)	chimico (m)	['kimiko]

archaeologist	archeologo (m)	[arkɛ'ɔlɔgo]
geologist	geologo (m)	[dʒe'ɔlɔgo]
researcher	ricercatore (m)	[ritʃerka'tɔrɛ]

| babysitter | baby-sitter (f) | [bɛbi'sitɛr] |
| teacher, educator | insegnante (m, f) | [inse'ɲjantɛ] |

editor	redattore (m)	[rɛdat'tɔrɛ]
editor-in-chief	redattore capo (m)	[rɛdat'tɔrɛ 'kapo]
correspondent	corrispondente (m)	[kɔrrispɔn'dɛntɛ]
typist (fem.)	dattilografa (f)	[datti'lɔgrafa]

designer	designer (m)	[di'zajnɛr]
computer expert	esperto (m) informatico	[ɛs'pɛrto infor'matiko]
programmer	programmatore (m)	[prɔgramma'tɔrɛ]
engineer (designer)	ingegnere (m)	[indʒe'ɲjerɛ]

sailor	marittimo (m)	[ma'rittimo]
seaman	marinaio (m)	[mari'najo]
rescuer	soccorritore (m)	[sɔkkorri'tɔrɛ]

firefighter	pompiere (m)	[pɔm'pjerɛ]
policeman	poliziotto (m)	[politsi'ɔtto]
watchman	guardiano (m)	[guardi'ano]
detective	detective (m)	[dɛ'tɛktiv]

customs officer	doganiere (m)	[dɔga'ɲjerɛ]
bodyguard	guardia (f) del corpo	[gu'ardia dɛʎ 'kɔrpo]
prison officer	guardia (f) carceraria	[gu'ardia kartʃe'raria]
inspector	ispettore (m)	[ispɛt'tɔrɛ]

sportsman	sportivo (m)	[spor'tivo]
trainer, coach	allenatore (m)	[allena'tɔrɛ]
butcher	macellaio (m)	[matʃe'ʎajo]
cobbler	calzolaio (m)	[kaʎtsɔ'ʎajo]
merchant	uomo (m) d'affari	[u'omo daf'fari]
loader (person)	caricatore (m)	[karika'tɔrɛ]

| fashion designer | stilista (m) | [sti'lista] |
| model (fem.) | modella (f) | [mɔ'dɛʎa] |

131. Occupations. Social status

| schoolboy | scolaro (m) | [skɔ'ʎarɔ] |
| student (college ~) | studente (m) | [stu'dɛntɛ] |

philosopher	filosofo (m)	[fi'lɜzɔfɔ]
economist	economista (m)	[ɛkɔnɔ'mista]
inventor	inventore (m)	[invɛn'tɔrɛ]

unemployed (n)	disoccupato (m)	[disɔkku'patɔ]
pensioner	pensionato (m)	[pɛnsiɔ'natɔ]
spy, secret agent	spia (f)	['spia]

prisoner	detenuto (m)	[dɛtɛ'nutɔ]
striker	scioperante (m)	[ʃopɛ'rantɛ]
bureaucrat	burocrate (m)	[bu'rɔkratɛ]
traveller	viaggiatore (m)	[wiadʒa'tɔrɛ]

homosexual	omosessuale (m)	[ɔmɔsɛssu'ale]
hacker	hacker (m)	['akɛr]
hippie	hippy	['ippi]

bandit	bandito (m)	[ban'ditɔ]
hit man, killer	sicario (m)	[si'kariɔ]
drug addict	drogato (m)	[drɔ'gatɔ]
drug dealer	trafficante (m) di droga	[traffi'kantɛ di 'drɔga]
prostitute (fem.)	prostituta (f)	[prɔsti'tuta]
pimp	magnaccia (m)	[ma'ɲjatʃa]

sorcerer	stregone (m)	[strɛ'gɔnɛ]
sorceress	strega (f)	['strɛga]
pirate	pirata (m)	[pi'rata]
slave	schiavo (m)	['skjavɔ]
samurai	samurai (m)	[samu'raj]
savage (primitive)	selvaggio (m)	[sɛʎ'vadʒɔ]

Sports

132. Kinds of sports. Sportspersons

sportsman	sportivo (m)	[spor'tivɔ]
kind of sport	sport (m)	[sport]
basketball	pallacanestro (m)	[paʎaka'nɛstrɔ]
basketball player	cestista (m)	[tʃes'tista]
baseball	baseball (m)	['bɛjzbɔl]
baseball player	giocatore (m) di baseball	[dʒoka'tɔrɛ di 'bɛjzbɔl]
football	calcio (m)	['kaʎtʃo]
football player	calciatore (m)	[kaʎtʃa'tɔrɛ]
goalkeeper	portiere (m)	[por'tʲerɛ]
ice hockey	hockey (m)	['ɔkkɛj]
ice hockey player	hockeista (m)	[ɔkkɛ'ista]
volleyball	pallavolo (m)	[paʎa'vɔlɔ]
volleyball player	pallavolista (m)	[paʎavɔ'lista]
boxing	pugilato (m)	[pudʒi'ʎatɔ]
boxer	pugile (m)	['pudʒile]
wrestling	lotta (f)	['lɔtta]
wrestler	lottatore (m)	[lɔtta'tɔrɛ]
karate	karate (m)	[ka'ratɛ]
karate fighter	karateka (m)	[kara'tɛka]
judo	judo (m)	['dʒudɔ]
judo athlete	judoista (m)	[dʒudɔ'ista]
tennis	tennis (m)	['tɛŋis]
tennis player	tennista (m)	[tɛ'ŋista]
swimming	nuoto (m)	[nu'ɔtɔ]
swimmer	nuotatore (m)	[nuɔta'tɔrɛ]
fencing	scherma (f)	['skɛrma]
fencer	schermitore (m)	[skɛrmi'tɔrɛ]
chess	scacchi (m pl)	['skakki]
chess player	scacchista (m)	[skak'kista]
alpinism	alpinismo (m)	[aʎpi'nizmɔ]
alpinist	alpinista (m)	[aʎpi'nista]
running	corsa (f)	['kɔrsa]

runner	corridore (m)	[korri'dorɛ]
athletics	atletica (f) leggera	[at'letika le'dʒera]
athlete	atleta (m)	[at'leta]

| horse riding | ippica (f) | ['ippika] |
| horse rider | fantino (m) | [fan'tinɔ] |

figure skating	pattinaggio (m) artistico	[patti'nadʒɔ ar'tistikɔ]
figure skater (masc.)	pattinatore (m)	[pattina'torɛ]
figure skater (fem.)	pattinatrice (f)	[pattinat'ritʃe]

weightlifting	pesistica (f)	[pɛ'zistika]
car racing	automobilismo (m)	[autɔmɔbi'lizmɔ]
racing driver	pilota (m)	[pi'lɔta]

| cycling | ciclismo (m) | [tʃik'lizmɔ] |
| cyclist | ciclista (m) | [tʃik'lista] |

long jump	salto (m) in lungo	['saʎtɔ in 'lyŋɔ]
pole vaulting	salto (m) con l'asta	['saʎtɔ kɔn 'ʎasta]
jumper	saltatore (m)	[saʎta'torɛ]

133. Kinds of sports. Miscellaneous

American football	football (m) americano	['futbɔʎ amɛri'kanɔ]
badminton	badminton (m)	['badmintɔn]
biathlon	biathlon (m)	['biatlɜn]
billiards	biliardo (m)	[bi'ʎardɔ]

bobsleigh	bob (m)	[bɔb]
bodybuilding	culturismo (m)	[kuʎtu'rizmɔ]
water polo	pallanuoto (m)	[paʎanu'ɔtɔ]
handball	pallamano (m)	[paʎa'manɔ]
golf	golf (m)	[gɔʎf]

rowing	canottaggio (m)	[kanɔt'tadʒɔ]
diving	immersione (f) subacquea	[immɛrsi'ɔnɛ su'bakvɛa]
cross-country skiing	sci (m) di fondo	[ɕi di 'fɔndɔ]
ping-pong	tennis (m) da tavolo	['tɛŋis da 'tavɔlɔ]

sailing	vela (f)	['vɛʎa]
rally	rally (m)	['rɛlli]
rugby	rugby (m)	['ragbi]
snowboarding	snowboard (m)	['znoubɔrd]
archery	tiro (m) con l'arco	['tirɔ kɔn 'ʎarkɔ]

134. Gym

barbell	bilanciere (m)	[biʎan'tʃerɛ]
dumbbells	manubri (m pl)	[ma'nubri]
training machine	attrezzo (m) sportivo	[att'rɛtsɔ spɔr'tivɔ]
bicycle trainer	cyclette (f)	[sik'lett]

treadmill	tapis roulant (m)	[tapiru'ʎan]
horizontal bar	sbarra (f)	['zbarra]
parallel bars	parallele (f pl)	[paral'lele]
vaulting horse	cavallo (m)	[ka'vallɔ]
mat (in gym)	materassino (m)	[matɛras'sinɔ]
skipping rope	corda (f) per saltare	['kɔrda pɛr saʎ'tarɛ]
aerobics	aerobica (f)	[aɛ'rɔbika]
yoga	yoga (m)	['jɔga]

135. Ice hockey

ice hockey	hockey (m)	['ɔkkɛj]
ice hockey player	hockeista (m)	[ɔkkɛ'ista]
to play ice hockey	giocare a hockey	[dʒɔ'karɛ a 'ɔkkɛj]
ice	ghiaccio (m)	['gjatʃɔ]
puck	disco (m)	['diskɔ]
ice hockey stick	bastone (m) da hockey	[bas'tɔnɛ da 'ɔkkɛj]
ice skates	pattini (m pl)	['pattini]
board	bordo (m)	['bɔrdɔ]
shot	tiro (m)	['tirɔ]
goaltender	portiere (m)	[por'tʲerɛ]
goal (score)	gol (m)	[gɔl]
to score a goal	segnare un gol	[sɛ'ɲarɛ un gɔl]
period	tempo (m)	['tɛmpɔ]
second period	secondo tempo (m)	[se'kɔndɔ 'tɛmrɔ]
substitutes bench	panchina (f)	[pa'ŋkina]

136. Football

football	calcio (m)	['kaʎtʃɔ]
football player	calciatore (m)	[kaʎtʃa'torɛ]
to play football	giocare a calcio	[dʒɔ'karɛ a 'kaʎtʃɔ]
major league	serie (f) A	['sɛriɛ a]
football club	società (f) calcistica	[sotʃɛ'ta kaʎ'tʃistika]
coach	allenatore (m)	[allena'torɛ]
owner, proprietor	proprietario (m)	[prɔpriɛ'tariɔ]
team	squadra (f)	[sku'adra]
team captain	capitano (m) di squadra	[kapi'tanɔ di sku'adra]
player	giocatore (m)	[dʒɔka'torɛ]
substitute	riserva (f)	[ri'sɛrva]
forward	attaccante (m)	[attak'kantɛ]
centre forward	centrocampista (m)	[tʃentrɔkam'pista]
striker, scorer	bomber (m)	['bɔmbɛr]
defender, back	terzino (m)	[tɛr'tsinɔ]

halfback	mediano (m)	[mɛdi'anɔ]
match	partita (f)	[par'tita]
to meet (vi, vt)	incontrarsi (vr)	[iŋkɔnt'rarsi]
final	finale (m)	[fi'nale]
semi-final	semifinale (m)	[sɛmifi'nale]
championship	campionato (m)	[kampiɔ'natɔ]

period, half	tempo (m)	['tɛmpɔ]
first period	primo tempo (m)	['primɔ 'tɛmpɔ]
half-time	intervallo (m)	[intɛr'vallɔ]

goal	porta (f)	['pɔrta]
goalkeeper	portiere (m)	[por't'erɛ]
goalpost	palo (m)	['palɔ]
crossbar	traversa (f)	[tra'vɛrsa]
net	rete (f)	['rɛtɛ]
to concede a goal	subire un gol	[su'birɛ un gɔl]

ball	pallone (m)	[pal'lɔnɛ]
pass	passaggio (m)	[pas'sadʒɔ]
kick	calcio (m), tiro (m)	['kaʎtʃɔ], ['tirɔ]
to kick (~ the ball)	tirare un calcio	[ti'rarɛ un 'kaʎtʃɔ]
free kick	calcio (m) di punizione	['kaʎtʃɔ di puni'ts'ɔnɛ]
corner kick	calcio (m) d'angolo	['kaʎtʃɔ 'daŋɔlɔ]

attack	attacco (m)	[at'takkɔ]
counterattack	contrattacco (m)	[kɔntrat'takkɔ]
combination	combinazione (f)	[kɔmbina'ts'ɔnɛ]

referee	arbitro (m)	['arbitrɔ]
to whistle (vi)	fischiare (vi)	[fis'kjarɛ]
whistle (sound)	fischio (m)	['fiskiɔ]
foul, misconduct	fallo (m)	['fallɔ]
to commit a foul	fare un fallo	['farɛ un 'fallɔ]
to send off	espellere dal campo	[ɛs'pɛllerɛ daʎ 'kampɔ]

yellow card	cartellino (m) giallo	[kartɛl'linɔ 'dʒallɔ]
red card	cartellino (m) rosso	[kartɛl'linɔ 'rɔssɔ]
disqualification	squalifica (f)	[skua'lifika]
to disqualify (vt)	squalificare (vt)	[skualifi'karɛ]

penalty kick	rigore (m)	[ri'gorɛ]
wall	barriera (f)	[bar'rjera]
to score (vi, vt)	segnare (vt)	[sɛ'ɲjarɛ]
goal (score)	gol (m)	[gɔl]
to score a goal	segnare un gol	[sɛ'ɲjarɛ un gɔl]

substitution	sostituzione (f)	[sɔstitu'ts'ɔnɛ]
to replace (vt)	sostituire (vt)	[sɔstitu'irɛ]
rules	regole (f pl)	['rɛgɔle]
tactics	tattica (f)	['tattika]

stadium	stadio (m)	['stadiɔ]
stand (at stadium)	tribuna (f)	[tri'buna]
fan, supporter	tifoso (m), fan (m)	[ti'fɔzɔ], [fan]
to shout (vi)	gridare (vi)	[gri'darɛ]

| scoreboard | tabellone (m) segnapunti | [tabɛl'lɔnɛ seɲja'punti] |
| score | punteggio (m) | [pun'tɛdʒɔ] |

defeat	sconfitta (f)	[skɔn'fitta]
to lose (not win)	perdere (vi)	['pɛrdɛrɛ]
draw	pareggio (m)	[pa'rɛdʒɔ]
to draw (vi)	pareggiare (vi)	[parɛ'dʒarɛ]

victory	vittoria (f)	[wit'tɔria]
to win (vi, vt)	vincere (vi)	['wintʃɛrɛ]
champion	campione (m)	[kampi'ɔnɛ]
best (adj)	migliore	[mi'ʎɔrɛ]
to congratulate (vt)	congratularsi (vr)	[kɔŋratu'ʎarsi]

commentator	commentatore (m)	[kɔmmɛnta'tɔrɛ]
to commentate (vt)	commentare (vt)	[kɔmmɛn'tarɛ]
broadcast	trasmissione (f)	[trazmissi'ɔnɛ]

137. Alpine skiing

skis	sci (m pl)	[ʃi]
to ski (vi)	sciare (vi)	[ʃi'arɛ]
mountain-ski resort	stazione (f) sciistica	[sta'tsʲonɛ ʃi'istika]
ski lift	sciovia (f)	[ʃiɔ'wia]

ski poles	bastoni (m pl) da sci	[bas'tɔni da ʃi]
slope	pendio (m)	[pɛn'diɔ]
slalom	slalom (m)	['zʎalɜm]

138. Tennis. Golf

golf	golf (m)	[gɔʎf]
golf club	golf club (m)	[gɔʎfk'lɛb]
golfer	golfista (m)	[gɔʎ'fista]
hole	buca (f)	['buka]
club	mazza (f) da golf	['matsa da gɔʎf]
golf trolley	carrello (m) da golf	[kar'rɛllɔ da gɔʎf]

tennis	tennis (m)	['tɛɲis]
tennis court	campo (m) da tennis	['kampɔ da 'tɛɲis]
serve	battuta (f)	[bat'tuta]
to serve (vt)	servire (vt)	[sɛr'wirɛ]
racket	racchetta (f)	[rak'kɛtta]
net	rete (f)	['rɛtɛ]
ball	palla (f)	['paʎa]

139. Chess

| chess | scacchi (m pl) | ['skakki] |
| chessmen | pezzi (m pl) degli scacchi | ['pɛtsi 'dɛʎi 'skakki] |

chess player	scacchista (m)	[skak'kista]
chessboard	scacchiera (f)	[skak'kjera]
chessman	pezzo (m)	['pɛtsɔ]

| White (white pieces) | Bianchi (m pl) | ['bjaŋki] |
| Black (black pieces) | Neri (m pl) | ['nɛri] |

pawn	pedina (f)	[pɛ'dina]
bishop	alfiere (m)	[aʎ'fjerɛ]
knight	cavallo (m)	[ka'vallɔ]
rook (castle)	torre (f)	['tɔrrɛ]
queen	regina (f)	[rɛ'dʒina]
king	re (m)	[rɛ]

move	mossa (m)	['mɔssa]
to move (vi, vt)	muovere (vt)	[mu'ɔvɛrɛ]
to sacrifice (vt)	sacrificare (vt)	[sakrifi'karɛ]
castling	arrocco (m)	[ar'rɔkkɔ]
check	scacco (m)	['skakkɔ]
checkmate	scacco matto (m)	['skakkɔ 'mattɔ]

chess tournament	torneo (m) di scacchi	[tɔr'nɛɔ di 'skakki]
Grand Master	gran maestro (m)	[gran ma'ɛstrɔ]
combination	combinazione (f)	[kɔmbina'tsʲɔnɛ]
game (in chess)	partita (f)	[par'tita]
draughts	dama (f)	['dama]

140. Boxing

boxing	pugilato (m), boxe (f)	[pudʒi'ʎatɔ], [bɔks]
fight (bout)	incontro (m)	[i'ŋkɔntrɔ]
boxing match	incontro (m) di boxe	[i'ŋkɔntrɔ di bɔks]
round (in boxing)	round (m)	['raund]

| ring | ring (m) | [riŋ] |
| gong | gong (m) | [gɔŋ] |

punch	pugno (m)	['puɲʲɔ]
knock-down	knock down (m)	[nɔk 'daun]
knockout	knock-out (m)	[nɔk 'aut]
to knock out	mettere knock-out	['mɛttɛrɛ nɔk 'aut]
boxing glove	guantone (m) da pugile	[guan'tɔnɛ da 'pudʒile]
referee	arbitro (m)	['arbitrɔ]

lightweight	peso (m) leggero	['pɛzɔ le'dʒɛrɔ]
middleweight	peso (m) medio	['pɛzɔ 'mɛdiɔ]
heavyweight	peso (m) massimo	['pɛzɔ 'massimɔ]

141. Sports. Miscellaneous

| Olympic Games | Giochi (m pl) Olimpici | ['dʒɔki ɔ'limpitʃi] |
| winner | vincitore (m) | [wintʃi'tɔrɛ] |

| to be winning | ottenere la vittoria | [otte'nɛrɛ ʎa wit'torija] |
| to win (vi) | vincere (vi) | ['wintʃerɛ] |

| leader | leader (m), capo (m) | ['lidɛr], ['kapo] |
| to lead (vi) | essere alla guida | ['ɛssɛrɛ 'aʎa gu'ida] |

first place	primo posto (m)	['primɔ 'pɔstɔ]
second place	secondo posto (m)	[sɛ'kɔndɔ 'pɔstɔ]
third place	terzo posto (m)	['tɛrtsɔ 'pɔstɔ]

medal	medaglia (f)	[mɛ'daʎja]
trophy	trofeo (m)	[trɔ'fɛɔ]
prize cup (trophy)	coppa (f)	['kɔppa]
prize (in game)	premio (m)	['prɛmiɔ]
main prize	primo premio (m)	['primɔ 'prɛmiɔ]

| record | record (m) | ['rɛkɔrd] |
| to set a record | stabilire un record | [stabi'lirɛ un 'rɛkɔrd] |

| final | finale (m) | [fi'nale] |
| final (adj) | finale | [fi'nale] |

| champion | campione (m) | [kampi'ɔnɛ] |
| championship | campionato (m) | [kampiɔ'natɔ] |

stadium	stadio (m)	['stadiɔ]
stand (at stadium)	tribuna (f)	[tri'buna]
fan, supporter	tifoso (m), fan (m)	[ti'fɔzɔ], [fan]
opponent, rival	avversario (m)	[avvɛr'sariɔ]

| start | partenza (f) | [par'tɛntsa] |
| finish line | traguardo (m) | [tragu'ardɔ] |

| defeat | sconfitta (f) | [skɔn'fitta] |
| to lose (not win) | perdere (vt) | ['pɛrdɛrɛ] |

referee	arbitro (m)	['arbitrɔ]
judges	giuria (f)	[dʒu'ria]
score	punteggio (m)	[pun'tɛdʒɔ]
draw	pareggio (m)	[pa'rɛdʒɔ]
to draw (vi)	pareggiare (vi)	[parɛ'dʒarɛ]
point	punto (m)	['puntɔ]
result (final score)	risultato (m)	[rizuʎ'tatɔ]

half-time	intervallo (m)	[intɛr'vallɔ]
doping	doping (m)	['dɔpiŋ]
to penalise (vt)	penalizzare (vt)	[penali'dzarɛ]
to disqualify (vt)	squalificare (vt)	[skualifi'karɛ]

apparatus	attrezzatura (f)	[attrɛtsa'tura]
javelin	giavellotto (m)	[dʒavɛl'lɔttɔ]
shot put ball	peso (m)	['pɛzɔ]
ball (snooker, etc.)	biglia (f)	['biʎja]

| aim (target) | obiettivo (m) | [ɔbjet'tivɔ] |
| target | bersaglio (m) | [bɛr'saʎɔ] |

to shoot (vi)	**sparare** (vi)	[spa'rarɛ]
precise (~ shot)	**preciso**	[prɛ'tʃizɔ]
trainer, coach	**allenatore** (m)	[allena'tɔrɛ]
to train (sb)	**allenare** (vt)	[alle'narɛ]
to train (vi)	**allenarsi** (vr)	[alle'narsi]
training	**allenamento** (m)	[allena'mɛntɔ]
gym	**palestra** (f)	[pa'lestra]
exercise (physical)	**esercizio** (m)	[ɛzɛr'tʃitsiɔ]
warm-up (of athlete)	**riscaldamento** (m)	[riskaʎda'mɛntɔ]

Education

142. School

school	scuola (f)	[sku'ɔʎa]
headmaster	direttore (m) di scuola	[diret'tɔrɛ di sku'ɔʎa]
pupil (boy)	allievo (m)	[a'ʎjevɔ]
pupil (girl)	allieva (f)	[a'ʎjeva]
schoolboy	scolaro (m)	[skɔ'ʎarɔ]
schoolgirl	scolara (f)	[skɔ'ʎara]
to teach (sb)	insegnare	[insɛ'ɲjarɛ]
to learn (language, etc.)	imparare (vt)	[impa'rarɛ]
to learn by heart	imparare a memoria	[impa'rarɛ a mɛ'mɔria]
to study (work to learn)	studiare (vi)	[studi'arɛ]
to be at school	frequentare la scuola	[frɛkuɛn'tarɛ la sku'ɔʎa]
to go to school	andare a scuola	[an'darɛ a sku'ɔʎa]
alphabet	alfabeto (m)	[aʎfa'bɛtɔ]
subject (at school)	materia (f)	[ma'tɛria]
classroom	classe (f)	['kʎassɛ]
lesson	lezione (f)	[le'tsʲɔnɛ]
playtime, break	ricreazione (f)	[rikrea'tsʲɔnɛ]
school bell	campanella (f)	[kampa'nɛʎa]
desk (for pupil)	banco (m)	['baŋkɔ]
blackboard	lavagna (f)	[ʎa'vaɲja]
mark	voto (m)	['vɔtɔ]
good mark	voto (m) alto	['vɔtɔ 'aʎtɔ]
bad mark	voto (m) basso	['vɔtɔ 'bassɔ]
to give a mark	dare un voto	['darɛ un 'vɔtɔ]
mistake	errore (m)	[ɛr'rɔrɛ]
to make mistakes	fare errori	['farɛ ɛr'rɔri]
to correct (an error)	correggere (vt)	[kɔr'rɛdʒerɛ]
crib	bigliettino (m)	[biʎjet'tinɔ]
homework	compiti (m pl)	['kɔmpiti]
exercise (in education)	esercizio (m)	[ɛzɛr'tʃitsiɔ]
to be present	essere presente	['ɛssɛrɛ prɛ'zɛntɛ]
to be absent	essere assente	['ɛssɛrɛ as'sɛntɛ]
to miss school	mancare le lezioni	[ma'ŋkarɛ le le'tsʲoni]
to punish (vt)	punire (vt)	[pu'nirɛ]
punishment	punizione (f)	[puni'tsʲɔnɛ]
conduct (behaviour)	comportamento (m)	[kɔmpɔrta'mɛntɔ]

school report	pagella (f)	[pa'dʒɛlla]
pencil	matita (f)	[ma'tita]
rubber	gomma (f) per cancellare	['gɔmma pɛr kantʃe'ʎarɛ]
chalk	gesso (m)	['dʒessɔ]
pencil case	astuccio (m) portamatite	[as'tutʃo portama'titɛ]

schoolbag	cartella (f)	[kar'tɛʎa]
pen	penna (f)	['pɛŋa]
exercise book	quaderno (m)	[kua'dɛrnɔ]
textbook	manuale (m)	[manu'ale]
compasses	compasso (m)	[kɔm'passɔ]

| to draw (a blueprint, etc.) | disegnare (vt) | [dizɛ'ɲjarɛ] |
| technical drawing | disegno (m) tecnico | [di'zɛɲɔ 'tɛknikɔ] |

poem	poesia (f)	[pɔɛ'zia]
by heart (adv)	a memoria	[a mɛ'mɔria]
to learn by heart	imparare a memoria	[impa'rarɛ a mɛ'mɔria]

school holidays	vacanze (f pl) scolastiche	[va'kantsɛ skɔ'ʎastikɛ]
to be on holiday	essere in vacanza	['ɛssɛrɛ in va'kantsa]
to spend holidays	passare le vacanze	[pas'sarɛ le va'kantsɛ]

test (at school)	prova (f) scritta	['prɔva 'skritta]
essay (composition)	composizione (f)	[kɔmpɔzi'tsʲɔnɛ]
dictation	dettato (m)	[dɛt'tatɔ]
exam	esame (m)	[ɛ'zamɛ]
to take an exam	sostenere un esame	[sɔstɛ'nɛmɛ un ɛ'zamɛ]
experiment (chemical ~)	esperimento (m)	[ɛspɛri'mɛntɔ]

143. College. University

academy	accademia (f)	[akka'dɛmia]
university	università (f)	[univɛrsi'ta]
faculty (section)	facoltà (f)	[fakɔʎ'ta]

student (masc.)	studente (m)	[stu'dɛntɛ]
student (fem.)	studentessa (f)	[studɛn'tɛssa]
lecturer (teacher)	docente (m, f)	[dɔ'tʃɛntɛ]

| lecture hall, room | aula (f) | ['auʎa] |
| graduate | diplomato (m) | [diplɔ'matɔ] |

| diploma | diploma (m) | [dip'lɔma] |
| dissertation | tesi (f) | ['tɛzi] |

| study (report) | ricerca (f) | [ri'tʃerka] |
| laboratory | laboratorio (m) | [ʎabɔra'tɔriɔ] |

| lecture | lezione (f) | [le'tsʲɔnɛ] |
| course mate | compagno (m) di corso | [kɔm'paɲɔ di 'kɔrsɔ] |

| scholarship | borsa (f) di studio | ['bɔrsa di 'studiɔ] |
| academic degree | titolo (m) accademico | ['titɔlɔ akka'dɛmikɔ] |

144. Sciences. Disciplines

mathematics	matematica (f)	[matɛ'matika]
algebra	algebra (f)	['aʎdʒebra]
geometry	geometria (f)	[dʒeɔmɛt'ria]
astronomy	astronomia (f)	[astronɔ'mia]
biology	biologia (f)	[biɔlɜ'dʒia]
geography	geografia (f)	[dʒeɔgra'fia]
geology	geologia (f)	[dʒeɔlɜ'dʒia]
history	storia (f)	['storia]
medicine	medicina (f)	[mɛdi'tʃina]
pedagogy	pedagogia (f)	[pɛdagɔ'dʒia]
law	diritto (m)	[di'rittɔ]
physics	fisica (f)	['fizika]
chemistry	chimica (f)	['kimika]
philosophy	filosofia (f)	[filɜzɔ'fia]
psychology	psicologia (f)	[psikɔlɜ'dʒia]

145. Writing system. Orthography

grammar	grammatica (f)	[gram'matika]
vocabulary	lessico (m)	['lessikɔ]
phonetics	fonetica (f)	[fɔ'nɛtika]
noun	sostantivo (m)	[sɔstan'tivɔ]
adjective	aggettivo (m)	[adʒet'tivɔ]
verb	verbo (m)	['vɛrbɔ]
adverb	avverbio (m)	[av'vɛrbiɔ]
pronoun	pronome (m)	[prɔ'nɔmɛ]
interjection	interiezione (f)	[intɛrje'tsɔnɛ]
preposition	preposizione (f)	[prɛpɔzi'tsɔnɛ]
root	radice (f)	[ra'ditʃe]
ending	desinenza (f)	[dɛzi'nɛntsa]
prefix	prefisso (m)	[prɛ'fissɔ]
syllable	sillaba (f)	['siʎaba]
suffix	suffisso (m)	[suf'fissɔ]
stress mark	accento (m)	[a'tʃentɔ]
apostrophe	apostrofo (m)	[a'postrofɔ]
full stop	punto (m)	['puntɔ]
comma	virgola (f)	['wirgɔʎa]
semicolon	punto (m) e virgola	['puntɔ ɛ 'wirgɔʎa]
colon	due punti	['duɛ 'punti]
ellipsis	puntini (m pl) di sospensione	[pun'tini di sɔspɛn'sɔnɛ]
question mark	punto (m) interrogativo	['puntɔ intɛrrɔga'tivɔ]
exclamation mark	punto (m) esclamativo	['puntɔ ɛskʎama'tivɔ]

inverted commas	virgolette (f pl)	[wirgɔ'lettɛ]
in inverted commas	tra virgolette	[tra wirgɔ'lettɛ]
parenthesis	parentesi (f pl)	[pa'rɛntɛzi]
in parenthesis	tra parentesi	[tra pa'rɛntɛzi]

hyphen	trattino (m)	[trat'tinɔ]
dash	lineetta (f)	[linɛ'ɛtta]
space (between words)	spazio (m)	['spatsiɔ]

| letter | lettera (f) | ['lettɛra] |
| capital letter | lettera (f) maiuscola | ['lettɛra ma'juskɔla] |

| vowel (n) | vocale (f) | [vɔ'kale] |
| consonant (n) | consonante (f) | [kɔnsɔ'nantɛ] |

sentence	proposizione (f)	[prɔpɔzi'tsʲɔnɛ]
subject	soggetto (m)	[sɔ'dʒettɔ]
predicate	predicato (m)	[prɛdi'katɔ]

line	riga (f)	['riga]
on a new line	a capo	[a 'kapɔ]
paragraph	capoverso (m)	[kapɔ'vɛrsɔ]

word	parola (f)	[pa'roʎa]
word group	gruppo (m) di parole	['gruppɔ di pa'rɔle]
expression	espressione (f)	[ɛsprɛssi'ɔnɛ]
synonym	sinonimo (m)	[si'nɔnimɔ]
antonym	antonimo (m)	[an'tɔnimɔ]

rule	regola (f)	['rɛgɔʎa]
exception	eccezione (f)	[ɛtʃe'tsʲɔnɛ]
correct (adj)	corretto	[kɔ'rɛttɔ]

conjugation	coniugazione (f)	[kɔɲjyga'tsʲɔnɛ]
declension	declinazione (f)	[dɛklina'tsʲɔnɛ]
nominal case	caso (m) nominativo	['kazɔ nɔmina'tivɔ]
question	domanda (f)	[dɔ'manda]
to underline (vt)	sottolineare (vt)	[sottolinɛ'arɛ]
dotted line	linea (f) tratteggiata	['linɛa trattɛ'dʒata]

146. Foreign languages

language	lingua (f)	['liŋua]
foreign (adj)	straniero	[stra'ɲjerɔ]
to study (vt)	studiare (vt)	[studi'arɛ]
to learn (language, etc.)	imparare (vt)	[impa'rarɛ]

to read (vi, vt)	leggere (vi, vt)	['ledʒerɛ]
to speak (vi, vt)	parlare (vi, vt)	[par'ʎarɛ]
to understand (vt)	capire (vt)	[ka'pirɛ]
to write (vt)	scrivere (vi, vt)	['skrivɛrɛ]

| fast (adv) | rapidamente | [rapida'mɛntɛ] |
| slowly (adv) | lentamente | [lenta'mɛntɛ] |

fluently (adv)	correntemente	[korrɛntɛ'mɛntɛ]
rules	regole (f pl)	['rɛgole]
grammar	grammatica (f)	[gram'matika]
vocabulary	lessico (m)	['lessiko]
phonetics	fonetica (f)	[fo'nɛtika]

textbook	manuale (m)	[manu'ale]
dictionary	dizionario (m)	[ditsʲo'nario]
teach-yourself book	manuale (m) autodidattico	[manu'ale autodi'dattiko]
phrasebook	frasario (m)	[fra'zario]

cassette	cassetta (f)	[kas'sɛtta]
videotape	videocassetta (f)	[widɛokas'sɛtta]
CD, compact disc	CD (m)	[tʃi'di]
DVD	DVD (m)	[divu'di]

alphabet	alfabeto (m)	[aʎfa'bɛto]
to spell (vt)	compitare (vt)	[kompi'tarɛ]
pronunciation	pronuncia (f)	[pro'nuntʃa]

accent	accento (m)	[a'tʃento]
with an accent	con un accento	[kon un a'tʃento]
without an accent	senza accento	['sɛntsa a'tʃento]

| word | vocabolo (m) | [vo'kabolo] |
| meaning | significato (m) | [siɲʲifi'kato] |

course (e.g. a French ~)	corso (m)	['korso]
to sign up	iscriversi (vr)	[isk'riversi]
teacher	insegnante (m, f)	[insɛ'ɲjantɛ]

translation (process)	traduzione (f)	[tradu'tsʲonɛ]
translation (text, etc.)	traduzione (f)	[tradu'tsʲonɛ]
translator	traduttore (m)	[tradut'torɛ]
interpreter	interprete (m)	[in'tɛrprɛtɛ]

| polyglot | poliglotta (m) | [polig'lɔtta] |
| memory | memoria (f) | [mɛ'moria] |

147. Fairy tale characters

Santa Claus	Babbo Natale (m)	['babbo na'tale]
Cinderella	Cenerentola (f)	[tʃenɛ'rɛntoʎa]
mermaid	sirena (f)	[si'rɛna]
Neptune	Nettuno (m)	[nɛt'tuno]

magician, wizard	mago (m)	['mago]
fairy	fata (f)	['fata]
magic (adj)	magico	['madʒiko]
magic wand	bacchetta (f) magica	[bak'kɛtta 'madʒika]

fairy tale	fiaba (f), favola (f)	['fjaba], ['favoʎa]
miracle	miracolo (m)	[mi'rakolo]
dwarf	nano (m)	['nano]

to turn into ...	trasformarsi in ...	[trasfor'marsi in]
ghost	fantasma (m)	[fan'tazma]
phantom	spettro (m)	['spɛttrɔ]
monster	mostro (m)	['mɔstrɔ]
dragon	drago (m)	['dragɔ]
giant	gigante (m)	[dʒi'gantɛ]

148. Zodiac Signs

Aries	Ariete (m)	[ari'ɛtɛ]
Taurus	Toro (m)	['tɔrɔ]
Gemini	Gemelli (m pl)	[dʒe'mɛlli]
Cancer	Cancro (m)	['kaŋkrɔ]
Leo	Leone (m)	[le'ɔnɛ]
Virgo	Vergine (f)	['vɛrdʒinɛ]

Libra	Bilancia (f)	[bi'ʎantʃa]
Scorpio	Scorpione (m)	[skɔr'pjɔnɛ]
Sagittarius	Sagittario (m)	[sadʒit'tarjɔ]
Capricorn	Capricorno (m)	[kapri'kɔrnɔ]
Aquarius	Acquario (m)	[aku'arjɔ]
Pisces	Pesci (m pl)	['pɛʃi]

character	carattere (m)	[ka'rattɛrɛ]
features of character	tratti (m pl) del carattere	['tratti dɛʎ ka'rattɛrɛ]
behaviour	comportamento (m)	[kɔmporta'mɛntɔ]
to tell fortunes	predire il futuro	[prɛ'dirɛ iʎ fu'turɔ]
fortune-teller	cartomante (f)	[kartɔ'mantɛ]
horoscope	oroscopo (m)	[ɔ'rɔskɔpɔ]

Arts

149. Theatre

theatre	teatro (m)	[tɛ'atrɔ]
opera	opera (f)	['ɔpɛra]
operetta	operetta (f)	[ɔpɛ'rɛtta]
ballet	balletto (m)	[bal'lettɔ]
playbill	cartellone (m)	[kartɛl'lɔnɛ]
theatrical company	compagnia (f) teatrale	[kɔmpa'nia tɛat'ralɛ]
tour	tournée (f)	[tur'nɛ]
to be on tour	andare in tournèe	[an'darɛ in tur'nɛ]
to rehearse (vi, vt)	fare le prove	['farɛ le 'prɔvɛ]
rehearsal	prova (f)	['prɔva]
repertoire	repertorio (m)	[rɛpɛr'tɔriɔ]
play	opera (f) teatrale	['ɔpɛra teat'ralɛ]
ticket	biglietto (m)	[bi'ʎjettɔ]
Box office	botteghino (m)	[bottɛ'ginɔ]
lobby, foyer	hall (m)	[ɔʎ]
coat check	guardaroba (f)	[guarda'rɔba]
cloakroom ticket	cartellino (m) del guardaroba	[kartɛl'linɔ deʎ guarda'rɔba]
binoculars	binocolo (m)	[bi'nɔkɔlɔ]
usher	maschera (f)	['maskɛra]
stalls	platea (f)	['pʎatɛa]
balcony	balconata (f)	[baʎkɔ'nata]
dress circle	prima galleria (f)	['prima galle'ria]
box	palco (m)	['paʎkɔ]
row	fila (f)	['fiʎa]
seat	posto (m)	['pɔstɔ]
audience	pubblico (m)	['pubblikɔ]
spectator	spettatore (m)	[spɛtta'tɔrɛ]
to clap (vi, vt)	battere le mani	['battɛrɛ le 'mani]
applause	applauso (m)	[app'ʎauzɔ]
ovation	ovazione (f)	[ova'ts'ɔnɛ]
stage	palcoscenico (m)	[paʎkɔ'ʃɛnikɔ]
curtain	sipario (m)	[si'pariɔ]
scenery	scenografia (f)	[ʃɛnɔgra'fia]
backstage	quinte (f pl)	[ku'intɛ]
scene (e.g. the last ~)	scena (f)	['ʃɛna]
act	atto (m)	['attɔ]
interval	intervallo (m)	[intɛr'vallɔ]

150. Cinema

actor	attore (m)	[at'tɔrɛ]
actress	attrice (f)	[att'ritʃe]
cinema (industry)	cinema (m)	['tʃinɛma]
film	film (m)	[fiʎm]
episode	puntata (f)	[pun'tata]
detective	film (m) giallo	[film 'dʒʲallɔ]
action film	film (m) d'azione	[fiʎm da'tsʲɔnɛ]
adventure film	film (m) d'avventure	[fiʎm davvɛn'turɛ]
science fiction film	film (m) di fantascienza	['fiʎm dɛ fanta'ʃɛntsa]
horror film	film (m) d'orrore	[fiʎm dɔr'rɔrɛ]
comedy film	film (m) comico	[fiʎm 'kɔmikɔ]
melodrama	melodramma (m)	[mɛlɜd'ramma]
drama	dramma (m)	['dramma]
fictional film	film (m) a soggetto	[fiʎm a sɔ'dʒettɔ]
documentary	documentario (m)	[dɔkumɛn'tariɔ]
cartoon	cartoni (m pl) animati	[kar'tɔni ani'mati]
silent films	cinema (m) muto	['tʃinɛma 'mutɔ]
role	parte (f)	['partɛ]
leading role	parte (f) principale	['partɛ printʃi'pale]
to play (vi, vt)	recitare (vi, vt)	[rɛtʃi'tarɛ]
film star	star (f), stella (f)	[star], ['stɛʎa]
well-known (adj)	noto	['nɔtɔ]
famous (adj)	famoso	[fa'mɔzɔ]
popular (adj)	popolare	[pɔpɔ'ʎarɛ]
script (screenplay)	sceneggiatura (m)	[ʃɛnɛdʒa'tura]
scriptwriter	sceneggiatore (m)	[ʃɛnɛdʒa'tɔrɛ]
film director	regista (m)	[rɛ'dʒista]
producer	produttore (m)	[prɔdut'tɔrɛ]
assistant	assistente (m)	[assis'tɛntɛ]
cameraman	cameraman (m)	[kamera'mɛn]
stuntman	controfigura (f)	[kɔntrɔfi'gura]
to shoot a film	girare un film	[dʒi'rarɛ un fiʎm]
audition, screen test	provino (m)	[prɔ'winɔ]
shooting	ripresa (f)	[rip'rɛza]
film crew	troupe (f) cinematografica	[trup tʃinɛmatɔg'rafika]
film set	set (m)	[sɛt]
camera	cinepresa (f)	[tʃinɛp'rɛza]
cinema	cinema (m)	['tʃinɛma]
screen (e.g. big ~)	schermo (m)	['skɛrmɔ]
to show a film	proiettare un film	[prɔjet'tarɛ un fiʎm]
soundtrack	colonna (f) sonora	[kɔ'lɜŋa sɔ'nɔra]
special effects	effetti (m pl) speciali	[ɛf'fɛtti spɛ'tʃali]
subtitles	sottotitoli (m pl)	[sɔttɔ'titɔli]

credits	**titoli** (m pl) **di coda**	['titoli di 'koda]
translation	**traduzione** (f)	[tradu'tsione]

151. Painting

art	**arte** (f)	['artε]
fine arts	**belle arti** (f pl)	['bεlle 'arti]
art gallery	**galleria** (f) **d'arte**	[galle'ria 'dartε]
art exhibition	**mostra** (f)	['mostra]
painting	**pittura** (f)	[pit'tura]
graphic art	**grafica** (f)	['grafika]
abstract art	**astrattismo** (m)	[astrat'tizmo]
impressionism	**impressionismo** (m)	[imprεssio'nizmo]
picture (painting)	**quadro** (m)	[ku'adro]
drawing	**disegno** (m)	[di'zεɲo]
poster	**cartellone** (m)	[kartεl'lonε]
illustration (picture)	**illustrazione** (f)	[illystra'tsione]
miniature	**miniatura** (f)	[minia'tura]
copy (of painting, etc.)	**copia** (f)	['kopia]
reproduction	**riproduzione** (f)	[riprodu'tsione]
mosaic	**mosaico** (m)	[mo'zaiko]
stained glass	**vetrata** (f)	[vεt'rata]
fresco	**affresco** (m)	[aff'rεsko]
engraving	**incisione** (f)	[intʃizi'onε]
bust (sculpture)	**busto** (m)	['busto]
sculpture	**scultura** (f)	[skuʎ'tura]
statue	**statua** (f)	['statua]
plaster of Paris	**gesso** (m)	['dʒesso]
plaster (as adj)	**in gesso**	[in 'dʒesso]
portrait	**ritratto** (m)	[rit'ratto]
self-portrait	**autoritratto** (m)	[autorit'ratto]
landscape	**paesaggio** (m)	[paε'zadʒo]
still life	**natura** (f) **morta**	[na'tura 'morta]
caricature	**caricatura** (f)	[karika'tura]
sketch	**abbozzo** (m)	[ab'botso]
paint	**colore** (m)	[ko'lorε]
watercolour	**acquerello** (m)	[akuε'rεllo]
oil (paint)	**olio** (m)	['oʎo]
pencil	**matita** (f)	[ma'tita]
Indian ink	**inchiostro** (m) **di china**	[in'kiostro di 'kina]
charcoal	**carbone** (m)	[kar'bonε]
to draw (vi, vt)	**disegnare** (vt)	[dizε'ɲarε]
to paint (vi, vt)	**dipingere** (vt)	[di'pindʒerε]
to pose (vi)	**posare** (vi)	[po'zarε]
artist's model (masc.)	**modello** (m)	[mo'dεllo]

artist's model (fem.)	modella (f)	[mɔ'dɛʎa]
artist (painter)	pittore (m)	[pit'tɔrɛ]
work of art	opera (f) d'arte	['ɔpɛra 'dartɛ]
masterpiece	capolavoro (m)	[kapoʎa'vorɔ]
workshop (of artist)	laboratorio (m)	[ʎabora'tɔriɔ]

canvas (cloth)	tela (f)	['tɛʎa]
easel	cavalletto (m)	[kaval'lettɔ]
palette	tavolozza (f)	[tavo'lɔʦa]

frame (of picture, etc.)	cornice (f)	[kor'niʧe]
restoration	restauro (m)	[rɛs'tauro]
to restore (vt)	restaurare (vt)	[rɛstau'rarɛ]

152. Literature & Poetry

literature	letteratura (f)	[lettɛra'tura]
author (writer)	autore (m)	[au'tɔrɛ]
pseudonym	pseudonimo (m)	[psɛu'dɔnimɔ]

book	libro (m)	['librɔ]
volume	volume (m)	[vo'lymɛ]
table of contents	sommario (m), indice (m)	[sɔm'mariɔ], ['indiʧɛ]
page	pagina (f)	['paʤina]
main character	protagonista (m)	[prɔtago'nista]
autograph	autografo (m)	[au'tɔgrafɔ]

short story	racconto (m)	[rak'kɔntɔ]
story (novella)	romanzo (m) breve	[rɔ'manʣɔ 'brɛvɛ]
novel	romanzo (m)	[rɔ'manʣɔ]
work (writing)	opera (f)	['ɔpɛra]
fable	favola (f)	['favoʎa]
detective novel	giallo (m)	['ʤallɔ]

poem (verse)	verso (m)	['vɛrsɔ]
poetry	poesia (f)	[poɛ'zia]
poem (epic, ballad)	poema (m)	[po'ɛma]
poet	poeta (m)	[po'ɛta]

fiction	narrativa (f)	[narra'tiva]
science fiction	fantascienza (f)	[fanta'ʃɛnʦa]
adventures	avventure (f pl)	[avvɛn'turɛ]
educational literature	letteratura (f) formativa	[lettɛra'tura forma'tiva]
children's literature	libri (m pl) per l'infanzia	['libri per lin'fansia]

153. Circus

circus	circo (m)	['ʧirkɔ]
big top (circus)	tendone (m) del circo	[tɛn'dɔnɛ dɛʎ 'ʧirkɔ]
programme	programma (m)	[prog'ramma]
performance	spettacolo (m)	[spɛt'takolɔ]
act (circus ~)	numero (m)	['numɛrɔ]

circus ring	arena (f)	[aˈrɛna]
pantomime (act)	pantomima (m)	[pantɔˈmima]
clown	pagliaccio (m)	[paˈʎjatʃɔ]

acrobat	acrobata (m)	[akˈrɔbata]
acrobatics	acrobatica (f)	[akrɔˈbatika]
gymnast	ginnasta (m)	[dʒiˈŋasta]
gymnastics	ginnastica (m)	[dʒiˈŋastika]
somersault	salto (m) mortale	[ˈsaʎtɔ mɔrˈtale]

strongman	forzuto (m)	[forˈtsutɔ]
animal-tamer	domatore (m)	[dɔmaˈtɔrɛ]
equestrian	cavallerizzo (m)	[kavalleˈridzɔ]
assistant	assistente (m)	[assisˈtɛntɛ]

stunt	acrobazia (f)	[akrɔbaˈtsia]
magic trick	gioco (m) di prestigio	[ˈdʒɔkɔ di prɛsˈtidʒɔ]
conjurer, magician	prestigiatore (m)	[prɛstidʒaˈtɔrɛ]

juggler	giocoliere (m)	[dʒɔkɔˈʎjerɛ]
to juggle (vi, vt)	giocolare (vi)	[dʒɔkɔˈʎarɛ]
animal trainer	ammaestratore (m)	[ammaɛstraˈtɔrɛ]
animal training	ammaestramento (m)	[ammaɛstraˈmɛntɔ]
to train (animals)	ammaestrare (vt)	[ammaɛstˈrarɛ]

154. Music. Pop music

music	musica (f)	[ˈmuzika]
musician	musicista (m)	[muziˈtʃista]
musical instrument	strumento (m) musicale	[struˈmɛntɔ musiˈkale]
to play ...	suonare ...	[suɔˈnarɛ]

guitar	chitarra (f)	[kiˈtarra]
violin	violino (m)	[wiɔˈlinɔ]
cello	violoncello (m)	[wiɔlɔnˈtʃellɔ]
double bass	contrabbasso (m)	[kɔntrabˈbassɔ]
harp	arpa (f)	[ˈarpa]

piano	pianoforte (m)	[pjanɔˈfɔrtɛ]
grand piano	pianoforte (m) a coda	[pjanɔˈfɔrtɛ a ˈkɔda]
organ	organo (m)	[ˈɔrganɔ]

wind instruments	strumenti (m pl) a fiato	[struˈmɛnti a ˈfjatɔ]
oboe	oboe (m)	[ˈɔbɔɛ]
saxophone	sassofono (m)	[sasˈsɔfɔnɔ]
clarinet	clarinetto (m)	[kʎariˈnɛttɔ]
flute	flauto (m)	[ˈfʎautɔ]
trumpet	tromba (f)	[ˈtrɔmba]

| accordion | fisarmonica (f) | [fizarˈmɔnika] |
| drum | tamburo (m) | [tamˈburɔ] |

| duo | duetto (m) | [duˈɛttɔ] |
| trio | trio (m) | [ˈtriɔ] |

quartet	quartetto (m)	[kuar'tɛtto]
choir	coro (m)	['kɔrɔ]
orchestra	orchestra (f)	[ɔr'kɛstra]
pop music	musica (f) pop	['muzika pɔp]
rock music	musica (f) rock	['muzika rɔk]
rock group	gruppo (m) rock	['gruppɔ rɔk]
jazz	jazz (m)	[dʒaz]
idol	idolo (m)	['idɔlɔ]
admirer, fan	ammiratore (m)	[ammira'tɔrɛ]
concert	concerto (m)	[kɔn'tʃertɔ]
symphony	sinfonia (f)	[sinfo'nia]
composition	composizione (f)	[kɔmpozi'tsɩɔnɛ]
to compose (write)	comporre (vt)	[kɔm'pɔrrɛ]
singing	canto (m)	['kantɔ]
song	canzone (f)	[kan'tsɔnɛ]
tune (melody)	melodia (f)	[mɛlɔ'dia]
rhythm	ritmo (m)	['ritmɔ]
blues	blues (m)	[blyz]
sheet music	note (f pl)	['nɔtɛ]
baton	bacchetta (f)	[bak'kɛtta]
bow	arco (m)	['arkɔ]
string	corda (f)	['kɔrda]
case (e.g. guitar ~)	custodia (f)	[kus'tɔdia]

Rest. Entertainment. Travel

155. Trip. Travel

tourism	turismo (m)	[tu'rizmo]
tourist	turista (m)	[tu'rista]
trip, voyage	viaggio (m)	['vjadʒo]
adventure	avventura (f)	[avvɛn'tura]
trip, journey	viaggio (m)	['vjadʒo]
holiday	vacanza (f)	[va'kantsa]
to be on holiday	essere in vacanza	['ɛssɛrɛ in va'kantsa]
rest	riposo (m)	[ri'pozo]
train	treno (m)	['trɛno]
by train	in treno	[in 'trɛno]
aeroplane	aereo (m)	[a'ɛrɛo]
by aeroplane	in aereo	[in a'ɛrɛo]
by car	in macchina	[in 'makkina]
by ship	in nave	[in 'navɛ]
luggage	bagaglio (m)	[ba'gaʎo]
suitcase, luggage	valigia (f)	[va'lidʒa]
luggage trolley	carrello (m)	[kar'rɛllo]
passport	passaporto (m)	[passa'porto]
visa	visto (m)	['wisto]
ticket	biglietto (m)	[bi'ʎjetto]
air ticket	biglietto (m) aereo	[bi'ʎjetto a'ɛrɛo]
guidebook	guida (f)	[gu'ida]
map	carta (f) geografica	['karta dʒeog'rafika]
area (rural ~)	località (f)	[lokali'ta]
place, site	luogo (m)	[ly'ogo]
exotica	ogetti (m pl) esotici	[o'dʒetti ɛ'zotitʃi]
exotic (adj)	esotico	[ɛ'zotiko]
amazing (adj)	sorprendente	[sorprɛn'dɛntɛ]
group	gruppo (m)	['gruppo]
excursion	escursione (f)	[ɛskursi'onɛ]
guide (person)	guida (f)	[gu'ida]

156. Hotel

hotel, inn	battaglia (f)	[bat'taʎja]
hotel	albergo, hotel (m)	[aʎ'bɛrgo], [o'tɛʎ]
motel	motel (m)	[mo'tɛʎ]

three-star (adj)	tre stelle	['trɛ 'stɛlle]
five-star	cinque stelle	['ʧiŋkuɛ 'stɛlle]
to stay (in hotel, etc.)	alloggiare (vi)	[allɔ'ʤarɛ]

room	camera (f)	['kamɛra]
single room	camera (f) singola	['kamɛra 'siŋɔʎa]
double room	camera (f) doppia	['kamɛra 'dɔppia]
to book a room	prenotare una camera	[prɛnɔ'tarɛ una 'kamera]

| half board | mezza pensione (f) | ['mɛʣa pɛnsi'ɔnɛ] |
| full board | pensione (f) completa | [pɛnsi'ɔnɛ kɔmp'leta] |

with bath	con bagno	[kɔn 'baɲɔ]
with shower	con doccia	[kɔn 'dɔʧa]
satellite television	televisione (f) satellitare	[tɛlewizi'ɔnɛ satɛlli'tarɛ]
air-conditioner	condizionatore (m)	[kɔndiʦiona'tɔrɛ]
towel	asciugamano (m)	[aʃuga'manɔ]
key	chiave (f)	['kjavɛ]

administrator	amministratore (m)	[amministra'tɔrɛ]
chambermaid	cameriera (f)	[kamɛ'rjera]
porter, bellboy	portabagagli (m)	[pɔrtaba'gaʎi]
doorman	portiere (m)	[pɔr'tʲerɛ]

restaurant	ristorante (m)	[ristɔ'rantɛ]
pub, bar	bar (m)	[bar]
breakfast	colazione (f)	[kɔʎa'ʦʲonɛ]
dinner	cena (f)	['ʧena]
buffet	buffet (m)	[buf'fɛ]

| lobby | hall (f) | [ɔʎ] |
| lift | ascensore (m) | [aʃɛn'sɔrɛ] |

| DO NOT DISTURB | NON DISTURBARE | [nɔn distur'barɛ] |
| NO SMOKING | VIETATO FUMARE! | [vje'tatɔ fu'marɛ] |

157. Books. Reading

book	libro (m)	['librɔ]
author	autore (m)	[au'tɔrɛ]
writer	scrittore (m)	[skrit'tɔrɛ]
to write (~ a book)	scrivere (vi, vt)	['skrivɛrɛ]

reader	lettore (m)	[let'tɔrɛ]
to read (vi, vt)	leggere (vi, vt)	['ledʒɛrɛ]
reading (activity)	lettura (f)	[let'tura]

| silently (to oneself) | in silenzio | [in si'lenʦio] |
| aloud (adv) | ad alta voce | [ad 'aʎta 'vɔʧe] |

to publish (vt)	pubblicare (vt)	[pubbli'karɛ]
publishing (process)	pubblicazione (f)	[publika'ʦʲonɛ]
publisher	editore (m)	[ɛdi'tɔrɛ]
publishing house	casa (f) editrice	['kaza ɛdit'riʧe]

to come out	**uscire** (vi)	[u'ʃirɛ]
release (of a book)	**uscita** (f)	[u'ʃita]
print run	**tiratura** (f)	[tira'tura]
bookshop	**libreria** (f)	[librɛ'ria]
library	**biblioteca** (f)	[biblio'tɛka]
story (novella)	**romanzo** (m) **breve**	[ro'mandzo 'brɛvɛ]
short story	**racconto** (m)	[rak'konto]
novel	**romanzo** (m)	[ro'mandzo]
detective novel	**giallo** (m)	['dʒallo]
memoirs	**memorie** (f pl)	[mɛ'moriɛ]
legend	**leggenda** (f)	[le'dʒenda]
myth	**mito** (m)	['mito]
poetry, poems	**poesia** (f), **versi** (m pl)	[poɛ'zia], ['vɛrsi]
autobiography	**autobiografia** (f)	[autobiogra'fia]
selected works	**opere** (f pl) **scelte**	['opɛrɛ 'ʃɛʎtɛ]
science fiction	**fantascienza** (f)	[fanta'ʃɛntsa]
title	**titolo** (m)	['titolo]
introduction	**introduzione** (f)	[introdu'tsɨonɛ]
title page	**frontespizio** (m)	[frontɛs'pitsɨo]
chapter	**capitolo** (m)	[ka'pitolo]
extract	**frammento** (m)	[fram'mɛnto]
episode	**episodio** (m)	[ɛpi'zodio]
plot (storyline)	**soggetto** (m)	[so'dʒetto]
contents	**contenuto** (m)	[kontɛ'nuto]
table of contents	**sommario** (m)	[som'mario]
main character	**protagonista** (m)	[protago'nista]
volume	**volume** (m)	[vo'lymɛ]
cover	**copertina** (f)	[kopɛr'tina]
binding	**rilegatura** (f)	[rilega'tura]
bookmark	**segnalibro** (m)	[sɛɲja'libro]
page	**pagina** (f)	['padʒina]
to flick through	**sfogliare** (vt)	[sfo'ʎjarɛ]
margins	**margini** (m pl)	['mardʒini]
annotation	**annotazione** (f)	[aɲota'tsɨonɛ]
footnote	**nota** (f)	['nota]
text	**testo** (m)	['tɛsto]
type, fount	**carattere** (m)	[ka'rattɛrɛ]
misprint, typo	**refuso** (m)	[rɛ'fuzo]
translation	**traduzione** (f)	[tradu'tsɨonɛ]
to translate (vt)	**tradurre** (vt)	[tra'durrɛ]
original (n)	**originale** (m)	[oridʒi'nale]
famous (adj)	**famoso**	[fa'mozo]
unknown (adj)	**sconosciuto**	[skono'ʃuto]
interesting (adj)	**interessante**	[intɛrɛs'santɛ]

bestseller	best seller (m)	[bes'tsɛller]
dictionary	dizionario (m)	[ditsɔ'narɔ]
textbook	manuale (m)	[manu'ale]
encyclopedia	enciclopedia (f)	[entʃiklɔpɛ'dia]

158. Hunting. Fishing

hunt (of animal)	caccia (f)	['katʃa]
to hunt (vi, vt)	cacciare (vt)	[ka'tʃarɛ]
hunter	cacciatore (m)	[katʃa'torɛ]

to shoot (vi)	sparare (vi)	[spa'rarɛ]
rifle	fucile (m)	[fu'tʃile]
bullet (cartridge)	cartuccia (f)	[kar'tutʃa]
shotgun pellets	pallini (m pl)	[pal'lini]

trap (e.g. bear ~)	tagliola (f)	[ta'ʎɔʎa]
snare (for birds, etc.)	trappola (f)	['trappɔʎa]
to fall into the trap	cadere in trappola	[ka'dɛrɛ in 'trappɔʎa]
to lay a trap	tendere una trappola	['tɛndɛrɛ una 'trappɔʎa]

poacher	bracconiere (m)	[brakkɔ'njɛrɛ]
game (in hunting)	cacciagione (m)	[katʃa'dʒɔnɛ]
hound	cane (m) da caccia	['kanɛ da 'katʃa]
safari	safari (m)	[sa'fari]
mounted animal	animale (m) impagliato	[ani'male impa'ʎjatɔ]

fisherman	pescatore (m)	[pɛska'torɛ]
fishing	pesca (f)	['pɛska]
to fish (vi)	pescare (vi)	[pɛs'karɛ]

fishing rod	canna (f) da pesca	['kaɲa da 'pɛska]
fishing line	lenza (f)	['lentsa]
hook	amo (m)	['amɔ]
float	galleggiante (m)	[galle'dʒantɛ]
bait	esca (f)	['ɛska]

| to cast a line | lanciare la canna | [ʎan'tʃarɛ ʎa 'kaɲa] |
| to bite (ab. fish) | abboccare (vi) | [abbɔk'karɛ] |

| catch (of fish) | pescato (m) | [pɛs'katɔ] |
| ice-hole | buco (m) nel ghiaccio | ['bukɔ nɛʎ 'gjatʃɔ] |

| net | rete (f) | ['rɛtɛ] |
| boat | barca (f) | ['barka] |

to net (catch with net)	prendere con la rete	['prɛndɛrɛ kɔn ʎa 'rɛtɛ]
to cast the net	gettare la rete	[dʒet'tarɛ ʎa 'rɛtɛ]
to haul in the net	tirare le reti	[ti'rarɛ le 'rɛti]
to fall into the net	cadere nella rete	[ka'dɛrɛ 'nɛʎa 'rɛtɛ]

whaler (person)	baleniere (m)	[bale'njɛrɛ]
whaler (vessel)	baleniera (f)	[bale'njera]
harpoon	rampone (m)	[ram'ponɛ]

159. Games. Billiards

billiards	biliardo (m)	[bi'ʎardɔ]
billiard room, hall	sala (f) da biliardo	['saʎa da bi'ʎardɔ]
ball	bilia (f)	['bilia]
to pocket a ball	imbucare (vt)	[imbu'karɛ]
cue	stecca (f) da biliardo	['stɛkka da bi'ʎardɔ]
pocket	buca (f)	['buka]

160. Games. Playing cards

diamonds	quadri (m pl)	[ku'adri]
spades	picche (f pl)	['pikkɛ]
hearts	cuori (m pl)	[ku'ɔri]
clubs	fiori (m pl)	['fɔri]
ace	asso (m)	['assɔ]
king	re (m)	[rɛ]
queen	donna (f)	['dɔɲa]
jack, knave	fante (m)	['fantɛ]
playing card	carta (f) da gioco	['karta da 'dʒɔkɔ]
cards	carte (f pl)	['kartɛ]
trump	briscola (f)	['briskɔʎa]
pack of cards	mazzo (m) di carte	['matsɔ di 'kartɛ]
point	punto (m)	['puntɔ]
to deal (vi, vt)	dare le carte	['darɛ le 'kartɛ]
to shuffle (cards)	mescolare (vt)	[mɛskɔ'ʎarɛ]
lead, turn (n)	turno (m)	['turnɔ]
cardsharp	baro (m)	['barɔ]

161. Casino. Roulette

casino	casinò (m)	[kazi'nɔ]
roulette (game)	roulette (f)	[ru'lett]
bet, stake	puntata (f)	[pun'tata]
to place bets	puntare su ...	[pun'tarɛ su]
red	rosso	['rɔssɔ]
black	nero (m)	['nɛrɔ]
to bet on red	puntare sul rosso	[pun'tarɛ suʎ 'rɔssɔ]
to bet on black	puntare sul nero	[pun'tarɛ suʎ 'nɛrɔ]
croupier (dealer)	croupier (m)	[kru'pje]
to turn the wheel	far girare la ruota	[far dʒi'rarɛ ʎa ru'ɔta]
rules (of game)	regole (f pl) del gioco	['rɛgɔle dɛʎ 'dʒɔkɔ]
chip	fiche (f)	[fiʃ]
to win (vi, vt)	vincere (vi, vt)	['wintʃerɛ]
winnings	vincita (f)	['wintʃita]

| to lose (~ 100 dollars) | perdere (vt) | ['pɛrdɛrɛ] |
| loss | perdita (f) | ['pɛrdita] |

player	giocatore (m)	[dʒɔka'tɔrɛ]
blackjack (card game)	black jack (m)	[blɛk dʒek]
game of dice	gioco (m) dei dadi	[dʒi'ɔkɔ dɛi 'dadi]
dice	dadi (m pl)	['dadi]
fruit machine	slot machine (f)	[zlɔt ma'ʃin]

162. Rest. Games. Miscellaneous

to take a walk	passeggiare (vi)	[passɛ'dʒarɛ]
walk, stroll	passeggiata (f)	[passɛ'dʒata]
road trip	gita (f)	['dʒita]
adventure	avventura (f)	[avvɛn'tura]
picnic	picnic (m)	['piknik]

game (chess, etc.)	gioco (m)	['dʒɔkɔ]
player	giocatore (m)	[dʒɔka'tɔrɛ]
game (one ~ of chess)	partita (f)	[par'tita]

collector (e.g. philatelist)	collezionista (m)	[kɔlletsio'nista]
to collect (vt)	collezionare (vt)	[kɔlletsio'narɛ]
collection	collezione (f)	[kɔlle'tsᴉɔnɛ]

crossword puzzle	cruciverba (m)	[krutʃi'vɛrba]
racecourse (hippodrome)	ippodromo (m)	[ip'pɔdromɔ]
discotheque	discoteca (f)	[diskɔ'tɛka]

| sauna | sauna (f) | ['sauna] |
| lottery | lotteria (f) | [lɔttɛ'ria] |

camping trip	campeggio (m)	[kam'pɛdʒɔ]
camp	campo (m)	['kampɔ]
tent (for camping)	tenda (f) da campeggio	['tɛnda da kam'pɛdʒɔ]
compass	bussola (f)	['bussɔʎa]
camper	campeggiatore (m)	[kampɛdʒa'tɔrɛ]

to watch (film, etc.)	guardare (vt)	[guar'darɛ]
viewer	telespettatore (m)	[tɛlespɛtta'tɔrɛ]
TV program	trasmissione (f)	[trazmissi'ɔnɛ]

163. Photography

| camera (photo) | macchina (f) fotografica | ['makkina fɔtɔg'rafika] |
| photo, picture | fotografia (f) | [fɔtɔgra'fia] |

photographer	fotografo (m)	[fɔ'tɔgrafɔ]
photo studio	studio (m) fotografico	['studio fɔtɔg'rafikɔ]
photo album	album (m) di fotografie	['aʎbum di fɔtɔgra'fiɛ]
camera lens	obiettivo (m)	[ɔbjet'tivɔ]
telephoto lens	teleobiettivo (m)	[tɛleobjet'tivɔ]

| filter | filtro (m) | ['fiʌtrɔ] |
| lens | lente (f) | ['lentɛ] |

optics (high-quality ~)	ottica (f)	['ɔttika]
diaphragm (aperture)	diaframma (m)	[diaf'ramma]
exposure time	tempo (m) di esposizione	['tɛmpɔ di ɛspɔzi'tsʲɔnɛ]
viewfinder	mirino (m)	[mi'rinɔ]

digital camera	fotocamera (f) digitale	[fotɔ'kamɛra didʒi'tale]
tripod	cavalletto (m)	[kaval'lettɔ]
flash	flash (m)	['flɛʃ]

to photograph (vt)	fotografare (vt)	[fotogra'farɛ]
to take pictures	fare foto	['farɛ 'fotɔ]
to be photographed	farsi fotografare	['farsi fotogra'farɛ]

focus	fuoco (m)	[fu'ɔkɔ]
to adjust the focus	mettere a fuoco	['mɛttɛrɛ a fu'ɔkɔ]
sharp, in focus (adj)	nitido	['nitidɔ]
sharpness	nitidezza (f)	[niti'dɛtsa]

| contrast | contrasto (m) | [kont'rastɔ] |
| contrasty (adj) | contrastato | [kontras'tatɔ] |

picture (photo)	foto (f)	['fotɔ]
negative (n)	negativa (f)	[nɛga'tiva]
film (a roll of ~)	pellicola (f) fotografica	[pɛl'likɔʎa fotog'rafika]
frame (still)	fotogramma (m)	[fotog'ramma]
to print (photos)	stampare (vt)	[stam'parɛ]

164. Beach. Swimming

beach	spiaggia (f)	['spjadʒa]
sand	sabbia (f)	['sabbja]
deserted (beach)	deserto	[dɛ'zɛrtɔ]

suntan	abbronzatura (f)	[abbrondza'tura]
to get a tan	abbronzarsi (vr)	[abbron'dzarsi]
tanned (adj)	abbronzato	[abbron'dzatɔ]
sunscreen	crema (f) solare	['krɛma sɔ'ʎarɛ]

bikini	bikini (m)	[bi'kini]
swimsuit, bikini	costume (m) da bagno	[kɔs'tumɛ da 'baɲɔ]
swim trunks	slip (m) da bagno	[zlip da 'baɲɔ]

swimming pool	piscina (f)	[pi'ʃina]
to swim (vi)	nuotare (vi)	[nuɔ'tarɛ]
shower	doccia (f)	['dotʃa]
to change (one's clothes)	cambiarsi (vr)	[kam'bjarsi]
towel	asciugamano (m)	[aʃuga'manɔ]

boat	barca (f)	['barka]
motorboat	motoscafo (m)	[motɔs'kafɔ]
water ski	sci (m) nautico	[ʃi 'nautikɔ]

pedalo	**pedalò** (m)	[pɛda'lɔ]
surfing	**surf** (m)	[sɛrf]
surfer	**surfista** (m)	[sur'fista]

scuba set	**autorespiratore** (m)	[autɔrɛspira'tɔrɛ]
flippers (swimfins)	**pinne** (f pl)	['pinɛ]
mask	**maschera** (f)	['maskɛra]
diver	**subacqueo** (m)	[su'bakvɛɔ]
to dive (vi)	**tuffarsi** (vr)	[tuf'farsi]
underwater (adv)	**sott'acqua**	[sɔ'takva]

beach umbrella	**ombrellone** (m)	[ɔmbrɛl'lɔnɛ]
beach chair	**sdraio** (f)	['zdrajo]
sunglasses	**occhiali** (m pl) **da sole**	[ɔk'kjali da 'sɔle]
air mattress	**materasso** (m) **ad aria**	[matɛ'rassɔ ad 'aria]

to play (amuse oneself)	**giocare** (vi)	[dʒɔ'karɛ]
to go for a swim	**fare il bagno**	['farɛ iʎ 'baɲɔ]

beach ball	**pallone** (m)	[pal'lɔnɛ]
to inflate (vt)	**gonfiare** (vt)	[gɔn'fjarɛ]
inflatable, air (adj)	**gonfiabile**	[gɔnfi'jabile]

wave	**onda** (f)	['ɔnda]
buoy	**boa** (f)	['bɔa]
to drown (ab. person)	**annegare** (vi)	[anɛ'garɛ]

to save, to rescue	**salvare** (vt)	[saʎ'varɛ]
lifejacket	**giubbotto** (m) **di salvataggio**	[dʒub'bɔttɔ di saʎva'tadʒɔ]
to observe, to watch	**osservare** (vt)	[ɔssɛr'varɛ]
lifeguard	**bagnino** (m)	[ba'ɲ'inɔ]

TECHNICAL EQUIPMENT. TRANSPORT

Technical equipment

165. Computer

computer	computer (m)	[kɔm'pjytɛr]
notebook, laptop	computer (m) portatile	[kɔm'pjytɛr pɔr'tatile]
to switch on	accendere (vt)	[a'tʃendɛrɛ]
to turn off	spegnere (vt)	['spɛɲjerɛ]
keyboard	tastiera (f)	[tas'tⁱera]
key	tasto (m)	['tastɔ]
mouse	mouse (m)	['maus]
mouse mat	tappetino (m) del mouse	[tap'pɛtinɔ dɛʎ 'maus]
button	tasto (m)	['tastɔ]
cursor	cursore (m)	[kur'sɔrɛ]
monitor	monitor (m)	['mɔnitɔr]
screen	schermo (m)	['skɛrmɔ]
hard disk	disco (m) rigido	['diskɔ 'ridʒidɔ]
hard disk volume	spazio (m) sul disco rigido	['spatsiɔ suʎ 'diskɔ 'ridʒidɔ]
memory	memoria (f)	[mɛ'mɔria]
random access memory	memoria (f) operativa	[mɛ'mɔria ɔpɛra'tiva]
file	file (m)	[fajl]
folder	cartella (f)	[kar'tɛʎa]
to open (vt)	aprire (vt)	[ap'rirɛ]
to close (vt)	chiudere (vt)	['kjydɛrɛ]
to save (vt)	salvare (vt)	[saʎ'varɛ]
to delete (vt)	eliminare (vt)	[ɛlimi'narɛ]
to copy (vt)	copiare (vt)	[kɔ'pjarɛ]
to sort (vt)	ordinare (vt)	[ɔrdi'narɛ]
to transfer (copy)	trasferire (vt)	[trasfɛ'rirɛ]
programme	programma (m)	[prɔg'ramma]
software	software (m)	['sɔftvɛa]
programmer	programmatore (m)	[prɔgramma'tɔrɛ]
to program (vt)	programmare (vt)	[prɔgram'marɛ]
hacker	hacker (m)	['akɛr]
password	password (f)	['passvɔrd]
virus	virus (m)	['wirus]
to find, to detect	trovare (vt)	[trɔ'varɛ]
byte	byte (m)	[bajt]

megabyte	megabyte (m)	['mɛgabajt]
data	dati (m pl)	['dati]
database	database (m)	['databɛjz]

cable (wire)	cavo (m)	['kavɔ]
to disconnect (vt)	sconnettere (vt)	[skɔ'ŋɛttɛrɛ]
to connect (sth to sth)	collegare (vt)	[kɔlle'garɛ]

166. Internet. E-mail

Internet	internet (m)	['intɛrnɛt]
browser	navigatore (m)	[nawiga'tɔrɛ]
search engine	motore (m) di ricerca	[mɔ'tɔrɛ di ri'tʃerka]
provider	provider (m)	[prɔ'vajdɛr]

web master	webmaster (m)	[uɛb'mastɛr]
website	sito web (m)	['sitɔ uɛb]
web page	pagina web (f)	['padʒina uɛb]

address	indirizzo (m)	[indi'ritsɔ]
address book	rubrica (f) indirizzi	[rub'rika indi'ritsi]

postbox	casella (f) di posta	[ka'zella di 'pɔsta]
post	posta (f)	['pɔsta]
full (adj)	battaglia (f)	[bat'taʎja]

message	messaggio (m)	[mes'sadʒɔ]
sender	mittente (m)	[mit'tɛntɛ]
to send (vt)	inviare (vt)	[inwi'arɛ]
sending (of mail)	invio (m)	[in'wiɔ]

receiver	destinatario (m)	[dɛstina'tariɔ]
to receive (vt)	ricevere (vt)	[ri'tʃevɛrɛ]

correspondence	corrispondenza (f)	[kɔrrispɔn'dɛntsa]
to correspond (vi)	essere in corrispondenza	['ɛssɛrɛ in kɔrrispɔn'dɛntsa]

file	file (m)	[fajl]
to download (vt)	scaricare (vt)	[skari'karɛ]
to create (vt)	creare (vt)	[krɛ'arɛ]
to delete (vt)	eliminare (vt)	[ɛlimi'narɛ]
deleted (adj)	eliminato	[ɛlimi'natɔ]

connection (ADSL, etc.)	connessione (f)	[kɔŋɛ's|ɔnɛ]
speed	velocità (f)	[vɛlɔtʃi'ta]
modem	modem (m)	['mɔdem]
access	accesso (m)	[a'tʃessɔ]
port (e.g. input ~)	porta (f)	['pɔrta]

connection (make a ~)	collegamento (m)	[kɔllega'mɛntɔ]
to connect (vi)	collegarsi a ...	[kɔlle'garsi a]

to select (vt)	scegliere (vt)	['ʃeʎjerɛ]
to search (for ...)	cercare (vt)	[tʃer'karɛ]

167. Electricity

electricity	elettricità (f)	[ɛlettriʧi'ta]
electrical (adj)	elettrico	[ɛ'lettriko]
electric power station	centrale (f) elettrica	[ʧent'rale ɛ'lettrika]
energy	energia (f)	[ɛnɛr'dʒia]
electric power	energia (f) elettrica	[ɛnɛr'dʒia ɛ'lettrika]
light bulb	lampadina (f)	[ʎampa'dina]
torch	torcia (f) elettrica	['tɔrʧa ɛ'lettrika]
street light	lampione (m)	[lam'pʲɔnɛ]
light	luce (f)	['lyʧe]
to turn on	accendere (vt)	[a'ʧendɛrɛ]
to turn off	spegnere (vt)	['spɛɲjerɛ]
to turn off the light	spegnere la luce	['spɛɲjerɛ ʎa 'lyʧe]
to burn out (vi)	fulminarsi (vr)	[fuʎmi'narsi]
short circuit	corto circuito (m)	['kɔrtɔ ʧir'kuitɔ]
broken wire	rottura (f)	[rɔt'tura]
contact	contatto (m)	[kɔn'tattɔ]
light switch	interruttore (m)	[intɛrrut'tɔrɛ]
socket outlet	presa (f) elettrica	['prɛza ɛ'lettrika]
plug	spina (f)	['spina]
extension lead	prolunga (f)	[prɔ'lyŋa]
fuse	fusibile (m)	[fu'zibile]
cable, wire	filo (m)	['filɔ]
wiring	impianto (m) elettrico	[impi'jantɔ ɛ'lettrikɔ]
ampere	ampere (m)	[am'pɛrɛ]
amperage	intensità di corrente	[intɛnsi'ta di kɔr'rɛntɛ]
volt	volt (m)	[vɔʎt]
voltage	tensione (f)	[tɛnsi'ɔnɛ]
electrical device	apparecchio (m) elettrico	[appa'rɛkkʲɔ ɛ'lettrikɔ]
indicator	indicatore (m)	[indika'tɔrɛ]
electrician	elettricista (m)	[ɛlettri'ʧista]
to solder (vt)	saldare (vt)	[saʎ'darɛ]
soldering iron	saldatoio (m)	[saʎda'tɔjo]
electric current	corrente (f)	[kɔr'rɛntɛ]

168. Tools

tool, instrument	utensile (m)	[utɛn'sile]
tools	utensili (m pl)	[utɛn'sili]
equipment (factory ~)	impianto (m)	[im'pjantɔ]
hammer	martello (m)	[mar'tɛllɔ]
screwdriver	giravite (m)	[dʒira'witɛ]
axe	ascia (f)	['aʃa]

saw	**sega** (f)	['sɛga]
to saw (vt)	**segare** (vt)	[sɛ'garɛ]
plane (tool)	**pialla** (f)	['pjaʎa]
to plane (vt)	**piallare** (vt)	[pja'ʎarɛ]
soldering iron	**saldatoio** (m)	[saʎda'tojo]
to solder (vt)	**saldare** (vt)	[saʎ'darɛ]
file (for metal)	**lima** (f)	['lima]
carpenter pincers	**tenaglie** (f pl)	[tɛ'naʎje]
combination pliers	**pinza** (f) **a punte piatte**	['pintsa a 'puntɛ 'pjattɛ]
chisel	**scalpello** (m)	[skaʎ'pɛllo]
drill bit	**punta** (f) **da trapano**	['punta da 'trapano]
electric drill	**trapano** (m) **elettrico**	['trapano ɛ'lettriko]
to drill (vi, vt)	**trapanare** (vt)	[trapa'narɛ]
knife	**coltello** (m)	[koʎ'tɛllo]
pocket knife	**temperino** (m)	[tɛmpɛ'rino]
folding (knife, etc.)	**pieghevole**	[pje'gɛvole]
blade	**lama** (f)	['ʎama]
sharp (blade, etc.)	**affilato**	[affi'ʎato]
blunt (adj)	**smussato**	[zmu'sato]
to become blunt	**smussarsi** (vr)	[zmus'sarsi]
to sharpen (vt)	**affilare** (vt)	[affi'ʎarɛ]
bolt	**bullone** (m)	[bul'lɔnɛ]
nut	**dado** (m)	['dado]
thread (of a screw)	**filettatura** (f)	[filetta'tura]
wood screw	**vite** (f)	['witɛ]
nail	**chiodo** (m)	[ki'ɔdɔ]
nailhead	**testa** (f) **di chiodo**	['tɛsta di ki'ɔdɔ]
ruler (for measuring)	**regolo** (m)	['rɛgolo]
tape measure	**nastro** (m) **metrico**	['nastro 'mɛtriko]
spirit level	**livella** (f)	[li'vella]
magnifying glass	**lente** (f) **d'ingradimento**	['lɛntɛ diŋrandi'mɛnto]
measuring instrument	**strumento** (m) **di misurazione**	[stru'mɛnto di mizura'tsʲɔnɛ]
to measure (vt)	**misurare** (vt)	[mizu'rarɛ]
scale (of thermometer, etc.)	**scala** (f) **graduata**	['skaʎa gradu'ata]
readings	**lettura, indicazione** (f)	[let'tura], [indika'tsʲɔnɛ]
compressor	**compressore** (m)	[komprɛs'sɔrɛ]
microscope	**microscopio** (m)	[mikrɔs'kɔpiɔ]
pump (e.g. water ~)	**pompa** (f)	['pompa]
robot	**robot** (m)	[rɔ'bɔ]
laser	**laser** (m)	['ʎazer]
spanner	**chiave** (f)	['kjavɛ]
adhesive tape	**nastro** (m) **adesivo**	['nastro adɛ'zivo]
glue	**colla** (f)	['koʎa]
emery paper	**carta** (f) **smerigliata**	['karta zmɛri'ʎjata]

spring	molla (f)	['mɔʎa]
magnet	magnete (m)	[ma'ɲjetɛ]
gloves	guanti (m pl)	[gu'anti]

rope	corda (f)	['kɔrda]
cord	cordone (m)	[kor'donɛ]
wire (e.g. telephone ~)	filo (m)	['filɔ]
cable	cavo (m)	['kavɔ]

sledgehammer	mazza (f)	['matsa]
crowbar	palanchino (m)	[paʎa'ŋkinɔ]
ladder	scala (f) a pioli	['skaʎa a pi'ɔli]
stepladder	scala (m) a libretto	['skaʎa a lib'rɛttɔ]

to screw (tighten)	avvitare (vt)	[avvi'tarɛ]
to unscrew, untwist (vt)	svitare (vt)	[zwi'tarɛ]
to tighten (vt)	stringere (vt)	['strindʒerɛ]
to glue, to stick	incollare (vt)	[iŋko'ʎarɛ]
to cut (vt)	tagliare (vt)	[ta'ʎʲarɛ]

malfunction (fault)	guasto (m)	[gu'astɔ]
repair (mending)	riparazione (f)	[ripara'tsʲonɛ]
to repair, to mend (vt)	riparare (vt)	[ripa'rarɛ]
to adjust (machine, etc.)	regolare (vt)	[rɛgo'ʎarɛ]

to check (to examine)	verificare (vt)	[vɛrifi'karɛ]
checking	controllo (m)	[kont'rollɔ]
readings	lettura, indicazione (f)	[let'tura], [indika'tsʲonɛ]

| reliable (machine) | sicuro | [si'kurɔ] |
| complicated (adj) | complesso | [komp'lessɔ] |

to rust (vi)	arrugginire (vi)	[arrudʒi'nirɛ]
rusty (adj)	arrugginito	[arrudʒi'nitɔ]
rust	ruggine (f)	['rudʒinɛ]

Transport

169. Aeroplane

aeroplane	aereo (m)	[a'ɛrɛɔ]
air ticket	biglietto (m) aereo	[bi'ʎjettɔ a'ɛrɛɔ]
airline	compagnia (f) aerea	[kɔmpa'nia a'ɛrɛa]
airport	aeroporto (m)	[aɛrɔ'pɔrtɔ]
supersonic (adj)	supersonico	[supɛr'sɔnikɔ]
captain	comandante (m)	[kɔman'dantɛ]
crew	equipaggio (m)	[ɛkui'padʒɔ]
pilot	pilota (m)	[pi'lɔta]
stewardess	hostess (f)	['ɔstɛss]
navigator	navigatore (m)	[nawiga'tɔrɛ]
wings	ali (f pl)	['ali]
tail	coda (f)	['kɔda]
cockpit	cabina (f)	[ka'bina]
engine	motore (m)	[mɔ'tɔrɛ]
undercarriage	carrello (m) d'atterraggio	[kar'rɛllɔ dattɛr'radʒɔ]
turbine	turbina (f)	[tur'bina]
propeller	elica (f)	['ɛlika]
black box	scatola (f) nera	['skatɔʎa 'nɛra]
control column	barra (f) di comando	['barra di kɔ'mandɔ]
fuel	combustibile (m)	[kɔmbus'tibile]
safety card	safety card (f)	['sɛjfti kard]
oxygen mask	maschera (f) ad ossigeno	['maskɛra ad ɔs'sidʒenɔ]
uniform	uniforme (f)	[uni'fɔrmɛ]
lifejacket	giubbotto (m) di salvataggio	[dʒub'bɔttɔ di saʎva'tadʒɔ]
parachute	paracadute (m)	[paraka'dutɛ]
takeoff	decollo (m)	[dɛ'kɔllɔ]
to take off (vi)	decollare (vi)	[dɛkɔ'ʎarɛ]
runway	pista (f) di decollo	['pista di dɛ'kɔllɔ]
visibility	visibilità (f)	[wizibili'ta]
flight (act of flying)	volo (m)	['vɔlɔ]
altitude	altitudine (f)	[aʎti'tudinɛ]
air pocket	vuoto (m) d'aria	[vu'ɔtɔ 'daria]
seat	posto (m)	['pɔstɔ]
headphones	cuffia (f)	['kuffˈa]
folding tray	tavolinetto (m) pieghevole	[tavɔli'nɛttɔ pje'gɛvole]
airplane window	oblò (m), finestrino (m)	[ɔb'lɔ], [finest'rinɔ]
aisle	corridoio (m)	[kɔrri'dɔjɔ]

170. Train

train	**treno** (m)	['trɛnɔ]
suburban train	**elettrotreno** (m)	[ɛlettrɔt'rɛnɔ]
fast train	**treno** (m) **rapido**	['trɛnɔ 'rapidɔ]
diesel locomotive	**locomotiva** (f) **diesel**	[lɔkɔmɔ'tiva 'dizɛʎ]
steam engine	**locomotiva** (f) **a vapore**	[lɔkɔmɔ'tiva a va'pɔrɛ]
coach, carriage	**carrozza** (f)	[kar'rɔtsa]
restaurant car	**vagone** (m) **ristorante**	[va'gɔnɛ ristɔ'rantɛ]
rails	**rotaie** (f pl)	[rɔ'taje]
railway	**ferrovia** (f)	[fɛrrɔ'wia]
sleeper (track support)	**traversa** (f)	[tra'vɛrsa]
platform (railway ~)	**banchina** (f)	[ba'ŋkina]
platform (~ 1, 2, etc.)	**binario** (m)	[bi'nariɔ]
semaphore	**semaforo** (m)	[sɛ'mafɔrɔ]
station	**stazione** (f)	[sta'tsɔnɛ]
train driver	**macchinista** (m)	[makki'nista]
porter (of luggage)	**portabagagli** (m)	[portaba'gaʎi]
train steward	**cuccettista** (m, f)	[kutʃet'tista]
passenger	**passeggero** (m)	[passɛ'dʒerɔ]
ticket inspector	**controllore** (m)	[kɔntrɔl'lɔrɛ]
corridor (in train)	**corridoio** (m)	[kɔrri'dojo]
emergency break	**freno** (m) **di emergenza**	['frɛnɔ di ɛmɛr'dʒentsa]
compartment	**scompartimento** (m)	[skɔmparti'mɛntɔ]
berth	**cuccetta** (f)	[ku'tʃetta]
upper berth	**cuccetta** (f) **superiore**	[ku'tʃetta supɛri'ɔrɛ]
lower berth	**cuccetta** (f) **inferiore**	[ku'tʃetta infɛri'ɔrɛ]
linen	**biancheria** (f) **da letto**	[biaŋke'ria da 'lɛttɔ]
ticket	**biglietto** (m)	[bi'ʎjettɔ]
timetable	**orario** (m)	[ɔ'rariɔ]
information display	**tabellone** (m) **orari**	[tabɛl'lɔnɛ ɔ'rari]
to leave, to depart	**partire** (vi)	[par'tirɛ]
departure (of train)	**partenza** (f)	[par'tentsa]
to arrive (ab. train)	**arrivare** (vi)	[arri'varɛ]
arrival	**arrivo** (m)	[ar'rivɔ]
to arrive by train	**arrivare con il treno**	[arri'varɛ kɔn iʎ 'trɛnɔ]
to get on the train	**salire sul treno**	[sa'lirɛ suʎ 'trɛnɔ]
to get off the train	**scendere dal treno**	['ʃendɛrɛ daʎ 'trɛnɔ]
train crash	**deragliamento** (m)	[dɛraʎja'mɛntɔ]
to be derailed	**deragliare** (vi)	[dɛra'ʎjarɛ]
steam engine	**locomotiva** (f) **a vapore**	[lɔkɔmɔ'tiva a va'pɔrɛ]
stoker, fireman	**fuochista** (m)	[fɔ'kista]
firebox	**forno** (m)	['fɔrnɔ]
coal	**carbone** (m)	[kar'bɔnɛ]

171. Ship

| ship | nave (f) | ['navɛ] |
| vessel | imbarcazione (f) | [imbarka'tsjonɛ] |

steamship	piroscafo (m)	[pi'rɔskafɔ]
riverboat	barca (f) fluviale	['barka fluwi'jale]
ocean liner	transatlantico (m)	[transat'lantikɔ]
cruiser	incrociatore (m)	[iŋkrɔtʃa'tɔrɛ]

yacht	yacht (m)	[jot]
tugboat	rimorchiatore (m)	[rimɔrkja'tɔrɛ]
barge	chiatta (f)	['kjatta]
ferry	traghetto (m)	[tra'gɛttɔ]

| sailing ship | veliero (m) | [vɛ'ʎjerɔ] |
| brigantine | brigantino (m) | [brigan'tinɔ] |

| ice breaker | rompighiaccio (m) | [rɔmpi'gjatʃɔ] |
| submarine | sottomarino (m) | [sɔttɔma'rinɔ] |

boat (flat-bottomed ~)	barca (f)	['barka]
dinghy	scialuppa (f)	[ʃa'luppa]
lifeboat	scialuppa (f) di salvataggio	[ʃa'lyppa di saʎva'tadʒɔ]
motorboat	motoscafo (m)	[mɔtɔs'kafɔ]

captain	capitano (m)	[kapi'tanɔ]
seaman	marittimo (m)	[ma'rittimɔ]
sailor	marinaio (m)	[mari'najo]
crew	equipaggio (m)	[ɛkui'padʒɔ]

boatswain	nostromo (m)	[nɔst'rɔmɔ]
ship's boy	mozzo (m) di nave	['mɔtsɔ di 'navɛ]
cook	cuoco (m)	[ku'ɔkɔ]
ship's doctor	medico (m) di bordo	['mɛdikɔ di 'bɔrdɔ]

deck	ponte (m)	['pɔntɛ]
mast	albero (m)	['aʎbɛrɔ]
sail	vela (f)	['vɛʎa]

hold	stiva (f)	['stiva]
bow (prow)	prua (f)	['prua]
stern	poppa (f)	['pɔppa]
oar	remo (m)	['rɛmɔ]
propeller	elica (f)	['ɛlika]

cabin	cabina (f)	[ka'bina]
wardroom	quadrato (m) degli ufficiali	[kuad'ratɔ dɛlli uffi'tʃali]
engine room	sala (f) macchine	['saʎa 'makkinɛ]
bridge	ponte (m) di comando	['pɔntɛ di kɔ'mandɔ]
radio room	cabina (f) radiotelegrafica	[ka'bina radiotɛleg'rafika]
wave (radio)	onda (f)	['ɔnda]
logbook	giornale (m) di bordo	[dʒɔr'nale di 'bɔrdɔ]
spyglass	cannocchiale (m)	[kaŋɔk'kjale]
bell	campana (f)	[kam'pana]

flag	bandiera (f)	[ban'djera]
rope (mooring ~)	cavo (m) d'ormeggio	['kavɔ dor'medʒɔ]
knot (bowline, etc.)	nodo (m)	['nɔdɔ]

| handrail | ringhiera (f) | [riŋ'ʲera] |
| gangway | passerella (f) | [passɛ'rɛʎa] |

anchor	ancora (f)	['aŋkɔra]
to weigh anchor	levare l'ancora	[le'varɛ 'ʎaŋkɔra]
to drop anchor	gettare l'ancora	[dʒet'tarɛ 'ʎaŋkɔra]
anchor chain	catena (f) dell'ancora	[ka'tɛna dɛʎ 'aŋkɔra]

port (harbour)	porto (m)	['pɔrtɔ]
wharf, quay	banchina (f)	[ba'ŋkina]
to berth (moor)	ormeggiarsi (vr)	[ɔrmɛ'dʒarsi]
to cast off	salpare (vi)	[saʎ'parɛ]

trip, voyage	viaggio (m)	['vjadʒɔ]
cruise (sea trip)	crociera (f)	[krɔ'tʃera]
course (route)	rotta (f)	['rɔtta]
route (itinerary)	itinerario (m)	[itinɛ'rariɔ]

fairway	tratto (m) navigabile	['trattɔ nawi'gabile]
shallows (shoal)	secca (f)	['sɛkka]
to run aground	arenarsi (vr)	[arɛ'narsi]

storm	tempesta (f)	[tɛm'pɛsta]
signal	segnale (m)	[sɛ'ɲjale]
to sink (vi)	affondare (vi)	[affon'darɛ]
Man overboard!	Uomo in mare!	[u'omɔ in 'marɛ]
SOS	SOS	['ɛssɛ ɔ 'ɛssɛ]
ring buoy	salvagente (m) anulare	[saʎva'dʒɛntɛ anu'larɛ]

172. Airport

airport	aeroporto (m)	[aɛrɔ'pɔrtɔ]
aeroplane	aereo (m)	[a'ɛrɛɔ]
airline	compagnia (f) aerea	[kɔmpa'nia a'ɛrɛa]
air-traffic controller	controllore (m) di volo	[kɔntrɔl'lɔrɛ di 'vɔlɔ]

departure	partenza (f)	[par'tɛntsa]
arrival	arrivo (m)	[ar'rivɔ]
to arrive (by plane)	arrivare (vi)	[arri'varɛ]

| departure time | ora (f) di partenza | ['ɔra di par'tɛntsa] |
| arrival time | ora (f) di arrivo | ['ɔra di ar'rivɔ] |

| to be delayed | essere ritardato | ['ɛssɛrɛ ritar'datɔ] |
| flight delay | volo (m) ritardato | ['vɔlɔ ritar'datɔ] |

information board	tabellone (m) orari	[tabɛl'lɔnɛ ɔ'rari]
information	informazione (f)	[informa'tsʲonɛ]
to announce (vt)	annunciare (vt)	[aɲun'tʃarɛ]
flight (e.g. next ~)	volo (m)	['vɔlɔ]

| customs | dogana (f) | [dɔ'gana] |
| customs officer | doganiere (m) | [dɔga'njerɛ] |

customs declaration	dichiarazione (f)	[dikjara'tsɨɔnɛ]
to fill in the declaration	riempire una dichiarazione	[riɛm'pirɛ una dikjara'tsɨɔnɛ]
passport control	controllo (m) passaporti	[kɔnt'rɔllɔ passa'pɔrti]

luggage	bagaglio (m)	[ba'gaʎɔ]
hand luggage	bagaglio (m) a mano	[ba'gaʎɔ a 'manɔ]
Lost Luggage Desk	Assistenza bagagli	[asis'tɛntsa ba'gaʎi]
luggage trolley	carrello (m)	[kar'rɛllɔ]

landing	atterraggio (m)	[attɛr'radʒɔ]
landing strip	pista (f) di atterraggio	['pista di attɛr'radʒɔ]
to land (vi)	atterrare (vi)	[attɛr'rarɛ]
airstairs	scaletta (f) dell'aereo	[ska'letta dɛʎ a'ɛrɛɔ]

check-in	check-in (m)	[ʧɛ'kin]
check-in desk	banco (m) del check-in	['baŋkɔ dɛʎ ʧɛ'kin]
to check-in (vi)	fare il check-in	['farɛ iʎ ʧɛ'kin]
boarding pass	carta (f) d'imbarco	['karta dim'barkɔ]
departure gate	porta (f) d'imbarco	['pɔrta dim'barkɔ]

transit	transito (m)	['tranzitɔ]
to wait (vt)	aspettare (vt)	[aspɛt'tarɛ]
departure lounge	sala (f) d'attesa	['saʎa dat'tɛza]
to see off	accompagnare (vt)	[akkɔmpa'ɲarɛ]
to say goodbye	congedarsi (vr)	[kɔndʒe'darsi]

173. Bicycle. Motorcycle

bicycle	bicicletta (f)	[biʧik'letta]
scooter	motorino (m)	[mɔtɔ'rinɔ]
motorbike	motocicletta (f)	[mɔtɔʧik'letta]

to go by bicycle	andare in bicicletta	[an'darɛ in biʧik'letta]
handlebars	manubrio (m)	[ma'nubriɔ]
pedal	pedale (m)	[pɛ'dale]
brakes	freni (m pl)	['frɛni]
saddle	sellino (m)	[sel'linɔ]

pump	pompa (f)	['pɔmpa]
luggage rack	portabagagli (m)	[pɔrtaba'gaʎi]
front lamp	fanale (m) anteriore	[fa'nalɛ antɛri'ɔrɛ]
helmet	casco (m)	['kaskɔ]

wheel	ruota (f)	[ru'ɔta]
mudguard	parafango (m)	[para'faŋɔ]
rim	cerchione (m)	[ʧer'kjɔnɛ]
spoke	raggio (m)	['radʒɔ]

Cars

174. Types of cars

car	automobile (f)	[auto'mobile]
sports car	auto (f) sportiva	['auto spor'tiva]
limousine	limousine (f)	[limu'zin]
off-road vehicle	fuoristrada (m)	[fuorist'rada]
convertible	cabriolet (m)	[kabrio'le]
minibus	pulmino (m)	[puʎ'mino]
ambulance	ambulanza (f)	[ambu'ʎantsa]
snowplough	spazzaneve (m)	[spatsa'nɛvɛ]
lorry	camion (m)	['kamion]
road tanker	autocisterna (f)	[autoʧis'tɛrna]
van (small truck)	furgone (m)	[fur'gonɛ]
road tractor	motrice (f)	[mot'riʧɛ]
trailer	rimorchio (m)	[ri'morkio]
comfortable (adj)	confortevole	[konfor'tɛvole]
second hand (adj)	di seconda mano	[di sɛ'konda 'mano]

175. Cars. Bodywork

bonnet	cofano (m)	['kofano]
wing	parafango (m)	[para'faŋo]
roof	tetto (m)	['tɛtto]
windscreen	parabrezza (m)	[parab'rɛdza]
rear-view mirror	retrovisore (m)	[rɛtrowi'zorɛ]
windscreen washer	lavacristallo (m)	[ʎava kris'tallo]
windscreen wipers	tergicristallo (m)	[tɛrdʒi kris'tallo]
side window	finestrino (m) laterale	[finɛst'rino ʎatɛ'rale]
window lift	alzacristalli (m)	[aʎtsakris'talli]
aerial	antenna (f)	[an'tɛŋa]
sun roof	tettuccio (m) apribile	[tɛt'tuʧo ap'ribile]
bumper	paraurti (m)	[para'urti]
boot	bagagliaio (m)	[baga'ʎjajo]
door	portiera (f)	[por'tiera]
door handle	maniglia (f)	[ma'niʎja]
door lock	serratura (f)	[sɛrra'tura]
number plate	targa (f)	['targa]
silencer	marmitta (f)	[mar'mitta]

| petrol tank | serbatoio (m) della benzina | [serba'tojo deʎa ben'dzina] |
| exhaust pipe | tubo (m) di scarico | ['tubɔ di 'skarikɔ] |

accelerator	acceleratore (m)	[atʃelera'tɔrɛ]
pedal	pedale (m)	[pɛ'dale]
accelerator pedal	pedale (m) dell'acceleratore	[pe'dalɛ dɛlatʃelera'tɔrɛ]

brake	freno (m)	['frɛnɔ]
brake pedal	pedale (m) del freno	[pɛ'dale dɛʎ 'frɛnɔ]
to slow down (to brake)	frenare (vi)	[frɛ'narɛ]
handbrake	freno (m) a mano	['frɛnɔ a 'manɔ]

clutch	frizione (f)	[fri'tsʲɔnɛ]
clutch pedal	pedale (m) della frizione	[pɛ'dale 'dɛʎa fri'tsʲɔnɛ]
clutch plate	disco (m) della frizione	['diskɔ 'dɛʎa fri'tsʲɔnɛ]
shock absorber	ammortizzatore (m)	[ammɔrtidza'tɔrɛ]

wheel	ruota (f)	[ru'ɔta]
spare tyre	ruota (f) di scorta	[ru'ɔta di 'skɔrta]
wheel cover (hubcap)	copriruota (m)	[kɔpriru'ɔta]

driving wheels	ruote (f pl) motrici	[ru'ɔtɛ mɔt'ritʃi]
front-wheel drive (as adj)	a trazione anteriore	[a tra'tsʲɔnɛ anteri'ɔrɛ]
rear-wheel drive (as adj)	a trazione posteriore	[a tra'tsʲɔnɛ pɔsteri'ɔrɛ]
all-wheel drive (as adj)	a trazione integrale	[a tra'tsʲɔnɛ integ'rale]

gearbox	scatola (f) del cambio	[ska'tɔla dɛʎ 'kambiɔ]
automatic (adj)	automatico	[autɔ'matikɔ]
mechanical (adj)	meccanico	[mɛk'kanikɔ]
gear lever	leva (f) del cambio	['leva dɛʎ 'kambʲɔ]

| headlight | faro (m) | ['farɔ] |
| headlights | luci (f pl), fari (m pl) | ['lytʃi], ['fari] |

dipped headlights	luci (f pl) anabbaglianti	['lytʃi anabba'ʎjanti]
full headlights	luci (f pl) abbaglianti	['lytʃi abba'ʎjanti]
brake light	luci (f pl) di arresto	['lytʃi di ar'rɛstɔ]

sidelights	luci (f pl) di posizione	['lytʃi di pɔzi'tsʲɔnɛ]
hazard lights	luci (f pl) di emergenza	['lytʃi di ɛmɛr'dʒɛntsa]
fog lights	fari (m pl) antinebbia	['fari anti'nɛbbia]
turn indicator	freccia (f)	['frɛtʃa]
reversing light	luci (f pl) di retromarcia	['lytʃi di rɛtrɔ'martʃa]

176. Cars. Passenger compartment

car inside	abitacolo (m)	[abi'takɔlɔ]
leather (as adj)	di pelle	[di 'pɛlle]
velour (as adj)	in velluto	[in vɛl'lytɔ]
upholstery	rivestimento (m)	[rivɛsti'mɛntɔ]

instrument (gage)	strumento (m) di bordo	[stru'mentɔ di 'bɔrdɔ]
dashboard	cruscotto (m)	[krus'kɔttɔ]
speedometer	tachimetro (m)	[ta'kimetrɔ]

needle (pointer)	lancetta (f)	[ʎanˈtʃetta]
mileometer	contachilometri (m)	[kɔntakiˈlɜmɛtri]
indicator (sensor)	indicatore (m)	[indikaˈtɔrɛ]
level	livello (m)	[liˈvɛllɔ]
warning light	spia (f) luminosa	[ˈspia lymiˈnɔza]

steering wheel	volante (m)	[vɔˈʎantɛ]
horn	clacson (m)	[ˈkʎaksɔn]
button	pulsante (m)	[puʎˈsantɛ]
switch	interruttore (m)	[intɛrrutˈtɔrɛ]

seat	sedile (m)	[sɛˈdile]
seat back	spalliera (f)	[spaˈʎjera]
headrest	appoggiatesta (m)	[appodʒaˈtɛsta]
seat belt	cintura (f) di sicurezza	[tʃinˈtura di sikuˈrɛtsa]
to fasten the belt	allacciare la cintura	[aʎaˈtʃarɛ ʎa tʃinˈtura]
adjustment (of seats)	regolazione (f)	[rɛgoʎaˈtsʲɔnɛ]

| airbag | airbag (m) | [ˈɛjrbɛg] |
| air-conditioner | condizionatore (m) | [kɔnditsionaˈtɔrɛ] |

radio	radio (f)	[ˈradiɔ]
CD player	lettore (m) CD	[letˈtɔrɛ tʃiˈdi]
to turn on	accendere (vt)	[aˈtʃendɛrɛ]
aerial	antenna (f)	[anˈtɛŋa]
glove box	vano (m) portaoggetti	[ˈvanɔ portaɔˈdʒetti]
ashtray	portacenere (m)	[portaˈtʃenɛrɛ]

177. Cars. Engine

motor	motore (m)	[mɔˈtɔrɛ]
diesel (as adj)	a diesel	[a ˈdizɛʎ]
petrol (as adj)	a benzina	[a benˈdzina]

engine volume	cilindrata (f)	[tʃilindˈrata]
power	potenza (f)	[pɔˈtɛntsa]
horsepower	cavallo vapore (m)	[kaˈvallo vaˈpɔrɛ]
piston	pistone (m)	[pisˈtɔnɛ]
cylinder	cilindro (m)	[tʃiˈlindrɔ]
valve	valvola (f)	[ˈvaʎvɔʎa]

injector	iniettore (m)	[iɲjetˈtɔrɛ]
generator	generatore (m)	[dʒenɛraˈtɔrɛ]
carburettor	carburatore (m)	[karburaˈtɔrɛ]
engine oil	olio (m) motore	[ˈɔlio mɔˈtɔrɛ]

radiator	radiatore (m)	[radiaˈtɔrɛ]
coolant	liquido (m) di raffreddamento	[ˈlikuidɔ di raffrɛdaˈmɛntɔ]
cooling fan	ventilatore (m)	[vɛntiʎaˈtɔrɛ]

battery (accumulator)	batteria (m)	[battɛˈria]
starter	motorino (m) d'avviamento	[mɔtɔˈrinɔ davwiaˈmɛntɔ]
ignition	accensione (f)	[atʃɛnsiˈɔnɛ]

sparking plug	candela (f) d'accensione	[kan'dɛʎa datʃɛnsi'ɔnɛ]
terminal (of battery)	morsetto (m)	[mɔr'sɛttɔ]
positive terminal	più (m)	['pju]
negative terminal	meno (m)	['menɔ]
fuse	fusibile (m)	[fu'zibile]

air filter	filtro (m) dell'aria	['fiʎtrɔ dɛʎ 'aria]
oil filter	filtro (m) dell'olio	['fiʎtrɔ dɛʎ 'ɔliɔ]
fuel filter	filtro (m) del carburante	['fiʎtrɔ dɛʎ karbu'rantɛ]

178. Cars. Crash. Repair

car accident	incidente (m)	[intʃi'dɛntɛ]
road accident	incidente (m) stradale	[intʃi'dɛntɛ stra'dale]
to run into ...	sbattere contro ...	['zbattɛrɛ 'kɔntrɔ]
to have an accident	avere un incidente	[a'vɛrɛ un intʃi'dɛntɛ]
damage	danno (m)	['danɔ]
intact (adj)	illeso	[il'lezɔ]

| to break down (vi) | essere rotto | ['ɛssɛrɛ 'rɔttɔ] |
| towrope | cavo (m) di rimorchio | ['kavɔ di ri'mɔrkiɔ] |

puncture	foratura (f)	[fɔra'tura]
to have a puncture	essere a terra	['ɛssɛrɛ a 'tɛrra]
to pump up	gonfiare (vt)	[gon'fjarɛ]
pressure	pressione (f)	[prɛssi'ɔnɛ]
to check (to examine)	verificare	[vɛrifi'karɛ]

repair	riparazione (f)	[ripara'tsʲɔnɛ]
auto repair shop	officina (f) meccanica	[ɔffi'tʃina me'kanika]
spare part	pezzo (m) di ricambio	['pɛtsɔ di ri'kambiɔ]
part	pezzo (m)	['pɛtsɔ]

bolt	bullone (m)	[bul'lɔnɛ]
screw bolt	bullone (m) a vite	[bul'lɔnɛ a 'witɛ]
nut	dado (m)	['dadɔ]
washer	rondella (f)	[rɔn'dɛʎa]
bearing	cuscinetto (m)	[kuʃi'nɛttɔ]

tube	tubo (m)	['tubɔ]
gasket, washer	guarnizione (f)	[guarni'tsʲɔnɛ]
cable, wire	filo (m), cavo (m)	['filɔ], ['kavɔ]

jack	cric (m)	[krik]
spanner	chiave (f)	['kjavɛ]
hammer	martello (m)	[mar'tɛllɔ]
pump	pompa (f)	['pompa]
screwdriver	giravite (m)	[dʒira'witɛ]

| fire extinguisher | estintore (m) | [ɛstin'tɔrɛ] |
| warning triangle | triangolo (m) d'emergenza | [tri'aŋɔlɔ dɛmɛr'dʒentsa] |

| to stall (vi) | spegnersi (vr) | ['spɛɲersi] |
| stalling | spegnimento (m) motore | [spɛɲi'mɛntɔ mɔ'tɔrɛ] |

to be broken	essere rotto	['ɛssɛrɛ 'rɔtto]
to overheat (vi)	surriscaldarsi (vr)	[surriskaʎ'darsi]
to be clogged up	intasarsi (vr)	[inta'zarsi]
to freeze up (pipes, etc.)	ghiacciarsi (vr)	[gja'ʧarsi]
to burst (vi, ab. tube)	spaccarsi (vr)	[spak'karsi]

pressure	pressione (f)	[prɛssi'ɔnɛ]
level	livello (m)	[li'vɛllɔ]
slack (~ belt)	lento	['lentɔ]

dent	ammaccatura (f)	[ammakka'tura]
abnormal noise (motor)	battito (m)	['battitɔ]
crack	fessura (f)	[fɛs'sura]
scratch	graffiatura (f)	[graffja'tura]

179. Cars. Road

road	strada (f)	['strada]
motorway	superstrada (f)	[supɛrst'rada]
highway	autostrada (f)	[autɔst'rada]
direction (way)	direzione (f)	[dirɛt'tsɪonɛ]
distance	distanza (f)	[dis'tantsa]

bridge	ponte (m)	['pɔntɛ]
car park	parcheggio (m)	[par'kɛʤɔ]
square	piazza (f)	['pjatsa]
road junction	svincolo (m)	['zwiŋkɔlɔ]
tunnel	galleria (f), tunnel (m)	[galle'ria], ['tuɲɛl]

petrol station	distributore (m) di benzina	[distribu'tɔrɛ di ben'ʣina]
car park	parcheggio (m)	[par'kɛʤɔ]
petrol pump	pompa (f) di benzina	['pompa di ben'ʣina]
auto repair shop	officina (f) meccanica	[ɔffi'ʧina me'kanika]
to fill up	fare benzina	['farɛ ben'ʣina]
fuel	carburante (m)	[karbu'rantɛ]
jerrycan	tanica (f)	['tanika]

asphalt	asfalto (m)	[as'faʎtɔ]
road markings	segnaletica (f) stradale	[sɛɲa'letika stra'dale]
kerb	cordolo (m)	['kɔrdɔlɔ]
guardrail	barriera (f) di sicurezza	[bar'rjera di siku'rɛtsa]
ditch	fosso (m)	['fɔssɔ]
roadside	ciglio (m) della strada	['ʧiʎɔ dɛlla 'strada]
lamppost	lampione (m)	[lam'pɪonɛ]

to drive (a car)	guidare, condurre	[gui'darɛ], [kɔn'durrɛ]
to turn (~ to the left)	girare (vi)	[ʤi'rarɛ]
to make a U-turn	fare un'inversione a U	['farɛ un invɛrsi'ɔnɛ a'u]
reverse	retromarcia (m)	[rɛtrɔ'marʧa]

to honk (vi)	suonare il clacson	[suɔ'narɛ iʎ 'kʎaksɔn]
honk (sound)	colpo (m) di clacson	['kɔʎpɔ di 'klaksɔn]
to get stuck	incastrarsi (vr)	[iŋkast'rarsi]
to spin (in mud)	impantanarsi (vr)	[impanta'narsi]

to cut, to turn off	spegnere (vt)	['spɛɲjerɛ]
speed	velocità (f)	[vɛlɜtʃi'ta]
to exceed the speed limit	superare i limiti di velocità	[supɛ'rarɛ i 'limiti di vɛlɜtʃi'ta]
to give a ticket	multare (vt)	[muʎ'tarɛ]
traffic lights	semaforo (m)	[sɛ'maforo]
driving licence	patente (f) di guida	[pa'tɛntɛ di gu'ida]

level crossing	passaggio (m) a livello	[pas'sadʒo a li'vɛllo]
crossroads	incrocio (m)	[iŋk'rotʃo]
zebra crossing	passaggio (m) pedonale	[pas'sadʒo pɛdo'nale]
bend, curve	curva (f)	['kurva]
pedestrian precinct	zona (f) pedonale	['dzona pɛdo'nale]

180. Signs

Highway Code	codice (m) stradale	['koditʃe stra'dale]
traffic sign	segnale (m) stradale	[sɛni'ale stra'dale]
overtaking	sorpasso (m)	[sor'passo]
curve	curva (f)	['kurva]
U-turn	inversione a U	[invɛrsi'onɛ a 'u]
roundabout	rotatoria (f)	[rota'toria]

No entry	divieto d'accesso	[di'vjeto da'tʃesso]
All vehicles prohibited	divieto di transito	[di'vjeto di 'tranzito]
No overtaking	divieto di sorpasso	[di'vjeto di sor'passo]
No parking	divieto di sosta	[di'vjeto di 'sosta]
No stopping	divieto di fermata	[di'vjeto di fer'mata]

dangerous curve	curva (f) pericolosa	['kurva pɛriko'lɜza]
steep descent	discesa (f) ripida	[di'ʃɛza 'ripida]
one-way traffic	senso (m) unico	['sɛnso 'uniko]
zebra crossing	passaggio (m) pedonale	[pas'sadʒo pɛdo'nale]
slippery road	strada (f) scivolosa	['strada ʃivo'lɜza]
GIVE WAY	dare la precedenza	['darɛ ʎa prɛtʃe'dɛntsa]

PEOPLE. LIFE EVENTS

Life events

181. Holidays. Event

celebration, holiday	festa (f)	['fɛsta]
national day	festa (f) nazionale	['fɛsta nats'ɔ'nale]
public holiday	festività (f) civile	[fɛstiwi'ta ʧi'wile]
to fete (celebrate)	festeggiare (vt)	[fɛstɛ'dʒarɛ]

event (happening)	avvenimento (m)	[avvɛni'mɛntɔ]
event (organized activity)	evento (m)	[ɛ'vɛntɔ]
banquet (party)	banchetto (m)	[ba'ŋkɛttɔ]
reception (formal party)	ricevimento (m)	[riʧewi'mɛntɔ]
feast	festino (m)	[fes'tinɔ]

anniversary	anniversario (m)	[aɲivɛr'sariɔ]
jubilee	giubileo (m)	[dʒubi'leɔ]
to celebrate (vt)	festeggiare (vt)	[fɛstɛ'dʒarɛ]

New Year	Capodanno (m)	[kapɔ'daŋɔ]
Happy New Year!	Buon Anno!	[buɔ'naŋɔ]

Christmas	Natale (m)	[na'tale]
Merry Christmas!	Buon Natale!	[bu'ɔn na'tale]
Christmas tree	Albero (m) di Natale	['aʎbɛrɔ di na'tale]
fireworks	fuochi (m pl) artificiali	[fu'ɔki artifi'ʧali]

wedding	nozze (f pl)	['nɔʦe]
groom	sposo (m)	['spɔzɔ]
bride	sposa (f)	['spɔza]

to invite (vt)	invitare (vt)	[inwi'tarɛ]
invitation card	invito (m)	[in'witɔ]

guest	ospite (m)	['ɔspitɛ]
to visit (go to see)	andare a trovare	[an'darɛ a trɔ'varɛ]
to greet the guests	accogliere gli invitati	[ak'kɔʎjerɛ ʎi inwi'tati]

gift, present	regalo (m)	[rɛ'galɔ]
to give (sth as present)	offrire (vt)	[ɔff'rirɛ]
to receive gifts	ricevere i regali	[ri'ʧevɛrɛ i rɛ'gali]
bouquet (of flowers)	mazzo (m) di fiori	['maʦɔ di 'fʲɔri]

greetings (New Year ~)	auguri (m pl)	[au'guri]
to congratulate (vt)	augurare (vt)	[augu'rarɛ]
greetings card	cartolina (f)	[kartɔ'lina]
to send a postcard	mandare una cartolina	[man'darɛ una kartɔ'lina]

to get a postcard	ricevere una cartolina	[ri'tʃevɛrɛ 'una kartɔ'lina]
toast	brindisi (m)	['brindizi]
to offer (a drink, etc.)	offrire (vt)	[ɔffʹrirɛ]
champagne	champagne (m)	[ʃam'paɲ]

to have fun	divertirsi (vr)	[divɛr'tirsi]
fun, merriment	allegria (f)	[alleg'ria]
joy (emotion)	gioia (f)	['dʒɔja]

| dance | danza (f), ballo (m) | ['dantsa], ['ballɔ] |
| to dance (vi, vt) | ballare (vi, vt) | [ba'ʎarɛ] |

| waltz | valzer (m) | ['vaʎtsɛr] |
| tango | tango (m) | ['taŋɔ] |

182. Funerals. Burial

cemetery	cimitero (m)	[tʃimi'tɛrɔ]
grave, tomb	tomba (f)	['tomba]
gravestone	pietra (f) tombale	['pjetra tom'bale]
fence	recinto (m)	[rɛ'tʃintɔ]
chapel	cappella (f)	[kap'pɛʎa]

death	morte (f)	['mɔrtɛ]
to die (vi)	morire (vi)	[mɔ'rirɛ]
the deceased	defunto (m)	[dɛ'funtɔ]
mourning	lutto (m)	['lyttɔ]

to bury (vt)	seppellire (vt)	[sɛppɛl'lirɛ]
undertakers	sede (f) di pompe funebri	['sɛdɛ di 'pompɛ 'funɛbri]
funeral	funerale (m)	[funɛ'rale]

wreath	corona (f) di fiori	[kɔ'rɔna di fi'ɔri]
coffin	bara (f)	['bara]
hearse	carro (m) funebre	['karrɔ 'funɛbrɛ]
shroud	lenzuolo (m) funebre	[lentsu'ɔlɔ 'funɛbrɛ]

funeral procession	corteo (m) funebre	[kɔr'tɛɔ 'funɛbrɛ]
cremation urn	urna (f) funeraria	['urna funɛ'raria]
crematorium	crematorio (m)	[krɛma'tɔriɔ]

obituary	necrologio (m)	[nɛkrɔ'lɔdʒɔ]
to cry (weep)	piangere (vi)	['pjandʒɛrɛ]
to sob (vi)	singhiozzare (vi)	[singɔ'tsarɛ]

183. War. Soldiers

platoon	plotone (m)	[plɔ'tɔnɛ]
company	compagnia (f)	[kɔmpa'nia]
regiment	reggimento (m)	[rɛdʒi'mɛntɔ]
army	esercito (m)	[ɛ'zɛrtʃitɔ]
division	divisione (f)	[diwizi'ɔnɛ]

| detachment | distaccamento (m) | [distakka'mɛntɔ] |
| host (army) | armata (f) | [ar'mata] |

| soldier | soldato (m) | [sɔʎ'datɔ] |
| officer | ufficiale (m) | [uffi'ʧale] |

private	soldato (m) semplice	[sɔʎ'datɔ 'sɛmpliʧe]
sergeant	sergente (m)	[sɛr'dʒentɛ]
lieutenant	tenente (m)	[tɛ'nɛntɛ]
captain	capitano (m)	[kapi'tanɔ]
major	maggiore (m)	[ma'dʒɔrɛ]
colonel	colonnello (m)	[kɔlɔ'ŋɛllɔ]
general	generale (m)	[dʒenɛ'rale]

sailor	marinaio (m)	[mari'najo]
captain	capitano (m)	[kapi'tanɔ]
boatswain	nostromo (m)	[nɔst'rɔmɔ]

artilleryman	artigliere (m)	[arti'ʎjerɛ]
paratrooper	paracadutista (m)	[parakadu'tista]
pilot	pilota (m)	[pi'lota]
navigator	navigatore (m)	[nawiga'tɔrɛ]
mechanic	meccanico (m)	[mɛk'kanikɔ]

pioneer (sapper)	geniere (m)	[dʒeni'erɛ]
parachutist	paracadutista (m)	[parakadu'tista]
scout	esploratore (m)	[ɛsplɔra'tɔrɛ]
sniper	cecchino (m)	[ʧek'kinɔ]

patrol (group)	pattuglia (f)	[pat'tuʎja]
to patrol (vt)	pattugliare (vt)	[pattu'ʎjarɛ]
sentry, guard	sentinella (f)	[sɛnti'nɛʎa]

warrior	guerriero (m)	[guɛr'rjerɔ]
hero	eroe (m)	[ɛ'rɔɛ]
heroine	eroina (f)	[ɛrɔ'ina]
patriot	patriota (m)	[patri'ɔta]

traitor	traditore (m)	[tradi'tɔrɛ]
deserter	disertore (m)	[dizɛr'tɔrɛ]
to desert (vi)	disertare (vi)	[dizɛr'tarɛ]

mercenary	mercenario (m)	[mɛrʧe'nariɔ]
recruit	recluta (f)	['rɛklyta]
volunteer	volontario (m)	[vɔlɔn'tariɔ]

dead	ucciso (m)	[u'ʧizɔ]
wounded (n)	ferito (m)	[fɛ'ritɔ]
prisoner of war	prigioniero (m) di guerra	[pridʒɔ'ɲjerɔ di gu'ɛrra]

184. War. Military actions. Part 1

| war | guerra (f) | [gu'ɛrra] |
| to be at war | essere in guerra | ['ɛssɛrɛ in gu'ɛrra] |

civil war	**guerra** (f) **civile**	[gu'ɛrra ʧi'wile]
treacherously (adv)	**perfidamente**	[pɛrfida'mɛntɛ]
declaration of war	**dichiarazione** (f) **di guerra**	[dik'ara'ts'ɔnɛ di gu'ɛrra]
to declare (~ war)	**dichiarare** (vt)	[dikja'rarɛ]
aggression	**aggressione** (f)	[aggrɛssi'ɔnɛ]
to attack (invade)	**attaccare** (vt)	[attak'karɛ]
to invade (vt)	**invadere** (vt)	[in'vadɛrɛ]
invader	**invasore** (m)	[inva'zɔrɛ]
conqueror	**conquistatore** (m)	[kɔŋkuista'tɔrɛ]
defence	**difesa** (f)	[di'fɛza]
to defend (a country, etc.)	**difendere** (vt)	[di'fɛndɛrɛ]
to defend oneself	**difendersi** (vr)	[di'fɛndɛrsi]
enemy	**nemico** (m)	[nɛ'mikɔ]
foe, adversary	**avversario** (m)	[avvɛr'sariɔ]
enemy (as adj)	**ostile**	[ɔs'tile]
strategy	**strategia** (f)	[stratɛ'dʒia]
tactics	**tattica** (f)	['tattika]
order	**ordine** (m)	['ɔrdinɛ]
command (order)	**comando** (m)	[kɔ'mandɔ]
to order (vt)	**ordinare** (vt)	[ɔrdi'narɛ]
mission	**missione** (f)	[mis's'ɔnɛ]
secret (adj)	**segreto**	[sɛg'rɛtɔ]
battle	**battaglia** (f)	[bat'taʎja]
combat	**combattimento** (m)	[kɔmbatti'mɛntɔ]
attack	**attacco** (m)	[at'takkɔ]
storming (assault)	**assalto** (m)	[as'saʎtɔ]
to storm (vt)	**assalire** (vt)	[assa'lirɛ]
siege (to be under ~)	**assedio** (m)	[as'sɛdiɔ]
offensive (n)	**offensiva** (f)	[ɔffɛn'siva]
to go on the offensive	**passare all'offensiva**	[pas'sarɛ allɔfɛn'siva]
retreat	**ritirata** (f)	[riti'rata]
to retreat (vi)	**ritirarsi** (vr)	[riti'rarsi]
encirclement	**accerchiamento** (m)	[atʃerkja'mɛntɔ]
to encircle (vt)	**accerchiare** (vt)	[atʃer'kjarɛ]
bombing (by aircraft)	**bombardamento** (m)	[bɔmbarda'mɛntɔ]
to drop a bomb	**lanciare una bomba**	[ʎan'ʧarɛ 'una 'bɔmba]
to bomb (vt)	**bombardare** (vt)	[bɔmar'darɛ]
explosion	**esplosione** (f)	[ɛsplɔzi'ɔnɛ]
shot	**sparo** (m)	['sparɔ]
to fire a shot	**sparare un colpo**	[spa'rarɛ un 'kɔʎpɔ]
shooting	**sparatoria** (f)	[spara'tɔria]
to take aim (at ...)	**puntare su ...**	[pun'tarɛ su]
to point (a gun)	**puntare** (vt)	[pun'tarɛ]

to hit (the target)	colpire (vt)	[koʎ'pirɛ]
to sink (~ a ship)	affondare (vt)	[affon'darɛ]
hole (in a ship)	falla (f)	['faʎa]
to founder, to sink (vi)	affondare (vi)	[affon'darɛ]

front (at war)	fronte (m)	['frontɛ]
rear (homefront)	retrovie (f pl)	[rɛtro'wie]
evacuation	evacuazione (f)	[ɛvakua'tsʲonɛ]
to evacuate (vt)	evacuare (vt)	[ɛvaku'arɛ]

trench	trincea (f)	[trin'tʃea]
barbed wire	filo (m) spinato	['filo spi'nato]
barrier (anti tank ~)	sbarramento (m)	[sbarra'mento]
watchtower	torretta (f) di osservazione	[tor'rɛtta di ɔsɛrva'tsʲonɛ]

hospital	ospedale (m) militare	[ɔspɛ'dale mili'tarɛ]
to wound (vt)	ferire (vt)	[fɛ'rirɛ]
wound	ferita (f)	[fɛ'rita]
wounded (n)	ferito (m)	[fɛ'rito]
to be injured	rimanere ferito	[rima'nɛrɛ fɛ'rito]
serious (wound)	grave	['gravɛ]

185. War. Military actions. Part 2

captivity	prigionia (f)	[pridʒo'nia]
to take captive	fare prigioniero	['farɛ pridʒo'njero]
to be in captivity	essere prigioniero	['ɛssɛrɛ pridʒo'njero]
to be taken prisoner	essere fatto prigioniero	['ɛssɛrɛ 'fatto pridʒo'njero]

concentration camp	campo (m) di concentramento	['kampo di kontʃentra'mento]
prisoner of war	prigioniero (m) di guerra	[pridʒo'njero di gu'ɛrra]
to escape (vi)	fuggire (vi)	[fu'dʒirɛ]

to betray (vt)	tradire (vt)	[tra'dirɛ]
betrayer	traditore (m)	[tradi'torɛ]
betrayal	tradimento (m)	[tradi'mento]

| to execute (shoot) | fucilare (vt) | [futʃi'ʎarɛ] |
| execution (shooting) | fucilazione (f) | [futʃiʎa'tsʲonɛ] |

equipment (uniform, etc.)	divisa (f) militare	[di'wiza mili'tarɛ]
shoulder board	spallina (f)	[spal'lina]
gas mask	maschera (f) antigas	['maskɛra anti'gas]

radio transmitter	radiotrasmettitore (m)	['radio transmetti'torɛ]
cipher, code	codice (m)	['koditʃe]
conspiracy	complotto (m)	[komp'lɔtto]
password	parola (f) d'ordine	[pa'roʎa 'dɔrdinɛ]

land mine	mina (f)	['mina]
to mine (road, etc.)	minare (vt)	[mi'narɛ]
minefield	campo (m) minato	['kampo mi'nato]
air-raid warning	allarme (m) aereo	[a'ʎarmɛ a'ɛrɛo]

alarm (warning)	allarme (m)	[a'ʎarmɛ]
signal	segnale (m)	[sɛ'ɲjale]
signal flare	razzo (m) di segnalazione	['radzo di sɛɲjaʎa'tsʲonɛ]

headquarters	quartier (m) generale	[kuar'tʲe dʒenɛ'rale]
reconnaissance	esplorazione (m)	[ɛsplɔra'tɔrɛ]
situation	situazione (f)	[situa'tsʲonɛ]
report	rapporto (m)	[rap'portɔ]
ambush	agguato (m)	[aggu'atɔ]
reinforcement (of army)	rinforzo (m)	[rin'fortsɔ]

target	bersaglio (m)	[bɛr'saʎʲɔ]
training area	terreno (m) di caccia	[tɛr'rɛnɔ di 'katʃa]
military exercise	manovre (f pl)	[ma'novrɛ]

panic	panico (m)	['panikɔ]
devastation	devastazione (f)	[dɛvasta'tsʲonɛ]
destruction, ruins	distruzione (m)	[distru'tsʲonɛ]
to destroy (vt)	distruggere (vt)	[dist'rudʒerɛ]

to survive (vi, vt)	sopravvivere (vi, vt)	[sɔprav'wivɛrɛ]
to disarm (vt)	disarmare (vt)	[dizar'marɛ]
to handle (~ a gun)	maneggiare (vt)	[manɛ'dʒarɛ]

Attention!	Attenti!	[at'tɛnti]
At ease!	Riposo!	[ri'pozɔ]

feat (of courage)	atto (m) eroico	['attɔ ɛ'rɔikɔ]
oath (vow)	giuramento (m)	[dʒura'mɛntɔ]
to swear (an oath)	giurare (vi)	[dʒu'rarɛ]

decoration (medal, etc.)	decorazione (f)	[dɛkɔra'tsʲonɛ]
to award (give medal to)	decorare qn	[dɛkɔ'rarɛ]
medal	medaglia (f)	[mɛ'daʎja]
order (e.g. ~ of Merit)	ordine (m)	['ɔrdinɛ]

victory	vittoria (f)	[wit'tɔria]
defeat	sconfitta (m)	[skɔn'fitta]
armistice	armistizio (m)	[armis'titsio]

banner (standard)	bandiera (f)	[ban'djera]
glory (honour, fame)	gloria (f)	['glɔria]
parade	parata (f)	[pa'rata]
to march (on parade)	marciare (vi)	[mar'tʃarɛ]

186. Weapons

weapons	armi (f pl)	['armi]
firearm	arma (f) da fuoco	['arma da fu'ɔkɔ]
cold weapons (knives, etc.)	arma (f) bianca	['arma 'bjaŋka]

chemical weapons	armi (f pl) chimiche	['armi 'kimikɛ]
nuclear (adj)	nucleare	[nukle'arɛ]
nuclear weapons	armi (f pl) nucleari	['armi nukle'ari]

| bomb | bomba (f) | ['bomba] |
| atomic bomb | bomba (f) atomica | ['bomba a'tomika] |

pistol (gun)	pistola (f)	[pis'toʎa]
rifle	fucile (m)	[fu'ʧile]
submachine gun	mitra (m)	['mitra]
machine gun	mitragliatrice (f)	[mitraʎjat'riʧe]

muzzle	bocca (f)	['bokka]
barrel	canna (f)	['kaɲa]
calibre	calibro (m)	['kalibro]

trigger	grilletto (m)	[gril'letto]
sight (aiming device)	mirino (m)	[mi'rino]
magazine	caricatore (m)	[karika'tore]
butt (of rifle)	calcio (m)	['kaʎʧo]

| hand grenade | bomba (f) a mano | ['bomba a 'mano] |
| explosive | esplosivo (m) | [ɛsplo'zivo] |

bullet	pallottola (f)	[pal'lɔttoʎa]
cartridge	cartuccia (f)	[kar'tuʧa]
charge	carica (f)	['karika]
ammunition	munizioni (f pl)	[muni'ʦ'oni]

bomber (aircraft)	bombardiere (m)	[bombar'djerɛ]
fighter	aereo (m) da caccia	[a'ɛrɛo da 'kaʧa]
helicopter	elicottero (m)	[ɛli'kottɛro]

anti-aircraft gun	cannone (m) antiaereo	[ka'ŋonɛ antia'ɛrɛo]
tank	carro (m) armato	['karro ar'mato]
tank gun	cannone (m)	[ka'ŋonɛ]

artillery	artiglieria (f)	[artiʎje'ria]
cannon	cannone (m)	[ka'ŋonɛ]
to lay (a gun)	mirare a ...	[mi'rarɛ a]

shell (projectile)	proiettile (m)	[pro'jettile]
mortar bomb	granata (f) da mortaio	[gra'nata da mor'tajo]
mortar	mortaio (m)	[mor'tajo]
splinter (of shell)	scheggia (f)	['skɛdʒa]

submarine	sottomarino (m)	[sottoma'rino]
torpedo	siluro (m)	[si'lyro]
missile	missile (m)	['missile]

to load (gun)	caricare (vt)	[kari'karɛ]
to shoot (vi)	sparare (vi)	[spa'rarɛ]
to take aim (at ...)	puntare su ...	[pun'tarɛ su]
bayonet	baionetta (f)	[bajo'nɛtta]

epee	spada (f)	['spada]
sabre (e.g. cavalry ~)	sciabola (f)	['ʃaboʎa]
spear (weapon)	lancia (f)	['ʎanʧa]
bow	arco (m)	['arko]
arrow	freccia (f)	['frɛʧa]

musket	moschetto (m)	[mɔs'kɛttɔ]
crossbow	balestra (f)	[ba'lestra]

187. Ancient people

primitive (prehistoric)	primitivo	[primi'tivɔ]
prehistoric (adj)	preistorico	[prɛis'tɔrikɔ]
ancient (~ civilization)	antico	[an'tikɔ]

Stone Age	Età (f) della pietra	[ɛ'ta 'dɛʎa 'pjetra]
Bronze Age	Età (f) del bronzo	[ɛ'ta dɛʎ 'brɔndzɔ]
Ice Age	epoca (f) glaciale	['ɛpɔka gʎa'tʃale]

tribe	tribù (f)	[tri'bu]
cannibal	cannibale (m)	[ka'ɲibale]
hunter	cacciatore (m)	[katʃa'tɔrɛ]
to hunt (vi, vt)	cacciare (vt)	[ka'tʃarɛ]
mammoth	mammut (m)	[mam'mut]

cave	caverna (f), grotta (f)	[ka'vɛrna], ['grɔtta]
fire	fuoco (m)	[fu'ɔkɔ]
campfire	falò (m)	[fa'lɔ]
rock painting	pittura (f) rupestre	[pit'tura ru'pɛstrɛ]

tool (e.g. stone axe)	strumento (m) di lavoro	[stru'mɛntɔ di ʎa'vɔrɔ]
spear	lancia (f)	['ʎantʃa]
stone axe	ascia (f) di pietra	['aʃa di 'pjetra]
to be at war	essere in guerra	['ɛssɛrɛ in gu'ɛrra]
to domesticate (vt)	addomesticare (vt)	[addɔmɛsti'karɛ]

idol	idolo (m)	['idɔlɔ]
to worship (vt)	idolatrare (vt)	[idɔʎat'rarɛ]
superstition	superstizione (f)	[supɛrsti'tsɨɔnɛ]
rite	rito (m)	['ritɔ]

evolution	evoluzione (f)	[ɛvɔly'tsɨɔnɛ]
development	sviluppo (m)	[zwi'lyppɔ]
disappearance	estinzione (f)	[ɛstin'tsɨɔnɛ]
to adapt oneself	adattarsi (vr)	[adat'tarsi]

archaeology	archeologia (f)	[arkɛɔlɔ'dʒia]
archaeologist	archeologo (m)	[arkɛ'ɔlɔgɔ]
archaeological (adj)	archeologico	[arkɛɔ'lɔdʒikɔ]
excavation site	sito (m) archeologico	['sitɔ arkɛɔ'lɔdʒikɔ]
excavations	scavi (m pl)	['skawi]
find (object)	reperto (m)	[rɛ'pɛrtɔ]
fragment	frammento (m)	[fram'mɛntɔ]

188. Middle Ages

people (population)	popolo (m)	['pɔpɔlɔ]
peoples	popoli (m pl)	['pɔpɔli]

| tribe | **tribù** (f) | [tri'bu] |
| tribes | **tribù** (f pl) | [tri'bu] |

barbarians	**barbari** (m pl)	['barbari]
Gauls	**galli** (m pl)	['galli]
Goths	**goti** (m pl)	['goti]
Slavs	**slavi** (m pl)	['zʎawi]
Vikings	**vichinghi** (m pl)	[wi'kiɲi]

| Romans | **romani** (m pl) | [rɔ'mani] |
| Roman (adj) | **romano** | [rɔ'manɔ] |

Byzantines	**bizantini** (m pl)	[bidzan'tini]
Byzantium	**Bisanzio** (m)	[bi'zansiɔ]
Byzantine (adj)	**bizantino**	[bidzan'tinɔ]

emperor	**imperatore** (m)	[impɛra'tɔrɛ]
leader, chief	**capo** (m)	['kapɔ]
powerful (~ king)	**potente**	[po'tɛntɛ]
king	**re** (m)	[rɛ]
ruler (sovereign)	**governante** (m)	[gɔvɛr'nantɛ]

knight	**cavaliere** (m)	[kava'ʎjere]
knightly (adj)	**cavalleresco**	[kavalle'rɛskɔ]
feudal lord	**feudatario** (m)	[fɛuda'tariɔ]
feudal (adj)	**feudale**	[fɛu'dale]
vassal	**vassallo** (m)	[vas'sallɔ]

duke	**duca** (m)	['duka]
earl	**conte** (m)	['kontɛ]
baron	**barone** (m)	[ba'rɔnɛ]
bishop	**vescovo** (m)	['vɛskɔvɔ]

armour	**armatura** (f)	[arma'tura]
shield	**scudo** (m)	['skudɔ]
sword	**spada** (f)	['spada]
visor	**visiera** (f)	[wi'zjera]
chain armour	**cotta** (f) **di maglia**	['kɔtta di 'maʎ'a]

| crusade | **crociata** (f) | [krɔ'ʧata] |
| crusader | **crociato** (m) | [krɔ'ʧatɔ] |

territory	**territorio** (m)	[tɛrri'tɔriɔ]
to attack (invade)	**attaccare** (vt)	[attak'karɛ]
to conquer (vt)	**conquistare** (vt)	[kɔŋkuis'tarɛ]
to occupy (invade)	**occupare** (vt)	[ɔkku'parɛ]

siege (to be under ~)	**assedio** (m)	[as'sɛdiɔ]
besieged (adj)	**assediato**	[assɛdi'atɔ]
to besiege (vt)	**assediare** (vt)	[assɛdi'arɛ]

inquisition	**inquisizione** (f)	[iŋkuizi'ts'ɔnɛ]
inquisitor	**inquisitore** (m)	[iŋkuizi'tɔrɛ]
torture	**tortura** (f)	[tor'tura]
cruel (adj)	**crudele**	[kru'dɛle]
heretic	**eretico** (m)	[ɛ'rɛtikɔ]

heresy	eresia (f)	[ɛrɛ'zia]
seafaring	navigazione (f)	[nawiga'tsʲɔnɛ]
pirate	pirata (m)	[pi'rata]
piracy	pirateria (f)	[piratɛ'ria]
boarding (attack)	arrembaggio (m)	[arrɛm'badʒɔ]
loot, booty	bottino (m)	[bɔt'tinɔ]
treasures	tesori (m)	[tɛ'zɔri]

discovery	scoperta (f)	[skɔ'pɛrta]
to discover (new land, etc.)	scoprire (vt)	[skɔp'rirɛ]
expedition	spedizione (f)	[spɛdi'tsʲɔnɛ]

musketeer	moschettiere (m)	[mɔskɛt'tʲerɛ]
cardinal	cardinale (m)	[kardi'nale]
heraldry	araldica (f)	[a'raʎdika]
heraldic (adj)	araldico	[a'raʎdikɔ]

189. Leader. Chief. Authorities

king	re (m)	[rɛ]
queen	regina (f)	[rɛ'dʒina]
royal (adj)	reale	[rɛ'ale]
kingdom	regno (m)	['rɛɲʲɔ]

| prince | principe (m) | ['printʃipɛ] |
| princess | principessa (f) | [printʃi'pɛssa] |

president	presidente (m)	[prɛzi'dɛntɛ]
vice-president	vicepresidente (m)	[witʃeprɛzi'dɛntɛ]
senator	senatore (m)	[sɛna'torɛ]

monarch	monarca (m)	[mɔ'narka]
ruler (sovereign)	governante (m)	[gɔvɛr'nantɛ]
dictator	dittatore (m)	[ditta'torɛ]
tyrant	tiranno (m)	[ti'raŋɔ]
magnate	magnate (m)	[ma'ɲʲatɛ]

director	direttore (m)	[dirɛt'torɛ]
chief	capo (m)	['kapɔ]
manager (director)	dirigente (m)	[diri'dʒɛntɛ]
boss	capo (m)	['kapɔ]
owner	proprietario (m)	[prɔpriɛ'tariɔ]

head (~ of delegation)	capo (m)	['kapɔ]
authorities	autorità (f pl)	[autɔri'ta]
superiors	superiori (m pl)	[supe'rʲɔri]

governor	governatore (m)	[gɔvɛrna'tɔrɛ]
consul	console (m)	['kɔnsɔle]
diplomat	diplomatico (m)	[diplɔ'matikɔ]
mayor	sindaco (m)	['sindakɔ]
sheriff	sceriffo (m)	[ʃɛ'riffɔ]
emperor	imperatore (m)	[impɛra'tɔrɛ]
tsar, czar	zar (m)	[tsar]

Pharaoh	faraone (m)	[fara'ɔnɛ]
khan	khan (m)	['kan]

190. Road. Way. Directions

road	strada (f)	['strada]
way (direction)	cammino (m)	[kam'minɔ]
highway	superstrada (f)	[supɛrst'rada]
motorway	autostrada (f)	[autost'rada]
trunk road	strada (f) statale	['strada sta'tale]
main road	strada (f) principale	['strada printʃi'pale]
dirt road	strada (f) sterrata	['strada ster'rata]
pathway	viottolo (m)	[wi'ɔttɔlɔ]
footpath	sentiero (m)	[sɛn'tʲerɔ]
Where?	Dove?	['dɔvɛ]
Where (to)?	Dove?	['dɔvɛ]
Where ... from?	Di dove?, Da dove?	[di 'dɔvɛ da 'dɔvɛ]
direction (way)	direzione (f)	[dirɛt'tsʲɔnɛ]
to point (~ the way)	indicare (vt)	[indi'karɛ]
to the left	a sinistra	[a si'nistra]
to the right	a destra	[a 'dɛstra]
straight ahead (adv)	dritto	['drittɔ]
back (e.g. to turn ~)	indietro	[in'djetrɔ]
bend, curve	curva (f)	['kurva]
to turn (~ to the left)	girare (vi)	[dʒi'rarɛ]
to make a U-turn	fare un'inversione a U	['farɛ un invɛrsi'ɔnɛ a'u]
to be visible	essere visibile	['ɛssɛrɛ wi'zibile]
to appear (come into view)	apparire (vi)	[appa'rirɛ]
stop, halt (in journey)	sosta (f)	['sɔsta]
to rest, to halt (vi)	riposarsi (vr)	[ripɔ'zarsi]
rest (pause)	riposo (m)	[ri'pɔzɔ]
to lose one's way	perdersi (vr)	['pɛrdɛrsi]
to lead to ... (ab. road)	portare verso ...	[pɔr'tarɛ 'vɛrsɔ]
to arrive at ...	raggiungere (vt)	[ra'dʒundʒerɛ]
stretch (of road)	tratto (m) di strada	['trattɔ di 'strada]
asphalt	asfalto (m)	[as'faʎtɔ]
kerb	cordolo (m)	['kɔrdɔlɔ]
ditch	fosso (m)	['fɔssɔ]
manhole	tombino (m)	[tɔm'binɔ]
roadside	ciglio (m) della strada	['tʃiʎɔ dɛlla 'strada]
pit, pothole	buca (f)	['buka]
to go (on foot)	andare (vi)	[an'darɛ]
to overtake (vt)	sorpassare (vt)	[sɔrpas'sarɛ]

| step (footstep) | passo (m) | ['passɔ] |
| on foot (adv) | a piedi | [a 'pjedi] |

to block (road)	sbarrare (vt)	[zbar'rarɛ]
boom barrier	sbarra (f)	['zbarra]
dead end	vicolo (m) cieco	['wikɔlɔ 'tʃjekɔ]

191. Breaking the law. Criminals. Part 1

bandit	bandito (m)	[ban'ditɔ]
crime	delitto (m)	[dɛ'littɔ]
criminal (person)	criminale (m)	[krimi'nale]

thief	ladro (m)	['ʎadrɔ]
to steal (vi, vt)	rubare (vi, vt)	[ru'barɛ]
stealing (larceny)	ruberia (f)	[rubɛ'ria]
theft	furto (m)	['furtɔ]

to kidnap (vt)	rapire (vt)	[ra'pirɛ]
kidnapping	rapimento (m)	[rapi'mɛntɔ]
kidnapper	rapitore (m)	[rapi'tɔrɛ]

| ransom | riscatto (m) | [ris'kattɔ] |
| to demand ransom | chiedere il riscatto | ['kjedɛrɛ iʎ ris'kattɔ] |

| to rob (vt) | rapinare (vt) | [rapi'narɛ] |
| robber | rapinatore (m) | [rapina'tɔrɛ] |

to extort (vt)	estorcere (vt)	[ɛs'tɔrtʃerɛ]
extortionist	estorsore (m)	[ɛstɔr'sɔrɛ]
extortion	estorsione (f)	[ɛstɔr'sʲɔnɛ]

to murder, to kill	uccidere (vt)	[u'tʃidɛrɛ]
murder	assassinio (m)	[assas'siniɔ]
murderer	assassino (m)	[assas'sinɔ]

gunshot	sparo (m)	['sparɔ]
to fire a shot	tirare un colpo	[ti'rarɛ un 'kɔʎpɔ]
to shoot down	abbattere (vt)	[ab'battɛrɛ]
to shoot (vi)	sparare (vi)	[spa'rarɛ]
shooting	sparatoria (f)	[spara'tɔria]

incident (fight, etc.)	incidente (m)	[intʃi'dɛntɛ]
fight, brawl	rissa (f)	['rissa]
Help!	Aiuto!	[a'jutɔ]
victim	vittima (f)	['wittima]

to damage (vt)	danneggiare (vt)	[danɛ'dʒarɛ]
damage	danno (m)	['danɔ]
dead body	cadavere (m)	[ka'davɛrɛ]
grave (~ crime)	grave	['gravɛ]

| to attack (vt) | aggredire (vt) | [aggrɛ'dirɛ] |
| to beat (dog, person) | picchiare (vt) | [pik'kjarɛ] |

to beat up	picchiare (vt)	[pik'kjarɛ]
to take (snatch)	sottrarre (vt)	[sott'rarrɛ]
to stab to death	accoltellare a morte	[akkoʎtɛ'ʎarɛ a 'mortɛ]
to maim (vt)	mutilare (vt)	[muti'ʎarɛ]
to wound (vt)	ferire (vt)	[fɛ'rirɛ]

blackmail	ricatto (m)	[ri'katto]
to blackmail (vt)	ricattare (vt)	[rikat'tarɛ]
blackmailer	ricattatore (m)	[rikatta'torɛ]

protection racket	estorsione (f)	[ɛstor'sjonɛ]
racketeer	estorsore (m)	[ɛstor'sorɛ]
gangster	gangster (m)	['gaŋstɛr]
mafia	mafia (f)	['mafia]

pickpocket	borseggiatore (m)	[borsɛdʒa'torɛ]
burglar	scassinatore (m)	[skassina'torɛ]
smuggling	contrabbando (m)	[kontrab'bando]
smuggler	contrabbandiere (m)	[kontrabban'djerɛ]

forgery	falsificazione (f)	[faʎsifika'tsjonɛ]
to forge (counterfeit)	falsificare (vt)	[faʎsifi'karɛ]
fake (forged)	falso, falsificato	['faʎso], [faʎsifi'kato]

192. Breaking the law. Criminals. Part 2

rape	stupro (m)	['stupro]
to rape (vt)	stuprare (vt)	[stup'rarɛ]
rapist	stupratore (m)	[stupra'torɛ]
maniac	maniaco (m)	[ma'niako]

prostitute (fem.)	prostituta (f)	[prosti'tuta]
prostitution	prostituzione (f)	[prostitu'tsjonɛ]
pimp	magnaccia (m)	[ma'ɲjatʃa]

| drug addict | drogato (m) | [dro'gato] |
| drug dealer | trafficante (m) di droga | [traffi'kantɛ di 'droga] |

to blow up (bomb)	far esplodere	[far ɛsp'lɔdɛrɛ]
explosion	esplosione (f)	[ɛsplozi'onɛ]
to set fire	incendiare (vt)	[intʃen'djarɛ]
incendiary (arsonist)	incendiario (m)	[intʃendi'ario]

terrorism	terrorismo (m)	[tɛrro'rizmo]
terrorist	terrorista (m)	[tɛrro'rista]
hostage	ostaggio (m)	[os'tadʒo]

to swindle (vt)	imbrogliare (vt)	[imbro'ʎjarɛ]
swindle	imbroglio (m)	[imb'roʎo]
swindler	imbroglione (m)	[imbroʎonɛ]

to bribe (vt)	corrompere (vt)	[kor'rompɛrɛ]
bribery	corruzione (f)	[korru'tsjonɛ]
bribe	bustarella (f)	[busta'rɛʎa]

poison	veleno (m)	[vɛ'lenɔ]
to poison (vt)	avvelenare (vt)	[avvɛle'narɛ]
to poison oneself	avvelenarsi (vr)	[avvɛle'narsi]

| suicide (act) | suicidio (m) | [sui'tʃidiɔ] |
| suicide (person) | suicida (m) | [sui'tʃida] |

to threaten (vt)	minacciare (vt)	[mina'tʃarɛ]
threat	minaccia (f)	[mi'natʃa]
to make an attempt	attentare (vi)	[attɛn'tarɛ]
attempt (attack)	attentato (m)	[attɛn'tatɔ]

| to steal (a car) | rubare (vt) | [ru'barɛ] |
| to hijack (a plane) | dirottare (vt) | [dirɔt'tarɛ] |

| revenge | vendetta (f) | [vɛn'dɛtta] |
| to avenge (vt) | vendicare (vt) | [vɛndi'karɛ] |

to torture (vt)	torturare (vt)	[tɔrtu'rarɛ]
torture	tortura (f)	[tɔr'tura]
to torment (vt)	maltrattare (vt)	[maʎtrat'tarɛ]

pirate	pirata (m)	[pi'rata]
hooligan	teppista (m)	[tɛp'pista]
armed (adj)	armato	[ar'matɔ]
violence	violenza (f)	[wiɔ'lentsa]

| spying (n) | spionaggio (m) | [spiɔ'nadʒɔ] |
| to spy (vi) | spiare (vi) | [spi'arɛ] |

193. Police. Law. Part 1

| justice | giustizia (f) | [dʒus'titsia] |
| court (court room) | tribunale (m) | [tribu'nale] |

judge	giudice (m)	['dʒuditʃe]
jurors	giurati (m)	[dʒu'rati]
jury trial	processo (m) con giuria	[prɔ'tʃessɔ kɔn dʒu'ria]
to judge (vt)	giudicare (vt)	[dʒudi'karɛ]

lawyer, barrister	avvocato (m)	[avvɔ'katɔ]
accused	imputato (m)	[impu'tatɔ]
dock	banco (m) degli imputati	['baŋkɔ 'deʎi impu'tati]

| charge | accusa (f) | [ak'kuza] |
| accused | accusato (m) | [akku'zatɔ] |

| sentence | condanna (f) | [kɔn'daŋa] |
| to sentence (vt) | condannare (vt) | [kɔnda'ŋarɛ] |

guilty (culprit)	colpevole (m)	[kɔʎ'pevɔle]
to punish (vt)	punire (vt)	[pu'nirɛ]
punishment	punizione (f)	[puni'tsʲɔnɛ]
fine (penalty)	multa (f), ammenda (f)	['muʎta], [am'mɛnda]

life imprisonment	ergastolo (m)	[ɛr'gastɔlɔ]
death penalty	pena (f) di morte	['pɛna di 'mɔrtɛ]
electric chair	sedia (f) elettrica	['sɛdja ɛ'lettrika]
gallows	impiccagione (f)	[impikka'dʒɔnɛ]

| to execute (vt) | giustiziare (vt) | [dʒustitsi'arɛ] |
| execution | esecuzione (f) | [ɛzɛku'tsʲɔnɛ] |

| prison, jail | prigione (f) | [pri'dʒɔnɛ] |
| cell | cella (f) | ['tʃeʎa] |

escort	scorta (f)	['skɔrta]
prison officer	guardia (f) carceraria	[gu'ardia kartʃe'raria]
prisoner	prigioniero (m)	[pridʒo'njerɔ]

| handcuffs | manette (f pl) | [ma'nɛttɛ] |
| to handcuff (vt) | mettere le manette | ['mɛttɛrɛ le ma'nɛttɛ] |

prison break	fuga (f)	['fuga]
to break out (vi)	fuggire (vi)	[fu'dʒirɛ]
to disappear (vi)	scomparire (vi)	[skompa'rirɛ]
to release (from prison)	liberare (vt)	[libɛ'rarɛ]
amnesty	amnistia (f)	[amnis'tia]

police	polizia (f)	[poli'tsia]
policeman	poliziotto (m)	[politsi'ɔttɔ]
police station	commissariato (m)	[kommissari'atɔ]
truncheon	manganello (m)	[maŋa'nɛllɔ]
loudspeaker	altoparlante (m)	[aʎtopar'ʎantɛ]

patrol car	macchina (f) di pattuglia	['makkina di pat'tuʎja]
siren	sirena (f)	[si'rɛna]
to turn on the siren	mettere la sirena	['mɛttɛrɛ ʎa si'rɛna]
siren call	suono (m) della sirena	[su'ɔnɔ 'dɛʎa si'rɛna]

crime scene	luogo (m) del crimine	[ly'ɔgɔ dɛʎ 'kriminɛ]
witness	testimone (m)	[tɛsti'mɔnɛ]
freedom	libertà (f)	[libɛr'ta]
accomplice	complice (m)	['komplitʃe]
to flee (vi)	fuggire (vi)	[fu'dʒirɛ]
trace (to leave a ~)	traccia (f)	['tratʃa]

194. Police. Law. Part 2

search (for a criminal)	ricerca (f)	[ri'tʃerka]
to look for ...	cercare (vt)	[tʃer'karɛ]
suspicion	sospetto (m)	[sos'pɛttɔ]
suspicious (suspect)	sospetto	[sos'pɛttɔ]
to stop (cause to halt)	fermare (vt)	[fɛr'marɛ]
to detain (keep in custody)	arrestare	[arrɛs'tarɛ]

case (lawsuit)	causa (f)	['kauza]
investigation	inchiesta (f)	[in'kjesta]
detective	detective (m)	[dɛ'tɛktiv]

investigator	investigatore (m)	[investiga'tɔrɛ]
version	versione (f)	[vɛrsi'ɔnɛ]
motive	movente (m)	[mɔ'vɛntɛ]
interrogation	interrogatorio (m)	[intɛrrɔga'tɔriɔ]
to interrogate (vt)	interrogare (vt)	[intɛrrɔ'garɛ]
to question (vt)	interrogare (vt)	[intɛrrɔ'garɛ]
checking (police ~)	controllo (m)	[kɔnt'rɔllɔ]
round-up	retata (f)	[rɛ'tata]
search (~ warrant)	perquisizione (f)	[pɛrkuizi'tsʲɔnɛ]
chase (pursuit)	inseguimento (m)	[insɛgui'mɛntɔ]
to pursue, to chase	inseguire (vt)	[insɛgu'irɛ]
to track (a criminal)	essere sulle tracce	['ɛssɛrɛ sullɛ 'tratʃɛ]
arrest	arresto (m)	[ar'rɛstɔ]
to arrest (sb)	arrestare	[arrɛs'tarɛ]
to catch (thief, etc.)	catturare (vt)	[kattu'rarɛ]
capture	cattura (f)	[kat'tura]
document	documento (m)	[dɔku'mɛntɔ]
proof (evidence)	prova (f)	['prɔva]
to prove (vt)	provare (vt)	[prɔ'varɛ]
footprint	impronta (f) del piede	[imp'rɔnta dɛʎ 'pjedɛ]
fingerprints	impronte (f pl) digitali	[imp'rɔntɛ didʒi'tali]
piece of evidence	elemento (m) di prova	[ɛle'mɛntɔ di 'prɔva]
alibi	alibi (m)	['alibi]
innocent (not guilty)	innocente	[iɲɔ'tʃɛntɛ]
injustice (unjust act)	ingiustizia (f)	[indʒus'titsia]
unjust, unfair (adj)	ingiusto	[in'dʒustɔ]
crime (adj)	criminale	[krimi'nale]
to confiscate (vt)	confiscare (vt)	[kɔnfis'karɛ]
drug (illegal substance)	droga (f)	['drɔga]
weapon, gun	armi (f pl)	['armi]
to disarm (vt)	disarmare (vt)	[dizar'marɛ]
to order (command)	ordinare (vt)	[ɔrdi'narɛ]
to disappear (vi)	sparire (vi)	[spa'rirɛ]
law	legge (f)	['ledʒe]
legal (adj)	legale	[le'gale]
illegal (adj)	illegale	[ille'gale]
responsibility	responsabilità (f)	[rɛspɔnsabili'ta]
responsible (adj)	responsabile	[rɛspɔn'sabile]

NATURE

The Earth. Part 1

195. Outer space

cosmos	cosmo (m)	['kɔzmɔ]
space (as adj)	cosmico, spaziale	['kɔzmikɔ], [spatsi'ale]
outer space	spazio (m) cosmico	['spatsiɔ 'kɔzmikɔ]
world	mondo (m)	['mɔndɔ]
universe	universo (m)	[uni'vɛrsɔ]
galaxy	galassia (f)	[ga'ʎassia]
star	stella (f)	['stɛʎa]
constellation	costellazione (f)	[kɔstɛʎa'tsɔnɛ]
planet	pianeta (m)	[pja'nɛta]
satellite	satellite (m)	[sa'tɛllitɛ]
meteorite	meteorite (m)	[mɛtɛɔ'ritɛ]
comet	cometa (f)	[kɔ'mɛta]
asteroid	asteroide (m)	[astɛ'rɔidɛ]
orbit	orbita (f)	['ɔrbita]
to rotate (vi)	ruotare (vi)	[ruɔ'tarɛ]
atmosphere	atmosfera (f)	[atmɔs'fɛra]
the Sun	il Sole	[iʎ 'sɔle]
solar system	sistema (m) solare	[sis'tɛma sɔ'ʎarɛ]
solar eclipse	eclisse (f) solare	[ɛk'lissɛ sɔ'ʎarɛ]
the Earth	la Terra	[ʎa 'tɛrra]
the Moon	la Luna	[ʎa 'lyna]
Mars	Marte (m)	['martɛ]
Venus	Venere (f)	['vɛnɛrɛ]
Jupiter	Giove (m)	['dʒɔvɛ]
Saturn	Saturno (m)	[sa'turnɔ]
Mercury	Mercurio (m)	[mɛr'kuriɔ]
Uranus	Urano (m)	[u'ranɔ]
Neptune	Nettuno (m)	[nɛt'tunɔ]
Pluto	Plutone (m)	[ply'tɔnɛ]
Milky Way	Via (f) Lattea	['wia 'ʎattɛa]
Great Bear	Orsa (f) Maggiore	['ɔrsa ma'dʒɔrɛ]
North Star	Stella (f) Polare	['stɛʎa pɔ'ʎarɛ]
Martian	marziano (m)	[martsi'anɔ]
extraterrestrial	extraterrestre (m)	[ɛkstratɛr'rɛstrɛ]

alien	alieno (m)	[a'ʎjenɔ]
flying saucer	disco (m) volante	['diskɔ vɔ'lantɛ]

spaceship	nave (f) spaziale	['navɛ spa'tsⁱale]
space station	stazione (f) spaziale	[sta'tsⁱonɛ spa'tsⁱale]
blast-off	lancio (m)	['ʎantʃo]

engine	motore (m)	[mɔ'torɛ]
nozzle	ugello (m)	[u'dʒellɔ]
fuel	combustibile (m)	[kɔmbus'tibile]

cockpit, flight deck	cabina (f) di pilotaggio	[ka'bina di pilɔ'tadʒiɔ]
aerial	antenna (f)	[an'tɛɲa]
porthole	oblò (m)	[ɔb'lɔ]
solar battery	batteria (f) solare	[battɛ'ria sɔ'ʎarɛ]
spacesuit	scafandro (m)	[ska'fandrɔ]

weightlessness	imponderabilità (f)	[impɔndɛrabili'ta]
oxygen	ossigeno (m)	[ɔs'sidʒenɔ]

docking (in space)	aggancio (m)	[ag'gantʃo]
to dock (vi, vt)	agganciarsi (vr)	[aggan'tʃarsi]

observatory	osservatorio (m)	[ɔssɛrva'toriɔ]
telescope	telescopio (m)	[tɛles'kopiɔ]
to observe (vt)	osservare (vt)	[ɔssɛr'varɛ]
to explore (vt)	esplorare (vt)	[ɛsplɔ'rarɛ]

196. The Earth

the Earth	la Terra	[ʎa 'tɛrra]
globe (the Earth)	globo (m) terrestre	['glɔbɔ tɛr'rɛstrɛ]
planet	pianeta (m)	[pja'nɛta]

atmosphere	atmosfera (f)	[atmɔs'fɛra]
geography	geografia (f)	[dʒeɔgra'fia]
nature	natura (f)	[na'tura]

globe (table ~)	mappamondo (m)	[mappa'mondɔ]
map	carta (f) geografica	['karta dʒeɔg'rafika]
atlas	atlante (m)	[at'ʎantɛ]

Europe	Europa (f)	[ɛu'rɔpa]
Asia	Asia (f)	['azia]

Africa	Africa (f)	['afrika]
Australia	Australia (f)	[aust'ralia]

America	America (f)	[a'mɛrika]
North America	America (f) del Nord	[a'mɛrika dɛʎ nɔrd]
South America	America (f) del Sud	[a'mɛrika dɛʎ sud]

Antarctica	Antartide (f)	[an'tartidɛ]
the Arctic	Artico (m)	['artikɔ]

197. Cardinal directions

north	**nord** (m)	[nɔrd]
to the north	**a nord**	[a nɔrd]
in the north	**al nord**	[aʎ nɔrd]
northern (adj)	**del nord**	[dɛʎ nɔrd]

south	**sud** (m)	[sud]
to the south	**a sud**	[a sud]
in the south	**al sud**	[aʎ sud]
southern (adj)	**del sud**	[dɛʎ sud]

west	**ovest** (m)	['ɔvɛst]
to the west	**a ovest**	[a ɔ'vɛst]
in the west	**all'ovest**	[aʎ 'ɔvɛst]
western (adj)	**dell'ovest, occidentale**	[dɛʎ 'ɔvɛst], [ɔʧidɛn'tale]

east	**est** (m)	[ɛst]
to the east	**a est**	[a ɛst]
in the east	**all'est**	[aʎ 'ɛst]
eastern (adj)	**dell'est, orientale**	[dɛ'ʎɛst], [ɔrien'tale]

198. Sea. Ocean

sea	**mare** (m)	['marɛ]
ocean	**oceano** (m)	[ɔ'ʧeanɔ]
gulf (bay)	**golfo** (m)	['gɔʎfɔ]
straits	**stretto** (m)	['strɛttɔ]

dry land	**terra** (f)	['tɛrra]
continent (mainland)	**continente** (m)	[kɔnti'nɛntɛ]
island	**isola** (f)	['izɔʎa]
peninsula	**penisola** (f)	[pɛ'nizɔʎa]
archipelago	**arcipelago** (m)	[arʧi'pɛʎagɔ]

bay	**baia** (f)	['baja]
harbour	**porto** (m)	['pɔrtɔ]
lagoon	**laguna** (f)	[ʎa'guna]
cape	**capo** (m)	['kapɔ]

atoll	**atollo** (m)	[a'tɔllɔ]
reef	**reef** (m)	[riːf]
coral	**corallo** (m)	[kɔ'rallɔ]
coral reef	**barriera** (f) **corallina**	[bar'rjera kɔral'lina]

deep (adj)	**profondo**	[prɔ'fondɔ]
depth (deep water)	**profondità** (f)	[profondi'ta]
abyss	**abisso** (m)	[a'bissɔ]
trench (e.g. Mariana ~)	**fossa** (f)	['fɔssa]

current, stream	**corrente** (f)	[kɔr'rɛntɛ]
to surround (bathe)	**circondare** (vt)	[ʧirkɔn'darɛ]
shore	**litorale** (m)	[litɔ'rale]

coast	costa (f)	['kɔsta]
high tide	alta marea (f)	['aʎta ma'rɛa]
low tide	bassa marea (f)	['bassa ma'rɛa]
sandbank	banco (m) di sabbia	['baŋkɔ di 'sabbia]
bottom	fondo (m)	['fondɔ]
wave	onda (f)	['ɔnda]
crest (~ of a wave)	cresta (f) dell'onda	['krɛsta dɛʎ 'ɔnda]
froth (foam)	schiuma (f)	['skjyma]
hurricane	uragano (m)	[ura'ganɔ]
tsunami	tsunami (m)	[ʦu'nami]
calm (dead ~)	bonaccia (f)	[bɔ'naʧa]
quiet, calm (adj)	tranquillo	[traŋku'illɔ]
pole	polo (m)	['pɔlɔ]
polar (adj)	polare	[pɔ'ʎarɛ]
latitude	latitudine (f)	[ʎati'tudinɛ]
longitude	longitudine (f)	[lɔndʒi'tudinɛ]
parallel	parallelo (m)	[paral'lelɔ]
equator	equatore (m)	[ɛkua'tɔrɛ]
sky	cielo (m)	['ʧelɔ]
horizon	orizzonte (m)	[ori'dzɔntɛ]
air	aria (f)	['aria]
lighthouse	faro (m)	['farɔ]
to dive (vi)	tuffarsi (vr)	[tuf'farsi]
to sink (ab. boat)	affondare (vi)	[affon'darɛ]
treasures	tesori (m)	[tɛ'zori]

199. Seas & Oceans names

Atlantic Ocean	Oceano (m) Atlantico	[ɔ'ʧeanɔ at'ʎantikɔ]
Indian Ocean	Oceano (m) Indiano	[ɔ'ʧeanɔ indi'anɔ]
Pacific Ocean	Oceano (m) Pacifico	[ɔ'ʧeanɔ pa'ʧifikɔ]
Arctic Ocean	mar (m) Glaciale Artico	[mar gʎa'ʧale 'artikɔ]
Black Sea	mar (m) Nero	[mar 'nɛrɔ]
Red Sea	mar (m) Rosso	[mar 'rɔssɔ]
Yellow Sea	mar (m) Giallo	[mar 'dʒallɔ]
White Sea	mar (m) Bianco	[mar 'bjaŋkɔ]
Caspian Sea	mar (m) Caspio	[mar 'kaspio]
Dead Sea	mar (m) Morto	[mar 'mortɔ]
Mediterranean Sea	mar (m) Mediterraneo	[mar mɛditɛr'ranɛɔ]
Aegean Sea	mar (m) Egeo	[mar ɛ'dʒeɔ]
Adriatic Sea	mar (m) Adriatico	[mar adri'atikɔ]
Arabian Sea	mar (m) Arabico	[mar a'rabikɔ]
Sea of Japan	mar (m) del Giappone	[mar dɛʎ dʒap'pɔnɛ]
Bering Sea	mare (m) di Bering	['marɛ di 'beriŋ]

South China Sea	mar (m) Cinese meridionale	[mar tʃi'nɛzɛ mɛridiɔ'nale]
Coral Sea	mar (m) dei Coralli	[mar 'dei kɔ'ralli]
Tasman Sea	mar (m) di Tasmania	[mar di taz'mania]
Caribbean Sea	mar (m) dei Caraibi	[mar dɛi kara'ibi]

| Barents Sea | mare (m) di Barents | ['marɛ di 'barɛnts] |
| Kara Sea | mare (m) di Kara | ['marɛ di 'kara] |

North Sea	mare (m) del Nord	['marɛ dɛʎ nɔrd]
Baltic Sea	mar (m) Baltico	[mar 'baʎtikɔ]
Norwegian Sea	mare (m) di Norvegia	['marɛ di nɔr'vɛdʒa]

200. Mountains

mountain	monte (m), montagna (f)	['mɔntɛ], [mɔn'taɲa]
mountain range	catena (f) montuosa	[ka'tɛna mɔntu'oza]
mountain ridge	crinale (m)	[kri'nale]

summit, top	cima (f)	['tʃima]
peak	picco (m)	['pikkɔ]
foot (of mountain)	piedi (m pl)	['pjedɛ]
slope (mountainside)	pendio (m)	[pɛn'diɔ]

volcano	vulcano (m)	[vuʎ'kanɔ]
active volcano	vulcano (m) attivo	[vuʎ'kanɔ at'tivɔ]
dormant volcano	vulcano (m) inattivo	[vuʎ'kanɔ inat'tivɔ]

eruption	eruzione (f)	[ɛru'tsiɔnɛ]
crater	cratere (m)	[kra'tɛrɛ]
magma	magma (m)	['magma]
lava	lava (f)	['ʎava]
molten (~ lava)	fuso	['fuzɔ]

canyon	canyon (m)	['kɛɲɔn]
gorge	gola (f)	['gɔʎa]
crevice	crepaccio (m)	[krɛ'patʃo]
pass, col	passo (m), valico (m)	['passɔ], ['valikɔ]
plateau	altopiano (m)	[aʎtɔ'pianɔ]
cliff	falesia (f)	[fa'lezija]
hill	collina (f)	[kɔl'lina]

glacier	ghiacciaio (m)	[gja'tʃajo]
waterfall	cascata (f)	[kas'kata]
geyser	geyser (m)	['gɛjzɛr]
lake	lago (m)	['ʎagɔ]

plain	pianura (f)	[pja'nura]
landscape	paesaggio (m)	[paɛ'zadʒɔ]
echo	eco (f)	['ɛkɔ]

alpinist	alpinista (m)	[aʎpi'nista]
rock climber	scalatore (m)	[skaʎa'tɔrɛ]
to conquer (in climbing)	conquistare (vt)	[kɔŋkuis'tarɛ]
climb (an easy ~)	scalata (f)	[ska'ʎata]

201. Mountains names

Alps	Alpi (f pl)	['aʎpi]
Mont Blanc	Monte (m) Bianco	['mɔntɛ 'bjaŋkɔ]
Pyrenees	Pirenei (m pl)	[pirɛ'nɛi]

Carpathians	Carpazi (m pl)	[kar'patsi]
Ural Mountains	gli Urali (m pl)	[ʎi u'rali]
Caucasus	Caucaso (m)	['kaukazɔ]
Elbrus	Monte (m) Elbrus	['mɔntɛ 'eʎbrus]

Altai	Monti (m pl) Altai	['mɔnti al'taj]
Tien Shan	Tien Shan (m)	[tʲɛn 'ʃan]
Pamir Mountains	Pamir (m)	[pa'mir]
Himalayas	Himalaia (m)	[ima'ʎaja]
Everest	Everest (m)	['ɛvɛrɛst]

| Andes | Ande (f pl) | ['andɛ] |
| Kilimanjaro | Kilimangiaro (m) | [kiliman'dʒarɔ] |

202. Rivers

river	fiume (m)	['fjymɛ]
spring (natural source)	fonte (f)	['fontɛ]
riverbed	letto (m)	['lettɔ]
basin	bacino (m)	[ba'tʃinɔ]
to flow into …	sfociare nel …	[sfɔ'tʃarɛ nɛʎ]

| tributary | affluente (m) | [affly'ɛntɛ] |
| bank (of river) | riva (f) | ['riva] |

current, stream	corrente (f)	[kɔr'rɛntɛ]
downstream (adv)	a valle	[a 'vallɛ]
upstream (adv)	a monte	[a 'mɔntɛ]

inundation	inondazione (f)	[inɔnda'tsʲɔnɛ]
flooding	piena (f)	['pjena]
to overflow (vi)	straripare (vi)	[strari'parɛ]
to flood (vt)	inondare (vt)	[inɔn'darɛ]

| shallows (shoal) | secca (f) | ['sɛkka] |
| rapids | rapida (f) | ['rapida] |

dam	diga (f)	['diga]
canal	canale (m)	[ka'nale]
reservoir (artificial lake)	bacino (m) di riserva	[ba'tʃinɔ di ri'zɛrva]
sluice, lock	chiusa (f)	['kjyza]

water body (pond, etc.)	bacino (m) idrico	[ba'tʃinɔ 'idrikɔ]
swamp, bog	palude (f)	[pa'lydɛ]
marsh	pantano (m)	[pan'tanɔ]
whirlpool	vortice (m)	['vortitʃe]
stream (brook)	ruscello (m)	[ru'ʃellɔ]

| drinking (ab. water) | potabile | [po'tabile] |
| fresh (~ water) | dolce | ['dɔʌʧe] |

| ice | ghiaccio (m) | ['gjaʧɔ] |
| to ice over | ghiacciarsi (vr) | [gja'ʧarsi] |

203. Rivers names

| Seine | Senna (f) | ['sɛŋa] |
| Loire | Loira (f) | ['lɜira] |

Thames	Tamigi (m)	[ta'miʤi]
Rhine	Reno (m)	['rɛnɔ]
Danube	Danubio (m)	[da'nubiɔ]

Volga	Volga (m)	['vɔʌga]
Don	Don (m)	[dɔn]
Lena	Lena (f)	['lena]

Yellow River	Fiume (m) Giallo	['fjymɛ 'ʤallɔ]
Yangtze	Fiume (m) Azzurro	['fjymɛ a'dzurrɔ]
Mekong	Mekong (m)	[mɛ'kɔn]
Ganges	Gange (m)	['ganʤe]

Nile	Nilo (m)	['nilɔ]
Congo	Congo (m)	['kɔŋɔ]
Okavango	Okavango	[ɔka'vaŋɔ]
Zambezi	Zambesi (m)	[dzam'bɛzi]
Limpopo	Limpopo (m)	['limpɔpɔ]

204. Forest

| forest | foresta (f) | [fo'rɛsta] |
| forest (as adj) | forestale | [forɛs'tale] |

thick forest	foresta (f) fitta	[fo'rɛsta 'fitta]
grove	boschetto (m)	[bos'kɛttɔ]
clearing	radura (f)	[ra'dura]

| thicket | roveto (m) | [rɔ'vɛtɔ] |
| scrubland | boscaglia (f) | [bos'kaʎja] |

| footpath | sentiero (m) | [sɛn'tʲerɔ] |
| gully | calanco (m) | [ka'laŋkɔ] |

tree	albero (m)	['aʌbɛrɔ]
leaf	foglia (f)	['foʎja]
leaves	fogliame (m)	[fo'ʎjamɛ]

falling leaves	caduta (f) delle foglie	[ka'duta 'dɛlle 'foʎje]
to fall (ab. leaves)	cadere (vi)	[ka'dɛrɛ]
top (of the tree)	cima (f)	['ʧima]

branch	ramo (m), ramoscello (m)	['ramɔ], [ramɔ'ʃɛllɔ]
bough	ramo (m)	['ramɔ]
bud (on shrub, tree)	gemma (f)	['dʒɛmma]
needle (of pine tree)	ago (m)	['agɔ]
fir cone	pigna (f)	['piɲja]

hollow (in a tree)	cavità (f)	[kawi'ta]
nest	nido (m)	['nidɔ]
burrow (animal hole)	tana (f)	['tana]

trunk	tronco (m)	['trɔŋkɔ]
root	radice (f)	[ra'ditʃe]
bark	corteccia (f)	[kɔr'tetʃa]
moss	musco (m)	['muskɔ]

to uproot (vt)	sradicare (vt)	[zradi'karɛ]
to chop down	abbattere (vt)	[ab'battɛrɛ]
to deforest (vt)	disboscare (vt)	[dizbɔs'karɛ]
tree stump	ceppo (m)	['tʃeppɔ]

campfire	falò (m)	[fa'lɔ]
forest fire	incendio (m) boschivo	[in'tʃɛndiɔ bɔs'kivɔ]
to extinguish (vt)	spegnere (vt)	['speɲjerɛ]

forest ranger	guardia (f) forestale	[gu'ardia fɔrɛs'tale]
protection	protezione (f)	[prɔtɛ'tsʲɔnɛ]
to protect (~ nature)	proteggere (vt)	[prɔ'tɛdʒerɛ]
poacher	bracconiere (m)	[brakkɔ'ɲjerɛ]
trap (e.g. bear ~)	tagliola (f)	[ta'ʎɔʎa]

| to gather, to pick (vt) | raccogliere (vt) | [rak'kɔʎjerɛ] |
| to lose one's way | perdersi (vr) | ['pɛrdɛrsi] |

205. Natural resources

natural resources	risorse (f pl) naturali	[ri'sɔrsɛ natu'rali]
minerals	minerali (m pl)	[minɛ'rali]
deposits	deposito (m)	[dɛ'pɔzitɔ]
field (e.g. oilfield)	giacimento (m)	[dʒatʃi'mɛntɔ]

to mine (extract)	estrarre (vt)	[ɛst'rarrɛ]
mining (extraction)	estrazione (f)	[ɛstra'tsʲɔnɛ]
ore	minerale (m) grezzo	[minɛ'rale 'grɛdzɔ]
mine (e.g. for coal)	miniera (f)	[mi'ɲjera]
mine shaft, pit	pozzo (m) di miniera	['pɔtsɔ di mi'ɲʲɛra]
miner	minatore (m)	[mina'tɔrɛ]

| gas | gas (m) | [gas] |
| gas pipeline | gasdotto (m) | [gas'dɔttɔ] |

oil (petroleum)	petrolio (m)	[pɛt'rɔliɔ]
oil pipeline	oleodotto (m)	[ɔleɔ'dɔttɔ]
oil rig	torre (f) di estrazione	['tɔrrɛ di ɛstra'tsʲɔnɛ]
derrick	torre (f) di trivellazione	['tɔrrɛ di trivɛʎa'tsʲɔnɛ]

tanker	petroliera (f)	[pɛtrɔ'ʎjera]
sand	sabbia (f)	['sabbja]
limestone	calcare (m)	[kaʎ'karɛ]
gravel	ghiaia (f)	['gjaja]
peat	torba (f)	['tɔrba]
clay	argilla (f)	[ar'dʒiʎa]
coal	carbone (m)	[kar'bɔnɛ]
iron	ferro (m)	['fɛrrɔ]
gold	oro (m)	['ɔrɔ]
silver	argento (m)	[ar'dʒentɔ]
nickel	nichel (m)	['nikɛʎ]
copper	rame (m)	['ramɛ]
zinc	zinco (m)	['dziŋkɔ]
manganese	manganese (m)	[maɲa'nɛzɛ]
mercury	mercurio (m)	[mɛr'kurjɔ]
lead	piombo (m)	['pjɔmbɔ]
mineral	minerale (m)	[minɛ'ralɛ]
crystal	cristallo (m)	[kris'tallɔ]
marble	marmo (m)	['marmɔ]
uranium	uranio (m)	[u'ranjɔ]

The Earth. Part 2

206. Weather

| weather | tempo (m) | ['tɛmpɔ] |
| weather forecast | previsione (f) del tempo | [prɛwizi'ɔnɛ dɛʎ 'tɛmpɔ] |

temperature	temperatura (f)	[tɛmpɛra'tura]
thermometer	termometro (m)	[tɛr'mɔmɛtrɔ]
barometer	barometro (m)	[ba'rɔmɛtrɔ]

humidity	umidità (f)	[umidi'ta]
heat (of summer)	caldo (m), afa (f)	['kaʎdɔ], ['afa]
hot (torrid)	molto caldo	['mɔʎtɔ 'kaʎdɔ]
it's hot	fa molto caldo	[fa 'mɔʎtɔ 'kaʎdɔ]

| it's warm | fa caldo | [fa 'kaʎdɔ] |
| warm (moderately hot) | caldo | ['kaʎdɔ] |

| it's cold | fa freddo | [fa 'frɛddɔ] |
| cold (adj) | freddo | ['frɛddɔ] |

sun	sole (m)	['sɔle]
to shine (vi)	splendere (vi)	['splendɛrɛ]
sunny (day)	di sole	[di 'sɔle]
to come up (vi)	levarsi (vr)	[lɛ'varsi]
to set (vi)	tramontare (vi)	[tramɔn'tarɛ]

cloud	nuvola (f)	['nuvɔʎa]
cloudy (adj)	nuvoloso	[nuvɔ'lзɔ]
rain cloud	nube (f) di pioggia	['nubɛ di 'pʲɔdʒa]
somber (gloomy)	nuvoloso	[nuvɔ'lзɔ]

rain	pioggia (f)	['pʲɔdʒa]
it's raining	piove	['pʲɔvɛ]
rainy (day)	piovoso	[pʲɔ'vɔzɔ]
to drizzle (vi)	piovigginare (vi)	[pʲowidʒi'narɛ]

pouring rain	pioggia (f) torrenziale	['pʲɔdʒa tɔrrɛntsi'ale]
downpour	acquazzone (m)	[akua'tsɔnɛ]
heavy (e.g. ~ rain)	forte	['fɔrtɛ]

| puddle | pozzanghera (f) | [pɔ'tsaŋɛra] |
| to get wet (in rain) | bagnarsi (vr) | [ba'ɲjarsi] |

| fog (mist) | foschia (f), nebbia (f) | [fɔs'kia], ['nɛbbia] |
| foggy | nebbioso | [nɛb'bʲɔzɔ] |

| snow | neve (f) | ['nɛvɛ] |
| it's snowing | nevica | ['nɛwika] |

207. Severe weather. Natural disasters

thunderstorm	temporale (m)	[tɛmpɔ'rale]
lightning (~ strike)	fulmine (f)	['fuʎminɛ]
to flash (vi)	lampeggiare (vi)	[ʎampɛ'dʒarɛ]
thunder	tuono (m)	[tu'ɔnɔ]
to thunder (vi)	tuonare (vi)	[tuɔ'narɛ]
it's thundering	tuona	[tu'ɔna]
hail	grandine (f)	['grandinɛ]
it's hailing	grandina	['grandina]
to flood (vt)	inondare (vt)	[inɔn'darɛ]
flood, inundation	inondazione (f)	[inɔnda'ʦɔnɛ]
earthquake	terremoto (m)	[tɛrrɛ'mɔtɔ]
tremor, quake	scossa (f)	['skɔssa]
epicentre	epicentro (m)	[ɛpi'ʧentrɔ]
eruption	eruzione (f)	[ɛru'ʦɔnɛ]
lava	lava (f)	['ʎava]
twister	tromba (f) d'aria	['trɔmba 'daria]
tornado	tornado (m)	[tor'nadɔ]
typhoon	tifone (m)	[ti'fɔnɛ]
hurricane	uragano (m)	[ura'ganɔ]
storm	tempesta (f)	[tɛm'pɛsta]
tsunami	tsunami (m)	[ʦu'nami]
cyclone	ciclone (m)	[ʧik'lɔnɛ]
bad weather	maltempo (m)	[maʎ'tɛmpɔ]
fire (accident)	incendio (m)	[in'ʧendiɔ]
disaster	disastro (m)	[di'zastrɔ]
meteorite	meteorite (m)	[mɛtɛɔ'ritɛ]
avalanche	valanga (f)	[va'ʎaŋa]
snowslide	slavina (f)	[zla'wina]
blizzard	tempesta (f) di neve	[tɛm'pɛsta di 'nɛvɛ]
snowstorm	bufera (f) di neve	['bufera di 'nɛvɛ]

208. Noises. Sounds

quiet, silence	silenzio (m)	[si'lenʦiɔ]
sound	suono (m)	[su'ɔnɔ]
noise	rumore (m)	[ru'mɔrɛ]
to make noise	far rumore	[far ru'mɔrɛ]
noisy (adj)	rumoroso	[rumɔ'rɔzɔ]
loudly (to speak, etc.)	forte, alto	['fɔrtɛ], ['aʎtɔ]
loud (voice, etc.)	alto, forte	['aʎtɔ], ['fɔrtɛ]
constant (continuous)	costante	[kɔs'tantɛ]

shout (n)	grido (m)	['grido]
to shout (vi)	gridare (vi)	[gri'darɛ]
whisper	sussurro (m)	[sus'surrɔ]
to whisper (vi, vt)	sussurrare (vi, vt)	[sussur'rarɛ]

barking (of dog)	abbaiamento (m)	[abaja'mɛntɔ]
to bark (vi)	abbaiare (vi)	[abba'jarɛ]

groan (of pain)	gemito (m)	['dʒemitɔ]
to groan (vi)	gemere (vi)	['dʒemɛrɛ]
cough	tosse (f)	['tɔssɛ]
to cough (vi)	tossire (vi)	[tɔs'sirɛ]

whistle	fischio (m)	['fiskiɔ]
to whistle (vi)	fischiare (vi)	[fis'kjarɛ]
knock (at the door)	bussata (f)	[bus'sata]
to knock (at the door)	bussare (vi)	[bus'sarɛ]

to crack (vi)	crepitare (vi)	[krɛpi'tarɛ]
crack (plank, etc.)	crepitio (m)	[krɛpi'tiɔ]

siren	sirena (f)	[si'rɛna]
whistle (factory's ~)	sirena (f) di fabbrica	[si'rɛna di 'fabrika]
to whistle (ship, train)	emettere un fischio	[ɛmɛt'tɛrɛ un 'fiskiɔ]
honk (signal)	colpo (m) di clacson	['koʎpɔ di 'klaksɔn]
to honk (vi)	clacsonare (vi)	[kʎaksɔ'narɛ]

209. Winter

winter (n)	inverno (m)	[in'vɛrnɔ]
winter (as adj)	invernale	[invɛr'nale]
in winter	d'inverno	[din'vɛrnɔ]

snow	neve (f)	['nɛvɛ]
it's snowing	nevica	['nɛwika]
snowfall	nevicata (f)	[nɛwi'kata]
snowdrift	mucchio (m) di neve	['mukkiɔ di 'nɛvɛ]

snowflake	fiocco (m) di neve	[fjokkɔ di 'nɛvɛ]
snowball	palla (f) di neve	['paʎa di 'nɛvɛ]
snowman	pupazzo (m) di neve	[pu'patsɔ di 'nɛvɛ]
icicle	ghiacciolo (m)	[gja'tʃolɔ]

December	dicembre (m)	[di'tʃembrɛ]
January	gennaio (m)	[dʒe'ŋajo]
February	febbraio (m)	[fɛbb'rajo]

heavy frost	gelo (m)	['dʒelɔ]
frosty (weather, air)	gelido	['dʒelidɔ]

below zero (adv)	sotto zero	['sɔtto 'dzɛrɔ]
first frost	primi geli (m pl)	['primi 'dʒeli]
hoarfrost	brina (f)	['brina]
cold (cold weather)	freddo (m)	['frɛddɔ]

it's cold	**fa freddo**	[fa 'freddɔ]
fur coat	**pelliccia** (f)	[pɛl'litʃa]
mittens	**manopole** (f pl)	[ma'nɔpɔle]

to fall ill	**ammalarsi** (vr)	[amma'ʎarsi]
cold (illness)	**raffreddore** (m)	[raffrɛd'dɔrɛ]
to catch a cold	**raffreddarsi** (vr)	[raffrɛd'darsi]

ice	**ghiaccio** (m)	['gjatʃɔ]
black ice	**ghiaccio** (m) **trasparente**	['gjatʃɔ traspa'rɛntɛ]
to ice over	**ghiacciarsi** (vr)	[gja'tʃarsi]
ice floe	**banco** (m) **di ghiaccio**	['baŋkɔ di 'gjatʃɔ]

skis	**sci** (m pl)	[ʃi]
skier	**sciatore** (m)	[ʃia'tɔrɛ]
to ski (vi)	**sciare** (vi)	[ʃi'arɛ]
to skate (vi)	**pattinare** (vi)	[patti'narɛ]

Fauna

210. Mammals. Predators

predator	predatore (m)	[prɛda'tɔrɛ]
tiger	tigre (f)	['tigrɛ]
lion	leone (m)	[le'ɔnɛ]
wolf	lupo (m)	['lypɔ]
fox	volpe (m)	['vɔʎpɛ]

jaguar	giaguaro (m)	[dʒagu'arɔ]
leopard	leopardo (m)	[leɔ'pardɔ]
cheetah	ghepardo (m)	[ge'pardɔ]

black panther	pantera (f)	[pan'tɛra]
puma	puma (f)	['puma]
snow leopard	leopardo (m) delle nevi	[leɔ'pardɔ 'dɛlle 'nɛwi]
lynx	lince (f)	['lintʃe]

coyote	coyote (m)	[kɔ'jotɛ]
jackal	sciacallo (m)	[ʃa'kallɔ]
hyena	iena (f)	['jena]

211. Wild animals

| animal | animale (m) | [ani'male] |
| beast (animal) | bestia (f) | ['bɛstia] |

squirrel	scoiattolo (m)	[skɔ'jattɔlɔ]
hedgehog	riccio (m)	['ritʃo]
hare	lepre (f)	['leprɛ]
rabbit	coniglio (m)	[kɔ'niʎɔ]

badger	tasso (m)	['tassɔ]
raccoon	procione (f)	[prɔ'tʃonɛ]
hamster	criceto (m)	[kri'tʃetɔ]
marmot	marmotta (f)	[mar'mɔtta]

mole	talpa (f)	['taʎpa]
mouse	topo (m)	['tɔpɔ]
rat	ratto (m)	['rattɔ]
bat	pipistrello (m)	[pipist'rɛllɔ]

ermine	ermellino (m)	[ɛrmɛl'linɔ]
sable	zibellino (m)	[dzibɛl'linɔ]
marten	martora (f)	['martɔra]
weasel	donnola (f)	['dɔŋɔʎa]
mink	visone (m)	[wi'zɔnɛ]

beaver	castoro (m)	[kas'tɔrɔ]
otter	lontra (f)	['lɔntra]
horse	cavallo (m)	[ka'vallɔ]
moose	alce (m)	['aʎʧe]
deer	cervo (m)	['ʧervɔ]
camel	cammello (m)	[kam'mɛllɔ]
bison	bisonte (m) americano	[bi'zɔntɛ ameri'kanɔ]
aurochs	bisonte (m) europeo	[bi'zɔntɛ eurɔ'pɛɔ]
buffalo	bufalo (m)	['bufalɔ]
zebra	zebra (f)	['dzɛbra]
antelope	antilope (f)	[an'tilɔpɛ]
roe deer	capriolo (m)	[kapri'ɔlɔ]
fallow deer	daino (m)	['dainɔ]
chamois	camoscio (m)	[ka'moʃɔ]
wild boar	cinghiale (m)	[ʧin'gjale]
whale	balena (f)	[ba'lena]
seal	foca (f)	['fɔka]
walrus	tricheco (m)	[tri'kɛkɔ]
fur seal	otaria (f)	[ɔ'taria]
dolphin	delfino (m)	[dɛʎ'finɔ]
bear	orso (m)	['ɔrsɔ]
polar bear	orso (m) bianco	['ɔrsɔ 'bjaŋkɔ]
panda	panda (m)	['panda]
monkey	scimmia (f)	['ʃimmʲa]
chimpanzee	scimpanzè (m)	[ʃimpan'dzɛ]
orangutan	orango (m)	[ɔ'raŋɔ]
gorilla	gorilla (m)	[gɔ'riʎa]
macaque	macaco (m)	[ma'kakɔ]
gibbon	gibbone (m)	[dʒib'bɔnɛ]
elephant	elefante (m)	[ɛle'fantɛ]
rhinoceros	rinoceronte (m)	[rinɔʧe'rɔntɛ]
giraffe	giraffa (f)	[dʒi'raffa]
hippopotamus	ippopotamo (m)	[ippɔ'pɔtamɔ]
kangaroo	canguro (m)	[ka'ŋurɔ]
koala (bear)	koala (m)	[kɔ'aʎa]
mongoose	mangusta (f)	[ma'ŋusta]
chinchilla	cincillà (f)	[ʧinʧi'ʎa]
skunk	moffetta (f)	[mɔf'fɛtta]
porcupine	istrice (m)	['istriʧe]

212. Domestic animals

cat	gatta (f)	['gatta]
tomcat	gatto (m)	['gattɔ]
dog	cane (m)	['kanɛ]

horse	cavallo (m)	[ka'vallɔ]
stallion	stallone (m)	[stal'lɜnɛ]
mare	giumenta (f)	[dʒu'mɛnta]

cow	mucca (f)	['mukka]
bull	toro (m)	['tɔrɔ]
ox	bue (m)	['buɛ]

sheep	pecora (f)	['pɛkɔra]
ram	montone (m)	[mɔn'tɔnɛ]
goat	capra (f)	['kapra]
billy goat, he-goat	caprone (m)	[kap'rɔnɛ]

| donkey | asino (m) | ['azinɔ] |
| mule | mulo (m) | ['mulɔ] |

pig	porco (m)	['pɔrkɔ]
piglet	porcellino (m)	[portʃel'linɔ]
rabbit	coniglio (m)	[kɔ'niʎɔ]

| hen (chicken) | gallina (f) | [gal'lina] |
| cock | gallo (m) | ['gallɔ] |

duck	anatra (f)	['anatra]
drake	maschio (m) dell'anatra	['maskiɔ dɛʎ 'anatra]
goose	oca (f)	['ɔka]

| stag turkey | tacchino (m) | [tak'kinɔ] |
| turkey (hen) | tacchina (f) | [tak'kina] |

domestic animals	animali (m pl) domestici	[ani'mali dɔ'mɛstitʃi]
tame (e.g. ~ hamster)	addomesticato	[addɔmɛsti'katɔ]
to tame (vt)	addomesticare (vt)	[addɔmɛsti'karɛ]
to breed (vt)	allevare (vt)	[alle'varɛ]

farm	fattoria (f)	[fattɔ'ria]
poultry	pollame (m)	[pɔ'ʎamɛ]
cattle	bestiame (m)	[bɛs'tjamɛ]
herd (cattle)	branco (m), mandria (f)	['braŋkɔ], ['mandria]

stable	scuderia (f)	[skudɛ'ria]
pigsty	porcile (m)	[pɔr'tʃile]
cowshed	stalla (f)	['stalla]
rabbit hutch	conigliera (f)	[kɔni'ʎjera]
hen house	pollaio (m)	[pɔ'ʎajo]

213. Dogs. Dog breeds

dog	cane (m)	['kanɛ]
sheepdog	cane (m) da pastore	['kanɛ da pas'tɔrɛ]
German shepherd dog	battaglia (f)	[bat'taʎja]
poodle	barbone (m)	[bar'bɔnɛ]
dachshund	bassotto (m)	[bas'sɔttɔ]
bulldog	bulldog (m)	[buʎ'dɔg]

boxer	boxer (m)	['bɔksɛr]
mastiff	mastino (m)	[mas'tino]
rottweiler	rottweiler (m)	[rɔt'vajler]
Doberman	dobermann (m)	[dɔbɛr'man]

basset	bassotto (m)	[bas'sɔttɔ]
bobtail	bobtail (m)	['bɔbtɛjl]
Dalmatian	dalmata (m)	['daʎmata]
cocker spaniel	cocker (m)	['kɔkkɛr]

| Newfoundland | terranova (m) | [tɛrra'nova] |
| Saint Bernard | sanbernardo (m) | [sanbɛr'nardɔ] |

husky	husky (m)	['aski]
Chow Chow	chow chow (m)	['ʧau 'ʧau]
spitz	volpino (m)	[vɔl'pinɔ]
pug	carlino (m)	[kar'linɔ]

214. Sounds made by animals

barking (n)	abbaiamento (m)	[abaja'mɛntɔ]
to bark (vi)	abbaiare (vi)	[abba'jarɛ]
to miaow (vi)	miagolare (vi)	[mjagɔ'ʎarɛ]
to purr (vi)	fare le fusa	['farɛ le 'fuza]

to moo (vi)	muggire (vi)	[mu'ʤirɛ]
to bellow (bull)	muggire (vi)	[mu'ʤirɛ]
to growl (vi)	ringhiare (vi)	[rin'gjarɛ]

howl (n)	ululato (m)	[uly'ʎatɔ]
to howl (vi)	ululare (vi)	[uly'ʎarɛ]
to whine (vi)	guaire (vi)	[gua'irɛ]

to bleat (sheep)	belare (vi)	[bɛ'ʎarɛ]
to oink, to grunt (pig)	grugnire (vi)	[gru'ɲirɛ]
to squeal (vi)	squittire (vi)	[skuit'tirɛ]

to croak (vi)	gracidare (vi)	[graʧi'darɛ]
to buzz (insect)	ronzare (vi)	[rɔn'dzarɛ]
to stridulate (vi)	frinire (vi)	[fri'nirɛ]

215. Young animals

cub	cucciolo (m)	['kuʧɔlɔ]
kitten	micino (m)	[mi'ʧinɔ]
baby mouse	topolino (m)	[tɔpɔ'linɔ]
pup, puppy	cucciolo (m) di cane	['kuʧɔlɔ di 'kanɛ]

leveret	leprotto (m)	[lep'rɔttɔ]
baby rabbit	coniglietto (m)	[kɔni'ʎjettɔ]
wolf cub	cucciolo (m) di lupo	['kuʧɔlɔ di 'lupɔ]
fox cub	cucciolo (m) di volpe	['kuʧɔlɔ di 'vɔʎpɛ]

bear cub	cucciolo (m) di orso	['kutʃolo di 'ɔrsɔ]
lion cub	cucciolo (m) di leone	['kutʃolo di le'ɔnɛ]
tiger cub	cucciolo (m) di tigre	[ku'tʃolo di 'tigrɛ]
elephant calf	elefantino (m)	[ɛlefan'tino]

piglet	porcellino (m)	[portʃel'lino]
calf (young cow, bull)	vitello (m)	[wi'tɛllo]
kid (young goat)	capretto (m)	[kap'rɛtto]
lamb	agnello (m)	[a'nɛllo]
fawn (deer)	cerbiatto (m)	[tʃer'bjatto]
young camel	cucciolo (m) di cammello	['kutʃolo di kam'mɛllo]

| baby snake | piccolo (m) di serpente | ['pikkolo di ser'pɛntɛ] |
| baby frog | piccolo (m) di rana | ['pikkolo di 'rana] |

nestling	uccellino (m)	[utʃel'lino]
chick (of chicken)	pulcino (m)	[puʎ'tʃino]
duckling	anatroccolo (m)	[anat'rokkolo]

216. Birds

bird	uccello (m)	[u'tʃello]
pigeon	colombo (m), piccione (m)	[ko'lɔmbo], [pi'tʃonɛ]
sparrow	passero (m)	['passɛro]
tit	cincia (f)	['tʃintʃa]
magpie	gazza (f)	['gatsa]

raven	corvo (m)	['kɔrvo]
crow	cornacchia (f)	[kor'nakkja]
jackdaw	taccola (f)	['takkoʎa]
rook	corvo (m) comune	['kɔrvo ko'munɛ]

duck	anatra (f)	['anatra]
goose	oca (f)	['ɔka]
pheasant	fagiano (m)	[fa'dʒano]

eagle	aquila (f)	['akuiʎa]
hawk	astore (m)	[as'tɔrɛ]
falcon	falco (m)	['faʎkɔ]
vulture	grifone (m)	[gri'fɔnɛ]
condor	condor (m)	['kɔndɔr]

swan	cigno (m)	['tʃiɲɔ]
crane	gru (f)	[gru]
stork	cicogna (f)	[tʃi'kɔɲa]

parrot	pappagallo (m)	[pappa'gallo]
hummingbird	colibrì (m)	[kolib'ri]
peacock	pavone (m)	[pa'vɔnɛ]

ostrich	struzzo (m)	['strutso]
heron	airone (m)	[ai'rɔnɛ]
flamingo	fenicottero (m)	[fɛni'kottɛro]
pelican	pellicano (m)	[pɛlli'kano]

nightingale	usignolo (m)	[uzi'nɔlo]
swallow	rondine (f)	['rondinɛ]

thrush	tordo (m)	['tordo]
song thrush	tordo (m) sasello	['tordo sa'zɛllo]
blackbird	merlo (m)	['mɛrlo]

swift	rondone (m)	[ron'donɛ]
lark	allodola (f)	[al'lɔdoʎa]
quail	quaglia (f)	[ku'aʎja]

woodpecker	picchio (m)	['pikkio]
cuckoo	cuculo (m)	['kukulo]
owl	civetta (f)	[ʧi'vɛtta]
eagle owl	gufo (m) reale	['gufo re'ale]
wood grouse	urogallo (m)	[uro'gallo]
black grouse	fagiano (m) di monte	[fadʒi'ano di 'montɛ]
partridge	pernice (f)	[pɛr'niʧe]

starling	storno (m)	['storno]
canary	canarino (m)	[kana'rino]
hazel grouse	francolino (m) di monte	[franko'lino di 'montɛ]
chaffinch	fringuello (m)	[friŋu'ɛllo]
bullfinch	ciuffolotto (m)	[ʧuffo'lotto]

seagull	gabbiano (m)	[gab'bjano]
albatross	albatro (m)	['aʎbatro]
penguin	pinguino (m)	[piŋu'ino]

217. Birds. Singing and sounds

to sing (vi)	cantare (vi)	[kan'tarɛ]
to call (animal, bird)	gridare (vi)	[gri'darɛ]
to crow (cock)	cantare, chicchiriare	[kan'tarɛ], [kikkiri'arɛ]
cock-a-doodle-doo	chicchirichì (m)	[kikkiri'ki]

to cluck (hen)	chiocciare (vi)	[kio'ʧarɛ]
to caw (vi)	gracchiare (vi)	[grak'kjarɛ]
to quack (duck)	fare qua qua	['farɛ ku'a ku'a]
to cheep (vi)	pigolare (vi)	[pigo'ʎarɛ]
to chirp, to twitter	cinguettare (vi)	[ʧiŋuɛt'tarɛ]

218. Fish. Marine animals

bream	abramide (f)	[ab'ramidɛ]
carp	carpa (f)	['karpa]
perch	perca (f)	['pɛrka]
catfish	pesce (m) gatto	['peʃe 'gatto]
pike	luccio (m)	['lyʧo]

salmon	salmone (m)	[saʎ'monɛ]
sturgeon	storione (m)	[stori'onɛ]

herring	aringa (f)	[a'riŋa]
Atlantic salmon	salmone (m)	[saʎ'mɔnɛ]
mackerel	scombro (m)	['skɔmbrɔ]
flatfish	sogliola (f)	['soʎɔʎa]

zander, pike perch	lucioperca (f)	[lyʧo'pɛrka]
cod	merluzzo (m)	[mɛr'lyʦɔ]
tuna	tonno (m)	['tɔŋɔ]
trout	trota (f)	['trota]

eel	anguilla (f)	[aŋu'iʎa]
electric ray	torpedine (f)	[tɔr'pɛdinɛ]
moray eel	murena (f)	[mu'rɛna]
piranha	piranha (f)	[pi'raɲia]

shark	squalo (m)	[sku'alɔ]
dolphin	delfino (m)	[dɛʎ'finɔ]
whale	balena (f)	[ba'lena]

crab	granchio (m)	['graŋkiɔ]
jellyfish	medusa (f)	[mɛ'duza]
octopus	polpo (m)	['pɔʎpɔ]

starfish	stella (f) marina	['stɛʎa ma'rina]
sea urchin	riccio (m) di mare	['riʧo di 'marɛ]
seahorse	cavalluccio (m) marino	[kaval'lyʧo ma'rinɔ]

oyster	ostrica (f)	['ɔstrika]
prawn	gamberetto (m)	[gambɛ'rɛttɔ]
lobster	astice (m)	['astiʧɛ]
spiny lobster	aragosta (f)	[ara'gɔsta]

219. Amphibians. Reptiles

| snake | serpente (m) | [sɛr'pɛntɛ] |
| venomous (snake) | velenoso | [vɛle'nɔzɔ] |

viper	vipera (f)	['wipɛra]
cobra	cobra (m)	['kɔbra]
python	pitone (m)	[pi'tɔnɛ]
boa	boa (m)	['bɔa]

grass snake	biscia (f)	['biʃa]
rattle snake	serpente (m) a sonagli	[sɛr'pɛntɛ a sɔ'naʎi]
anaconda	anaconda (f)	[ana'kɔnda]

lizard	lucertola (f)	[ly'ʧertoʎa]
iguana	iguana (f)	[igu'ana]
monitor lizard	varano (m)	[va'ranɔ]
salamander	salamandra (f)	[saʎa'mandra]
chameleon	camaleonte (m)	[kamale'ɔntɛ]
scorpion	scorpione (m)	[skɔr'piɔnɛ]
turtle	tartaruga (f)	[tarta'ruga]
frog	rana (f)	['rana]

| toad | rospo (m) | ['rɔspɔ] |
| crocodile | coccodrillo (m) | [kɔkkɔd'rillɔ] |

220. Insects

insect	insetto (m)	[in'sɛttɔ]
butterfly	farfalla (f)	[far'faʎa]
ant	formica (f)	[fɔr'mika]
fly	mosca (f)	['mɔska]
mosquito	zanzara (f)	[dzan'dzara]
beetle	scarabeo (m)	[skara'bɛɔ]

wasp	vespa (f)	['vɛspa]
bee	ape (f)	['apɛ]
bumblebee	bombo (m)	['bɔmbɔ]
gadfly	tafano (m)	[ta'fanɔ]

| spider | ragno (m) | ['raɲ'ɔ] |
| spider's web | ragnatela (f) | [raɲja'tɛʎa] |

dragonfly	libellula (f)	[li'bɛllyʎa]
grasshopper	cavalletta (f)	[kaval'letta]
moth (night butterfly)	farfalla (f) notturna	[far'faʎa nɔt'turna]

cockroach	scarafaggio (m)	[skara'fadʒɔ]
tick	zecca (f)	['tsɛkka]
flea	pulce (f)	['puʎtʃe]
midge	moscerino (m)	[mɔʃɛ'rinɔ]

locust	locusta (f)	[lɜ'kusta]
snail	lumaca (f)	[ly'maka]
cricket	grillo (m)	['grillɔ]
firefly	lucciola (f)	['lytʃɔʎa]
ladybird	coccinella (f)	[kɔtʃi'nɛʎa]
cockchafer	maggiolino (m)	[madʒɔ'linɔ]

leech	sanguisuga (f)	[saɲui'zuga]
caterpillar	bruco (m)	['brukɔ]
earthworm	verme (m)	['vɛrmɛ]
larva	larva (m)	['ʎarva]

221. Animals. Body parts

beak	becco (m)	['bɛkkɔ]
wings	ali (f pl)	['ali]
foot (of bird)	zampa (f)	['dzampa]
feathering	piumaggio (m)	[pʲu'madʒɔ]
feather	penna (f), piuma (f)	['pɛɲa], ['pʲuma]
crest	cresta (f)	['krɛsta]

| gill | branchia (f) | ['brankja] |
| spawn | uova (f pl) | [u'ova] |

larva	larva (f)	['ʎarva]
fin	pinna (f)	['piɲa]
scales (of fish, reptile)	squama (f)	[sku'ama]

fang (of wolf, etc.)	zanna (f)	['tzaɲa]
paw (e.g. cat's ~)	zampa (f)	['dzampa]
muzzle (snout)	muso (m)	['muzɔ]
mouth (of cat, dog)	bocca (f)	['bɔkka]
tail	coda (f)	['kɔda]
whiskers	baffi (m pl)	['baffi]

| hoof | zoccolo (m) | ['dzɔkkɔlɔ] |
| horn | corno (m) | ['kɔrnɔ] |

carapace	carapace (f)	[kara'patʃɛ]
shell (of mollusc)	conchiglia (f)	[kɔ'ŋkiʎja]
eggshell	guscio (m) dell'uovo	['guɕɔ dɛʎ u'ovɔ]

| hair (e.g. dog's ~) | pelo (m) | ['pɛlɔ] |
| pelt | pelle (f) | ['pɛlle] |

222. Actions of animals

| to fly (vi) | volare (vi) | [vɔ'ʎarɛ] |
| to make circles | volteggiare (vi) | [vɔʎtɛ'dʒarɛ] |

| to fly away | volare via | [vɔ'ʎarɛ 'wia] |
| to flap (~ the wings) | battere le ali | ['battɛrɛ le 'ali] |

| to peck (vi) | beccare (vi) | [bɛk'karɛ] |
| to sit on (vt) | covare (vt) | [kɔ'varɛ] |

| to hatch out (vi) | sgusciare (vi) | [zgu'ʃarɛ] |
| to build the nest | fare il nido | ['farɛ iʎ 'nidɔ] |

to slither, to crawl	strisciare (vi)	[stri'ʃarɛ]
to sting, to bite (insect)	pungere (vt)	['pundʒɛrɛ]
to bite (ab. animal)	mordere (vt)	['mɔrdɛrɛ]

to sniff (vt)	fiutare (vt)	[fjy'tarɛ]
to bark (vi)	abbaiare (vi)	[abba'jarɛ]
to hiss (snake)	sibilare (vi)	[sibi'larɛ]

| to scare (vt) | spaventare (vt) | [spavɛn'tarɛ] |
| to attack (vt) | attaccare (vt) | [attak'karɛ] |

to gnaw (bone, etc.)	rodere (vt)	['rɔdɛrɛ]
to scratch (with claws)	graffiare (vt)	[graf'fjarɛ]
to hide (vi)	nascondersi (vr)	[nas'kɔndɛrsi]

to play (kittens, etc.)	giocare (vi)	[dʒɔ'karɛ]
to hunt (vi, vt)	cacciare (vt)	[ka'tʃarɛ]
to hibernate (vi)	ibernare (vi)	[iber'narɛ]
to become extinct	estinguersi (vr)	[ɛs'tiŋuɛrsi]

223. Animals. Habitats

habitat	ambiente (m) naturale	[am'bjentɛ natu'ralɛ]
migration	migrazione (f)	[migra'tsjonɛ]
mountain	monte (m), montagna (f)	['montɛ], [mon'taɲa]
reef	reef (m)	[ri:f]
cliff	falesia (f)	[fa'lezija]
forest	foresta (f)	[fo'rɛsta]
jungle	giungla (f)	['dʒuŋʎa]
savanna	savana (f)	[sa'vana]
tundra	tundra (f)	['tundra]
steppe	steppa (f)	['stɛppa]
desert	deserto (m)	[dɛ'zɛrto]
oasis	oasi (f)	['ɔazi]
sea	mare (m)	['marɛ]
lake	lago (m)	['ʎago]
ocean	oceano (m)	[ɔ'tʃeano]
swamp	palude (f)	[pa'ludɛ]
freshwater (adj)	di acqua dolce	[di 'akua 'doʎtʃe]
pond	stagno (m)	['staɲo]
river	fiume (m)	['fjymɛ]
den	tana (f)	['tana]
nest	nido (m)	['nidɔ]
hollow (in a tree)	cavità (f)	[kawi'ta]
burrow (animal hole)	tana (f)	['tana]
anthill	formicaio (m)	[formi'kajo]

224. Animal care

zoo	zoo (m)	['dzɔ:]
nature reserve	riserva (f) naturale	[ri'sɛrva natu'ralɛ]
breeder, breed club	allevatore (m)	[alleva'torɛ]
open-air cage	gabbia (f) all'aperto	['gabbja aʎ a'pɛrto]
cage	gabbia (f)	['gabbja]
kennel	canile (m)	[ka'nilɛ]
dovecot	piccionaia (f)	[pitʃo'naja]
aquarium	acquario (m)	[aku'ariɔ]
dolphinarium	delfinario (m)	[dɛʎfi'nariɔ]
to breed (animals)	allevare (vt)	[alle'varɛ]
brood, litter	cucciolata (f)	[kutʃo'lata]
to tame (vt)	addomesticare (vt)	[addomɛsti'karɛ]
feed (for animal)	mangime (m)	[man'dʒimɛ]
to feed (vt)	dare da mangiare	['darɛ da man'dʒarɛ]
to train (animals)	ammaestrare (vt)	[ammaɛst'rarɛ]

pet shop	negozio (m) di animali	[nɛ'gotsio di ani'mali]
muzzle (for dog)	museruola (f)	[muzɛru'ɔʎa]
collar	collare (m)	[ko'ʎarɛ]
name (of animal)	nome (m)	['nɔmɛ]
pedigree (of dog)	pedigree (m)	['pɛdigri]

225. Animals. Miscellaneous

pack (wolves)	branco (m)	['braŋkɔ]
flock (birds)	stormo (m)	['stɔrmɔ]
shoal (fish)	banco (m)	['baŋkɔ]
herd of horses	mandria (f)	['mandria]

| male (n) | maschio (m) | ['maskiɔ] |
| female | femmina (f) | ['fɛmmina] |

hungry (adj)	affamato	[affa'matɔ]
wild (adj)	selvatico	[sɛʎ'vatikɔ]
dangerous (adj)	pericoloso	[pɛrikɔ'lɜzɔ]

226. Horses

| horse | cavallo (m) | [ka'vallɔ] |
| breed (race) | razza (f) | ['ratsa] |

| foal (of horse) | puledro (m) | [pu'ledrɔ] |
| mare | giumenta (f) | [dʒu'mɛnta] |

mustang	mustang (m)	['mustaŋ]
pony (small horse)	pony (m)	['pɔni]
draught horse	cavallo (m) da tiro pesante	[ka'vallɔ da 'tirɔ pɛ'zantɛ]

| mane | criniera (f) | [kri'njera] |
| tail | coda (f) | ['kɔda] |

hoof	zoccolo (m)	['dzɔkkɔlɔ]
horseshoe	ferro (m) di cavallo	['fɛrrɔ di ka'vallɔ]
to shoe (vt)	ferrare (vt)	[fɛr'rarɛ]
blacksmith	fabbro (m)	['fabbrɔ]

saddle	sella (f)	['sɛʎa]
stirrup	staffa (f)	['staffa]
bridle	briglia (f)	['briʎja]
reins	redini (m pl)	['rɛdini]
whip (for riding)	frusta (f)	['frusta]

rider	fantino (m)	[fan'tinɔ]
to break in (horse)	scozzonare (vt)	[skɔtsɔ'narɛ]
to saddle (vt)	sellare (vt)	[sɛ'ʎarɛ]
to mount a horse	montare in sella	[mɔn'tarɛ in 'sɛʎa]
gallop	galoppo (m)	[ga'lɜppɔ]
to gallop (vi)	galoppare (vi)	[galɜp'parɛ]

| trot (n) | **trotto** (m) | ['trɔtto] |
| at a trot (adv) | **al trotto** | [aʎ 'trɔtto] |

| racehorse | **cavallo** (m) **da corsa** | [ka'vallɔ da 'kɔrsa] |
| races | **corse** (f pl) | ['kɔrsɛ] |

stable	**scuderia** (f)	[skudɛ'ria]
to feed (vt)	**dare da mangiare**	['darɛ da man'dʒarɛ]
hay	**fieno** (m)	['fjenɔ]
to water (animals)	**abbeverare** (vt)	[abbɛvɛ'rarɛ]
to wash (horse)	**lavare** (vt)	[ʎa'varɛ]
to hobble (vt)	**impastoiare** (vt)	[impastɔ'jarɛ]

horse-drawn cart	**carro** (m)	['karrɔ]
to graze (vi)	**pascolare** (vi)	[paskɔ'ʎarɛ]
to neigh (vi)	**nitrire** (vi)	[nit'rirɛ]
to jib, to kick out	**dare un calcio**	['darɛ un 'kaʎʧɔ]

Flora

227. Trees

tree	albero (m)	['aʎbɛrɔ]
deciduous (adj)	deciduo	[dɛ'ʧiduɔ]
coniferous (adj)	conifero	[kɔ'nifɛrɔ]
evergreen (adj)	sempreverde	[sɛmprɛ'vɛrdɛ]
apple tree	melo (m)	['mɛlɔ]
pear tree	pero (m)	['pɛrɔ]
sweet cherry tree	ciliegio (m)	[ʧi'ʎjedʒɔ]
sour cherry tree	amareno (m)	[ama'rɛnɔ]
plum tree	prugno (m)	['pruɲɔ]
birch	betulla (f)	[bɛ'tuʎa]
oak	quercia (f)	[ku'ɛrʧa]
linden tree	tiglio (m)	['tiʎɔ]
aspen	pioppo (m) tremolo	['pʲɔppɔ 'trɛmɔlɔ]
maple	acero (m)	['aʧerɔ]
spruce	abete (m)	[a'bɛtɛ]
pine	pino (m)	['pinɔ]
larch	larice (m)	['ʎariʧe]
fir	abete (m) bianco	[a'bɛtɛ 'bjaŋkɔ]
cedar	cedro (m)	['ʧedrɔ]
poplar	pioppo (m)	['pʲɔppɔ]
rowan	sorbo (m)	['sɔrbɔ]
willow	salice (m)	['saliʧe]
alder	alno (m)	['aʎnɔ]
beech	faggio (m)	['fadʒɔ]
elm	olmo (m)	['ɔʎmɔ]
ash (tree)	frassino (m)	['frassinɔ]
chestnut	castagno (m)	[kas'taɲɔ]
magnolia	magnolia (f)	[ma'ɲʲɔlia]
palm tree	palma (f)	['paʎma]
cypress	cipresso (m)	[ʧip'rɛssɔ]
mangrove	mangrovia (f)	[maŋ'rɔwia]
baobab	baobab (m)	[baɔ'bab]
eucalyptus	eucalipto (m)	[ɛuka'liptɔ]
sequoia	sequoia (f)	[sɛku'ɔja]

228. Shrubs

bush	cespuglio (m)	[ʧes'puʎɔ]
shrub	arbusto (m)	[ar'bustɔ]

| grapevine | vite (f) | ['witɛ] |
| vineyard | vigneto (m) | [wiˈɲjetɔ] |

raspberry bush	lampone (m)	[ʎamˈpɔnɛ]
redcurrant bush	ribes (m) rosso	[ˈribɛs ˈrɔssɔ]
gooseberry bush	uva (f) spina	[ˈuva ˈspina]

acacia	acacia (f)	[aˈkatʃa]
barberry	crespino (m)	[krɛsˈpino]
jasmine	gelsomino (m)	[dʒeʎsɔˈminɔ]

juniper	ginepro (m)	[dʒiˈnɛprɔ]
rosebush	roseto (m)	[roˈzɛtɔ]
dog rose	rosa (f) canina	[ˈroza kaˈnina]

229. Mushrooms

mushroom	fungo (m)	[ˈfuŋɔ]
edible mushroom	fungo (m) commestibile	[ˈfuŋɔ kɔmmɛsˈtibile]
toadstool	fungo (m) velenoso	[ˈfuŋɔ vɛleˈnɔzɔ]
cap (of mushroom)	cappello (m)	[kapˈpɛllɔ]
stipe (of mushroom)	gambo (m)	[ˈgambo]

cep, penny bun	porcino (m)	[porˈtʃino]
orange-cap boletus	boleto (m) rufo	[bɔˈletɔ ˈrufo]
birch bolete	porcinello (m)	[portʃiˈnɛllɔ]
chanterelle	gallinaccio (m)	[galliˈnatʃɔ]
russula	rossola (f)	[ˈrɔssɔʎa]

morel	spugnola (f)	[ˈspuɲɔʎa]
fly agaric	ovolaccio (m)	[ɔvɔˈlatʃɔ]
death cap	fungo (m) moscario	[ˈfuŋɔ mɔsˈkariɔ]

230. Fruits. Berries

apple	mela (f)	[ˈmɛʎa]
pear	pera (f)	[ˈpɛra]
plum	prugna (f)	[ˈpruɲja]

strawberry	fragola (f)	[ˈfragɔʎa]
sour cherry	amarena (f)	[amaˈrɛna]
sweet cherry	ciliegia (f)	[tʃiˈʎjedʒa]
grape	uva (f)	[ˈuva]

raspberry	lampone (m)	[ʎamˈpɔnɛ]
blackcurrant	ribes (m) nero	[ˈribɛs ˈnɛrɔ]
redcurrant	ribes (m) rosso	[ˈribɛs ˈrɔssɔ]
gooseberry	uva (f) spina	[ˈuva ˈspina]
cranberry	mirtillo (m) di palude	[mirˈtillɔ di paˈlydɛ]

| orange | arancia (f) | [aˈrantʃa] |
| tangerine | mandarino (m) | [mandaˈrinɔ] |

pineapple	ananas (m)	[ana'nas]
banana	banana (f)	[ba'nana]
date	dattero (m)	['dattɛro]

lemon	limone (m)	[li'mɔnɛ]
apricot	albicocca (f)	[aʎbi'kɔkka]
peach	pesca (f)	['pɛska]
kiwi	kiwi (m)	['kiwi]
grapefruit	pompelmo (m)	[pɔm'pɛʎmɔ]

berry	bacca (f)	['bakka]
berries	bacche (f pl)	['bakkɛ]
cowberry	mirtillo (m) rosso	[mir'tillo 'rɔssɔ]
wild strawberry	fragola (f) di bosco	['fragɔʎa di 'bɔskɔ]
bilberry	mirtillo (m)	[mir'tillɔ]

231. Flowers. Plants

| flower | fiore (m) | ['fjɔrɛ] |
| bouquet (of flowers) | mazzo (m) di fiori | ['matso di 'fjori] |

rose (flower)	rosa (f)	['rɔza]
tulip	tulipano (m)	[tuli'panɔ]
carnation	garofano (m)	[ga'rɔfanɔ]
gladiolus	gladiolo (m)	[gʎa'diɔlɔ]

cornflower	fiordaliso (m)	[fjorda'lizɔ]
bluebell	campanella (f)	[kampa'nɛʎa]
dandelion	soffione (m)	[sɔf'fjonɛ]
camomile	camomilla (f)	[kamɔ'miʎa]

aloe	aloe (m)	['alɜɛ]
cactus	cactus (m)	['kaktus]
rubber plant, ficus	ficus (m)	['fikus]

lily	giglio (m)	['dʒiʎ'ɔ]
geranium	geranio (m)	[dʒe'raniɔ]
hyacinth	giacinto (m)	[dʒa'ʧintɔ]

mimosa	mimosa (f)	[mi'mɔza]
narcissus	narciso (m)	[nar'ʧizɔ]
nasturtium	nasturzio (m)	[nas'turtsiɔ]

orchid	orchidea (f)	[ɔrki'dɛa]
peony	peonia (f)	[pɛ'ɔnia]
violet	viola (f)	[wi'ɔʎa]

pansy	viola (f) del pensiero	[wi'ɔʎa dɛʎ pɛn'sjerɔ]
forget-me-not	nontiscordardimé (m)	[nɔntiskɔrdardi'mɛ]
daisy	margherita (f)	[margɛ'rita]

poppy	papavero (m)	[pa'pavɛrɔ]
hemp	canapa (f)	['kanapa]
mint	menta (f)	['menta]

lily of the valley	**mughetto** (m)	[mu'gɛtto]
snowdrop	**bucaneve** (m)	[buka'nɛvɛ]
nettle	**ortica** (f)	[ɔr'tika]
sorrel	**acetosa** (f)	[atʃe'toza]
water lily	**ninfea** (f)	[nin'fɛa]
fern	**felce** (f)	['fɛʎtʃe]
lichen	**lichene** (m)	[li'kɛnɛ]
tropical glasshouse	**serra** (f)	['sɛrra]
grass lawn	**prato** (m) **erboso**	['prato ɛr'bɔzɔ]
flowerbed	**aiuola** (f)	[aju'ɔʎa]
plant	**pianta** (f)	['pjanta]
grass	**erba** (f)	['ɛrba]
blade of grass	**filo** (m) **d'erba**	['filɔ 'dɛrba]
leaf	**foglia** (f)	['foʎja]
petal	**petalo** (m)	['pɛtalɔ]
stem	**stelo** (m)	['stɛlɔ]
tuber	**tubero** (m)	['tubɛrɔ]
young plant (shoot)	**germoglio** (m)	[dʒer'mɔʎ'ɔ]
thorn	**spina** (f)	['spina]
to blossom (vi)	**fiorire** (vi)	[fjo'rirɛ]
to fade, to wither	**appassire** (vi)	[appas'sirɛ]
smell (odour)	**odore** (m), **profumo** (m)	[ɔ'dɔrɛ], [prɔ'fumɔ]
to cut (flowers)	**tagliare** (vt)	[ta'ʎiarɛ]
to pick (a flower)	**cogliere** (vt)	['kɔʎjerɛ]

232. Cereals, grains

grain	**grano** (m)	['granɔ]
cereals (plants)	**cereali** (m pl)	[tʃerɛ'ali]
ear (of barley, etc.)	**spiga** (f)	['spiga]
wheat	**frumento** (m)	[fru'mɛntɔ]
rye	**segale** (f)	['sɛgale]
oats	**avena** (f)	[a'vɛna]
millet	**miglio** (m)	['miʎ'ɔ]
barley	**orzo** (m)	['ɔrtsɔ]
maize	**mais** (m)	['mais]
rice	**riso** (m)	['rizɔ]
buckwheat	**grano** (m) **saraceno**	['granɔ sara'tʃenɔ]
pea	**pisello** (m)	[pi'zɛllɔ]
kidney bean	**fagiolo** (m)	[fa'dʒɔlɔ]
soya	**soia** (f)	['sɔja]
lentil	**lenticchie** (f pl)	[len'tikkje]
beans (broad ~)	**fave** (f pl)	['favɛ]

233. Vegetables. Greens

| vegetables | ortaggi (m pl) | [ɔr'tadʒi] |
| greens | verdura (f) | [vɛr'dura] |

tomato	pomodoro (m)	[pɔmɔ'dɔrɔ]
cucumber	cetriolo (m)	[ʧetri'ɔlɔ]
carrot	carota (f)	[ka'rɔta]
potato	patata (f)	[pa'tata]
onion	cipolla (f)	[ʧi'pɔʎa]
garlic	aglio (m)	['aʎɔ]

cabbage	cavolo (m)	['kavɔlɔ]
cauliflower	cavolfiore (m)	[kavɔʎ'fɔrɛ]
Brussels sprouts	cavoletti (m pl) di Bruxelles	[kavɔ'letti di bruk'sɛʎ]
broccoli	broccolo (m)	['brɔkkɔlɔ]

beetroot	barbabietola (f)	[barba'bjetɔʎa]
aubergine	melanzana (f)	[mɛʎan'ʦana]
marrow	zucchina (f)	[dzuk'kina]
pumpkin	zucca (f)	['dzukka]
turnip	rapa (f)	['rapa]

parsley	prezzemolo (m)	[prɛ'ʦemɔlɔ]
dill	aneto (m)	[a'nɛtɔ]
lettuce	lattuga (f)	[ʎat'tuga]
celery	sedano (m)	['sɛdanɔ]
asparagus	asparago (m)	[as'paragɔ]
spinach	spinaci (m pl)	[spi'naʧi]

pea	pisello (m)	[pi'zɛllɔ]
beans	fave (f pl)	['favɛ]
maize	mais (m)	['mais]
kidney bean	fagiolo (m)	[fa'dʒɔlɔ]

bell pepper	peperone (m)	[pepɛ'rɔnɛ]
radish	ravanello (m)	[rava'nɛllɔ]
artichoke	carciofo (m)	[kar'ʧɔfɔ]

REGIONAL GEOGRAPHY

Countries. Nationalities

234. Western Europe

Europe	**Europa** (f)	[eu'rɔpa]
European Union	**Unione** (f) **Europea**	[uni'ɔnɛ ɛurɔ'pɛa]
European (n)	**europeo** (m)	[ɛurɔ'pɛɔ]
European (adj)	**europeo**	[ɛurɔ'pɛɔ]
Austria	**Austria** (f)	['austria]
Austrian (masc.)	**austriaco** (m)	[aust'riakɔ]
Austrian (fem.)	**austriaca** (f)	[aust'riaka]
Austrian (adj)	**austriaco**	[aust'riakɔ]
Great Britain	**Gran Bretagna** (f)	[gran brɛ'taɲa]
England	**Inghilterra** (f)	[iɲiʎ'tɛrra]
British (masc.)	**britannico** (m), **inglese** (m)	[bri'tanikɔ], [iŋ'lezɛ]
British (fem.)	**britannica** (f), **inglese** (f)	[bri'tanika], [iŋ'lezɛ]
English, British (adj)	**inglese**	[iŋ'lezɛ]
Belgium	**Belgio** (m)	['bɛʎdʒɔ]
Belgian (masc.)	**belga** (m)	['bɛʎga]
Belgian (fem.)	**belga** (f)	['bɛʎga]
Belgian (adj)	**belga** (adj)	['bɛʎga]
Germany	**Germania** (f)	[dʒer'mania]
German (masc.)	**tedesco** (m)	[tɛ'dɛskɔ]
German (fem.)	**tedesca** (f)	[tɛ'dɛska]
German (adj)	**tedesco** (adj)	[tɛ'dɛskɔ]
Netherlands	**Paesi Bassi** (m pl)	[pa'ɛzi 'bassi]
Holland	**Olanda** (f)	[ɔ'ʎanda]
Dutchman	**olandese** (m)	[ɔʎan'dɛzɛ]
Dutchwoman	**olandese** (f)	[ɔʎan'dɛzɛ]
Dutch (adj)	**olandese** (adj)	[ɔʎan'dɛzɛ]
Greece	**Grecia** (f)	['grɛtʃa]
Greek (masc.)	**greco** (m)	['grɛkɔ]
Greek (fem.)	**greca** (f)	['grɛka]
Greek (adj)	**greco** (adj)	['grɛkɔ]
Denmark	**Danimarca** (f)	[dani'marka]
Dane (masc.)	**danese** (m)	[da'nɛzɛ]
Dane (fem.)	**danese** (f)	[da'nɛzɛ]
Danish (adj)	**danese** (adj)	[da'nɛzɛ]
Ireland	**Irlanda** (f)	[ir'ʎanda]
Irishman	**irlandese** (m)	[irʎan'dɛzɛ]

| Irishwoman | irlandese (f) | [irˈanˈdɛzɛ] |
| Irish (adj) | irlandese (adj) | [irˈanˈdɛzɛ] |

Iceland	Islanda (f)	[izˈʌanda]
Icelander (masc.)	islandese (m)	[izʌanˈdɛzɛ]
Icelander (fem.)	islandese (f)	[izʌanˈdɛzɛ]
Icelandic (adj)	islandese (adj)	[izʌanˈdɛzɛ]

Spain	Spagna (f)	[ˈspaɲˈa]
Spaniard (masc.)	spagnolo (m)	[spaɲˈɔlɔ]
Spaniard (fem.)	spagnola (f)	[spaɲˈɔʎa]
Spanish (adj)	spagnolo (adj)	[spaɲˈɔlɔ]

Italy	Italia (f)	[iˈtalia]
Italian (masc.)	italiano (m)	[itaˈʎjanɔ]
Italian (fem.)	italiana (f)	[itaˈʎjana]
Italian (adj)	italiano (adj)	[itaˈʎjanɔ]

Cyprus	Cipro (m)	[ˈtʃiprɔ]
Cypriot (masc.)	cipriota (m)	[tʃipriˈɔta]
Cypriot (fem.)	cipriota (f)	[tʃipriˈɔta]
Cypriot (adj)	cipriota (adj)	[tʃipriˈɔta]

Malta	Malta (f)	[ˈmaʎta]
Maltese (masc.)	maltese (m)	[maʎˈtɛzɛ]
Maltese (fem.)	maltese (f)	[maʎˈtɛzɛ]
Maltese (adj)	maltese (adj)	[maʎˈtɛzɛ]

Norway	Norvegia (f)	[nɔrˈvɛdʒa]
Norwegian (masc.)	norvegese (m)	[nɔrveˈdʒezɛ]
Norwegian (fem.)	norvegese (f)	[nɔrveˈdʒezɛ]
Norwegian (adj)	norvegese (adj)	[nɔrveˈdʒezɛ]

Portugal	Portogallo (f)	[pɔrtɔˈgallɔ]
Portuguese (masc.)	portoghese (m)	[pɔrtɔˈgɛzɛ]
Portuguese (fem.)	portoghese (f)	[pɔrtɔˈgɛzɛ]
Portuguese (adj)	portoghese (adj)	[pɔrtɔˈgɛzɛ]

Finland	Finlandia (f)	[finˈʌandia]
Finn (masc.)	finlandese (m)	[finʌanˈdɛzɛ]
Finn (fem.)	finlandese (f)	[finʌanˈdɛzɛ]
Finnish (adj)	finlandese (adj)	[finʌanˈdɛzɛ]

France	Francia (f)	[ˈfrantʃa]
Frenchman	francese (m)	[franˈtʃezɛ]
Frenchwoman	francese (f)	[franˈtʃezɛ]
French (adj)	francese (adj)	[franˈtʃezɛ]

Sweden	Svezia (f)	[ˈzvɛtsia]
Swede (masc.)	svedese (m)	[zvɛˈdɛzɛ]
Swede (fem.)	svedese (f)	[zvɛˈdɛzɛ]
Swedish (adj)	svedese (adj)	[zvɛˈdɛzɛ]

Switzerland	Svizzera (f)	[ˈzwitsɛra]
Swiss (masc.)	svizzero (m)	[ˈzwitsɛrɔ]
Swiss (fem.)	svizzera (f)	[ˈzwitsɛra]

Swiss (adj)	**svizzero** (adj)	['zwitsɛrɔ]
Scotland	**Scozia** (f)	['skɔtsia]
Scottish (masc.)	**scozzese** (m)	[skɔ'tsɛzɛ]
Scottish (fem.)	**scozzese** (f)	[skɔ'tsɛzɛ]
Scottish (adj)	**scozzese** (adj)	[skɔ'tsɛzɛ]

Vatican	**Vaticano** (m)	[vati'kanɔ]
Liechtenstein	**Liechtenstein** (m)	['liktɛnstajn]
Luxembourg	**Lussemburgo** (m)	[lyssɛm'burgɔ]
Monaco	**Monaco** (m)	['mɔnakɔ]

235. Central and Eastern Europe

Albania	**Albania** (f)	[aʎba'nia]
Albanian (masc.)	**albanese** (m)	[aʎba'nɛzɛ]
Albanian (fem.)	**albanese** (f)	[aʎba'nɛzɛ]
Albanian (adj)	**albanese** (adj)	[aʎba'nɛzɛ]

Bulgaria	**Bulgaria** (f)	[buʎga'ria]
Bulgarian (masc.)	**bulgaro** (m)	['buʎgarɔ]
Bulgarian (fem.)	**bulgara** (f)	['buʎgara]
Bulgarian (adj)	**bulgaro** (adj)	['buʎgarɔ]

Hungary	**Ungheria** (f)	[uŋɛ'ria]
Hungarian (masc.)	**ungherese** (m)	[uŋɛ'rɛzɛ]
Hungarian (fem.)	**ungherese** (f)	[uŋɛ'rɛzɛ]
Hungarian (adj)	**ungherese** (adj)	[uŋɛ'rɛzɛ]

Latvia	**Lettonia** (f)	[let'tonia]
Latvian (masc.)	**lettone** (m)	['lettɔnɛ]
Latvian (fem.)	**lettone** (f)	['lettɔnɛ]
Latvian (adj)	**lettone** (adj)	['lettɔnɛ]

Lithuania	**Lituania** (f)	[litu'ania]
Lithuanian (masc.)	**lituano** (m)	[litu'anɔ]
Lithuanian (fem.)	**lituana** (f)	[litu'ana]
Lithuanian (adj)	**lituano** (adj)	[litu'anɔ]

Poland	**Polonia** (f)	[pɔ'lɔnia]
Pole (masc.)	**polacco** (m)	[pɔ'ʎakkɔ]
Pole (fem.)	**polacca** (f)	[pɔ'ʎakka]
Polish (adj)	**polacco** (adj)	[pɔ'ʎakkɔ]

Romania	**Romania** (f)	[rɔma'nia]
Romanian (masc.)	**rumeno** (m)	[ru'mɛnɔ]
Romanian (fem.)	**rumena** (f)	[ru'mɛna]
Romanian (adj)	**rumeno** (adj)	[ru'mɛnɔ]

Serbia	**Serbia** (f)	['sɛrbia]
Serbian (masc.)	**serbo** (m)	['sɛrbɔ]
Serbian (fem.)	**serba** (f)	['sɛrba]
Serbian (adj)	**serbo** (adj)	['sɛrbɔ]
Slovakia	**Slovacchia** (f)	[zlɔ'vakkia]
Slovak (masc.)	**slovacco** (m)	[zlɔ'vakkɔ]

| Slovak (fem.) | slovacca (f) | [zlɔ'vakka] |
| Slovak (adj) | slovacco (adj) | [zlɔ'vakkɔ] |

Croatia	Croazia (f)	[krɔ'atsia]
Croatian (masc.)	croato (m)	[krɔ'atɔ]
Croatian (fem.)	croata (f)	[krɔ'ata]
Croatian (adj)	croato (adj)	[krɔ'atɔ]

Czech Republic	Repubblica (f) Ceca	[rɛ'pubblika 'ʧeka]
Czech (masc.)	ceco (m)	['ʧekɔ]
Czech (fem.)	ceca (f)	['ʧeka]
Czech (adj)	ceco (adj)	['ʧekɔ]

Estonia	Estonia (f)	[ɛs'tonia]
Estonian (masc.)	estone (m)	['ɛstonɛ]
Estonian (fem.)	estone (f)	['ɛstonɛ]
Estonian (adj)	estone (adj)	['ɛstonɛ]

Bosnia-Herzegovina	Bosnia-Erzegovina (f)	['bɔznia ɛrtsɛ'gɔwina]
Macedonia	Macedonia (f)	[matʃe'dɔnia]
Slovenia	Slovenia (f)	[zlɔ'vɛnia]
Montenegro	Montenegro (m)	[montɛ'nɛgrɔ]

236. Former USSR countries

Azerbaijan	Azerbaigian (m)	[azɛrbaj'dʒan]
Azerbaijani (masc.)	azerbaigiano (m)	[azɛrbaj'dʒanɔ]
Azerbaijani (fem.)	azerbaigiana (f)	[azɛrbaj'dʒana]
Azerbaijani (adj)	azerbaigiano (adj)	[azɛrbaj'dʒanɔ]

Armenia	Armenia (f)	[ar'mɛnia]
Armenian (masc.)	armeno (m)	[ar'mɛnɔ]
Armenian (fem.)	armena (f)	[ar'mɛna]
Armenian (adj)	armeno (adj)	[ar'mɛnɔ]

Belarus	Bielorussia (f)	[bjelɔ'russia]
Belarusian (masc.)	bielorusso (m)	[bjelɔ'russɔ]
Belarusian (fem.)	bielorussa (f)	[bjelɔ'russa]
Belarusian (adj)	bielorusso (adj)	[bjelɔ'russɔ]

Georgia	Georgia (f)	[dʒe'ɔrdʒa]
Georgian (masc.)	georgiano (m)	[dʒeor'dʒanɔ]
Georgian (fem.)	georgiana (f)	[dʒeor'dʒana]
Georgian (adj)	georgiano (adj)	[dʒeor'dʒanɔ]

Kazakhstan	Kazakistan (m)	[ka'zakistan]
Kazakh (masc.)	kazaco (m)	[ka'zakɔ]
Kazakh (fem.)	kazaca (f)	[ka'zaka]
Kazakh (adj)	kazaco (adj)	[ka'zakɔ]

Kirghizia	Kirghizistan (m)	[kir'gizistan]
Kirghiz (masc.)	kirghiso (m)	[kir'gizɔ]
Kirghiz (fem.)	kirghisa (f)	[kir'giza]
Kirghiz (adj)	kirghiso (adj)	[kir'gizɔ]

Moldavia	Moldavia (f)	[mɔʎ'dawia]
Moldavian (masc.)	moldavo (m)	[mɔʎ'davɔ]
Moldavian (fem.)	moldava (f)	[mɔʎ'dava]
Moldavian (adj)	moldavo (adj)	[mɔʎ'davɔ]

Russia	Russia (f)	['russia]
Russian (masc.)	russo (m)	['russɔ]
Russian (fem.)	russa (f)	['russa]
Russian (adj)	russo (adj)	['russɔ]

Tajikistan	Tagikistan (m)	[ta'dʒikistan]
Tajik (masc.)	tagico (m)	['tadʒikɔ]
Tajik (fem.)	tagica (f)	['tadʒika]
Tajik (adj)	tagico (adj)	['tadʒikɔ]

Turkmenistan	Turkmenistan (m)	[turk'mɛnistan]
Turkmen (masc.)	turkmeno (m)	[turk'mɛnɔ]
Turkmen (fem.)	turkmena (f)	[turk'mɛna]
Turkmenian (adj)	turkmeno (adj)	[turk'mɛnɔ]

Uzbekistan	Uzbekistan (m)	[uz'bɛkistan]
Uzbek (masc.)	usbeco (m)	[uz'bɛkɔ]
Uzbek (fem.)	usbeca (f)	[uz'bɛka]
Uzbek (adj)	usbeco (adj)	[uz'bɛkɔ]

Ukraine	Ucraina (f)	[uk'raina]
Ukrainian (masc.)	ucraino (m)	[uk'rainɔ]
Ukrainian (fem.)	ucraina (f)	[uk'raina]
Ukrainian (adj)	ucraino (adj)	[uk'rainɔ]

237. Asia

| Asia | Asia (f) | ['azia] |
| Asian (adj) | asiatico (adj) | [azi'atikɔ] |

Vietnam	Vietnam (m)	['vjetnam]
Vietnamese (masc.)	vietnamita (m)	[vjetna'mita]
Vietnamese (fem.)	vietnamita (f)	[vjetna'mita]
Vietnamese (adj)	vietnamita (adj)	[vjetna'mita]

India	India (f)	['india]
Indian (masc.)	indiano (m)	[indi'anɔ]
Indian (fem.)	indiana (f)	[indi'ana]
Indian (adj)	indiano (adj)	[indi'anɔ]

Israel	Israele (m)	[izra'ɛle]
Israeli (masc.)	israeliano (m)	[izraɛli'anɔ]
Israeli (fem.)	israeliana (f)	[izraɛli'ana]
Israeli (adj)	israeliano (adj)	[izraɛli'anɔ]

Jew (n)	ebreo (m)	[ɛb'rɛɔ]
Jewess (n)	ebrea (f)	[ɛb'rɛa]
Jewish (adj)	ebraico (adj)	[ɛb'raikɔ]
China	Cina (f)	['tʃina]

Chinese (masc.)	cinese (m)	[ʧi'nɛzɛ]
Chinese (fem.)	cinese (f)	[ʧi'nɛzɛ]
Chinese (adj)	cinese (adj)	[ʧi'nɛzɛ]
Korean (masc.)	coreano (m)	[kɔrɛ'anɔ]
Korean (fem.)	coreana (f)	[kɔrɛ'ana]
Korean (adj)	coreano (adj)	[kɔrɛ'anɔ]
Lebanon	Libano (m)	['libanɔ]
Lebanese (masc.)	libanese (m)	[liba'nɛzɛ]
Lebanese (fem.)	libanese (f)	[liba'nɛzɛ]
Lebanese (adj)	libanese (adj)	[liba'nɛzɛ]
Mongolia	Mongolia (f)	[mɔ'ŋɔlia]
Mongolian (masc.)	mongolo (m)	['mɔŋɔlɔ]
Mongolian (fem.)	mongola (f)	['mɔŋɔʎa]
Mongolian (adj)	mongolo (adj)	['mɔŋɔlɔ]
Malaysia	Malesia (f)	[ma'lezia]
Malaysian (masc.)	malese (m)	[ma'lezɛ]
Malaysian (fem.)	malese (f)	[ma'lezɛ]
Malaysian (adj)	malese (adj)	[ma'lezɛ]
Pakistan	Pakistan (m)	['pakistan]
Pakistani (masc.)	pakistano (m)	[pakis'tanɔ]
Pakistani (fem.)	pakistana (f)	[pakis'tana]
Pakistani (adj)	pakistano (adj)	[pakis'tanɔ]
Saudi Arabia	Arabia Saudita (f)	[a'rabia sau'dita]
Arab (masc.)	arabo (m), saudita (m)	['arabɔ], [sau'dita]
Arab (fem.)	araba (f), saudita (f)	['araba], [sau'dita]
Arabian (adj)	arabo (adj)	['arabɔ]
Thailand	Tailandia (f)	[taj'landia]
Thai (masc.)	tailandese (m)	[tajlan'dɛzɛ]
Thai (fem.)	tailandese (f)	[tajlan'dɛzɛ]
Thai (adj)	tailandese (adj)	[tajlan'dɛzɛ]
Taiwan	Taiwan (m)	[taj'van]
Taiwanese (masc.)	taiwanese (m)	[tajva'nɛzɛ]
Taiwanese (fem.)	taiwanese (f)	[tajva'nɛzɛ]
Taiwanese (adj)	taiwanese (adj)	[tajva'nɛzɛ]
Turkey	Turchia (f)	[tur'kia]
Turk (masc.)	turco (m)	['turkɔ]
Turk (fem.)	turca (f)	['turka]
Turkish (adj)	turco (adj)	['turkɔ]
Japan	Giappone (m)	[dʒap'pɔnɛ]
Japanese (masc.)	giapponese (m)	[dʒappɔ'nɛzɛ]
Japanese (fem.)	giapponese (f)	[dʒappɔ'nɛzɛ]
Japanese (adj)	giapponese (adj)	[dʒappɔ'nɛzɛ]
Afghanistan	Afghanistan (m)	[af'ganistan]
Bangladesh	Bangladesh (m)	['baŋʎadɛʃ]
Indonesia	Indonesia (f)	[indɔ'nɛzia]

Jordan	Giordania (f)	[dʒor'dania]
Iraq	Iraq (m)	['irak]
Iran	Iran (m)	['iran]
Cambodia	Cambogia (f)	[kam'bodʒa]
Kuwait	Kuwait (m)	[ku'vɛjt]

Laos	Laos (m)	['ʎaɔs]
Myanmar	Birmania (f)	[bir'mania]
Nepal	Nepal (m)	[nɛ'paʎ]
United Arab Emirates	Emirati (m pl) Arabi	[ɛmi'rati 'arabi]

Syria	Siria (f)	['siria]
Palestine	Palestina (f)	[pales'tina]
South Korea	Corea (f) del Sud	[kɔ'rɛa dɛʎ sud]
North Korea	Corea (f) del Nord	[kɔ'rɛa dɛʎ nɔrd]

238. North America

United States of America	Stati (m pl) Uniti d'America	['stati u'niti da'mɛrika]
American (masc.)	americano (m)	[amɛri'kanɔ]
American (fem.)	americana (f)	[amɛri'kana]
American (adj)	americano (adj)	[amɛri'kanɔ]

Canada	Canada (m)	['kanada]
Canadian (masc.)	canadese (m)	[kana'dɛzɛ]
Canadian (fem.)	canadese (f)	[kana'dɛzɛ]
Canadian (adj)	canadese (adj)	[kana'dɛzɛ]

Mexico	Messico (m)	['messikɔ]
Mexican (masc.)	messicano (m)	[messi'kanɔ]
Mexican (fem.)	messicana (f)	[messi'kana]
Mexican (adj)	messicano (adj)	[messi'kanɔ]

239. Central and South America

Argentina	Argentina (f)	[ardʒen'tina]
Argentinian (masc.)	argentino (m)	[ardʒen'tinɔ]
Argentinian (fem.)	argentina (f)	[ardʒen'tina]
Argentinian (adj)	argentino (adj)	[ardʒen'tinɔ]

Brazil	Brasile (m)	[bra'zile]
Brazilian (masc.)	brasiliano (m)	[brazi'ʎjanɔ]
Brazilian (fem.)	brasiliana (f)	[brazi'ʎjana]
Brazilian (adj)	brasiliano (adj)	[brazi'ʎjanɔ]

Colombia	Colombia (f)	[kɔ'lɔmbia]
Colombian (masc.)	colombiano (m)	[kɔlɔm'bjanɔ]
Colombian (fem.)	colombiana (f)	[kɔlɔm'bjana]
Colombian (adj)	colombiano (adj)	[kɔlɔm'bjanɔ]

| Cuba | Cuba (f) | ['kuba] |
| Cuban (masc.) | cubano (m) | [ku'banɔ] |

Cuban (fem.)	cubana (f)	[ku'bana]
Cuban (adj)	cubano (adj)	[ku'banɔ]

Chile	Cile (m)	['ʧile]
Chilean (masc.)	cileno (m)	[ʧi'lenɔ]
Chilean (fem.)	cilena (f)	[ʧi'lena]
Chilean (adj)	cileno (adj)	[ʧi'lenɔ]

Bolivia	Bolivia (f)	[bɔ'liwia]
Venezuela	Venezuela (f)	[vɛnɛʦu'ɛʎa]
Paraguay	Paraguay (m)	[paragu'aj]
Peru	Perù (m)	[pɛ'ru]

Suriname	Suriname (m)	[suri'namɛ]
Uruguay	Uruguay (m)	[urugu'aj]
Ecuador	Ecuador (m)	[ɛkva'dɔr]

The Bahamas	le Bahamas	[le ba'amas]
Haiti	Haiti (m)	[a'iti]
Dominican Republic	Repubblica (f) Dominicana	[rɛ'pubblika domini'kana]
Panama	Panama (m)	['panama]
Jamaica	Giamaica (f)	[ʤa'majka]

240. Africa

Egypt	Egitto (m)	[ɛ'ʤittɔ]
Egyptian (masc.)	egiziano (m)	[ɛʤiʦi'anɔ]
Egyptian (fem.)	egiziana (f)	[ɛʤiʦi'ana]
Egyptian (adj)	egiziano (adj)	[ɛʤiʦi'anɔ]

Morocco	Marocco (m)	[ma'rɔkkɔ]
Moroccan (masc.)	marocchino (m)	[marɔk'kinɔ]
Moroccan (fem.)	marocchina (f)	[marɔk'kina]
Moroccan (adj)	marocchino (adj)	[marɔk'kinɔ]

Tunisia	Tunisia (f)	[tuni'zia]
Tunisian (masc.)	tunisino (m)	[tuni'zinɔ]
Tunisian (fem.)	tunisina (f)	[tuni'zina]
Tunisian (adj)	tunisino (adj)	[tuni'zinɔ]

Ghana	Ghana (m)	['gana]
Zanzibar	Zanzibar	['dzandzibar]
Kenya	Kenya (m)	['kɛnia]
Libya	Libia (f)	['libia]
Madagascar	Madagascar (m)	[madagas'kar]

Namibia	Namibia (f)	[na'mibia]
Senegal	Senegal (m)	[sɛnɛ'gaʎ]
Tanzania	Tanzania (f)	[tan'dzania]
South Africa	Repubblica (f) Sudafricana	[rɛ'pubblika sudafri'kana]

African (masc.)	africano (m)	[afri'kanɔ]
African (fem.)	africana (f)	[afri'kana]
African (adj)	africano (adj)	[afri'kanɔ]

241. Australia. Oceania

Australia	Australia (f)	[aust'ralia]
Australian (masc.)	australiano (m)	[australi'ano]
Australian (fem.)	australiana (f)	[australi'ana]
Australian (adj)	australiano (adj)	[australi'ano]

New Zealand	Nuova Zelanda (f)	[nu'ova dze'ʎanda]
New Zealander (masc.)	neozelandese (m)	[neɔdzeʎan'dɛze]
New Zealander (fem.)	neozelandese (f)	[neɔdzeʎan'dɛze]
New Zealand (as adj)	neozelandese (adj)	[neɔdzeʎan'dɛze]

| Tasmania | Tasmania (f) | [taz'mania] |
| French Polynesia | Polinesia (f) Francese | [pɔli'nɛzia fran'ʧeze] |

242. Cities

Amsterdam	Amsterdam	['amstɛrdam]
Ankara	Ankara	['aŋkara]
Athens	Atene	[a'tɛnɛ]
Baghdad	Baghdad	[bag'dad]
Bangkok	Bangkok	[baŋ'kɔk]
Barcelona	Barcellona	[barʧel'lɔna]

Beijing	Pechino	[pe'kinɔ]
Beirut	Beirut	['bejrut]
Berlin	Berlino	[ber'linɔ]
Bombay, Mumbai	Bombay, Mumbai	[bɔm'bej], [mum'baj]
Bonn	Bonn	[bɔŋ]

Bordeaux	Bordeaux	[bɔr'dɔ]
Bratislava	Bratislava	[bratiz'ʎava]
Brussels	Bruxelles	[bruk'sɛʎ]
Bucharest	Bucarest	['bukarɛst]
Budapest	Budapest	['budapɛst]

Cairo	Il Cairo	[iʎ 'kairɔ]
Calcutta	Calcutta	[kaʎ'kutta]
Chicago	Chicago	[ʧi'kagɔ]
Copenhagen	Copenaghen	[kɔpe'nagɛn]

Dar-es-Salaam	Dar es Salaam	[dar ɛs sala'am]
Delhi	Delhi	['dɛli]
Dubai	Dubai	[du'bai]
Dublin	Dublino	[dub'linɔ]
Düsseldorf	Düsseldorf	['dyssɛʎdɔrf]

Florence	Firenze	[fi'rɛnʦɛ]
Frankfurt	Francoforte	[fraŋkɔ'fɔrtɛ]
Geneva	Ginevra	[dʒi'nɛvra]

| The Hague | L'Aia | ['ʎaja] |
| Hamburg | Amburgo | [am'burgɔ] |

Hanoi	Hanoi	[a'nɔj]
Havana	L'Avana	[ʎa'vana]
Helsinki	Helsinki	['ɛʎsiŋki]
Hiroshima	Hiroshima	[irɔ'ʃima]
Hong Kong	Hong Kong	['ɔŋkɔŋ]

Istanbul	Istanbul	['istanbuʎ]
Jerusalem	Gerusalemme	[dʒeruza'lemmɛ]
Kiev	Kiev	['kiev]
Kuala Lumpur	Kuala Lumpur	[ku'aʎa 'lympur]
Lisbon	Lisbona	[liz'bɔna]
London	Londra	['lɔndra]
Los Angeles	Los Angeles	[lɔs 'ɛndʒeles]
Lyons	Lione	[li'ɔnɛ]

Madrid	Madrid	[mad'rid]
Marseille	Marsiglia	[mar'siʎja]
Mexico City	Città del Messico	[tʃit'ta dɛʎ 'mɛssikɔ]
Miami	Miami	[ma'jami]
Montreal	Montreal	[mɔnrɛ'aʎ]
Moscow	Mosca	['mɔska]
Munich	Monaco di Baviera	['mɔnakɔ di bawi'era]

Nairobi	Nairobi	[naj'rɔbi]
Naples	Napoli	['napɔli]
New York	New York	[ɲjy 'jork]
Nice	Nizza	['nitsa]
Oslo	Oslo	['ɔzlɔ]
Ottawa	Ottawa	[ɔt'tava]

Paris	Parigi	[pa'ridʒi]
Prague	Praga	['praga]
Rio de Janeiro	Rio de Janeiro	['riɔ dɛ ʒa'nɛjrɔ]
Rome	Roma	['rɔma]

Saint Petersburg	San Pietroburgo	[san pjetrɔ'burgɔ]
Seoul	Seoul	[sɛ'uʎ]
Shanghai	Shanghai	[ʃa'ŋaj]
Singapore	Singapore	[siŋa'pɔrɛ]
Stockholm	Stoccolma	[stɔk'kɔʎma]
Sydney	Sidney	[sid'nɛj]

Taipei	Taipei	[taj'pɛj]
Tokyo	Tokio	['tɔkiɔ]
Toronto	Toronto	[tɔ'rɔntɔ]
Venice	Venezia	[vɛ'nɛtsia]
Vienna	Vienna	['vjeŋa]
Warsaw	Varsavia	[var'sawia]
Washington	Washington	[u'oʃiŋtɔn]

243. Politics. Government. Part 1

| politics | politica (f) | [pɔ'litika] |
| political (adj) | politico (adj) | [pɔ'litikɔ] |

politician	politico (m)	[po'litiko]
state (country)	stato (m)	['stato]
citizen	cittadino (m)	[tʃitta'dino]
citizenship	cittadinanza (f)	[tʃittadi'nantsa]

| national emblem | emblema (m) nazionale | [ɛmb'lema natsʲo'nale] |
| national anthem | inno (m) nazionale | ['iŋo natsʲo'nale] |

government	governo (m)	[go'vɛrno]
head of state	capo (m) di Stato	['kapo di 'stato]
parliament	parlamento (m)	[parʎa'mɛnto]
party	partito (m)	[par'tito]

| capitalism | capitalismo (m) | [kapita'lizmo] |
| capitalist (adj) | capitalistico | [kapita'listiko] |

| socialism | socialismo (m) | [sotʃia'lizmo] |
| socialist (adj) | socialista | [sotʃia'lista] |

communism	comunismo (m)	[komu'nizmo]
communist (adj)	comunista	[komu'nista]
communist (n)	comunista (m)	[komu'nista]

democracy	democrazia (f)	[dɛmokra'tsia]
democrat	democratico (m)	[dɛmok'ratiko]
democratic (adj)	democratico	[dɛmok'ratiko]
Democratic party	partito (m) democratico	[par'tito dɛmok'ratiko]

liberal (n)	liberale (m)	[libɛ'rale]
Liberal (adj)	liberale (adj)	[libɛ'rale]
conservative (n)	conservatore (m)	[konsɛrva'torɛ]
conservative (adj)	conservatore (adj)	[konsɛrva'torɛ]

republic (n)	repubblica (f)	[rɛ'pubblika]
republican (n)	repubblicano (m)	[rɛpubbli'kano]
Republican party	partito (m) repubblicano	[par'tito rɛpubbli'kano]

poll, elections	elezioni (f pl)	[ɛle'tsʲoni]
to elect (vt)	eleggere (vt)	[ɛ'ledʒerɛ]
elector, voter	elettore (m)	[ɛlet'torɛ]
election campaign	campagna (f) elettorale	[kam'paŋja ɛletto'rale]

voting (n)	votazione (f)	[vota'tsʲonɛ]
to vote (vi)	votare (vi)	[vo'tarɛ]
suffrage, right to vote	diritto (m) di voto	[di'ritto di 'voto]

candidate	candidato (m)	[kandi'dato]
to be a candidate	candidarsi (vr)	[kandi'darsi]
campaign	campagna (f)	[kam'paŋja]

| opposition (as adj) | d'opposizione | [doppozi'tsʲonɛ] |
| opposition (n) | opposizione (f) | [oppozi'tsʲonɛ] |

visit	visita (f)	['wizita]
official visit	visita (f) ufficiale	['wizita uffi'tʃale]
international (adj)	internazionale	[intɛrnatsʲo'nale]

| negotiations | trattative (f pl) | [tratta'tivɛ] |
| to negotiate (vi) | negoziare (vi) | [nego'tsjarɛ] |

244. Politics. Government. Part 2

society	società (f)	[sotʃie'ta]
constitution	costituzione (f)	[kostitu'tsʲɔnɛ]
power (political control)	potere (m)	[po'tɛrɛ]
corruption	corruzione (f)	[korru'tsʲɔnɛ]

| law (justice) | legge (f) | ['ledʒe] |
| legal (legitimate) | legittimo | [le'dʒittimɔ] |

| justice (fairness) | giustizia (f) | [dʒus'titsia] |
| just (fair) | giusto | ['dʒustɔ] |

committee	comitato (m)	[komi'tatɔ]
bill (draft of law)	disegno (m) di legge	[di'zeɲʲɔ di 'ledʒe]
budget	bilancio (m)	[bi'ʎantʃo]
policy	politica (f)	[po'litika]
reform	riforma (f)	[ri'fɔrma]
radical (adj)	radicale	[radi'kale]

power (strength, force)	forza (f), potenza (f)	['fortsa], [po'tɛntsa]
powerful (adj)	potente	[po'tɛntɛ]
supporter	sostenitore (m)	[sostɛni'tɔrɛ]
influence	influenza (f)	[infly'ɛntsa]

regime (e.g. military ~)	regime (m)	[rɛ'dʒimɛ]
conflict	conflitto (m)	[konf'littɔ]
conspiracy (plot)	complotto (m)	[komp'lɔttɔ]
provocation	provocazione (f)	[provoka'tsʲɔnɛ]

to overthrow (regime, etc.)	rovesciare (vt)	[rove'ʃarɛ]
overthrow (of government)	rovesciamento (m)	[roveʃa'mɛntɔ]
revolution	rivoluzione (f)	[rivoly'tsʲɔnɛ]

| coup d'état | colpo (m) di Stato | ['koʎpɔ di 'statɔ] |
| military coup | golpe (m) militare | ['goʎpɛ mili'tarɛ] |

crisis	crisi (f)	['krizi]
economic recession	recessione (f) economica	[rɛtʃessi'ɔnɛ ɛko'nɔmika]
demonstrator (protester)	manifestante (m)	[manifɛs'tantɛ]
demonstration	manifestazione (f)	[manifɛsta'tsʲɔnɛ]
martial law	legge (f) marziale	['ledʒe martsi'ale]
military base	base (f) militare	['bazɛ mili'tarɛ]

| stability | stabilità (f) | [stabili'ta] |
| stable (adj) | stabile | ['stabile] |

exploitation	sfruttamento (m)	[sfrutta'mɛntɔ]
to exploit (workers)	sfruttare (vt)	[sfrut'tarɛ]
racism	razzismo (m)	[ra'tsizmɔ]
racist	razzista (m)	[ra'tsista]

| fascism | fascismo (m) | [fa'ʃizmɔ] |
| fascist | fascista (m) | [fa'ʃista] |

245. Countries. Miscellaneous

foreigner	straniero (m)	[stra'ɲjerɔ]
foreign (adj)	straniero (adj)	[stra'ɲjerɔ]
abroad (adv)	all'estero	[a'ʎ'ɛstɛrɔ]

emigrant	emigrato (m)	[ɛmig'ratɔ]
emigration	emigrazione (f)	[ɛmigra'tsʲɔnɛ]
to emigrate (vi)	emigrare (vi)	[ɛmig'rarɛ]

the West	Ovest (m)	['ɔvɛst]
the East	Est (m)	[ɛst]
the Far East	Estremo Oriente (m)	[ɛst'rɛmɔ ɔri'ɛntɛ]

civilization	civiltà (f)	[ʧiwiʎ'ta]
humanity (mankind)	umanità (f)	[umani'ta]
world (earth)	mondo (m)	['mɔndɔ]
peace	pace (f)	['paʧe]
worldwide (adj)	mondiale	[mɔn'dʲale]

homeland	patria (f)	['patria]
people (population)	popolo (m)	['pɔpɔlɔ]
population	popolazione (f)	[popoʎa'tsʲɔnɛ]
people (a lot of ~)	gente (f)	['ʤentɛ]
nation (people)	nazione (f)	[na'tsʲɔnɛ]
generation	generazione (f)	[ʤenɛra'tsʲɔnɛ]

territory (area)	territorio (m)	[tɛrri'tɔriɔ]
region	regione (f)	[rɛ'ʤɔnɛ]
state (part of a country)	stato (m)	['statɔ]
tradition	tradizione (f)	[tradi'tsʲɔnɛ]
custom (tradition)	costume (m)	[kɔs'tumɛ]
ecology	ecologia (f)	[ɛkɔlɜ'ʤia]

Indian (Native American)	indiano (m)	[indi'anɔ]
Gipsy (masc.)	zingaro (m)	['ʣiŋarɔ]
Gipsy (fem.)	zingara (f)	['ʣiŋara]
Gipsy (adj)	di zingaro	[di 'ʣiŋarɔ]

empire	impero (m)	[im'pɛrɔ]
colony	colonia (f)	[kɔ'lɔnia]
slavery	schiavitù (f)	[skjawi'tu]
invasion	invasione (f)	[inva'zʲɔnɛ]
famine	carestia (f)	[karɛs'tia]

246. Major religious groups. Confessions

| religion | religione (f) | [rɛli'ʤɔnɛ] |
| religious (adj) | religioso | [rɛli'ʤɔzɔ] |

belief (in God)	fede (f)	['fɛdɛ]
to believe (in God)	credere (vi)	['krɛdɛrɛ]
believer	credente (m)	[krɛ'dɛntɛ]

| atheism | ateismo (m) | [atɛ'izmɔ] |
| atheist | ateo (m) | ['atɛɔ] |

Christianity	cristianesimo (m)	[kristia'nɛzimɔ]
Christian (n)	cristiano (m)	[kristi'anɔ]
Christian (adj)	cristiano (adj)	[kristi'anɔ]

Catholicism	Cattolicesimo (m)	[kattɔli'ʧezimɔ]
Catholic (n)	cattolico (m)	[kat'tɔlikɔ]
Catholic (adj)	cattolico (adj)	[kat'tɔlikɔ]

Protestantism	Protestantesimo (m)	[prɔtɛntan'tɛsimɔ]
Protestant Church	Chiesa (f) protestante	['kjeza protɛs'tantɛ]
Protestant	protestante (m)	[prɔtɛs'tantɛ]

Orthodoxy	Ortodossia (f)	[ɔrtɔdɔs'sija]
Orthodox Church	Chiesa (f) ortodossa	['kjeza ɔrtɔ'dɔssa]
Orthodox	ortodosso (m)	[ɔrtɔ'dɔssɔ]

Presbyterianism	Presbiterianesimo (m)	[prɛsbitɛria'nɛzimɔ]
Presbyterian Church	Chiesa (f) presbiteriana	['kjeza prɛsbitɛri'ana]
Presbyterian (n)	presbiteriano (m)	[prɛsbitɛri'anɔ]

| Lutheranism | Luteranesimo (m) | [lytɛra'nɛzimɔ] |
| Lutheran | luterano (m) | [lytɛ'ranɔ] |

| Baptist Church | confessione (f) battista | [kɔnfɛssi'ɔnɛ bat'tista] |
| Baptist | battista (m) | [bat'tista] |

| Anglican Church | Chiesa (f) anglicana | ['kjeza aŋli'kana] |
| Anglican | anglicano (m) | [aŋli'kanɔ] |

| Mormonism | Mormonismo (m) | [mɔrmɔ'nizmɔ] |
| Mormon | mormone (m) | [mɔr'mɔnɛ] |

| Judaism | giudaismo (m) | [ʤuda'izmɔ] |
| Jew | ebreo (m) | [ɛb'rɛɔ] |

| Buddhism | buddismo (m) | [bud'dizmɔ] |
| Buddhist | buddista (m) | [bud'dista] |

| Hinduism | Induismo (m) | [indu'izmɔ] |
| Hindu | induista (m) | [indu'ista] |

Islam	Islam (m)	['izʎam]
Muslim (n)	musulmano (m)	[musuʎ'manɔ]
Muslim (adj)	musulmano	[musuʎ'manɔ]

Shiism	sciismo (m)	[ʃi'izmɔ]
Shiite (n)	sciita (m)	[ʃi'ita]
Sunni (religion)	sunnismo (m)	[su'ŋizmɔ]
Sunnite (n)	sunnita (m)	[su'ŋita]

247. Religions. Priests

priest	**prete** (m)	['prɛtɛ]
the Pope	**Papa** (m)	['papa]
monk, friar	**monaco** (m)	['mɔnakɔ]
nun	**monaca** (f)	['mɔnaka]
pastor	**pastore** (m)	[pas'tɔrɛ]
abbot	**abate** (m)	[a'batɛ]
vicar	**vicario** (m)	[wi'kariɔ]
bishop	**vescovo** (m)	['vɛskɔvɔ]
cardinal	**cardinale** (m)	[kardi'nalɛ]
preacher	**predicatore** (m)	[prɛdika'tɔrɛ]
preaching	**predica** (f)	['prɛdika]
parishioners	**parrocchiani** (m)	[parrɔk'kjani]
believer	**credente** (m)	[krɛ'dɛntɛ]
atheist	**ateo** (m)	['atɛɔ]

248. Faith. Christianity. Islam

Adam	**Adamo**	[a'damɔ]
Eve	**Eva**	['ɛva]
God	**Dio** (m)	['diɔ]
the Lord	**Signore** (m)	[si'ɲɔrɛ]
the Almighty	**Onnipotente** (m)	[ɔɲipo'tɛntɛ]
sin	**peccato** (m)	[pɛk'katɔ]
to sin (vi)	**peccare** (vi)	[pɛk'karɛ]
sinner (masc.)	**peccatore** (m)	[pɛkka'tɔrɛ]
sinner (fem.)	**peccatrice** (f)	[pɛkkat'ritʃe]
hell	**inferno** (m)	[in'fɛrnɔ]
paradise	**paradiso** (m)	[para'dizɔ]
Jesus	**Gesù**	[dʒe'su]
Jesus Christ	**Gesù Cristo**	[dʒe'su 'kristɔ]
the Holy Spirit	**Spirito** (m) **Santo**	['spiritɔ 'santɔ]
the Saviour	**Salvatore** (m)	[saʎva'tɔrɛ]
the Virgin Mary	**Madonna**	[ma'dɔɲa]
the Devil	**Diavolo** (m)	['diavɔlɔ]
devil's (adj)	**del diavolo**	[dɛʎ 'diavɔlɔ]
Satan	**Satana** (m)	['satana]
satanic (adj)	**satanico**	[sa'tanikɔ]
angel	**angelo** (m)	['andʒelɔ]
guardian angel	**angelo** (m) **custode**	['andʒelɔ kus'tɔdɛ]
angelic (adj)	**angelico**	[an'dʒelikɔ]

apostle	apostolo (m)	[a'pɔstɔlɔ]
archangel	arcangelo (m)	[ar'kandʒelɔ]
the Antichrist	Anticristo (m)	[antik'ristɔ]

Church	Chiesa (f)	['kjeza]
Bible	Bibbia (f)	['bibbja]
biblical (adj)	biblico	['biblikɔ]

Old Testament	Vecchio Testamento (m)	['vɛkkiɔ tɛsta'mɛntɔ]
New Testament	Nuovo Testamento (m)	[nu'ɔvɔ tɛsta'mɛntɔ]
Gospel	Vangelo (m)	[van'dʒelɔ]
Holy Scripture	Sacra Scrittura (f)	['sakra skrit'tura]
heaven	Il Regno dei Cieli	[iʎ 'reɲɔ dɛi 'tʃeli]

Commandment	comandamento (m)	[kɔmanda'mɛntɔ]
prophet	profeta (m)	[prɔ'fɛta]
prophecy	profezia (f)	[prɔfɛ'tsia]

Allah	Allah	[a'la]
Mohammed	Maometto	[maɔ'mɛtɔ]
the Koran	Corano (m)	[kɔ'ranɔ]

mosque	moschea (f)	[mɔs'kɛa]
mullah	mullah (m)	[mul'la]
prayer	preghiera (f)	[prɛ'gjera]
to pray (vi, vt)	pregare (vi, vt)	[prɛ'garɛ]

pilgrimage	pellegrinaggio (m)	[pɛllegri'nadʒɔ]
pilgrim	pellegrino (m)	[pɛlleg'rinɔ]
Mecca	La Mecca (f)	[ʎa 'mɛkka]

church	chiesa (f)	['kjeza]
temple	tempio (m)	['tɛmplɔ]
cathedral	cattedrale (f)	[kattɛd'rale]
Gothic (adj)	gotico	['gɔtikɔ]
synagogue	sinagoga (f)	[sina'gɔga]
mosque	moschea (f)	[mɔs'kɛa]

chapel	cappella (f)	[kap'pɛʎa]
abbey	abbazia (f)	[abba'tsia]
convent	convento (m) di suore	[kɔn'vɛntɔ di su'ɔrɛ]
monastery	monastero (m)	[mɔnas'tɛrɔ]

bell (in church)	campana (f)	[kam'pana]
bell tower	campanile (m)	[kampa'nile]
to ring (ab. bells)	suonare (vi)	[suɔ'narɛ]

cross	croce (f)	['krɔtʃe]
cupola (roof)	cupola (f)	['kupɔʎa]
icon	icona (f)	[i'kɔna]

soul	anima (f)	['anima]
fate (destiny)	destino (m), sorte (f)	[dɛs'tinɔ], ['sɔrtɛ]
evil (n)	male (m)	['male]
good (n)	bene (m)	['bɛnɛ]
vampire	vampiro (m)	[vam'pirɔ]

witch (sorceress)	strega (f)	['strɛga]
demon	demone (m)	['dɛmonɛ]
devil	diavolo (m)	['diavɔlɔ]
spirit	spirito (m)	['spiritɔ]
redemption (giving us ~)	redenzione (f)	[rɛdɛn'tsiɔnɛ]
to redeem (vt)	redimere (vt)	[rɛ'dimɛrɛ]
church service, mass	messa (f)	['messa]
to say mass	dire la messa	['dirɛ ʎa 'messa]
confession	confessione (f)	[kɔnfɛssi'ɔnɛ]
to confess (vi)	confessarsi (vr)	[kɔnfɛs'sarsi]
saint (n)	santo (m)	['santɔ]
sacred (holy)	sacro	['sakrɔ]
holy water	acqua (f) santa	['akua 'santa]
ritual (n)	rito (m)	['ritɔ]
ritual (adj)	rituale	[ritu'ale]
sacrifice	sacrificio (m)	[sakri'fitʃɔ]
superstition	superstizione (f)	[supɛrsti'tsiɔnɛ]
superstitious (adj)	superstizioso	[supɛrstitsi'ozɔ]
afterlife	vita (f) dell'oltretomba	['wita del ɔltre'tɔmba]
eternal life	vita (f) eterna	['wita ɛ'tɛrna]

MISCELLANEOUS

249. Various useful words

background (green ~)	**sfondo** (m)	['sfɔndɔ]
balance (of situation)	**bilancio** (m)	[bi'ʎantʃɔ]
barrier (obstacle)	**barriera** (f)	[bar'rjera]
base (basis)	**base** (f)	['bazɛ]
beginning	**inizio** (m)	[i'nitsiɔ]
category	**categoria** (f)	[katɛgɔ'ria]
cause (reason)	**causa** (f)	['kauza]
choice	**scelta** (f)	['ʃɛʎta]
coincidence	**coincidenza** (f)	[kɔintʃi'dɛntsa]
comfortable (~ chair)	**comodo**	['kɔmɔdɔ]
comparison	**confronto** (m)	[kɔnf'rɔntɔ]
compensation	**compenso** (m)	[kɔm'pɛnsɔ]
degree (extent, amount)	**grado** (m)	['gradɔ]
development	**sviluppo** (m)	[zwi'lyppɔ]
difference	**differenza** (f)	[diffɛ'rɛntsa]
effect (e.g. of drugs)	**effetto** (m)	[ɛf'fɛttɔ]
effort (exertion)	**sforzo** (m)	['sfɔrtsɔ]
element	**elemento** (m)	[ɛle'mɛntɔ]
end (finish)	**termine** (m)	['tɛrminɛ]
example (illustration)	**esempio** (m)	[ɛ'zɛmpjɔ]
fact	**fatto** (m)	['fattɔ]
frequent (adj)	**frequente**	[frɛku'ɛntɛ]
growth (development)	**crescita** (f)	['krɛʃita]
help	**aiuto** (m)	[a'jutɔ]
ideal	**ideale** (m)	[idɛ'ale]
kind (sort, type)	**genere** (m)	['dʒenɛrɛ]
labyrinth	**labirinto** (m)	[ʎabi'rintɔ]
mistake, error	**errore** (m)	[ɛr'rɔrɛ]
moment	**momento** (m)	[mɔ'mɛntɔ]
object (thing)	**oggetto** (m)	[ɔ'dʒettɔ]
obstacle	**ostacolo** (m)	[ɔs'takɔlɔ]
original (original copy)	**originale** (m)	[ɔridʒi'nale]
part (~ of sth)	**parte** (f)	['partɛ]
particle, small part	**particella** (f)	[parti'tʃeʎa]
pause (break)	**pausa** (f)	['pauza]
position	**posizione** (f)	[pɔzi'tsjɔnɛ]
principle	**principio** (m)	[prin'tʃipjɔ]
problem	**problema** (m)	[prɔb'lema]

process	processo (m)	[pro'tʃessɔ]
progress	progresso (m)	[prɔg'rɛssɔ]
property (quality)	proprietà (f)	[proprie'ta]

| reaction | reazione (f) | [rɛa'tsɨɔnɛ] |
| risk | rischio (m) | ['riskiɔ] |

secret	segreto (m)	[sɛg'rɛtɔ]
section (sector)	sezione (f)	[sɛ'tsɨɔnɛ]
series	serie (f)	['sɛrie]
shape (outer form)	forma (f)	['fɔrma]
situation	situazione (f)	[situa'tsɨɔnɛ]

solution	soluzione (f)	[sɔly'tsɨɔnɛ]
standard (adj)	standard	['standar]
standard (level of quality)	standard (m)	['standar]
stop (pause)	pausa (f)	['pauza]
style	stile (m)	['stile]
system	sistema (m)	[sis'tɛma]

table (chart)	tabella (f)	[ta'bɛʎa]
tempo, rate	ritmo (m)	['ritmɔ]
term (word, expression)	termine (m)	['tɛrminɛ]
thing (object, item)	cosa (f)	['kɔza]
truth	verità (f)	[vɛri'ta]
turn (please wait your ~)	turno (m)	['turnɔ]
type (sort, kind)	tipo (m)	['tipɔ]

urgent (adj)	urgente	[ur'dʒɛntɛ]
urgently	urgentemente	[urdʒɛntɛ'mɛntɛ]
utility (usefulness)	utilità (f)	[utili'ta]
variant (alternative)	variante (f)	[vari'antɛ]
way (means, method)	modo (m)	['mɔdɔ]
zone	zona (f)	['dzɔna]

250. Modifiers. Adjectives. Part 1

additional (adj)	supplementare	[supplemen'tarɛ]
ancient (~ civilization)	antico	[an'tikɔ]
artificial (adj)	artificiale	[artifi'tʃale]

back, rear (adj)	posteriore	[postɛri'ɔrɛ]
bad (adj)	cattivo	[kat'tivɔ]
beautiful (~ palace)	magnifico	[ma'ɲifikɔ]
beautiful (person)	bello	['bɛllɔ]
big (in size)	grande	['grandɛ]
bitter (taste)	amaro	[a'marɔ]
blind (sightless)	cieco	['tʃekɔ]

calm, quiet (adj)	tranquillo	[traŋku'illɔ]
careless (negligent)	noncurante	[noŋku'rantɛ]
caring (~ father)	premuroso	[prɛmu'rozɔ]
central (adj)	centrale	[tʃent'rale]
cheap (adj)	a buon mercato	[a bu'ɔn mɛr'katɔ]

cheerful (adj)	allegro	[al'legrɔ]
children's (adj)	per bambini	[pɛr bam'bini]
civil (~ law)	civile	[tʃi'wile]

clandestine (secret)	clandestino	[kʎandɛs'tinɔ]
clean (free from dirt)	pulito	[pu'litɔ]
clear (explanation, etc.)	chiaro	['kjarɔ]
clever (intelligent)	intelligente	[intɛlli'dʒentɛ]
closed (adj)	chiuso	['kjyzɔ]
cloudless (sky)	sereno	[sɛ'rɛnɔ]

cold (drink, weather)	freddo	['frɛddɔ]
compatible (adj)	compatibile	[kɔmpa'tibile]
contented (adj)	contento	[kɔn'tɛntɔ]
continuous (adj)	continuo	[kɔn'tinuɔ]
continuous (incessant)	ininterrotto	[inintɛ'rɔttɔ]
cool (weather)	fresco	['frɛskɔ]

dangerous (adj)	pericoloso	[pɛrikɔ'lɔzɔ]
dark (room)	buio, scuro	['bujo], ['skurɔ]
dead (not alive)	morto	['mɔrtɔ]
dense (fog, smoke)	denso	['dɛnsɔ]

different (adj)	diverso	[di'vɛrsɔ]
difficult (decision)	difficile	[dif'fitʃile]
difficult (problem, task)	complicato	[kɔmpli'katɔ]
dim, faint (light)	fievole	['fjevɔle]

dirty (not clean)	sporco	['spɔrkɔ]
distant (faraway)	distante	[dis'tantɛ]
distant (in space)	lontano	[lɔn'tanɔ]
dry (climate, clothing)	secco	['sɛkkɔ]

easy (not difficult)	facile	['fatʃile]
empty (glass, room)	vuoto	[vu'ɔtɔ]
exact (amount)	preciso	[prɛ'tʃizɔ]
excellent (adj)	eccellente	[ɛtʃe'lentɛ]
excessive (adj)	eccessivo	[ɛtʃes'sivɔ]
expensive (adj)	caro	['karɔ]
exterior (adj)	esterno	[ɛs'tɛrnɔ]

fast (quick)	veloce, rapido	[vɛ'lɔtʃe], ['rapidɔ]
fatty (food)	grasso	['grassɔ]
fertile (land, soil)	fertile	['fɛrtile]
flat (~ panel display)	piatto	['pjattɔ]
flat (e.g. ~ surface)	piatto	['pjattɔ]

foreign (adj)	straniero	[stra'ɲjerɔ]
fragile (china, glass)	fragile	['fradʒile]
free (at no cost)	gratuito	[gra'tuitɔ]
free (unrestricted)	libero	['libɛrɔ]

fresh (~ water)	dolce	['dɔʎtʃe]
fresh (e.g. ~ bred)	fresco	['frɛskɔ]
frozen (food)	surgelato	[surdʒe'latɔ]
full (completely filled)	pieno	['pjenɔ]

good (book, etc.)	buono	[bu'ɔnɔ]
good (kindhearted)	buono	[bu'ɔnɔ]
grateful (adj)	grato	['gratɔ]

happy (adj)	felice	[fɛ'litʃe]
hard (not soft)	duro	['durɔ]
heavy (in weight)	pesante	[pɛ'zantɛ]

hostile (adj)	ostile	[ɔs'tile]
hot (adj)	caldo	['kaʎdɔ]
huge (adj)	enorme	[ɛ'nɔrmɛ]
humid (adj)	umido	['umidɔ]
hungry (adj)	affamato	[affa'matɔ]

ill (sick, unwell)	malato	[ma'ʎatɔ]
incomprehensible	incomprensibile	[iŋkɔmprɛn'sibile]

immobile (adj)	immobile	[im'mɔbile]
important (adj)	importante	[impɔr'tantɛ]
impossible (adj)	impossibile	[impɔs'sibile]

indispensable (adj)	indispensabile	[indispɛn'sabile]
inexperienced (adj)	inesperto	[inɛs'pɛrtɔ]
insignificant (adj)	insignificante	[insinifi'kantɛ]
interior (adj)	interno	[in'tɛrnɔ]
joint (~ decision)	collegiale	[kɔlle'dʒale]

last (e.g. ~ week)	scorso	['skɔrsɔ]
last (final)	ultimo	['uʎtimɔ]
left (e.g. ~ side)	sinistro	[si'nistrɔ]
legal (legitimate)	legale	[le'gale]

light (in weight)	leggero	[le'dʒerɔ]
light (pale color)	chiaro, tenue	['kjarɔ], ['tɛnuɛ]
limited (adj)	limitato	[limi'tatɔ]
liquid (fluid)	liquido	['likuidɔ]
long (e.g. ~ way)	lungo	['luŋɔ]
loud (voice, etc.)	alto, forte	['aʎtɔ], ['fɔrtɛ]
low (voice)	basso	['bassɔ]

251. Modifiers. Adjectives. Part 2

main (principal)	principale	[printʃi'pale]
matt (paint)	opaco	[ɔ'pakɔ]
meticulous (job)	meticoloso, accurato	[mɛtikɔ'lozɔ], [akku'ratɔ]
mysterious (adj)	misterioso	[mistɛri'ozɔ]

narrow (street, etc.)	stretto	['strɛttɔ]
native (of country)	nativo	[na'tivɔ]
necessary (adj)	necessario	[nɛtʃe'sarɔ]
negative (adj)	negativo	[nɛga'tivɔ]
neighbouring (adj)	vicino, prossimo	[wi'tʃinɔ], ['prɔssimɔ]
nervous (adj)	nervoso	[nɛr'vozɔ]
new (adj)	nuovo	[nu'ɔvɔ]

next (e.g. ~ week)	successivo	[sutʃes'sivɔ]
nearby	vicino, accanto	[wi'tʃinɔ], [a'kantɔ]
nice (kind)	gentile	[dʒen'tile]
nice (voice)	gradevole	[gra'dɛvɔle]

normal (adj)	normale	[nɔr'male]
not big (adj)	non molto grande	[nɔn 'mɔʎtɔ 'grandɛ]
not clear (adj)	poco chiaro	['pɔkɔ 'kjarɔ]
not difficult (adj)	non difficile	[nɔn di'fitʃile]

obligatory (adj)	obbligatorio	[ɔbbliga'tɔriɔ]
old (house)	vecchio	['vɛkkiɔ]
open (adj)	aperto	[a'pɛrtɔ]
opposite (adj)	opposto	[ɔp'pɔstɔ]
ordinary (usual)	comune, normale	[kɔ'munɛ], [nɔr'male]
original (unusual)	originale	[ɔridʒi'nale]

past (recent)	passato	[pas'satɔ]
permanent (adj)	permanente	[pɛrma'nɛntɛ]
personal (adj)	personale	[pɛrsɔ'nale]
polite (adj)	gentile	[dʒen'tile]
poor (not rich)	povero	['pɔvɛrɔ]
possible (adj)	possibile	[pɔs'sibile]
poverty-stricken (adj)	molto povero	['mɔltɔ 'pɔvɛrɔ]

present (current)	presente	[prɛ'zɛntɛ]
principal (main)	principale	[printʃi'pale]
private (~ jet)	privato	[pri'vatɔ]
probable (adj)	probabile	[prɔ'babile]

public (open to all)	pubblico	['pubblikɔ]
punctual (person)	puntuale	[puntu'ale]
quiet (tranquil)	calmo	['kaʎmɔ]

rare (adj)	raro	['rarɔ]
raw (uncooked)	crudo	['krudɔ]
right (not left)	destro	['dɛstrɔ]
right, correct (adj)	giusto	['dʒustɔ]
ripe (fruit)	maturo	[ma'turɔ]
risky (adj)	rischioso	[ris'k'ɔzɔ]

sad (~ look)	triste	['tristɛ]
sad (depressing)	triste, mesto	['tristɛ], ['mɛstɔ]
safe (not dangerous)	sicuro	[si'kurɔ]
salty (food)	salato	[sa'ʎatɔ]
satisfied (customer)	soddisfatto	[sɔddis'fattɔ]
second hand (adj)	di seconda mano	[di sɛ'kɔnda 'manɔ]

shallow (water)	poco profondo	['pɔkɔ prɔ'fɔndɔ]
sharp (blade, etc.)	affilato	[affi'ʎatɔ]
short (in length)	corto	['kɔrtɔ]
short, short-lived (adj)	breve	['brɛvɛ]
short-sighted (adj)	miope	['miɔpɛ]

| significant (notable) | notevole | [nɔ'tɛvɔle] |
| similar (adj) | simile | ['simile] |

simple (easy)	semplice	['sɛmplitʃe]
slim (person)	magro	['magro]
small (in size)	piccolo	['pikkɔlɔ]
smooth (surface)	liscio	['liʃo]
soft (to touch)	morbido	['mɔrbidɔ]
solid (~ wall)	solido	['sɔlidɔ]
somber, gloomy (adj)	fosco	['fɔskɔ]
sour (flavour, taste)	acido, agro	['atʃidɔ], ['agrɔ]
spacious (house, etc.)	spazioso	[spatsi'ɔzɔ]
special (adj)	speciale	[spɛ'tʃale]
straight (line, road)	dritto	['drittɔ]
strong (person)	forte	['fɔrtɛ]
stupid (foolish)	stupido	['stupidɔ]
convenient (adj)	idoneo	[i'dɔnɛɔ]
sunny (day)	di sole	[di 'sɔle]
superb, perfect (adj)	perfetto	[per'fɛttɔ]
swarthy (adj)	bruno	['brunɔ]
sweet (sugary)	dolce	['dɔʎtʃe]
tanned (adj)	abbronzato	[abbrɔn'dzatɔ]
tasty (adj)	buono, gustoso	[bu'ɔnɔ], [gus'tɔzɔ]
tender (affectionate)	dolce, tenero	['dɔʎtʃe], ['tɛnɛrɔ]
the highest (adj)	il più alto	[iʎ pi'ju 'aʎtɔ]
the most important	il più importante	[iʎ pjy impɔr'tantɛ]
the nearest	il più vicino	[iʎ pi'ju wi'tʃinɔ]
the same, equal (adj)	uguale	[ugu'ale]
thick (e.g. ~ fog)	fitto	['fittɔ]
thick (wall, slice)	spesso	['spɛssɔ]
tired (exhausted)	stanco	['stankɔ]
tiring (adj)	faticoso	[fati'kozɔ]
too thin (emaciated)	molto magro	['mɔʎtɔ 'magrɔ]
transparent (adj)	trasparente	[traspa'rɛntɛ]
unique (exceptional)	unico	['unikɔ]
various (adj)	differente	[diffɛ'rɛntɛ]
warm (moderately hot)	caldo	['kaʎdɔ]
wet (e.g. ~ clothes)	bagnato	[ba'ɲjatɔ]
whole (entire, complete)	intero	[in'tɛrɔ]
wide (e.g. ~ road)	largo	['ʎargɔ]
young (adj)	giovane	['dʒɔvanɛ]

MAIN 500 VERBS

252. Verbs A-C

to accompany (vt)	accompagnare (vt)	[akkɔmpa'ɲjarɛ]
to accuse (vt)	accusare (vt)	[akku'zarɛ]
to act (take action)	agire (vi)	[a'dʒirɛ]

to add (supplement)	aggiungere (vt)	[a'dʒundʒarɛ]
to address (speak to)	rivolgersi a ...	[ri'vɔʎdʒersi a]
to admire (vi)	ammirare (vi)	[ammi'rarɛ]
to advertise (vt)	pubblicizzare (vt)	[pubbliʧi'dzarɛ]
to advise (vt)	consigliare (vt)	[kɔnsi'ʎjarɛ]

to affirm (vt)	affermare (vt)	[affɛr'marɛ]
to agree (say yes)	essere d'accordo	['ɛssɛrɛ dak'kɔrdɔ]
to allow (sb to do sth)	autorizzare (vt)	[autɔri'dzarɛ]
to allude (vi)	alludere (vi)	[al'lydɛrɛ]

to amputate (vt)	amputare (vt)	[ampu'tarɛ]
to make angry	far arrabbiare	[far arra'bʲarɛ]
to answer (vi, vt)	rispondere (vi, vt)	[ris'pɔndɛrɛ]

to apologize (vi)	scusarsi (vr)	[sku'zarsi]
to appear (come into view)	apparire (vi)	[appa'rirɛ]
to applaud (vi, vt)	applaudire (vi, vt)	[appʎau'dirɛ]
to appoint (assign)	nominare (vt)	[nɔmi'narɛ]
to approach (come nearer)	avvicinarsi (vr)	[avwiʧi'narsi]

to arrive (ab. train)	arrivare (vi)	[arri'varɛ]
to ask (~ sb to do sth)	chiedere, domandare	['kjedɛrɛ], [dɔman'darɛ]
to aspire to ...	aspirare (vi)	[aspi'rarɛ]
to assist (help)	assistere (vt)	[as'sistɛrɛ]

to attack (mil.)	attaccare (vt)	[attak'karɛ]
to attain (objectives)	raggiungere (vt)	[ra'dʒundʒɛrɛ]
to avenge (vt)	vendicare (vt)	[vɛndi'karɛ]
to avoid (danger, task)	evitare (vt)	[ɛwi'tarɛ]
to award (give medal to)	decorare qn	[dɛkɔ'rarɛ]

to bath (~ one's baby)	far fare il bagno	[far 'farɛ iʎ 'baɲʲɔ]
to battle (vi)	combattere (vi)	[kɔm'battɛrɛ]

to be (~ on the table)	stare (vi)	['starɛ]
to be (vi)	essere (vi)	['ɛssɛrɛ]

to be afraid	avere paura	[a'vɛrɛ pa'ura]
to be angry (with ...)	essere arrabbiato con ...	['ɛssɛrɛ arrab'bjatɔ kɔn]
to be at war	essere in guerra	['ɛssɛrɛ in gu'ɛrra]
to be based (on ...)	basarsi su ...	[ba'zarsi su]

to be bored	annoiarsi (vr)	[aɲɔ'jarsi]
to be convinced	convincersi (vr)	[kɔn'wintʃersi]
to be enough	bastare (vi)	[bas'tarɛ]
to be envious	invidiare (vt)	[inwidi'arɛ]
to be indignant	indignarsi (vr)	[indi'ɲjarsi]
to be interested in ...	interessarsi di ...	[intɛrɛs'sarsi di]
to be lying down	essere sdraiato	['ɛssɛrɛ zdra'jatɔ]

to be needed	essere necessario	['ɛssɛrɛ nɛtʃɛs'sariɔ]
to be perplexed	essere perplesso	['ɛssɛrɛ pɛrp'lessɔ]
to be preserved	essere conservato	['ɛssɛrɛ kɔnsɛr'vatɔ]
to be required	occorrere (vi)	[ɔk'kɔrrɛrɛ]
to be surprised	stupirsi (vr)	[stu'pirsi]
to be worried	essere preoccupato	['ɛssɛrɛ prɛɔkku'patɔ]

to beat (dog, person)	picchiare (vt)	[pik'kjarɛ]
to become (e.g. ~ old)	diventare, divenire	[divɛn'tarɛ], [dɛvɛ'nirɛ]
to become pensive	diventare pensieroso	[diwen'tarɛ penzie'rɔzɔ]
to behave (vi)	comportarsi (vr)	[kɔmpor'tarsi]

to believe (think)	credere (vt)	['krɛdɛrɛ]
to belong to ...	appartenere (vi)	[appartɛ'nɛrɛ]
to berth (moor)	ormeggiarsi (vr)	[ɔrmɛ'dʒarsi]
to blind (of flash of light)	abbagliare (vt)	[abba'ʎjarɛ]
to blow (wind)	soffiare (vi)	[sof'fjarɛ]
to blush (vi)	arrossire (vi)	[arrɔs'sirɛ]

to boast (vi)	vantarsi (vr)	[van'tarsi]
to borrow (money)	prendere in prestito	['prɛndɛrɛ in 'prɛstitɔ]
to break (branch, toy, etc.)	rompere (vt)	['rompɛrɛ]
to snap (vi, ab. rope)	scoppiare (vi)	[skɔp'pʲarɛ]

to breathe (vi)	respirare (vi)	[rɛspi'rarɛ]
to bring (sth)	portare (vt)	[por'tarɛ]
to burn (paper, logs)	bruciare (vt)	[bru'tʃarɛ]
to buy (purchase)	comprare (vt)	[kɔmp'rarɛ]
to call (for help)	chiamare (vt)	[kja'marɛ]
to calm down (vt)	calmare (vt)	[kaʎ'marɛ]
can (v aux)	potere (vi)	[po'tɛrɛ]
to cancel (call off)	annullare (vt)	[aɲu'ʎarɛ]

to cast off	salpare (vi)	[saʎ'parɛ]
to catch (e.g. ~ a ball)	afferrare (vt)	[affer'rarɛ]
to catch sight (of ...)	intravedere (vt)	[intrawe'dɛrɛ]
to cause ...	essere causa di ...	['ɛssɛrɛ 'kauza di]

to change (~ one's opinion)	cambiare (vt)	[kam'bjarɛ]
to change (exchange)	scambiare (vt)	[skam'bjarɛ]
to charm (vt)	incantare (vt)	[iŋkan'tarɛ]
to choose (select)	scegliere (vt)	['ʃeʎjerɛ]
to chop off (with an axe)	tagliare (vt)	[ta'ʎarɛ]

to clean (from dirt)	pulire (vt)	[pu'lirɛ]
to clean (shoes, etc.)	pulirsi (vr)	[pu'lirsi]
to clean (tidy)	fare le pulizie	['farɛ le puli'tsiɛ]
to close (vt)	chiudere (vt)	['kjydɛrɛ]

to comb one's hair	pettinarsi (vr)	[pɛtti'narsi]
to come down (the stairs)	scendere (vi)	['ʃɛndɛrɛ]
to come in (enter)	entrare (vi)	[ɛnt'rarɛ]
to come out (book)	uscire (vi)	[u'ʃirɛ]

to compare (vt)	confrontare (vt)	[kɔnfrɔn'tarɛ]
to compensate (vt)	compensare (vt)	[kɔmpɛn'sarɛ]
to compete (vi)	competere (vi)	[kɔm'pɛtɛrɛ]

to compile (~ a list)	compilare (vt)	[kɔmpi'ʎarɛ]
to complain (vi, vt)	lamentarsi (vr)	[ʎamɛn'tarsi]
to complicate (vt)	complicare (vt)	[kɔmpli'karɛ]
to compose (music, etc.)	comporre (vt)	[kɔm'pɔrrɛ]
to compromise (vt)	compromettere (vt)	[kɔmprɔ'mɛttɛrɛ]

to concentrate (vi)	concentrarsi (vr)	[kɔnʧɛnt'rarsi]
to confess (criminal)	confessarsi (vr)	[kɔnfɛs'sarsi]
to confuse (mix up)	confondere (vt)	[kɔn'fɔndɛrɛ]
to congratulate (vt)	congratularsi (vr)	[kɔŋratu'ʎarsi]

to consult (doctor, expert)	consultare (vt)	[kɔnsuʎ'tarɛ]
to continue (~ to do sth)	continuare (vt)	[kɔntinu'arɛ]
to control (vt)	controllare (vt)	[kɔntro'ʎarɛ]
to convince (vt)	convincere (vt)	[kɔn'winʧɛrɛ]

to cooperate (vi)	collaborare (vi)	[kɔʎabɔ'rarɛ]
to coordinate (vt)	coordinare (vt)	[kɔ:rdi'narɛ]
to correct (an error)	correggere (vt)	[kɔr'rɛdʒɛrɛ]
to cost (vt)	costare (vt)	[kɔs'tarɛ]

to count (money, etc.)	contare (vt)	[kɔn'tarɛ]
to count on ...	contare su ...	[kɔn'tarɛ su]
to crack (ceiling, wall)	screpolarsi (vi)	[skrɛpɔ'ʎarsi]
to create (vt)	creare (vt)	[krɛ'arɛ]
to cry (weep)	piangere (vi)	['pjandʒɛrɛ]
to cut off (with a knife)	tagliare (vt)	[ta'ʎiarɛ]

253. Verbs D-G

to dare (~ to do sth)	osare (vt)	[ɔ'zarɛ]
to date from ...	risalire a ...	[resa'lirɛ a]
to deceive (vi, vt)	ingannare (vt)	[iŋa'ŋarɛ]
to decide (~ to do sth)	decidere (vt)	[dɛ'ʧidɛrɛ]

to decorate (tree, street)	decorare (vt)	[dɛkɔ'rarɛ]
to dedicate (book, etc.)	dedicare (vt)	[dɛdi'karɛ]
to defend (a country, etc.)	difendere (vt)	[di'fɛndɛrɛ]
to defend oneself	difendersi (vr)	[di'fɛndɛrsi]

to demand (request firmly)	esigere (vt)	[ɛ'zidʒɛrɛ]
to denounce (vt)	denunciare (vt)	[dɛnun'ʧarɛ]
to deny (vt)	negare (vt)	[nɛ'garɛ]
to depend on ...	dipendere da ...	[di'pɛndɛrɛ da]
to deprive (vt)	privare (vt)	[pri'varɛ]

to deserve (vt)	meritare (vt)	[mɛri'tarɛ]
to design (machine, etc.)	progettare (vt)	[prodʒet'tarɛ]
to desire (want, wish)	desiderare (vt)	[dɛzidɛ'rarɛ]
to despise (vt)	disprezzare (vt)	[disprɛ'tsarɛ]
to destroy (documents, etc.)	distruggere (vt)	[dist'rudʒerɛ]

to differ (from sth)	essere diverso da ...	['ɛssɛrɛ di'vɛrsɔ da]
to dig (tunnel, etc.)	scavare (vt)	[ska'varɛ]
to direct (point the way)	indirizzare (vt)	[indiri'tsarɛ]

to disappear (vi)	sparire (vi)	[spa'rirɛ]
to discover (new land, etc.)	scoprire (vt)	[skɔp'rirɛ]
to discuss (vt)	discutere (vt)	[dis'kutɛrɛ]
to distribute (leaflets, etc.)	distribuire (vt)	[distribu'irɛ]
to disturb (vt)	disturbare (vt)	[distur'barɛ]

| to dive (vi) | tuffarsi (vr) | [tuf'farsi] |
| to divide (math) | dividere (vt) | [di'widɛrɛ] |

to do (vt)	fare (vt)	['farɛ]
to do the laundry	fare il bucato	['farɛ iʎ bu'katɔ]
to double (increase)	raddoppiare (vt)	[raddɔp'pjarɛ]
to doubt (have doubts)	dubitare (vi)	[dubi'tarɛ]

to draw a conclusion	trarre una conclusione	['trarrɛ una kɔŋklyzi'ɔnɛ]
to dream (daydream)	sognare (vi)	[sɔ'ɲjarɛ]
to dream (in sleep)	sognare (vi)	[sɔ'ɲjarɛ]

to drink (vi, vt)	bere (vi, vt)	['bɛrɛ]
to drive a car	guidare, condurre	[gui'darɛ], [kɔn'durrɛ]
to drive away	cacciare via	[ka'tʃarɛ 'wia]

to drop (let fall)	lasciar cadere	[ʎa'ʃar ka'dɛrɛ]
to drown (ab. person)	annegare (vi)	[anɛ'garɛ]
to dry (clothes, hair)	asciugare (vt)	[aʃu'garɛ]

to eat (vi, vt)	mangiare (vi, vt)	[man'dʒarɛ]
to eavesdrop (vi)	origliare (vi)	[ori'ʎjarɛ]
to enter (on the list)	iscrivere (vt)	[isk'rivɛrɛ]
to entertain (amuse)	divertire (vt)	[divɛr'tirɛ]
to equip (fit out)	equipaggiare (vt)	[ɛkuipa'dʒarɛ]

to examine (proposal)	esaminare (vt)	[ɛzami'narɛ]
to exchange (sth)	scambiarsi (vr)	[skam'bjarsi]
to exclude, to expel	escludere (vt)	[ɛsk'lydɛrɛ]
to excuse (forgive)	scusare (vt)	[sku'zarɛ]
to exist (vi)	esistere (vi)	[ɛ'zistɛrɛ]

to expect (anticipate)	aspettarsi (vr)	[aspɛt'tarsi]
to expect (foresee)	prevedere (vt)	[prɛvɛ'dɛrɛ]
to explain (vt)	spiegare (vt)	[spje'garɛ]
to express (vt)	esprimere (vt)	[ɛsp'rimɛrɛ]
to extinguish (a fire)	estinguere (vt)	[ɛs'tiŋuɛrɛ]

| to fall in love (with ...) | innamorarsi di ... | [iɲamɔ'rarsi di] |
| to fancy (vt) | piacere (vi) | [pja'tʃerɛ] |

to feed (provide food)	**dare da mangiare**	['darɛ da man'dʒarɛ]
to fight (against the enemy)	**battersi** (vr)	['battɛrsi]
to fight (vi)	**picchiarsi** (vr)	[pik'kjarsi]

to fill (glass, bottle)	**riempire** (vt)	[riɛm'pirɛ]
to find (~ lost items)	**trovare** (vt)	[tro'varɛ]
to finish (vt)	**finire, terminare** (vt)	[fi'nirɛ], [tɛrmi'narɛ]
to fish (vi)	**pescare** (vi)	[pɛs'karɛ]
to fit (ab. dress, etc.)	**stare bene**	['starɛ 'bɛnɛ]

to flatter (vt)	**adulare** (vt)	[adu'ʎarɛ]
to fly (bird, plane)	**volare** (vi)	[vɔ'ʎarɛ]

to follow … (come after)	**seguire** (vt)	[sɛgu'irɛ]
to forbid (vt)	**vietare** (vt)	[vje'tarɛ]
to force (compel)	**costringere** (vt)	[kɔst'rindʒerɛ]
to forget (vi, vt)	**dimenticare** (vt)	[dimɛnti'karɛ]
to forgive (pardon)	**perdonare** (vt)	[pɛrdɔ'narɛ]
to form (constitute)	**formare** (vt)	[for'marɛ]

to get dirty (vi)	**sporcarsi** (vr)	[spor'karsi]
to get infected (with …)	**contagiarsi** (vr)	[kɔnta'dʒarsi]
to get irritated	**irritarsi** (vr)	[irri'tarsi]
to get married	**sposarsi** (vr)	[spɔ'zarsi]
to get rid of …	**liberarsi** (vr)	[libɛ'rarsi]
to get tired	**stancarsi** (vr)	[sta'ŋkarsi]
to get up (arise from bed)	**alzarsi** (vr)	[aʎ'tsarsi]

to give a hug, to hug (vt)	**abbracciare** (vt)	[abbra'tʃarɛ]
to give in (yield to)	**arrendersi** (vr)	[ar'rɛndɛrsi]

to go (by car, etc.)	**andare** (vi)	[an'darɛ]
to go (on foot)	**camminare** (vi)	[kammi'narɛ]
to go for a swim	**fare il bagno**	['farɛ iʎ 'baɲɔ]
to go out (for dinner, etc.)	**uscire** (vi)	[u'ʃirɛ]
to go to bed	**andare a letto**	[an'darɛ a 'lettɔ]

to greet (vt)	**salutare** (vt)	[saly'tarɛ]
to grow (plants)	**coltivare** (vt)	[kɔʎti'varɛ]
to guarantee (vt)	**garantire** (vt)	[garan'tirɛ]
to guess right	**indovinare** (vt)	[indowi'narɛ]

254. Verbs H-M

to hand out (distribute)	**distribuire** (vt)	[distribu'irɛ]
to hang (curtains, etc.)	**appendere** (vt)	[ap'pɛndɛrɛ]

to have (vt)	**avere** (vt)	[a'vɛrɛ]
to have a bath	**fare un bagno**	['farɛ un 'baɲɔ]
to have a try	**tentare** (vt)	[tɛn'tarɛ]
to have breakfast	**fare colazione**	['farɛ kɔʎa'tsɂonɛ]
to have dinner	**cenare** (vi)	[tʃe'narɛ]
to have fun	**divertirsi** (vr)	[divɛr'tirsi]
to have lunch	**pranzare** (vi)	[pran'tsarɛ]

to head (group, etc.)	capeggiare (vt)	[kapɛ'dʒarɛ]
to hear (vt)	sentire (vt)	[sɛn'tirɛ]
to heat (vt)	scaldare (vt)	[skaʎ'darɛ]
to help (vt)	aiutare (vt)	[aju'tarɛ]

to hide (vt)	nascondere (vt)	[nas'kondɛrɛ]
to hire (e.g. ~ a boat)	noleggiare (vt)	[nole'dʒarɛ]
to hire (staff)	assumere (vt)	[as'sumɛrɛ]
to hope (vi, vt)	sperare (vi, vt)	[spɛ'rarɛ]

to hunt (for food, sport)	cacciare (vt)	[ka'tʃarɛ]
to hurry (vi)	avere fretta	[a'vɛrɛ 'frɛtta]
to hurry (sb)	mettere fretta a ...	[mɛt'tɛrɛ 'frɛtta a]

to imagine (to picture)	immaginare (vt)	[immadʒi'narɛ]
to imitate (vt)	imitare (vt)	[imi'tarɛ]
to implore (vt)	supplicare (vt)	[suppli'karɛ]
to import (vt)	importare (vt)	[impɔr'tarɛ]

to increase (vi)	aumentare (vi)	[aumɛn'tarɛ]
to increase (vt)	aumentare (vt)	[aumɛn'tarɛ]
to infect (vt)	contagiare (vt)	[kɔnta'dʒarɛ]
to influence (vt)	influire (vt)	[infly'irɛ]

to inform (~ sb about ...)	informare di ...	[infɔr'marɛ di]
to inform (vt)	informare (vt)	[infɔr'marɛ]
to inherit (vt)	ereditare (vt)	[ɛrɛdi'tarɛ]
to inquire (about ...)	scoprire (vt)	[skɔp'rirɛ]

to insist (vi, vt)	insistere (vi)	[in'sistɛrɛ]
to inspire (vt)	ispirare (vt)	[ispi'rarɛ]
to instruct (teach)	dare istruzioni	['darɛ istru'tsʲoni]
to insult (offend)	insultare (vt)	[insuʎ'tarɛ]

to interest (vt)	interessare (vt)	[intɛrɛs'sarɛ]
to intervene (vi)	intervenire (vi)	[intɛrvɛ'nirɛ]
to introduce (present)	far conoscere	[far kɔ'noʃɛrɛ]
to invent (machine, etc.)	inventare (vt)	[invɛn'tarɛ]
to invite (vt)	invitare (vt)	[inwi'tarɛ]

to iron (laundry)	stirare (vt)	[sti'rarɛ]
to irritate (annoy)	irritare (vt)	[irri'tarɛ]
to isolate (vt)	isolare (vt)	[izɔ'ʎarɛ]

| to join (political party, etc.) | aderire a ... | [adɛ'rirɛ] |
| to joke (be kidding) | scherzare (vi) | [skɛr'tsarɛ] |

to keep (old letters, etc.)	tenere (vt)	[tɛ'nɛrɛ]
to keep silent	tacere (vi)	[ta'tʃerɛ]
to kill (vt)	uccidere (vt)	[u'tʃidɛrɛ]
to knock (at the door)	bussare (vi)	[bus'sarɛ]
to know (sb)	conoscere (vt)	[kɔ'noʃɛrɛ]
to know (sth)	sapere (vt)	[sa'pɛrɛ]

| to laugh (vi) | ridere (vi) | ['ridɛrɛ] |
| to launch (start up) | avviare (vt) | [av'vʲarɛ] |

to leave (~ for Mexico)	**partire** (vi)	[par'tirɛ]
to leave (forget)	**lasciare** (vt)	[ʎa'ʃarɛ]
to leave (spouse)	**lasciare** (vt)	[ʎa'ʃarɛ]

to liberate (city, etc.)	**liberare** (vt)	[libɛ'rarɛ]
to lie (tell untruth)	**mentire** (vi)	[men'tirɛ]
to light (campfire, etc.)	**accendere** (vt)	[a'tʃendɛrɛ]
to light up (illuminate)	**illuminare** (vt)	[illymi'narɛ]

to limit (vt)	**limitare** (vt)	[limi'tarɛ]
to listen (vi)	**ascoltare** (vi)	[askɔʎ'tarɛ]
to live (~ in France)	**abitare** (vi)	[abi'tarɛ]
to live (exist)	**vivere** (vi)	['wivɛrɛ]

to load (gun)	**caricare** (vt)	[kari'karɛ]
to load (vehicle, etc.)	**caricare** (vt)	[kari'karɛ]
to look (I'm just ~ing)	**guardare** (vi)	[guar'darɛ]
to look for ... (search)	**cercare** (vt)	[tʃer'karɛ]
to look like (resemble)	**assomigliare a ...**	[assɔmi'ʎjarɛ a]

to lose (umbrella, etc.)	**perdere** (vt)	['pɛrdɛrɛ]
to love (sb)	**amare** (vt)	[a'marɛ]
to love (sth)	**gradire** (vt)	[gra'dirɛ]
to lower (blind, head)	**abbassare** (vt)	[abbas'sarɛ]

to make (~ dinner)	**fare, preparare**	['farɛ], [prepa'rarɛ]
to make a mistake	**sbagliare** (vi)	[zba'ʎjarɛ]
to make copies	**fare copie**	['farɛ 'kɔpje]
to make easier	**semplificare** (vt)	[sɛmplifi'karɛ]
to make the acquaintance	**fare la conoscenza di ...**	['farɛ ʎa kɔnɔ'ʃɛntsa di]
to make use (of ...)	**usare** (vt)	[u'zarɛ]

to manage, to run	**dirigere** (vt)	[di'ridʒerɛ]
to mark (make a mark)	**segnare** (vt)	[sɛ'ɲjarɛ]
to mean (signify)	**significare** (vt)	[siɲ'ifi'karɛ]
to memorize (vt)	**memorizzare** (vt)	[mɛmori'dzarɛ]
to mention (talk about)	**menzionare** (vt)	[mentsɪɔ'narɛ]

to miss (school, etc.)	**mancare le lezioni**	[ma'ŋkarɛ le le'tsɪɔni]
to mix (combine, blend)	**mescolare** (vt)	[mɛskɔ'ʎarɛ]
to mock (deride)	**canzonare** (vt)	[kantsɔ'narɛ]
to move (wardrobe, etc.)	**spostare** (vt)	[spɔs'tarɛ]
to multiply (math)	**moltiplicare** (vt)	[mɔʎtipli'karɛ]
must (v aux)	**dovere** (v aux)	[dɔ'vɛrɛ]

255. Verbs N-S

to name, to call (vt)	**chiamare** (vt)	[kja'marɛ]
to negotiate (vi)	**negoziare** (vi)	[nego'tsjarɛ]
to note (write down)	**prendere nota**	['prɛndɛrɛ 'nɔta]
to notice (see)	**accorgersi** (vr)	[ak'kɔrdʒersi]

to obey (vi, vt)	**obbedire** (vi)	[ɔbbɛ'dirɛ]
to object (vi, vt)	**obiettare** (vt)	[ɔbjet'tarɛ]

to observe (see)	osservare (vt)	[ɔssɛr'varɛ]
to offend (vt)	offendere (vt)	[ɔf'fɛndɛrɛ]
to omit (word, phrase)	omettere (vt)	[ɔ'mɛttɛrɛ]
to open (vt)	aprire (vt)	[ap'rirɛ]
to order (in restaurant)	ordinare (vt)	[ɔrdi'narɛ]
to order (mil.)	comandare	[kɔman'darɛ]
to organize (concert, party)	organizzare (vt)	[ɔrgani'dzarɛ]
to overestimate (vt)	sopravvalutare (vt)	[sɔpravvaly'tarɛ]
to own (possess)	possedere (vt)	[pɔssɛ'dɛrɛ]
to participate (vi)	partecipare (vi)	[partɛtʃi'parɛ]
to pass (go beyond)	sorpassare (vt)	[sɔrpas'sarɛ]
to pay (vi, vt)	pagare (vi, vt)	[pa'garɛ]
to peep, to spy on	spiare (vt)	[spi'arɛ]
to penetrate (vt)	penetrare (vi)	[pɛnɛt'rarɛ]
to permit (vt)	permettere (vt)	[pɛr'mɛttɛrɛ]
to pick (flowers)	cogliere (vt)	['kɔʎjerɛ]
to place (put, set)	collocare (vt)	[kɔllɔ'karɛ]
to plan (~ to do sth)	pianificare (vt)	[pjanifi'karɛ]
to play (actor)	recitare (vt)	[rɛtʃi'tarɛ]
to play (children)	giocare (vi)	[dʒɔ'karɛ]
to point (~ the way)	indicare (vt)	[indi'karɛ]
to pour (liquid)	versare (vt)	[vɛr'sarɛ]
to pray (vi, vt)	pregare (vi, vt)	[prɛ'garɛ]
to predominate (vi)	prevalere (vi)	[prɛva'lerɛ]
to prefer (vt)	preferire (vt)	[prɛfɛ'rirɛ]
to prepare (~ a plan)	preparare (vt)	[prɛpa'rarɛ]
to present (sb to sb)	presentare (vt)	[prɛzɛn'tarɛ]
to preserve (peace, life)	preservare (vt)	[prɛzɛr'varɛ]
to progress (move forward)	avanzare (vi)	[avan'tsarɛ]
to promise (vt)	promettere (vt)	[prɔ'mɛttɛrɛ]
to pronounce (vt)	pronunciare (vt)	[prɔnun'tʃarɛ]
to propose (vt)	proporre (vt)	[prɔ'pɔrrɛ]
to protect (e.g. ~ nature)	proteggere (vt)	[prɔ'tɛdʒɛrɛ]
to protest (vi)	protestare (vi)	[prɔtɛs'tarɛ]
to prove (vt)	provare (vt)	[prɔ'varɛ]
to provoke (vt)	provocare (vt)	[prɔvɔ'karɛ]
to pull (~ the rope)	tirare (vt)	[ti'rarɛ]
to punish (vt)	punire (vt)	[pu'nirɛ]
to push (~ the door)	spingere (vt)	['spindʒɛrɛ]
to put away (vt)	mettere via	['mɛttɛrɛ 'wia]
to put in (insert)	inserire (vt)	[insɛ'rirɛ]
to put in order	mettere in ordine	['mɛttɛrɛ in 'ɔrdinɛ]
to put, to place	mettere (vt)	['mɛttɛrɛ]
to quote (cite)	citare (vt)	[tʃi'tarɛ]
to reach (arrive at)	raggiungere (vt)	[ra'dʒundʒɛrɛ]
to read (vi, vt)	leggere (vi, vt)	['lɛdʒɛrɛ]

| to realise (achieve) | realizzare (vt) | [reali'dzarɛ] |
| to recall (~ one's name) | ricordarsi di | [rikɔr'darsi di] |

to recognize (admit)	ammettere (vt)	[am'mɛtɛrɛ]
to recognize (identify sb)	riconoscere (vt)	[riko'noʃɛrɛ]
to recommend (vt)	raccomandare (vt)	[rakkoman'darɛ]
to recover (~ from flu)	guarire (vi)	[gua'rirɛ]

to redo (do again)	rifare (vt)	[ri'farɛ]
to reduce (speed, etc.)	ridurre (vt)	[ri'durrɛ]
to refuse (~ sb)	rifiutare (vt)	[rifjy'tarɛ]
to regret (be sorry)	rammaricarsi (vr)	[ramari'karsi]

to remember (vt)	ricordare (vt)	[rikɔr'darɛ]
to remind of ...	ricordare (vt)	[rikɔr'darɛ]
to remove (~ a stain)	rimuovere (vt)	[rimu'ɔvɛrɛ]
to remove (~ an obstacle)	eliminare (vt)	[ɛlimi'narɛ]
to rent (sth from sb)	affittare (vt)	[affit'tarɛ]

to repair (mend)	riparare (vt)	[ripa'rarɛ]
to repeat (say again)	ripetere (vt)	[ri'pɛtɛrɛ]
to report (make a report)	fare un rapporto	['farɛ un rap'pɔrtɔ]
to reproach (vt)	rimproverare (vt)	[rimprovɛ'rarɛ]

to reserve, to book	prenotare (vt)	[prɛno'tarɛ]
to restrain (hold back)	trattenere (vt)	[trattɛ'nɛrɛ]
to return (come back)	ritornare (vi)	[ritor'narɛ]
to risk, to take a risk	rischiare (vi, vt)	[ris'kjarɛ]
to rub off (erase)	cancellare (vt)	[kantʃe'ʎarɛ]
to run (move fast)	correre (vi)	['kɔrrɛrɛ]

to satisfy (please)	soddisfare (vt)	[sɔddis'farɛ]
to save (rescue)	salvare (vt)	[saʎ'varɛ]
to say (~ thank you)	dire (vt)	['dirɛ]
to scold (vt)	sgridare (vt)	[zgri'darɛ]
to scratch (with claws)	graffiare (vt)	[graf'fjarɛ]

to select (to pick)	selezionare (vt)	[selets'o'narɛ]
to sell (goods)	vendere (vt)	['vɛndɛrɛ]
to send (a letter)	inviare (vt)	[inwi'arɛ]
to send back (vt)	rimandare (vt)	[riman'darɛ]

to sense (danger)	sentire (vt)	[sɛn'tirɛ]
to sentence (vt)	condannare (vt)	[kɔnda'ŋarɛ]
to serve (in restaurant)	servire (vt)	[sɛr'wirɛ]
to settle (a conflict)	regolare (vt)	[rɛgo'ʎarɛ]

to shake (vt)	scuotere (vt)	[sku'ɔtɛrɛ]
to shave (vi)	rasarsi (vr)	[ra'zarsi]
to shine (vi)	splendere (vi)	['splendɛrɛ]
to shiver (with cold)	tremare (vi)	[trɛ'marɛ]

to shoot (vi)	sparare (vi)	[spa'rarɛ]
to shout (vi)	gridare (vi)	[gri'darɛ]
to show (to display)	mostrare (vt)	[mɔst'rarɛ]
to shudder (vi)	sussultare (vi)	[susuʎ'tarɛ]

to sigh (vi)	sospirare (vi)	[sɔspi'rarɛ]
to sign (document)	firmare (vt)	[fir'marɛ]
to signify (mean)	significare (vt)	[siɲifi'karɛ]
to simplify (vt)	semplificare (vt)	[sɛmplifi'karɛ]

to sin (vi)	peccare (vi)	[pɛk'karɛ]
to sit (be sitting)	sedere (vi)	[sɛ'dɛrɛ]
to sit down (vi)	sedersi (vr)	[sɛ'dɛrsi]

to smash (~ a bug)	schiacciare (vt)	[skia'ʧarɛ]
to smell (have odour)	emanare odore	[ɛma'narɛ ɔ'dorɛ]
to smell (sniff at)	odorare (vt)	[ɔdo'rarɛ]
to smile (vi)	sorridere (vi)	[sor'ridɛrɛ]

to solve (problem)	risolvere (vt)	[ri'zɔʎvɛrɛ]
to sow (seed, crop)	seminare (vt)	[sɛmi'narɛ]
to spill (liquid)	rovesciare (vt)	[rɔvɛ'ʃarɛ]
to spill out (flour, etc.)	spargersi (vr)	['spardʒersi]
to spit (vi)	sputare (vi)	[spu'tarɛ]
to emit (smell)	emanare (vt)	[ɛma'narɛ]

to stand (toothache, cold)	sopportare (vt)	[sɔppor'tarɛ]
to start (begin)	cominciare (vt)	[kɔmin'ʧarɛ]
to steal (money, etc.)	rubare (vt)	[ru'barɛ]

to stop (cease)	cessare (vt)	[ʧes'sarɛ]
to stop (for pause, etc.)	fermarsi (vr)	[fɛr'marsi]
to stop talking	smettere di parlare	['zmɛttɛrɛ di par'larɛ]

to strengthen	rafforzare (vt)	[raffor'tsarɛ]
to stroke (caress)	accarezzare (vt)	[akkarɛ'tsarɛ]
to study (vt)	studiare (vt)	[studi'arɛ]
to suffer (feel pain)	soffrire (vt)	[sɔff'rirɛ]
to support (cause, idea)	sostenere (vt)	[sɔstɛ'nɛrɛ]
to suppose (assume)	supporre (vt)	[sup'porrɛ]

to surface (ab. submarine)	emergere (vi)	[ɛ'mɛrdʒerɛ]
to surprise (amaze)	sorprendere (vt)	[sorp'rɛndɛrɛ]
to suspect (vt)	sospettare (vt)	[sɔspɛt'tarɛ]
to swim (vi)	nuotare (vi)	[nuɔ'tarɛ]
to switch on (vt)	accendere (vt)	[a'ʧendɛrɛ]

256. Verbs T-W

to take (get hold of)	prendere (vt)	['prɛndɛrɛ]
to take a rest	riposarsi (vr)	[ripɔ'zarsi]
to take aim (at ...)	mirare, puntare	[mi'rarɛ], [pun'tarɛ]
to take away	portare via	[por'tarɛ 'wia]

to take off (aeroplane)	decollare (vi)	[dɛkɔ'ʎarɛ]
to take off (remove)	togliere (vt)	['tɔʎjerɛ]
to take pictures	fare foto	['farɛ 'foto]
to talk to ...	parlare con ...	[par'ʎarɛ kɔn]
to teach (give lessons)	insegnare (vt)	[insɛ'ɲarɛ]

to tear off (vt)	strappare (vt)	[strap'parɛ]
to tell (story, joke)	raccontare (vt)	[rakkɔn'tarɛ]
to thank (vt)	ringraziare (vt)	[riŋratsi'arɛ]
to think (believe)	pensare (vi)	[pɛn'sarɛ]
to think (vi, vt)	pensare (vi, vt)	[pɛn'sarɛ]
to threaten (vt)	minacciare (vt)	[mina'ʧarɛ]
to throw (stone)	gettare (vt)	[ʤet'tarɛ]
to tie to ...	legare (vt)	[le'garɛ]
to tie up (prisoner)	legare (vt)	[le'garɛ]
to tire (make tired)	stancare (vt)	[sta'nakrɛ]
to touch (one's arm, etc.)	toccare (vt)	[tɔk'karɛ]
to tower (over ...)	sovrastare (vi)	[sɔvras'tarɛ]
to train (animals)	ammaestrare (vt)	[ammaɛst'rarɛ]
to train (vi)	allenarsi (vr)	[alle'narsi]
to train (sb)	allenare (vt)	[alle'narɛ]
to transform (vt)	trasformare (vt)	[trasfor'marɛ]
to translate (vt)	tradurre (vt)	[tra'durrɛ]
to treat (patient, illness)	curare (vt)	[ku'rarɛ]
to trust (vt)	fidarsi (vt)	[fi'darsi]
to try (attempt)	tentare (vt)	[tɛn'tarɛ]
to turn (~ to the left)	girare (vi)	[ʤi'rarɛ]
to turn away (vi)	girare lo sguardo	[ʤi'rarɛ lo zgu'ardɔ]
to turn off (the light)	spegnere (vt)	['spɛɲɛrɛ]
to turn over (stone, etc.)	capovolgere (vt)	[kapɔ'vɔʎʤɛrɛ]
to underestimate (vt)	sottovalutare (vt)	[sɔttɔvaly'tarɛ]
to underline (vt)	sottolineare (vt)	[sɔttɔlinɛ'arɛ]
to understand (vt)	capire (vt)	[ka'pirɛ]
to undertake (vt)	intraprendere (vt)	[intrap'rɛndɛrɛ]
to unite (vt)	unire (vt)	[u'nirɛ]
to untie (vt)	slegare (vt)	[zle'garɛ]
to use (phrase, word)	utilizzare (vt)	[utili'dzarɛ]
to vaccinate (vt)	vaccinare (vt)	[vatʃi'narɛ]
to vote (vi)	votare (vi)	[vɔ'tarɛ]
to wait (vt)	aspettare (vt)	[aspɛt'tarɛ]
to wake (sb)	svegliare (vt)	[zvɛ'ʎjarɛ]
to want (wish, desire)	volere (vt)	[vɔ'lerɛ]
to warn (of the danger)	avvertire (vt)	[avwɛr'tirɛ]
to wash (clean)	lavare (vt)	[ʎa'varɛ]
to water (plants)	innaffiare (vt)	[iɲaf'fjarɛ]
to wave (the hand)	agitare la mano	[adʒi'tarɛ ʎa 'manɔ]
to weigh (have weight)	pesare (vi)	[pɛ'zarɛ]
to work (vi)	lavorare (vi)	[ʎavɔ'rarɛ]
to worry (make anxious)	preoccupare (vt)	[prɛɔkku'parɛ]
to worry (vi)	preoccuparsi (vr)	[prɛɔkku'parsi]

to wrap (parcel, etc.)	**incartare** (vt)	[iŋkar'tarɛ]
to wrestle (sport)	**lottare** (vi)	[lɔt'tarɛ]
to write (vt)	**scrivere** (vi, vt)	['skrivɛrɛ]
to write down	**annotare** (vt)	[aŋɔ'tarɛ]

Printed in Great Britain
by Amazon.co.uk, Ltd.,
Marston Gate.